Artist,
Audience,
Accomplice

# Artist,
# Audience,
# Accomplice

**Sydney
Stutterheim**

Ethics & Authorship

in Art of the 1970s & 1980s

DUKE UNIVERSITY PRESS *Durham & London* 2024

© 2024 DUKE UNIVERSITY PRESS
All rights reserved
Project Editor: Ihsan Taylor
Designed by Matthew Tauch
Typeset in Garamond Premier Pro by
Westchester Publishing Services

Library of Congress Cataloging-in-Publication Data
Names: Stutterheim, Sydney, [date] author.
Title: Artist, audience, accomplice : ethics and authorship in art
    of the 1970s and 1980s / Sydney Stutterheim.
Description: Durham : Duke University Press, 2024. | Includes
    bibliographical references and index.
Identifiers: LCCN 2023046397 (print)
LCCN 2023046398 (ebook)
ISBN 9781478030690 (paperback)
ISBN 9781478026433 (hardcover)
ISBN 9781478059677 (ebook)
Subjects: LCSH: Burden, Chris, 1946–2015. | Wilke, Hannah. |

Kippenberger, Martin, 1953–1997. | O'Grady, Lorraine. |
Arts and morals. | Arts and society. | Authorship. | Audiences
in art. | BISAC: ART / History / Contemporary (1945-) |
PERFORMING ARTS / General
Classification: LCC NX180.E8 S78 2024 (print) | LCC NX180.E8
    (ebook) | DDC 306.4/709047—dc23/eng/20240506
LC record available at https://lccn.loc.gov/2023046397
LC ebook record available at https://lccn.loc.gov/2023046398

# Contents

# Acknowledgments

This project would not have been possible without the support and guidance—both visible and invisible—provided by colleagues, mentors, peers, family, and friends.

It is the greatest honor to publish my first book with Duke University Press. To Ihsan Taylor, Ryan Kendall, Chad Royal, James Moore, and the rest of the team at the Press, thank you for expertly shepherding this book to completion. My deepest thanks are reserved for Ken Wissoker, whose commitment to supporting innovative ideas and his fierce advocacy of his authors is unparalleled. Ken, thank you for believing in me, and this project, as I found my way through it.

I would also like to thank the anonymous readers of my manuscript, who brought compelling insights to the project and pushed my scholarship in new directions that were both surprising and enlightening.

Specific thanks goes to David Joselit, who has offered both practical and intellectual support throughout the writing process. So much of how I think about art has been profoundly shaped by him.

The conceptual origins of this project, and its subsequent development, have been greatly informed by a range of individuals, including Andy Avini, Claire Bishop, Ross Bleckner, Will Cotton, Abigail Lapin Dardashti, Cathy Davidson, Rose Dergan, Gabriel Florenz, Romy Golan, Trever Hagen, Branden Joseph, and Nicholas Weber. Additionally, I'd like to thank the librarians and archivists—especially those at the Wellesley College Archives and Special Collections, Museum of Modern Art Archives, Mina Rees Library, New York Public Library, Avery Architectural and Fine Arts Library, and Getty Research Institute—who kindly gave their time and energies in helping me track down research materials.

I am grateful for the tremendous generosity of those who lent their support to the book through their participation in interviews, their willingness to answer questions, or their continued engagement with the project; this list includes Mowry Baden, Jeffrey Deitch, Regina Fiorito, Lisa

Franzen, Phyllis Lutjeans, Lorraine O'Grady, Nancy Rubins, Marsie Scharlatt, Andrew Scharlatt, and Yayoi Shionoiri.

Additionally, acknowledgment is due to those who made the time for, and dedication to, this book possible: Dakota Arkin Cafourek, Sabine Avini, Edie Brickell, Jaclyn Burney, Cheryl Camerieri, Maggie Conlon, Anne Ellis, Josephine Kilroy, Shelly Kramer, Mosha Lündstrom Halbert, Adriana Mather, Tiffany Obser, and Priscilla Vasquez.

My deepest thanks are reserved for my family, for their patience and support. Nanette Stutterheim and Victoria, Bill, and Billy Brock: thank you for being there for me, unequivocally.

I am infinitely appreciative of my husband, CJ Camerieri, whose intelligence and unwavering love sustained me throughout this tremendous undertaking. It is an understatement to say that I could not have done this without you. And to my two daughters, Celine and Annika, who bring me peace and happiness in ways that I never knew before.

Finally, this book is dedicated to my late father, Mario Jose Stutterheim, who believed in the pursuit of intellectual curiosity above all.

# Introduction

**On the evening of November 12, 1972,** artist Chris Burden was arrested by the Los Angeles Police Department (LAPD). According to the police, an anonymous motorist driving down La Cienega Boulevard in Los Angeles reported a cadaver covered in a canvas tarpaulin lying alongside parked cars in the street, which forced oncoming vehicles to swerve to avoid collision. By the time officers arrived at the "crime scene," located directly in front of the Riko Mizuno Gallery, the two fifteen-minute flares that were set around the body to warn oncoming traffic had begun to extinguish, leaving the unidentified subject in a vulnerable position. Shortly thereafter, additional police appeared and a "young deputy [told] people to clear the street, [asking] 'Anybody here see this thing happen?'"[1]

Given the approximately three-hundred-person crowd that had gathered, it seemed peculiar that not even one had witnessed the accident firsthand. According to performance artist Barbara T. Smith—who had been in attendance at the nearby gallery—after an unfruitful attempt at locating eyewitnesses, one officer tentatively approached the body and removed the cloth covering. Finding an unharmed male subject, the officer "asked if he was OK and what he was doing. He told them he was an artist doing his 'piece.' They arrested him."[2] After spending the night in jail, Burden was released on his own recognizance.

Although the legal charge of "causing a false emergency to be reported" for *Deadman* (1972) was directed toward the artist alone, Burden's actions staged in the public domain produced a test revealing the involvement—and potential accountability—of the other people present as well.[3] A network of individuals became embroiled in the subsequent lawsuit and three-day trial that resulted from his performance: gallery associates, friends, attorneys, and even unrelated passersby. By deliberately compelling witting or unwitting auxiliary participants to take on expanded roles beyond that of a traditional viewing audience, such as serving as his witnesses in the ensuing trial, Burden produced a largely unauthorized relay of legal and ethical responsibility to subjects whose presence has been largely overlooked in descriptions or analyses of such artworks.

*Artist, Audience, Accomplice: Ethics and Authorship in Art of the 1970s and 1980s* corrects this gap. It positions the role of accomplice as a new figure in histories of performance, participation, and appropriation art in the United States and Western Europe during the 1970s and 1980s that allows us to revise the relations of property, agency, and authorship that have been assumed in those fields. Taking the work of Chris Burden, Hannah Wilke, Martin Kippenberger, and Lorraine O'Grady as case studies, I argue that these artists exploit the ambiguities between clearly delineated roles of art-ist and viewer by mobilizing a range of significant but often discounted auxiliary participants—such as assistants, documenters, romantic partners, and institutional workers—to rethink existing models of the social in favor of a networked yet hierarchical collectivity. Frequently engaging in what can be broadly characterized as illicit artistic strategies, these artists test the limits of authorial accountability and agency by delegating ethically com-promised actions to figures who work constitutively alongside the nominal artist in a role that I theorize as the *accomplice*.

The accomplice is a type of agent who shares in the responsibility for artworks that are often centered on tactics of legal or ethical disobedience while the recognition of her or his authorial position in the artistic produc-tion is deliberately obscured, diminished, or overlooked. This is evident in a range of projects, including *TV Hijack*, a 1972 performance in which Burden took an interviewer hostage on live cable-access TV while his as-sistants destroyed the only record of the broadcasted events; and *So Help Me Hannah: Snatch-Shots with Ray Guns* (1978), in which Wilke—with the help of her photographer—used covert tactics to document evidence of gender-based limitations experienced throughout her career. During the 1980s, Kippenberger accumulated a network of studio assistants whose labor he would deliberately undermine or exploit in the service of promot-ing his public persona, while O'Grady developed a performance character to stage unauthorized, guerrilla-like interventions in art institutions that both exposed the inequities of gender and racial representation perpetu-ating her exclusions from such spaces and sought potential allies for her cause. Using theorizations of distributed agency across a network—in other words, shared accountability for the ethical or legal consequences of a work—I contend that Burden, Wilke, Kippenberger, and O'Grady used accomplices to make visible the tensions and contradictions of various rights of the subject at stake in the 1970s and 1980s.

In my view, art practices during this time demonstrate a substantial exploration of non-audience participation; additionally, there is a marked interest in extending late 1960s Conceptual art's legal designations of authorship into inquiries about subjects' rights and other conferrals of authority through legal means. The resulting shifts in the nature of the relationship between the artist and auxiliary figures whose contributions differ from those of audiences are demonstrated in this investigation's four main case studies: gallery owners became implicated in potential crimes (Burden), private relations became public in the process of disclosing inequitable access to shared personal history and authorial attribution (Wilke), assistants were hired to be deliberately undermined in an artist's studio (Kippenberger), and an artist's performance character assumed primary responsibility for acts of trespassing into the white- and male-dominated art world undertaken in an effort to seek supporters (O'Grady). While these artists were not alone in making work that explores illicit actions in the context of art during the 1970s and 1980s, a tactic often used to expose the cultural norms around, and acceptance of, violence in daily life, the artists I discuss deliberately use accomplices in their endeavors to expand on questions of responsibility and power over other individuals that were opened up in the 1960s with delegated labor practices and Conceptualist investigations of aesthetic property.

The work of these four artists should also be contextualized as an extension of ideas concerning the increased involvement of audiences and interpretive agency given to performers in the late 1950s and 1960s, such as in Allan Kaprow's Happenings or Fluxus event scores. These works might also serve as a prehistory to post-1989 participatory practices, particularly those that stage projects with antagonistic social relations. However, in many existing discussions of participation in art, the audience or hired labor often acts under the auspices of the artist, behaving as a proxy. In contrast, I present a three-point model of "auxiliary participation," in that the accomplices (1) tend to remain within the domain of authority of the nominal artist while they are not necessarily hired, nor are they centrally visible as performers in the work of art; (2) may not have agreed to the full terms of their engagement (which is often centered on unethical or illicit actions); and (3) participate not because an artist is engaging audiences collaboratively in the creative process but because the artist is producing manipulative situations based on power differentials. The role of the accomplice provides different insights than that of audience participation in that its unique position—neither creator nor viewer—blurs the line between the nominal artist's private domain and the audience's public, through which questions concerning the thresholds of individual rights get staged and evaluated.

At first glance, the centrality of Burden's body in the performative intervention *Deadman* might seem to reassert the physical presence and personal preoccupations of the nominal artist that are said to characterize much of the best-known art of the 1970s and 1980s in the United States and Western Europe. Many of the most iconic images from these two decades ostensibly indicate a pronounced emphasis on the individual subject in art: a shirtless Burden having been nailed through his palms to the rear hood of a Volkswagen Beetle; Wilke's photographic self-portraits in which she glamorously modeled herself for the camera; Kippenberger's mythologized persona that was proliferated across paintings, sculptures, and ephemera using simulations of expressive content; and O'Grady's appearance at the New Museum in the guise of an alter ego, a former beauty pageant queen turned art-world vigilante known as "Mlle Bourgeoise Noire." Returning to a paradigm of the artistic genius or auteur following a period in which the artist's subjective experience was deemphasized in 1960s Pop, Minimalist, and Conceptual art, these images suggest that the creator—and she or he alone—is paramount, in line with the characterizations of the widespread desires for individual satisfaction that dominated the so-called Me and Greed decades of the 1970s and 1980s. However, as this book will demonstrate, this narrative of art practices from these two decades in which self-interested art became predominant fails to account for an important history of participation that evades conventional classification.

Art historian Anne M. Wagner succinctly characterized the slippage between the artist and audience as a general condition of performance and video art during the 1970s, writing: "what was performed in performance, what was observed in video, are the uncertainties that by 1970 or thereabouts had begun to accumulate around 'artist' and 'viewer' as art's two essential correlative terms."[4] Building on Rosalind Krauss's influential essay "Video: The Aesthetics of Narcissism" (1976), Wagner argues that in the case of many examples of performance art around 1970, "their self-absorption (what Krauss called narcissism) is conjoined with an especially aggressive—we can rightly say coercive—posture toward the viewer, by which a new awareness and mode of vision might be urged."[5] While Wagner modified Krauss's reading of narcissism as the dominant feature of such practices, her own analysis suggests—but stops short of—closely examining the expanded levels of involvement on the part of the audience in the related performance practices of the period. Looking to the immediate performance history out of which her opening example emerged (Bill Viola's 1976 *He Weeps for You*), Wagner identifies the period of the early 1970s as the moment when "behavior and coercion meant everything to the making of art, with both the artist and viewer feeling the pressure like never before."[6]

Throughout this decade, artists working in the burgeoning fields of performance and video art became interested in how their role might intersect with the public in other, more surreptitious, ways: whether Vito Acconci confessing private fantasies in *Seedbed* (1972), Laurie Anderson documenting voyeuristic behavior in *Fully Automated Nikon (Object/Objection/Objectivity)* (1973), or Sophie Calle surveilling an unsuspecting subject in *Suite Vénitienne* (1980). These artistic endeavors presented a newly strained relationship between the artist and viewer, while also suggesting an expansion of potential roles for participation that exceed the categorical binary of artistic author and spectator. Reframing Wagner's inquiry through a "third term" outside the artist/viewer dichotomy, I contend that artists during the 1970s and 1980s produced work that precisely began testing the parameters of that relationship. The present study asserts that much art from the 1970s and 1980s indeed needed other people, although these might not be those whom we initially suspect or recognize.

### Legality in Concert

Just as the most famous American crime of the 1970s—the Watergate scandal—involved a clandestine network of accomplices who broke into the Democratic National Committee headquarters in June 1972 on behalf of then president Richard M. Nixon, the present study analyzes a concurrent set of art practices in which artists embroiled other individuals in the responsibility for covert and often unethical actions directed by the nominal artist. The very nature of visibility became a primary concern during the 1970s: questions arose regarding who was being represented and what was at stake in attaining or maintaining such observable presence. In the United States and parts of Western Europe, the activism generated by the New Left during the 1960s had begun to splinter by the end of the decade, the result of a post-1968 disillusionment that manifested itself through factionalism and mounting private concerns through the following decade. Given the backdrop of growing neoconservatism and the Vietnam War draft, the nature of individual rights began to gain urgency—whether in terms of women's, gay, or civil rights; intellectual property or privacy legislation; and aesthetic and critical debates over one's self, property, and representation. However, rising calls for representation coincided with a growing mistrust of those same mechanisms, recognizing them as traps that provoke surveillance, categorization, and control as much as enhanced political power. These dual effects of visibility play out in terms of the accomplice, as its entrance as a subject resulted in increased agency but also potential accountability shared with the nominal artist.

While the negotiation of a subject's rights was widely discussed on a social level over the historical period of the 1970s and 1980s, it is important to note that there was also significant legislation passed in US courts during this time regarding the scope of accountability for another's actions, otherwise known as accomplice liability.[7] In legal terms, the accomplice is defined as an auxiliary role in which an individual provides assistance to another in the commission of a crime and therefore shares culpability for the resulting charges: "whoever commits an offense against the United States or aids, abets, counsels, commands, induces or procures its commission, is punishable as a principal."[8]

The legal context of the role of the accomplice is critical to consider in light of legislation that was put into effect during this period regarding shared complicity and the twofold aspects of defining a criminal offense.[9] Both an *actus reus* ("guilty act") and *mens rea* ("guilty mind") are required in order to convict an individual—there must be a demonstration of deliberate actions (*actus reus*) as well as the intention to behave in an illicit manner (*mens rea*).[10] In 1971, the National Commission on Reform of Federal Criminal Laws, which was established to study the criminal justice system, submitted its final report to Congress. One of the commission's main proposals concerned the development of a more systematic application of *mens rea*, an argument that was later partially addressed in the Criminal Code Reform Act of 1977. Until this point, common law had stipulated that a principal must be convicted for an accomplice to be complicit as well; in the 1970s, the law determined that an accomplice's indirect involvement could result in complete culpability for another's actions, even if the principal was not convicted.[11]

Although the concept of accomplice liability offers a useful departure point into rethinking the conventional subject positions and forms of agency in art critical and historical analyses, it is important to note that the figure of the accomplice examined in this book only draws inspiration from the potentials of such a paradigm. Thanks to the dismissal of the events around Burden's *Deadman*, none of the artists discussed in this book commit actual crimes. Nonetheless, the fact that a significant number of performances during the 1970s engaged with aspects of criminality in the name of art—a tendency that Acconci discusses in his 1991 essay "Some Notes on Illegality in Art"—necessitates some consideration.[12] The present study is informed by texts that offer legal perspectives on aesthetic questions, which emphasize the need to interrogate the complete range of agents involved in an artwork's production in terms of ethics, authority, responsibility, and ownership.[13] The recourse to conceivably illicit actions in art practices and the way that the framework of art could potentially be used to nullify problematic conduct enacted on another individual demonstrates the fundamental arbitrariness of law—a point that has critical stakes beyond an artistic context.

### Legality in Art

At the start of the 1970s, a set of artists working in the United States and Western Europe began undertaking violent, potentially illicit, or otherwise unethical behavior—such as being shot in the arm by a friend, enacting self-mutilation, or becoming the subject of a live audience's physical and emotional demands—in the name of art. While the motivations for such actions might be attributed to the widespread violence and dramatic political transformations that characterized this period—including the ongoing US military intervention in Vietnam; the Kent State shootings; a surge of international terrorism; and the overthrow of military dictatorships in Greece, Portugal, and Spain—early 1970s performance art has nonetheless often been characterized as the culmination of an avant-garde progression in which artists moved beyond well-worn artistic tactics to engage audiences by using spectacular shock effects frequently taking place through the performing artist's own body. *Artist, Audience, Accomplice* complicates such claims by reconceiving unethical or deviant actions as a critical tactic deployed not merely for provocation but also to explore the thresholds of authorial property and agency.

Against the dominant critical analysis that situates potentially illegal artistic actions within a trajectory of increasingly avant-garde gestures,

I contend that the possible legal and ethical violations found in the work of these artist case studies provide ways of reconstituting the established roles of art as property and artist as agent in an artwork. At a time when both subject and image were undergoing extreme regulation, the figure of the accomplice put pressure on the threshold of the self as property against the legal boundaries that delineate what belongs to a subject and what belongs to a public. In other words, these artists amended Conceptual art's interrogation of *objects* as artistic property to instead test the boundaries of the authorial agency over *subjects* mobilizing a vast network of previously unseen actors embedded in each work. Artists' perceived illicit or otherwise unethical actions must therefore be understood not as aggrandized provocations for shock effect but rather as tactical investigations of new forms of artistic ownership that no longer occurred exclusively on the level of the object but rather on that of the subject as well.[14]

According to historian Bruce Schulman, the expansive public transformations of American life in the 1960s had, by the following decade, dissolved into small, independent communities driven by personal interests. In his estimation, the long 1970s—defined as the period between 1969 and 1984—marked a turning point in the United States, during which entrepreneurial self-interest and an emerging new political majority in the South and Southwest, which favored small government and reduced social services, gained traction. With diminished faith in authority and the public sphere, Americans began pursuing principles of self-reliance—which materialized in alternatives to the 1960s valuation of social solidarity and collective public obligations toward one's fellow citizens within the national community.[15]

Sovereignty became an integral part of the social, political, and economic discourses of the 1970s and 1980s. In 1973, approximately two hundred Native Americans began a seventy-one-day-long occupation of Wounded Knee in South Dakota; their demands for Indigenous sovereignty and treaty rights led to violent conflict with federal authorities, leaving two dead. That same year, the US Supreme Court ruled in favor of abortion rights in the landmark case *Roe v. Wade*, effectively protecting women's self-governance over their own bodies. Following the Paris Peace Accords that were signed in January 1973, the United States ceased its direct military involvement in Vietnam, and active conscription into the US Armed Forces ended. Yet the concept of personal sovereignty also assumed meaning beyond bodily integrity; self-ownership, or the idea of the self as a form of property, became a crucial part of the ideology behind right-wing libertarianism, neoliberalism, and free-market capitalism that expanded and took hold in the United States by the 1980s.

A similar shift occurred in the history of art. The height of the 1960s was characterized by a supposed democratization of art—as seen in the everyday aesthetic of Pop art and the attempts at integrating audiences in Happenings—that nonetheless maintained traditional formulations of authorial control. By the end of the decade, some artists became less interested in generating work for broad audiences, instead developing ways of engaging a more limited group of spectators while opening the production processes to auxiliary agents. While the types of art practices seen during the early 1970s increasingly involved others in what might at first appear to be more equitable distributions of labor and responsibility—a photographer documenting live performances conducted exclusively for the camera, for instance—the fact that the resulting artwork nonetheless remained credited to a single artist brings up a contradiction that recurs throughout this book and is worth a brief mention. Despite my best efforts to develop a critical language that describes the roles of other auxiliary agents operating within a work of art, it is perhaps impossible to avoid perpetuating the single-author model in some capacity—an issue that is reflected in the "case study" structure of this book. This paradox is undoubtably a product of the ongoing focus in art historical discourse on artistic originality and innovation. However, it also draws attention to the complex power dynamics between the nominal artist and other subjects that continue to affirm traditional formulations of creative expression that are structured centrifugally from a single conceptual center, as well as the fundamental limitations between artistic intentionality and the final effect of one's work. By examining four artists and their accomplices who collectively put pressure on this strict formulation of authorship, my book is an attempt to begin to imagine alternative possibilities.

For the purposes of this study, one of the most important aspects of Conceptual art to emerge was the exploration of legalistic determinations conferring an artist's authority. Both Minimalist and Conceptual art practices often involved few, if not singular, individuals performing delegated tasks conducted in the name of the artist—such as Donald Judd hiring industrial fabricators to produce his three-dimensional objects or Sol LeWitt creating instructional directives that textually declared how to execute his work by others. The limited network of associates involved with a work's execution in these cases expanded the traditional formulation of either singular or collaborative art production, approaching a model in between—one that notably relied on determinations made through legal means. By taking seriously the performative power vested in Marcel Duchamp's readymades—in that naming a work of art becomes the creative authorial act—artists developed strategies for testing out other ways of defining their authorial parameters and legitimacy through labor contracts, certificates of authenticity, and notarized statements.[16] For instance, Robert Morris's prescient *Statement of Aesthetic Withdrawal* (1963), in which the artist sought recourse from the State of New York in formally deauthorizing his work *Litanies* through a notarized statement after failing to receive payment from a collector for said work, stands as an example of the ways in which artists used the law to define their authorial power over aesthetic property in place of concrete material object production.

The legal emphasis of such conceptual projects culminated in 1971, when gallerist and Conceptual art impresario Seth Siegelaub, along with the attorney Robert Projansky, developed "The Artist's Reserved Rights Transfer and Sale Agreement" (ARRTSA). Recognizing the urgent need for legal articulation in artworks that became increasingly immaterial or ephemeral, such as Conceptual and performance art, Siegelaub provided a formal framework for protecting artists' economic interests in their intellectual property. The basic concept of granting artists more financial control over their work that was expressed in ARRTSA became codified in further revisions to the US Copyright Act in 1976 intended to protect emergent forms of intellectual property that arose with new media technologies.

While the ambitions of Siegelaub's groundbreaking document promised new protections for artists, the self-generated, grassroots nature of the contract did not result in systemic change; at the time of ARRTSA's introduction in the early 1970s, many of the artists who signed the agreement ended up becoming blacklisted by collectors, limiting the scope of the agreement's power. It wasn't until 1990—when the US Congress passed the Visual Artists Rights Act (VARA), which granted the clearest and most comprehensive articulation of a creator's rights concerning works of visual art—that a clear and universal legal standard was established communicating the enduring power of artistic authorship over one's creative visual production that persists even after a work leaves the artist's studio and enters the art market. As such, the ambiguity of such questions that remained undefined during the nineteen-year span between the 1971 publication of ARRTSA in *Studio International* and VARA's federal legislation in 1990 marks precisely the period of this book's study, during which the accomplice appeared in art practices that explored similar inquiries about authorial control and rights over aesthetic property.

During the 1970s and 1980s, artists began adopting what resembled highly individualized practices—such as the prominent display of the performer in so-called body art or Neo-Expressionist painting—that belied a network of supporting associates required to execute the work. While the emphasis on legal determinations of authorship that characterized late 1960s Conceptualism largely dropped out of subsequent discussions of art practices that immediately followed, I contend that considerations of legal questions evolved in ways that proved useful for artists who were exploring new models of participation. This recourse to the legal, coupled with the involvement of a network of auxiliary associates, was notably featured in other works from this period as well; in 1978, Tehching Hsieh began his first major durational performance, *One Year Performance 1978–1979 (Cage Piece)*, in which he incarcerated himself in a makeshift jail cell for an entire year. During that time, apart from occasional audience viewing periods, Hsieh interacted with only two individuals, who became necessary figures in the work's execution: an associate of Hsieh's brought daily sustenance, removed the artist's waste, and took a single photograph of the artist each day, while a lawyer notarized the piece and confirmed the successful execution of the terms of the work, including Hsieh's continual confinement.[17] Given that these agents performed tasks within a networked yet hierarchical working model of distributed agency to maintain the incarceration of the artist under his direction, Hsieh's reliance on such figures demonstrates a wider shift in art practices during this time toward non-audience participation as well as an interest in extending Conceptual art's legal designations into inquiries about subjects' rights and the conferral of authority through legal means that relates to the primary case-study artists analyzed here.

### Typologies and Responsibilities

Each of the four chapters of this book examines a different typology of the accomplice: *abettors*, *partners*, *assistants*, and *preservers*. The accomplice provides a useful model as it allows us to probe the actions and agents that occur beyond the scope of the typical artist-audience framework, which would otherwise remain undetected. Looking at a distinct set of legal theories in each chapter—chapter 1 expands on the discussion of criminality and accomplice liability, chapter 2 looks at publicity and privacy rights, chapter 3 focuses on intellectual property law, and chapter 4 explores trespassing within tort law—provides a means of drawing out the networks of delegated responsibility from which the accomplice emerges as a key player.

The accomplice paradigm allows for an analysis of a basic question that recurs throughout the book: to what extent is a person responsible for another's actions? As an accessory to a crime who legally shares equal culpability with a perpetrator, a network of *abettors* appears in Burden's work through their (often coerced) involvement with potentially illicit or unethical actions undertaken by the nominal artist. That is, Burden seeks to distribute responsibility for artworks that frequently test the outermost limits of criminal liability using his abettors, but only in a way that maintains sole authorship. Such creative action mobilizes auxiliary agents and is contingent on their participation. In contrast to Burden, Wilke uses techniques of exposure through possible violations of publicity and privacy laws to create *partners* from individuals who refused to engage in equitable relationships, whether personal or professional; she imposes shared accountability to reconfigure the gendered hierarchies of authorial recognition and agency. The *assistants* examined in chapter 3 describe those agents who assume largely traditional roles working in an artist's studio. However, rather than executing directions in the service of the nominal artist, Kippenberger develops a two-pronged and contradictory mode of delegation: giving assistants the opportunity to assume control over their actions while also demanding their obedience to subvert it, often in potential violation of their own intellectual property rights. Exceeding the conventional boundaries of an artist-assistant relationship, Kippenberger creates a centripetal working model in which all output feeds back into his public image. O'Grady's experience of the largely segregated mainstream New York art world of the early 1980s led to her formulation of a self-generated performance persona; Mlle Bourgeoise Noire became her primary operative in pursuit of potential accomplices who took the form of *preservers*. Drawing inspiration from Martin Heidegger's definition of the term as "presenters, critics, and audiences" that O'Grady cited as particularly influential to her thinking about her practice in 1983, the preservers in this chapter describe the prospective allies—including gallerists, curators, art critics, and nonart audiences—whom O'Grady sought to exhibit, document, discuss, or view her work, despite the potential risks involved in the act of preservation for Black artists and audiences in this context.

Given the ways in which the artists analyzed in this book utilize individuals as accomplices, the question of ethics for the projects discussed is complex. While the nature of artworks in which accomplices are used is often necessarily exploitative and based on power differentials, it is *through* such inequitable relations that the accomplice emerges as a viable subject position. The very nature of participatory art—using other individuals as a constitutive part of an artwork—brings up important considerations about ethics, authorship, and responsibility. As art historian Claire Bishop has articulated, the frequent partiality by critics, curators, and audiences toward projects based on collaborative, democratic, and consensual inter-actions often limits the engagement with artistic strategies in which un-ethical or self-interested actions are deliberately forged. Therefore, often the assessment of participatory art falls to ethical considerations, such as the extent of equitable collaboration staged in the work, which precludes more nuanced understandings of the potential value of participatory art to ask critical questions about accountability, authorship, and agency that appear in more unequal situations.[18]

Like Bishop, I believe that successful art does not need to follow an ameliorative agenda and that its value does not rest on such aspirations. In *Artificial Hells: Participatory Art and the Politics of Spectatorship* (2012), she emphasizes the need for new language to describe a broader network of what she calls "co-existing authorial positions" in visual art, much like the various constitutive, yet independently recognized, roles found in the worlds of music, film, theater, and fashion—such as director, writer, makeup artist, stylist, and so on.[19] By theorizing a new subject position that is mutually constituted by certain responsibilities held by both artist and audience alike, my research aims to introduce language for expanded authorial models, albeit in hierarchical and distributed terms.

To this end, the accomplice paradigm shows how artists who stage exploitative relations allow us to think about the self and other (as neither autonomous nor collective), shared responsibility, and non-sovereign rela-tions in new ways. In contrast to participatory projects in which equitable collaboration with audiences or traditionally hired labor is performed as a central component, the works described in this book that stage hierar-chical differentials between the artist and accomplices arguably perform a critical role in exposing individuals who have typically been left out of such agential possibilities—with the aim that in recognizing them, a possible transformation of power may ultimately emerge. But we might ask, do the accomplices want to be found, and what does finding them actually do for our understandings of these works? In my estimation, the legal framework allows us to trace responsibility in artworks to people who are conventionally invisible in the established binary of artist and audience, thereby destabilizing the artistic author as it is currently understood. By looking for accomplices through a legal lens, the ways in which agency and accountability are dispersed under an artist's authority becomes clearer.

## Performance, Participation, and Collaboration

Several scholars have presented models of analysis or provided important theoretical backgrounds that have shaped my conceptualization of the accomplice. Peggy Phelan has argued that the innate power of performance resides in its ability to evade conscription into representation, noting the dual effects of visibility in both negative and positive terms.[20] For Phelan, the exceptional strength of performance art derives from its fundamental ability to resist visual reproduction, and therefore commodification, by remaining "unmarked"—a model that shares certain similarities with the operations of the accomplices. The fact that accomplices first appear concomitantly during a surge of performance work in the early 1970s might indicate that the medium uniquely provided a way to circumvent traditional valuations of presence and representation that served the accomplices as well. Just as Phelan "attempts to find a theory of value for that which is not 'really' there, which cannot be surveyed within the boundaries of the putative real," I use the accomplices to expose a blind spot within current art historical constructions that omit a range of significant but often discounted labor staged through deliberate power differentials.[21]

Body art in the late 1960s and early 1970s has often been portrayed as an extension of critiques introduced by Conceptual art against the commodification of the art object and traditional object-based materials as signifiers of authorial property (a.k.a. "dematerialization") by using the artist's own body as both subject and object, as defined by critic Willoughby Sharp in the inaugural issue of *Avalanche* in 1970.[22] For art historians such as Amelia Jones, body art practices—of which Wilke is a key example—dissolve the hierarchies between artist and viewer to produce an intersubjective engagement that "instantiate[s] the dislocation or decentering of the Cartesian subject of modernism."[23] However, such interpretations elide the ways that many of these performances in fact pivot on distributed forms of responsibility and agency among a wide range of participants and constitute a set of consequences that extend beyond a work's ostensible actions.

Although collaborative authorship or expanded social involvement has been examined in various art historical contexts—notably experimentations with audience participation such as 1960s Happenings and Fluxus event scores and post-1989 US and European participatory and installation art practices—many of these critical debates (for instance, those by curators such as Nicolas Bourriaud and Maria Lind) have centered on projects that reflect optimistically democratic or egalitarian values.[24] Following the work of Bishop and Frazer Ward, I instead focus my attention on authored projects in which the involvement of auxiliary figures is deliberately manipulated.[25]

Despite their typical categorization within the genres of body art, feminist performance, and Neo-Expressionist painting—all of which are thought to center on the physical or conceptual actions of the nominal artist—I contend that the art practices analyzed in this book represent a new subgenre of participatory art, defined by Bishop as artworks in which "people constitute the central artistic medium and material."[26] The omission of the accomplices presents the work of artists like Burden, Wilke, Kippenberger, and O'Grady as total and exclusive, whereas in fact it was more relational and fluid. By restructuring the social parameters of artworks to include auxiliary agents, the theorization of the accomplices in the present study intersects with, yet nonetheless expands, the existing literature on participation.

Bishop developed the concept of "delegated performance," which provides an important model for describing the way that artists use other individuals through deliberately manipulative, aggressive, or otherwise unethical means. Within the framework of the so-called social turn in contemporary art after 1989, delegated performance designates an artist's tendency to hire nonprofessionals to perform in their place. Bishop argues that these practices differ from models of employment often found in other contexts, such as theater, in which individuals are hired by directors to play specific roles in their artistic vision, including writer, makeup artist, stylist, and so on; rather, she considers artworks for which artists largely "hire people to perform *their own socioeconomic category*, be this on the basis of gender, class, ethnicity, age, disability, or (more rarely) profession."[27] However, while Bishop offers a critical examination of hierarchical artistic delegation in which hired performers are subjected to ethically questionable

actions directed by the artist—such as her example of Santiago Sierra paying minimum-wage workers to perform demeaning or embarrassing activities as an exploration of exploitative labor practices in economic exchange
systems—she specifically distinguishes such tendencies from "a tradition
of performance from the late 1960s and early 1970s" exemplified by the
work of Burden, Acconci, and Gina Pane, "in which work is undertaken
by the artists themselves."[28]

My argument proceeds from the scholarly investigation put forth
in Bishop's inquiry; however, I expand her analysis to include alternative
forms of participation that emerged in early 1970s performance art and
that evolved through the 1980s. The artworks studied in this book digress
from existing models of participation in three important ways: (1) the accomplices are not readily visible as key operatives; (2) their involvement
is often not voluntary; and (3) they occupy a thoroughly distinct subject
position—neither emerging from traditional audiences nor acting as extensions of the artist, as is the case with hired performers who work in
the place of or within the domain of the artist. While Bishop describes
performance art from the 1970s and 1980s as characterized by artists using
"their *own* bodies as the medium and material of the work, often with a
corresponding emphasis on physical and psychological transgression," I instead argue that the artists analyzed in *Artist, Audience, Accomplice* notably
mobilized the involvement of secondary agents whose participation comes
into view because of said transgressive elements.[29]

The historical background for outsourcing—defined as contracting
work to others—intersects with participatory art practices throughout the
twentieth century. Such a working model diverges from expanded audience involvement in that hired artistic labor is sourced from agents working within the domain of authority of the nominal artist. The context for
such forms of delegation can be traced to John Cage's experimental composition techniques, in which a score is repeatable by other individuals and
no longer privileges the notion of a singular authentic performance. For
artists experimenting in the first half of the 1960s, such as Simone Forti,
Yoko Ono, and La Monte Young, scoring became more than the directives on the page as performers were tasked with bringing outside elements
into the realm of traditional notation. The tacit agreement between the
artist and the performer became expanded and codified by the late 1960s
through certificates of authenticity or contractual arrangements seen in
Conceptual art practices, which extended to actual legal regulation by the
start of the following decade. For example, in the late 1960s, artists such as

Joseph Kosuth, John Baldessari, and Lawrence Weiner began using documentation and information as their artistic material in the production of alternative, language-based forms of artworks. The pieces created by these artists emphasized authorial intention as the primary marker of authenticity while simultaneously probing distributed accountability for the work that was shared among other agents.

Complicating the dichotomy between the "traditional conception of the artist as an autonomous agent" and collaborative authorship, in which authorial recognition is shared among two or more individuals, this book's investigation maintains a focus on hierarchical relationships between nominal artists and their network of accomplices.[30] While artistic collaboration has been the subject of occasional exhibitions, including Cynthia McCabe's *Artistic Collaboration in the Twentieth Century* at the Hirshhorn Museum in 1984; curators Susan Sollins and Nina Castelli Sundell's traveling exhibition *Team Spirit* in 1991; and What, How & for Whom / whw's *Collective Creativity* at the Fridericianum in Kassel in 2005, these shows focus on jointly or communally authored works. In contrast, my approach to analyzing these artworks is framed, at least in part, by feminist scholarly literature that considers unseen forms of collaboration and labor, often by female artists, whose role in artistic production was obscured.[31] Most notably, Anne M. Wagner's analysis of Georgia O'Keeffe, Lee Krasner, and Eva Hesse in her 1996 book *Three Artists (Three Women)* was an early source of inspiration for this project for negotiating the gender dynamics and social hierarchies in marital relationships between two artists, as was performance scholar Shannon Jackson's cogent analysis of Mierle Laderman Ukeles's work and practice in *Social Works: Performing Art, Supporting Publics*.

### Authorship and Ownership

The breakdown of the presumed neutrality between artist and audience in the 1970s was indicative of a larger shift concerning the possibilities of expanded roles for individuals beyond that binary. This marked a radical transformation in existing authorial frameworks, many of which had been well established for centuries, centered on the obfuscation of a vast body of auxiliary labor that affirmed the primacy of a singular, autonomous author. In the twentieth century, the authorial subject became paradoxically disrupted and further reinforced as modernism brought the interrelated issues of authorship, originality, and aesthetic property to the fore of artistic debate. Artists became increasingly recognized for their unique contributions, yet the legacy of the readymade—a creative act centered on the artist's designation of a found object as art—necessitated the legitimating power of the artist's authority more than ever.

While the immediate post–World War II period largely signaled a recommitment to the Romantic conception of the artist-genius by using one's medium to convey personal expression (as in the cultic myth of personality generated around Abstract Expressionists such as Jackson Pollock), during the 1960s artists began exploring means of decentering their authorial role in artistic practices through techniques of delegation and deskilling. For example, artists such as Andy Warhol and Frank Stella developed methods of sharing labor among a variety of individual agents working under the nominal artist's direction, whether in the form of Warhol's Factory assistants or the Minimalist employment of off-site industrial fabricators for the production of work that effaced visible evidence of the artist's subjective input or "hand," thereby eroding the typical authorial hierarchies and recalibrating the authorial function to a largely conceptual role.[32]

The late 1950s and early 1960s also marked a moment of transition from medium-specific works to the formulation of projects involving greater audience participation, such as environmental installations, which in turn necessitated alternative methods of artistic evaluation and theorization.[33] Across performances, Fluxus events or directives, and Happenings, many artists—including George Brecht, VALIE EXPORT, and Yoko Ono—solicited the participation of their viewers, disrupting the presumed passivity of such a role to enact a more invested, embodied exchange. Artists such as Kaprow incorporated the audience into the realization of his Happenings, at times to menacing or otherwise violent ends, applying the viewer's own personal and unscripted reaction to a set of actions or circumstances as the work's primary material.[34] These early experiments with harnessing individuals as what Susan Sontag called "material objects" prefigured the shift to 1970s so-called body art, in which artists such as Pane and Acconci used their own physicality as their principal medium, often with transgressive undertones.[35]

Whether through audiences becoming integrally involved as key actors in Happenings, the viewer's perceptual experience assuming a greater constitutive role in viewing Minimalist objects, or the explicit solicitation of bystanders to become contributors through Conceptualist directives or

Fluxus event scores, the 1960s marked a decade of increased participation by individuals who would be considered something other than the nominal artist. Despite their divergent methods, such artistic paradigms presented a destabilization of the unitary authority of the primary creator in a work of art that was being discussed concurrently by poststructuralist thinkers during the end of the 1960s. Perhaps most famously, the 1967 publication of Roland Barthes's landmark "Death of the Author" essay disrupted authorial sovereignty over a work's meaning, allowing instead for the possibilities of interpretive exchange controlled by the reader or spectator. Barthes posited an alternative model of interpretation—one that undid the universality of an author-imposed narrative, rejected the conflation of artwork and author, and deemphasized individual subjectivity as the ultimate locus of meaning. Despite Barthes's influence in critical theory and beyond, this formulation of the "birth of the reader" maintained a conventional binary between artist and viewer (or author and reader) as the two operative subject positions.[36]

While Barthes and other poststructuralists were against the unilateral singularity of a narrative imposed by an author in favor of what was seen as more equitable interpretive exchanges, some scholars and writers began to question the authority of the author altogether and what was at stake in dismantling it. As Barthes and others interrogated the power held by the author as the sole determinant of meaning, the timing of such inquiries—at a moment when marginalized voices were finally able to assume authorial roles or occupy positions of subjective power, albeit of a still limited scope—felt suspect to many important thinkers, including Linda Nochlin, Nancy Hartsock, Luce Irigaray, and Gayatri Chakravorty Spivak.[37]

By inhabiting a decentered subject position apart from that of both the artist and the audience, the accomplice presents a potential alternative to the paradigmatic binary that might offer an untraditional means of retaining agency and power for those previously underrepresented. Yet dealing with the accomplice's significance requires a different approach than simply acknowledging its presence or restoring such individuals unproblematically to the position of sovereign authorial subjects. Just as Griselda Pollock expressed in 1996 when critiquing the limitations of using a monographic approach to study the work of women artists ("we could not begin to speak of the women artists we would re-excavate from dusty basements and forgotten encyclopedias using the existing languages of art history or criticism"), I believe that exploring artwork with the rhetoric and reality of legality in mind heightens our awareness of previously undisclosed links of responsibility by exposing auxiliary individuals whose role was otherwise unidentified or only partially recognized.[38] Nochlin, Spivak, and others desire not to impart representation onto those previously excluded from such visibility but to show *how* such representations have been heretofore ideologically conditioned to silence certain subjects. Similarly, I do not argue that accomplices should be co-credited artistic authors or occupy equal footing as the nominal author but that their presence allows us to better understand the ways in which existing models of authorship, based on a dichotomous relationship with an audience, fail to allow for other forms of agency and responsibility to emerge in our understanding of art.

### Abettors, Partners, Assistants, Preservers

This book charts how the poststructuralist destabilization of the Romantic formulation of the creative author in the late 1960s opened up the possibility for the accomplice to emerge in two directions: white male artists developed the accomplice to posit an alternative form of authorship using other individuals in a manner that retains authorial agency and recognition; while in contrast, the experience of having been an accomplice became a weapon wielded by women artists and artists of color to reclaim forms of power that had been refused or abrogated. Therefore, the selection of my four case-study artists allows for a discussion of discrepancies in the way artists mobilize accomplices based on racial and gender privileges. Both Burden's and Kippenberger's abilities to perform illicit or ethically compromised actions in the name of art speak to the ways in which white men often evade surveillance and legal regulation when compared with artists of other racial and gender identities. For instance, Burden's invocations of criminal liability with his accomplices and Kippenberger's exploitations of his assistants through potential transgressions of intellectual property law to explore questions of responsibility, control, and aesthetic property demonstrate the ease with which such actions could be enacted by those whose experiences rested in positions of power. In contrast, given the gendered disparities in power and authorial recognition, Wilke turned to the law in the form of publicity and privacy rights in her work as part of a strategy for recovering accreditation from which she felt deliberately excluded—a condition all too familiar to the white feminist context in which her work was situated. For O'Grady, deploying her Mlle Bourgeoise Noire performance character became a necessary framework for trespassing—metaphorically breaking and entering—into spaces from which she was still excluded on account of ongoing racism and sexism in the white-run art world on her hunt for potential preserver-accomplices.

In chapter 1, I argue that Burden's often violent or provocative performance and video works produced during the 1970s—including some canonical examples of body art performed singularly for the camera, without a live audience—did not pivot exclusively on the performing artist's body. I instead contend that these pieces strategically brought into visibility a network of previously unrecognized participants, whom I term *abettors*, as a consequence of their shared ethical responsibility. That is, the tactics undertaken in Burden's work from this period were deployed to test the limits of artistic ownership and agency by compelling auxiliary agents to perform actions that would bring about distributed culpability for legal or ethical noncompliance. By focusing attention on the figures whose involvement would not typically be accounted for in traditional narratives of Burden's work, the social and temporal boundaries of the artistic projects become reformulated.

Centering on five primary artworks by Burden that took place over the course of a decade—*Deadman* (1972), *TV Hijack* (1972), *747* (1973), *Doomed* (1975), and *Diamonds Are Forever* (1981)—the artistic exploration of the limits of shared accountability takes on a particular resonance in the context of shifting debates over the scope and definition of individual rights during the 1970s that were being negotiated in both legal and aesthetic domains. Considering performance art literature and contemporaneous legislation regarding accomplice liability in the United States as well as extensive primary and secondary source material, I organize the chapter around the different types of accomplices that perform integral but often overlooked roles in Burden's work, such as his assistants, partners, documenters, security guards, and institutional representatives.

Against the background of second-wave white feminist demands for representation during the 1970s (what Chela Sandoval has referred to as "hegemonic feminism"), chapter 2 focuses on the ways in which Wilke developed various techniques of exposure to reveal evidence of shared responsibility for artistic production by publicly disclosing private behaviors or relationships.[39] The chapter is organized around a set of artworks that employ performance, video, and photography to seek artistic agency and credit from which she felt excluded throughout her career, exploring how claims for female agency in the context of white feminism intersected with debates regarding publicity, privacy, and intellectual property law throughout the 1970s. It is worth noting, however, that Wilke's attempts to repair gender-based inequities by seeking equal recognition to men speaks to her position as a white middle-class artist in the United States guided by a branch of feminism that did not particularly account for questions of class and race.

Wilke's term *snatch-shot*, which she used to subtitle her 1979 *So Help Me Hannah* photographs, encapsulates a key aspect of her broader working practice. I argue that the *snatch-shot* becomes a useful term to describe how she develops a countermodel of photography that reversed the actions of capturing and rendering a model immobile under the camera's objectification and instead used the medium to reveal indications of gendered distributions of artistic authority, labor, and recognition. By staging her sexuality and her frequently nude body for the camera, Wilke solicited male attention as a means of reclaiming authority over its unilateral hold over artistic representation. For instance, in her performance *Intercourse with . . .* (1977), she performed a striptease for the camera that exposed black stickers applied directly on her skin spelling out the initials of notable individuals in her life to draw attention to deliberate exclusions she had experienced and put them on public record. By exploiting the intimate access to her lovers and associates, Wilke indirectly revealed evidence of her presence that had otherwise been obscured in the lives and works of notable art-world figures, such as her former romantic and professional partner Claes Oldenburg.

Chapter 3 investigates Martin Kippenberger's unique, and rather infamous, relationship with his assistants. Following a brief period in which he explored collaborative artistic production, in the late 1980s Kippenberger developed a strategic mode of employment by hiring various artists to work under his authority at his art studio. Yet instead of having these assistants successfully execute tasks following his direction, Kippenberger developed a new formula for artist-assistant relations characterized by the nonproductive and deliberately exploitative participation of subjects as well as a decentralized overproduction and proliferation of images that ultimately, and paradoxically, reaffirmed his personal celebrity.

Considering the enormous artistic output produced by Kippenberger during the late 1980s—paintings, sculptures, installations, photography, posters, drawings, and event invitations—as well as his larger-than-life artistic persona and extensive self-promotion, I analyze how he develops an alternative authorial model that greatly differs from the traditional artist-assistant working relationship. This was achieved by actively soliciting his assistants' subjectivity while also creating various forms of disruption that would thwart their execution of tasks or potentially undermine their intellectual property rights. To this end, he set in motion two interlocking feedback loops of image remediation and social delegation. Rather than harnessing the talents and abilities of the auxiliary forms of hired labor, Kippenberger reversed the helpful but subordinate role that assistants typically played by introducing three forms of disruption that I term *error, residual individuality*, and *waste*. In so doing, Kippenberger shifts the central artistic procedure—such as creating a painting—to causing interference between the two major cycles of remediation and delegation, establishing a model of authorship that acts as an interruptive mechanism while also cultivating an expanded public artistic persona.

Chapter 4 examines how O'Grady strategically developed her Mlle Bourgeoise Noire performance character to stage a sequence of prescient public performances over a three-year period beginning in 1980 that critiqued various aspects of the contemporary art world as experienced through the lens of a Black middle-class woman artist. Adapting a term that Mlle Bourgeoise Noire used to describe one of her most famous interventions—*invasion*—I argue that this performance persona became O'Grady's primary operative to conduct various forms of conceptual "trespassings" into art institutions and private spaces in her pursuit of potential accomplices. Her actions as Mlle Bourgeoise Noire strategically targeted a range of shifting adversaries: Black artists making "well-behaved" art that adhered to values set by the white-dominated art world, the art institutions in New York that perpetuated their own hegemonic whiteness, second-wave white feminists who failed to account for the intersectional experience of Black women, and the latent sexism pervasive in the predominantly male art world. By choosing the word *trespassing*, I aim to draw out the more complex ways that O'Grady-as-Mlle Bourgeoise Noire attempted to move undetected—as will be discussed in terms of her curatorial work for *The Black and White Show*, her unsolicited letters to other Black artists, and a participatory work staged at a Harlem parade in 1983 known as *Art Is . . .* —in addition to her more public performative intervention at Just Above Midtown in 1980 and the reprisal of this project at the New Museum in 1981. Given O'Grady's restricted access to the mainstream art world at the time, I argue that unlike performance personas made by white male artists, for instance, for whom acceptance was readily available, O'Grady's development of Mlle Bourgeoise Noire was motivated by a desire to infiltrate mainstream art institutions and discourses to seek out those who might become allies in disrupting the art world's continued segregation, which was reflected in the lack of racial diversity for exhibiting artists and audiences alike.

This chapter differs in that it charts O'Grady's pursuit of auxiliary agents to serve as accomplices in the form of preservers rather than her active mobilization of them—as was true of previous case studies in this book. Instead, I contend that she tactically developed the Mlle Bourgeoise Noire character to perform a similar role to that of the accomplices—sharing in accountability for potential risks while maintaining a hierarchical power structure under the direction of the nominal artist—while she sought out other individuals willing to assume that responsibility on her behalf. This strategic distinction between O'Grady and the other case-study artists discussed in this book can be attributed to the serious consequences at stake for Black artists and their artistic accomplices: that to engage in simulations of, or flirtations with, illicit behavior in the context of the early 1980s in New York would likely result in greater punitive measures, while explicit critiques of the ongoing racism that pervaded mainstream art institutions might result in retaliatory gestures that could have profound personal effects for those involved.

Collectively, these four chapters introduce different formulations of the accomplice that have implications for the shifting hierarchies among artistic subjects and objects, notions of aesthetic property or ownership, and the limits of individual agency. The multiple ways that accomplices are constituted as sharing in the responsibility for ethically or even legally questionable projects demonstrate one of the core issues at stake concerning the possible consequences of expanding one's artistic material to include actual human subjects. I argue that these artists, rather than undermining culture or extant cultural values, invoked alternative models of shared accountability and agency that restructure the role of the author in order to interrogate new potential capacities for the social. By opening the established binary between the categorical subject positions of artist and audience to account for operatives whose presence continually slips out of view, *Artist, Audience, Accomplice* calls for a redistribution of power dynamics, a recalibration of visibility, and a reformulation of existing models of participation. It calls forth allies and adversaries who have been waiting in the margins of history.

# Abettors

**In 1974, Chris Burden** released *Chris Burden 71–73*. This self-published book cataloged twenty-three early performances with terse narrative descriptions of works coupled with black-and-white documentary photographs. The account of his 1971 performance *Shoot* reads as follows: "At 7:45 p.m. I was shot in the left arm by a friend. The bullet was a copper jacket 22 long rifle. My friend was standing about fifteen feet from me."[1] This rather neutral explanation is accompanied by thirteen photographs of the performance taken primarily by Alfred Lutjeans, including three of the best-known images of Burden from this series: preparing himself as the shooter takes aim, clutching his side as blood drips down his arm from the wound (fig. 1.1), and staring into the camera as his arm is wrapped in a makeshift bandage (fig. 1.2). Following the performance, these images became the key documentation of *Shoot* and were circulated widely in the mass media as reports of Burden's work gained notoriety.

In the catalog, a full-page photograph faces the artist's written description of *Shoot*: two figures opposite each other in an empty gallery space (fig. 1.3). On the left side of the frame is Burden. His image is blurred, captured in motion at the moment he was shot. His feet, firmly planted in a wide-legged stance, shift backward as his arms, which were once by his side, move in front of his torso and clutch the site of the gunshot wound. On the right side of the frame is Burden's unnamed shooter, whose physical stillness is registered in the relative clarity of his image.[2] The long hair of the marksman, captured in three-quarter profile from the camera, obscures his face. Due to the brevity of the action, the weapon itself is entirely invisible, leaving an indeterminate shadow in its place.

While reproductions of *Shoot* have typically been limited to these few select photographs, the other images included as official documentation of this work open the boundaries of the performance in important ways. The following pages of the 1974 catalog include ten other photographs that capture the artist's wife, Barbara, and various friends working

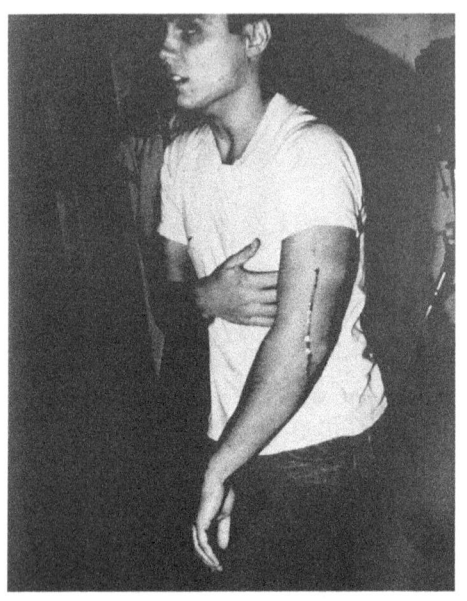

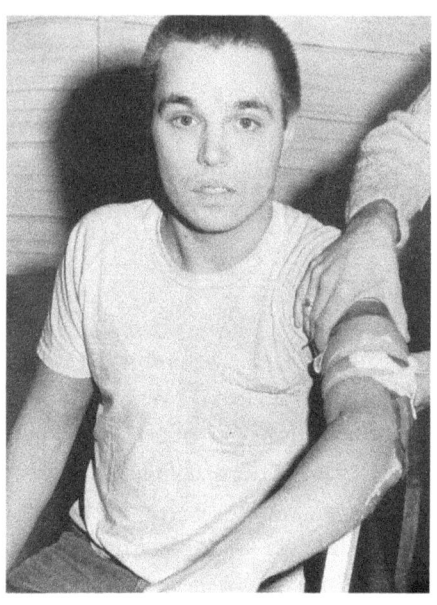

**1.01** Chris Burden, *Shoot*, November 19, 1971. F Space, Santa Ana, California. Photograph by Alfred Lutjeans.

**1.02** Chris Burden, *Shoot*, November 19, 1971. F Space, Santa Ana, California. Photograph by Alfred Lutjeans.

on the preparation of the piece and responding to the act of Burden being shot. In one of these photographs, Chris stands with Barbara (who was also his uncredited videographer) as they prepare a camera for additional documentation. In another, various individuals present at the performance wrap a makeshift tourniquet and bandage out of packing tape and towels around Burden's arm. The last image depicts four young, casually dressed women posing for the camera in front of the garage door of the F Space gallery with Burden nowhere to be seen (fig. 1.4). These photographs offer support to Burden's claim that "the violence part really wasn't that important, it was just a crux to make all the mental stuff happen . . . the anticipation, how you dealt with the anticipation. Physically it was no big deal."[3]

While both Burden's text and photographs emphasize the codependency of the shooter and the performing artist, reports in the media directed their attention toward Burden alone. The catalog was released in the wake of a series of dramatic articles published about Burden's performances, particularly the infamous 1973 *New York Times* article "He Got Shot—for His Art."[4] As art historian Amelia Jones points out, "most articles on Burden's work from the 1970s . . . begin with a sensationalizing description of

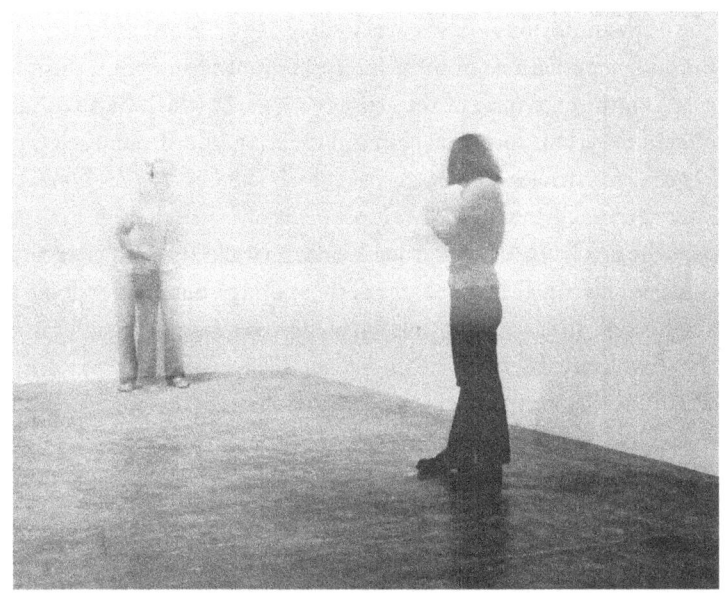

**1.03**   Chris Burden, *Shoot*, November 19, 1971. F Space, Santa
Ana, California. Photograph by Alfred Lutjeans.

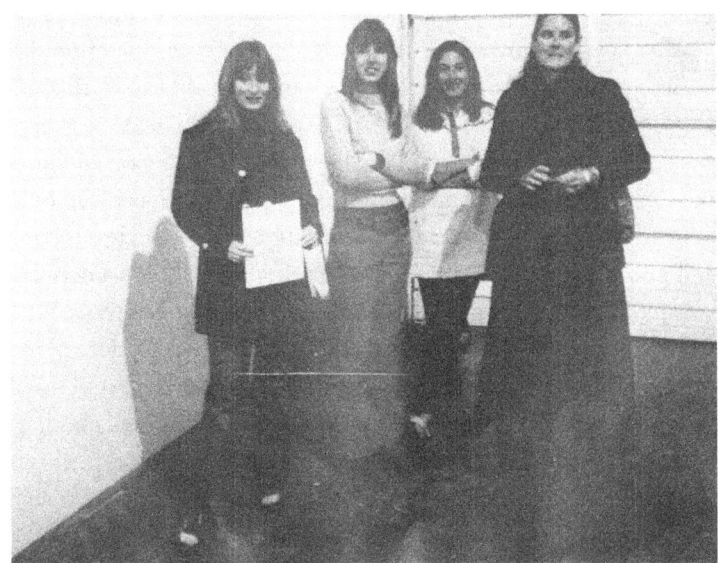

**1.04**   Chris Burden, *Shoot*, November 19, 1971. F Space, Santa
Ana, California. Photograph by Alfred Lutjeans.

one of the notorious violent acts he staged as performance art."[5] Despite Burden's repudiations of these interpretations of his work, the media focused on the extremity of the artist's actions, in which he often subjected himself to various corporeal pain and suffering.[6] Burden himself explained: "Those first articles in *Esquire*, *Newsweek*, the *Los Angeles Times*, and the interview on Channel 9 in LA. It pisses me off when they only take the first slice, the first level. 'Chris Burden, man who walks through glass . . .' I mean, come on! It's true I've done some of those things, but I'm not doing them as a circus act."[7] Regardless of Burden's repeated insistence that his intent was not "frivolous exhibitionism," narratives that foreground the violence of his actions have continued to be perpetuated through the present day.[8]

In a 1975 magazine interview, Burden explained that he chose to use black-and-white photographs for the documentation of his early performances in order to deflect attention from the blood and gore of the principal action, suggesting that the significance of these works might also reside elsewhere.[9] In fact, the initial intention was for the marksman to merely graze Burden's arm, which would have left a minimal physical trace.[10] What becomes most evident in the documentation of *Shoot* included in *Chris Burden 71–73*, taken in its entirety, is the extent to which the performance—typically described as the precise action of Burden being shot—in fact expands socially and temporally to include a variety of auxiliary participants who were involved in the events before and after the bullet's trajectory from rifle to artist's arm. In fact, the work could arguably be said to continue beyond the confines of the F Space gallery—into Burden's subsequent trip to a local hospital, where he gave a "domestic dispute" as the official reason for his injury. Not only having embroiled the marksman in any potential criminal charges that would result but his wife and photographer as well, Burden's actions opened onto a network of coconspirators, including Barbara and Lutjeans, among others.[11] While their respective roles are not readily visible in traditional narrations of the work's content, the significance of their involvement is the subject of this chapter.

Critical attention is often paid to the rather limited number of Burden's performances that involve pain or danger to himself; this has precluded an approach that takes a sustained measure of projects such as *220* (1971), *Jaizu* (1972), *Match Piece* (1972), and *Dos Equis* (1972), in which Burden enacted potential legal or ethical transgressions that affected other individuals.[12] For example, in *220*, F Space was filled with twelve inches of water as Burden and three other participants each sat atop their own fourteen-foot ladders that were scattered throughout the gallery. Burden then dropped a 220-volt live electric line into the water, forcing those present to remain precariously in position overnight until Burden's wife arrived the following morning to cut the circuit breaker. Prohibiting any nonparticipating audience on site, Burden tested both the physical endurance and mental culpability that would determine the fate of those present. In *Dos Equis*, Burden placed two sixteen-foot X-shaped wooden sculptures that he had soaked in gasoline across both lanes of Laguna Canyon Road at 2 a.m.; he then set them on fire, causing unsuspecting car traffic to be blocked. Burden himself left the site of the work before having encountered any potential viewers, as he later explained: "the intended audience for that piece was the one guy driving down the road who saw it first."[13] These examples invite an alternative interpretation of the artist's performance practice from this period that would account for projects by Burden that have been largely ignored in favor of works that fit within the art historical categorization of "body art."

While Burden's physical presence is certainly essential to many of his performances, the social network and the surrounding events that often exceed the work's documentation are critical yet frequently overlooked components of such pieces. By redefining the parameters of his work to not simply pivot on the artist's body or image alone, I contend that the involvement of other agents (who are neither the artist nor the audience) and the events that occur before and after the "central" actions of a piece are crucial to understanding the actual works themselves. Moving beyond explicitly illegal transgressions, an expanded sense of the term *accomplice* becomes a useful model for articulating the subject position of other individuals whose role within Burden's work has been heretofore overlooked yet who ultimately shared responsibility with the nominal artist.

This chapter explores the relationship between Burden's ongoing tactics of civil disobedience and his mobilization of a network of auxiliary participants who became willingly or unwillingly involved in the execution of his performance work, broadly construed. I use the term *abettor* to analyze the ways in which Burden's actions compelled a network of individuals to take on an expanded role in which they would aid the artist during the execution of unethical tasks undertaken in the name of art. The chapter is organized around the positions of various abettors, drawing upon a specialized common-law term defined as "one who commands, advises, instigates, or encourages another to commit a crime. A person who, being present, incites another to commit a crime, and thus becomes a principal. To be an abettor, the accused must have instigated or advised the commission of a crime or been present for the purpose of assisting in its commission; he or she must share criminal intent with which the crime was committed."[14] Much like the auxiliary role of the accomplice—who shares responsibility with but is ultimately distinct from the nominal artist that I theorize in this book—an abettor occupies a discrete position from that of the principal agent, while being equally subject to potential incrimination. Rather than exploiting the media spectacle of perceived delinquency in his work (a position that the artist himself repeatedly refuted), Burden assessed the ethical "accountability for the conduct of another person" in the context of art to demonstrate the complexity regarding the limit point of a subject's rights, an issue that became particularly significant in both aesthetic and legal debates in the 1970s.[15]

Focusing on four less-analyzed works by the artist—*TV Hijack* (1972), *747* (1973), *Doomed* (1975), and *Diamonds Are Forever* (1981)—along with *Deadman* (1972), I interpret Burden's manipulation of the agency and shared responsibility of his accomplices as a reflection of tensions around the changing definitions of individual rights in both aesthetic and legal spheres. In performances such as *747* or *TV Hijack*, Burden coerced, threatened, or otherwise terrorized auxiliary participants or audiences in a manner that replicated the social and political violence dominating the news of the 1970s, while in *Deadman* their relative involvement was psychologically generated. However, despite the differences in construction of these works, in all cases Burden tested the limits of his accomplices through his engagement with concepts of illegality, which could have implications for others as equally culpable abettors.

The recognition of the abettors in Burden's work reconceptualizes the construction and boundaries of the performative interventions so that their actual stakes can become visible. In other words, the way that Burden strategically staged illicit actions brought to light the broad network of differential agency among various auxiliary agents that is embedded but often obscured in the production, circulation, or exhibition of artworks. Therefore, I argue that Burden staged artworks that engaged illicit tactics in the context of art to expose the cultural norms around violence. However, his interest in involving the accomplices in such endeavors was to explore new questions about responsibility and authorial power that emerged in the wake of delegated labor practices of the 1960s.

This book offers the first theorization of an intermediary subject position between artist and audience, an occupant of a provisionary space distinct from the general audience that emerges in 1970s art. Yet some art historians, like Frazer Ward, have previously explored alternative ways of opening this binary—notably in discussions of Burden's work. In his essay "Gray Zone: Watching *Shoot*" (2001) and later book *No Innocent Bystanders: Performance Art and Audience* (2012), Ward argues that the 1971 performance of *Shoot* "limned the public as an arena of responsibility, of dilemma and decision—as an ethical realm."[16] However, Ward does not fully pursue a sustained examination of the ethical and legal implications of the auxiliary participants who lie outside the arena of the audience.[17] Therefore, while Ward's text provides important analyses of issues concerning "how art imagines its audiences, and the possibilities of their transformation," the subject of my chapter is how Burden's works are more than what they ostensibly seem to be—for example, the artist being shot by a marksman—by involving a network of implicated players (who are neither artist nor audience) that I term *abettors*.[18]

Legally defined, abettors are a particular subtype of the accomplice who share in criminal culpability for illicit actions conducted by primary offenders in their presence; they "aid and abet" when a crime is being planned or executed. The abettor can therefore be distinguished from an accessory, for instance, due to the abettor's typical involvement *during* a criminal action rather than *after* the crime took place. Burden, I argue, uses the framework of criminal liability to put pressure on the conditions of live performance and participation—asking what the potential implications of being present for, or helping, an artist execute a work of art might be—as well as the legal systems that were used to uphold Conceptualist transformations of the art object. That is, taking seriously art historical analyses of how art began to require more legal articulation of aesthetic ownership and authorship as the object became "contingent" in the late 1960s, in this chapter I examine how artists such as Burden extended this logic to other *subjects* using the framework of criminal law to address questions of an individual's agency and responsibility for another person.[19]

Instead of reading Burden's often violent or extreme actions in his performances from the early to mid-1970s as aggrandized avant-garde provocations, I situate his legal and ethical transgressions as strategic deployments to thrust a wider constellation of previously unrecognized participants into visibility. Burden exploits the legal responsibility that was assigned to the auxiliary agents in his performances to conduct a critical examination of an alternative form of aesthetic property that occurred through the body of the other. Modifying Conceptual art's interrogation of concepts of aesthetic ownership by expanding the traditional art object to a social network, Burden offers the rights of his abettors in their place.

**Abettors on Trial**

On February 21, 1973, Burden entered the Beverly Hills Municipal Courthouse—accompanied by his attorney—to face charges of causing a false emergency to be reported during the performative intervention known as *Deadman*. The prosecution, led by Deputy District Attorney Robert Savitt, called for testimony by the two officers who had arrived at the scene of Burden's piece three months prior. Based on the officers' accounts, Savitt sought a guilty verdict due to what he saw as a conscious manipulation of events to cause alarm—which constituted an unlawful action in the court of law.

Despite the ongoing flirtation with illegality that runs throughout much of Burden's performance work, *Deadman* was the only piece where an actual crime was charged and, as such, the one situation in which auxiliary agents could be indicted as legal accomplices to Burden. Considering the expanded circumstances of the trial as constitutive to the piece, *Deadman* foregrounds the agency and accountability of Burden's abettors, opening a relay of ethical and legal involvement moving beyond the conventional responsibility assumed by an audience. Suddenly, a variety of individuals who played an integral role in the work's construction—such as friends, professional colleagues, and legal representatives—became discernible operatives whose participation resulted in potential complicity in its consequences.

In a 1974 interview with Liza Béar for *Avalanche*, Burden discussed the transformation of audience participation in his recent work, with Béar noting:

> Everyone's getting very conscious of what . . . some of the issues in performance are, right? And it seems to me that it's gone way beyond being a display in front of an audience. And increasingly the audience is more prepared and is somehow implicated in the work. . . . No one can avoid being used somehow and used in a most intimate way, even though it's imaginary. I'm just trying to get at some of the different ways in which audiences are part of the performance now . . . [20]

By staging a situation in which auxiliary agents were coerced to act quickly in the face of potential legal incrimination because of their logistical support, aid, counsel, or defense of the artist, Burden presented a distinct scenario in which these individuals, previously unrecognized as participants in the artist's work, became his abettors.

There are conflicting narratives regarding the initial interaction between members of the art-world audience and the police during the evening of *Deadman*'s performance. For instance, according to Peter Plagens, who observed the piece firsthand while he was on assignment for the *New York Times*, both an unidentified critic and a curator had to jump to Burden's defense as he was being arrested and led to the squad car. Plagens (in reportage-style shorthand) explained how they had to "step forward, tell deputy who they are, who artist is, what this is. Deputy says, everything considered, [he] cannot lie down in the middle of La Cienega Boulevard creating traffic hazard."[21]

The limited art historical discussions of *Deadman* have largely situated the parameters of this project around the body of the artist as he lay in the street until the authorities arrived.[22] These examinations overlook the events that occurred before and after the approximately fifteen-minute action as well as the unacknowledged participation of various figures whose role and responsibility were crucial to the events that would unfold. As with *Shoot*, Burden included documentation for *Deadman* that exceeded the events that occurred on the night of November 12, 1972; his description of the piece in *Chris Burden 71–73* also notably includes mention of his arrest and subsequent trial.[23] Moreover, to accompany his narrative, Burden incorporated four images—only one of which corresponds to the typical description of *Deadman* as ending with the arrival of the police in front of the Mizuno Gallery—which therefore serve as evidence of the expanded scope of the performance itself beyond its conventional parameters.

The first photograph is the most canonical, depicting the artist lying on the street under the tarpaulin, alongside a parked vehicle (fig. 1.5). Burden's head is located near the car's tire and flanked by two flares that emit a white glow. As the image taken by Gary Beydler is framed, it is unclear whether the car has stopped unrelatedly or if it was the cause of the "crime scene" depicted. The second image—a photograph by Chuck Arnoldi—captures the moment of Burden's arrest. The photograph, shot from behind, shows the handcuffed artist directed into the awaiting police car as various bystanders look on (fig. 1.6). The third photograph, by performance artist Barbara T. Smith, depicts an anxious-looking Burden within the courthouse accompanied by his lawyer (fig. 1.7).

The fourth and final image is a courtroom drawing by Smith in which the artist is shown seated beside his lawyer as they face the judge

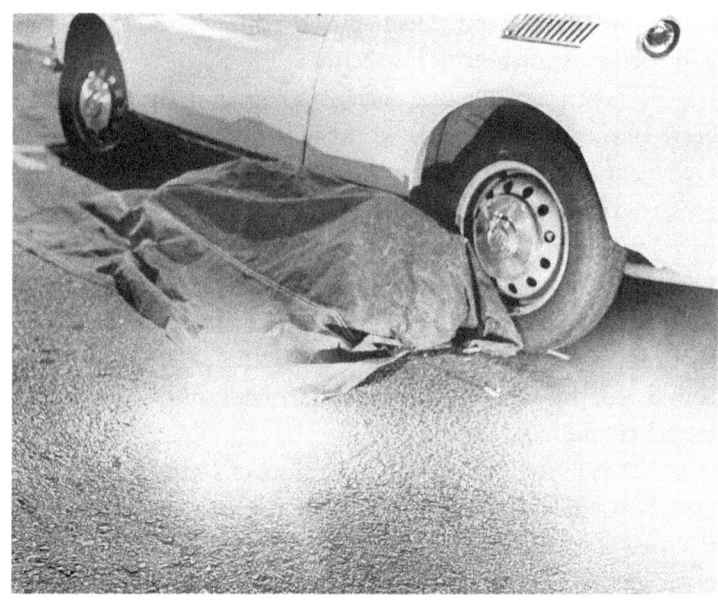

**1.05**   Chris Burden, *Deadman*, November 12, 1972. Riko Mizuno Gallery, Los Angeles, California. Photograph by Gary Beydler.

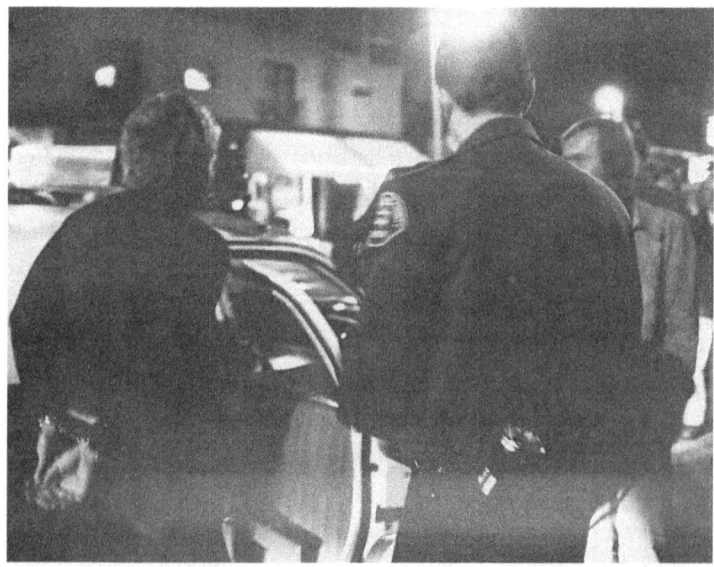

**1.06**   Chris Burden, *Deadman*, November 12, 1972. Arrest outside Riko Mizuno Gallery, Los Angeles, California. Photograph by Chuck Arnoldi.

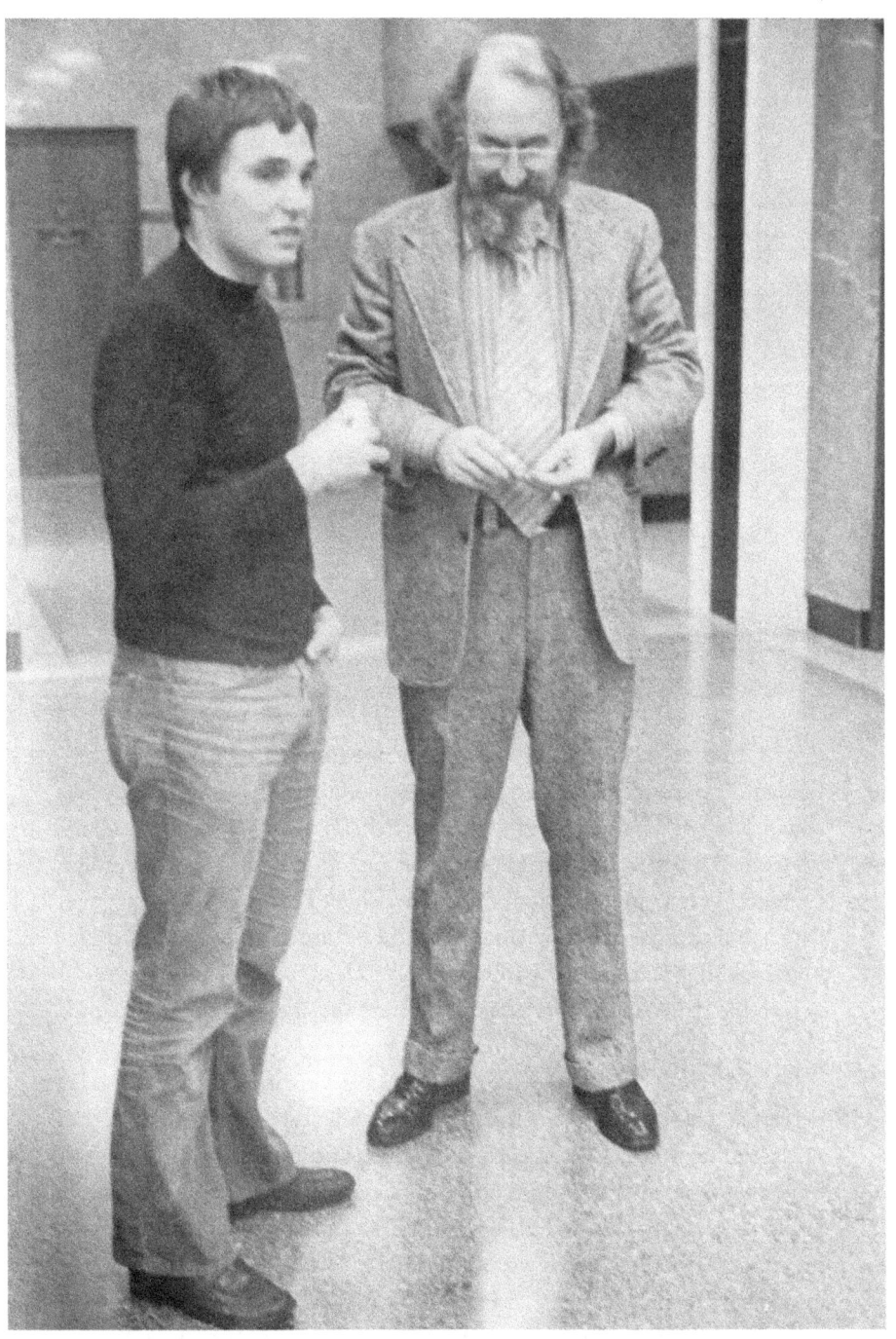

**1.07**  Chris Burden, *Deadman*, 1972. Beverly Hills Courthouse, Los Angeles, California. Photograph by Barbara T. Smith.

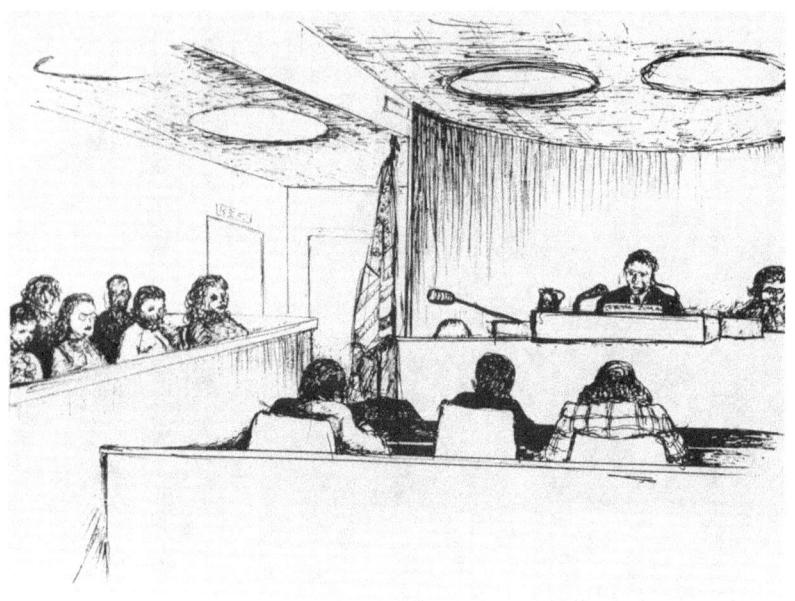

**1.08**    Chris Burden, *Deadman*, 1972. Drawing by Barbara T. Smith.

during Burden's trial (fig. 1.8). From her position seated behind the defendant in the audience, Smith illustrates those individuals present at the courthouse yet does not note their names in her drawing. Instead, she identifies them on the verso: six members of the jury, a court reporter, judge George Zucher, and one lawyer on either side of the artist—deputy DA Savitt and defense attorney James G. Butler. Burden's inclusion of these multiple images for the documentation of *Deadman* offers further evidence that the scope of this performance expands beyond the events and participants present on the evening of his arrest.

Smith—who had photographed a few of Burden's early performances—assumed the role of a public advocate for the artist in the press leading up to the artist's three-day trial at the Beverly Hills Courthouse. In response to the substantial public criticism that Burden received, Smith went so far as to write a series of three separate statements defending his performance, which were published in *Artweek* over the following months.[24] The first article, "Art Piece Brings Arrest," gives her preliminary account of the events comprising the *Deadman* performance. In it, Smith holds her fellow audience members accountable for the events that transpired, pointing out that "although many of the persons present hold positions of responsibility in the art community, no one effectively prevented the arrest or enlightened the officers."[25] Supporting this claim, in a 1972 letter to Smith, an unidentified sculptor named Michael describes the hypocrisy of the art-world bystanders present at *Deadman*: "too bad about no one putting up money for his bail—but I'm not surprised at all—I think it's neat that they were confronted with an opportunity to support someone and let it go. . . . It shows where their heads are."[26]

The response to Smith's article caused such a controversy that on February 10, 1973, the *Artweek* editors published a series of letters-to-the-editor that reproached Burden's work as well as Smith's defense of *Deadman*. The "Editor's Mail Bag" included disgruntled notes that went so far as to compare the artist to Nazi Heinrich Himmler, as well as refusals to renew *Artweek* subscriptions on account of the inclusion of Burden's performance and Smith's response to the work. Enjoying the intense reader engagement, the publication invited Smith to present a counter-retort.

In her second written piece, Smith defended Burden's innocence by shifting focus to the responsibility shared by those present at the performance when confronted with police intervention. Condemning the audience's passive response, she states: "his piece became a vehicle for everyone else's trip, to use as they saw fit and needed for their own self-esteem."[27] For example, one curator declared the work to be "the best piece done anywhere this year," another "left to have a beer," while an unnamed museum director "became the protective inquirer, phoning the police to determine exactly what was going to happen to Burden."[28] Furthermore, she points out in Burden's defense that "he set the flares beside his body to protect himself, not to call false attention to a supposed accident and 'play games' with the police. This was a formal art event. The persons there were invited, and the gallery knew what he was going to do."[29]

In her first article, Smith had highlighted a crucial feature of the audience's response to the work: "the fact that after Burden had placed himself under the car and set the scene, and before the crowd came out of the gallery to see it, several persons walked by and saw the 'accident' but seemed neither curious nor alarmed."[30] Smith's statement suggests that the blithe passivity of the viewers who observed his action also potentially engendered an ethical and legal dilemma that might result in their abetment of a potential crime. Given that both the art-world onlookers and unsuspecting pedestrians largely refrained from intervening in the work, their inaction perpetuated risks for both the living artist and the drivers swerving to avoid him.

Yet the unwitting participants' general lack of involvement might be attributed to their disbelief in the circumstances, the assumption that someone else had already taken care of the matter, or simply general apathy when faced with a body lying in the street. After all, the tarp over Burden's body suggested that he was not in critical need of medical care but rather was beyond the point of assistance. Once the police intervened, the responsibility of those present shifted to the legal defense and protection of Burden's rights against the LAPD's jurisdiction. The auxiliary participants' reaction to the circumstances thus brought them into proximity with potential culpability as they knowingly or unknowingly left the site of the performance and Burden's subsequent arrest.

At Burden's trial, the defense attorney called forth three witnesses to the stand: Riko Mizuno, Helene Winer, and Jane Livingston. According to Plagens, gallery owner Mizuno had been in charge of directing the art audience to leave the gallery space and move into the street in order to view *Deadman*.[31] Given the legal definition of accomplice liability, which implicates those who induce the commission of a criminal offense, Mizuno's role in the execution of *Deadman* suggests a shared responsibility for the work's outcome that was tested not only on the night of the performance but also in the court of law.

Mizuno was an early supporter of Burden, allowing him to stage *Deadman* as part of a week of performance and film that included the work of Chuck Arnoldi, Jud Fine, Ed Moses, and Tom Wudl. As a result of exhibiting this work and soliciting viewers for Burden's performance, her involvement as Burden's Los Angeles gallerist expanded to something more akin to that of an abettor. Her authority as a known gallery owner was exploited (1) to attract an audience for the piece, (2) to direct them to leave the gallery building to view the work on the street, and (3) to negotiate with the resulting legal authorities both on the night of the performance and at the subsequent trial. Whether or not the actions that comprised *Deadman* would be legally considered a crime would be predicated on the testimony of figures like Mizuno.

According to Smith in her subsequent article "Burden Case Tried, Dismissed," Mizuno was the first witness called by the defense. In her testimony, Mizuno emphasized that she and the artist jointly discussed the piece prior to its execution, even considering the possibility of police intervention, which they determined to be unlikely given the artistic context.[32] While Burden did not typically give advance notice of his performances and often organized participants largely through word of mouth, the fact that *Deadman* was one of the few works by the artist to date to be staged "in" a commercial gallery meant that Mizuno was aware of the work's parameters and therefore knowingly agreed to go ahead despite potential legal implications.

The next witness was Helene Winer, the former director of the Pomona College gallery and an art critic for the *Los Angeles Times*.[33] Later noting that she was likely asked to serve as a witness for the defense "probably because I was one of the only people at the event who wasn't an artist and had a respectable job," Winer recounts that on the stand, she underscored "that despite the resemblance to an accident scene, I did not think that it could be mistaken for one or posed any danger to the artist or to cars driving on the street. While this was not an entirely honest testimony, it was not far off."[34]

Finally, the Los Angeles County Museum of Art curator Jane Livingston took the stand. Her defense of Burden's work touched on the way in which he used legal transgressions in his performances to explore shared responsibility with others. Smith described Livingston's statement as expressing how "artists, like Chris, use their bodies in a way that is a direct experience for the artist himself and incidentally perhaps for other people."[35] According to Smith's account, Livingston also stressed that *Deadman* was conceptually in line with other works by the artist in which he foregrounded a "generally passive use of his body achieving the maximum amount of psychic reaction, a simple act with complex ramifications."[36] While Livingston focused on the centrality of Burden's body, her recognition of the work as opening outward to involve the experience of others suggests that expanded forms of accountability in the work were at least unconsciously acknowledged.

James G. Butler, Burden's defense attorney, was a Los Angeles–based drug products lawyer as well as a prominent art collector during the late 1960s and 1970s.[37] Butler's legal reputation was built on his participation in significant class-action civil cases against pharmaceutical companies and on being the founder of the Compton NAACP in 1955. Although his identity has not been attributed in scholarly or critical texts on Burden's performances to date, he plays a significant role in *Deadman*.[38]

Despite being charged with the criminal offense of falsely signaling a police emergency, based on his use of flares, Burden faced accusations by the district attorney during his trial that he was exploiting the circumstances for fame, publicity, and money, or simply playing a hoax. Butler's defense strategy was to explain the artistic context for *Deadman*, offer evidence that Burden was an established artist (despite being only three years out of his MFA), and provide a brief overview of the significance of performance and Conceptual art for the jury. According to Smith, Butler "argued the necessity for an avant-garde which challenges current ideas of what art and life is about, saying that such challenges are part of the right of free speech and that this right must leave room for controversial ideas."[39] Butler denied accusations of the artist's criminal intent, stressing that lying in the street and setting up flares was—in itself—lawful. His closing statements added that the police had overreacted without thorough investigation; Butler therefore claimed that they "had caused the emergency report and the law does not deal with a false emergency, but only with a false report of an emergency."[40] Furthermore, he emphasized that "the police had never ascertained at all if indeed any emergency existed."[41]

This last point is significant. The lack of a proper police investigation at *Deadman* necessitates an acknowledgment of the artist's white privilege—upon which his engagement with illegality was often predicated. The fact that the primary suspect for a "crime" that occurred in a white, middle-class neighborhood in Los Angeles was a young man of a similar demographic allowed Burden to engage with tactics of criminality in ways that artists from marginalized groups could not readily or safely access.

This is particularly clear when compared with the contemporaneous work of the Chicano artist collective Asco, whose LA-based performances of the early 1970s used similar tactics of public intervention with radically different results. For instance, Asco's *Decoy Gang War Victim* (1974; fig. 1.9) also comprised a fake crime scene, with one member—Glugio Nicandro, also known as Gronk—playing the role of a cadaver lying on the pavement. While Burden staged *Deadman* on a main throughfare in the predominantly white area of West Hollywood, where it received immediate police involvement, *Decoy Gang War Victim* was staged multiple times in largely Chicano neighborhoods struggling with local gang violence. Anticipating the lack of art audiences or even police presence, *Decoy Gang War Victim* was photographed by Asco member Harry Gamboa Jr., whose images were then distributed to the mainstream local media with a caption suggesting the victim was a gang member. Gamboa explained the motivations in *Art-forum* in 2011: "The project was a response to the incendiary tabloid-style journalism of the two major Los Angeles newspapers, which often listed the names, addresses, workplaces, and gang affiliations of the victims or their family members in an effort to maintain high levels of reciprocal gang

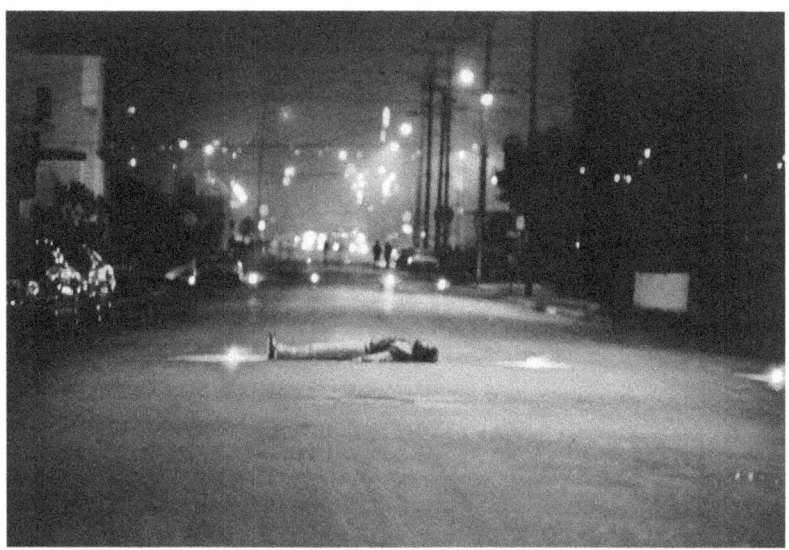

**1.09**  Asco, *Decoy Gang War Victim*, 1974. Chromogenic print, 16 × 20 in.
Photograph by Harry Gamboa Jr.

violence, thus selling more newspapers. The desired effect of *Decoy Gang War Victim* was ... to rob the newspapers of their daily list of victims."[42]

The fact that law enforcement did not intervene in the staging of the Asco work, as was the case within minutes for Burden, highlights the racial discrepancies over police protection affecting marginalized communities in Los Angeles at the time. Burden's deliberate choice to stage *Deadman* in a highly populated throughfare also speaks to his relative confidence in being able to negotiate potential legal fallout from the events that might transpire from his work. Moreover, Burden had a substantial network of associates to protect him, as his witnesses called to the stand had proven; these abettors mark a significant contrast to the lack of onlookers and police involvement for Asco's work.

Despite their contextual differences, both Burden and Asco put forth a simulation of a fatally injured person at a time when the rights of the body had recently undergone—or were undergoing—substantial public debate and legal battles. Burden would later produce sculptural works that addressed authoritative power and police violence; for instance, *L.A.P.D. Uniforms* (1993), in which he created thirty enlarged replicas of Los Angeles Police Department uniforms and installed them along the perimeter of an exhibition space to visually suggest an impenetrable cordon, was made in the wake of widespread social unrest that erupted in 1992 following the acquittal of Los Angeles police officers on charges of excessive force for brutally beating Rodney King.

Other Los Angeles–based artists working in the early 1970s shared this interest in how the representation of the body intersected with the court of law. David Hammons, for instance, created *Injustice Case* (1970; fig. 1.10) as part of his series of body prints in which he coated his clothed form in margarine and imprinted a record of his body on a sheet that was then dusted with pigment. This work depicts a figure bound and gagged; Hammons staged himself in the image of the Black Panther leader Bobby Seale, who was denied both an attorney of his choice and the opportunity to represent himself while on trial for conspiracy in 1969 as part of the Chicago Eight. When Seale contested such silencing, the judge—operating in a closed courtroom without cameras—ordered that Seale be physically restrained in front of the jury deciding the trial. When *Injustice Case* was first shown at the Brockman Gallery in Los Angeles, the work appeared inside a glass case with a judge's gavel—dramatizing the disturbing scope of legal power that hung over Seale's proceedings.[43] Even seen without such details, Hammons's portrayal of the courtroom scene in *Injustice Case* bears witness to an event in which photographic documentation was explicitly banned.

Returning to Burden's trial, after a full day of deliberation, the twelve jurors could not come to a unanimous decision, resulting in a hung jury. While the D.A. sought a retrial, Judge Zucher decided to dismiss the case due to the fact that he believed "Chris was a serious artist, had intended no emergency, nor was his art merely a prank, and that he did not deserve further inconvenience in as much as he was being tried under the wrong section of the law and he was not a criminal."[44] According to follow-up discussions with the jury, despite a 9–3 verdict in favor of conviction, three jurors cited reasonable doubt over whether Burden had knowingly caused a false emergency, which led to the case being thrown out.

Although charges against Burden were ultimately dropped, the legal dimension that underlies this work and Burden's deliberate involvement of auxiliary participants recurs in other key performances by the artist conducted over the following years. By placing his freedom in the hands of the jury, *Deadman* serves as a key example of distributed agency: rather than being centered exclusively on his personal actions, the work in fact comprised a network of individuals whose authority and culpability were tested under the purview of the law. If prosecuted, those who abetted the artist in

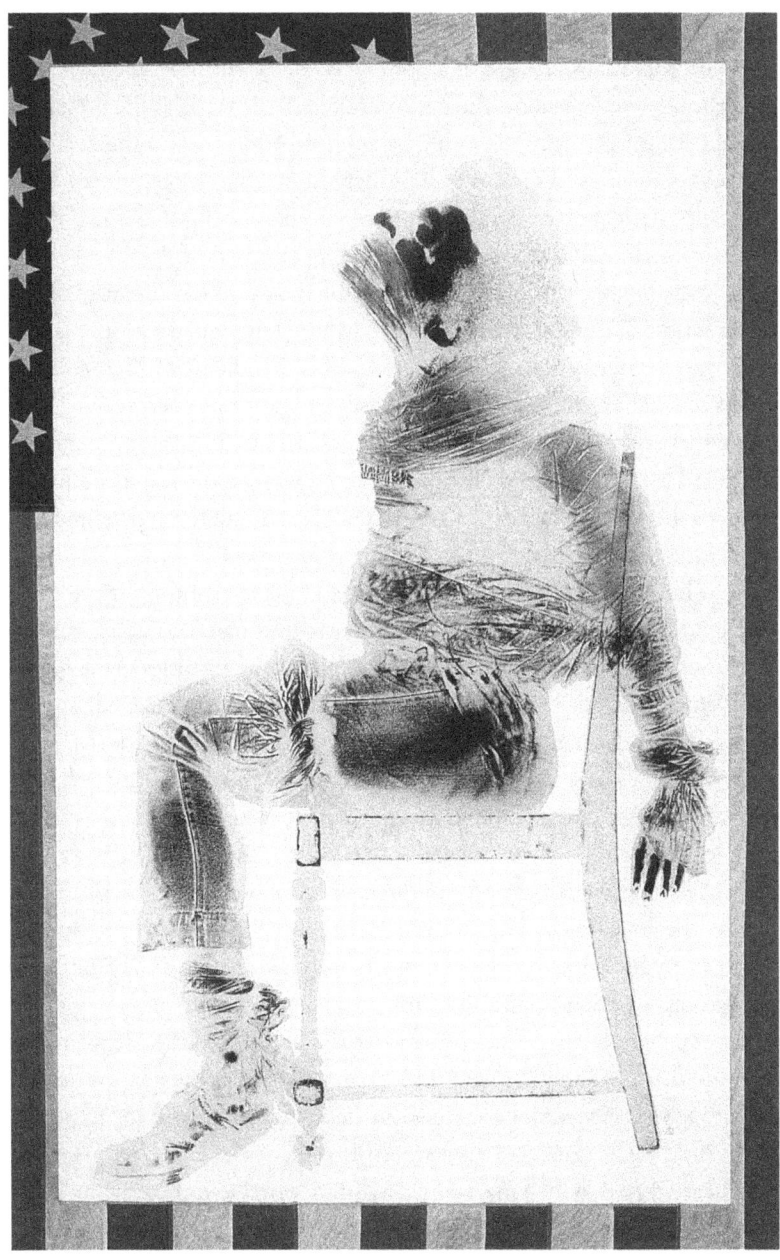

**1.10**     David Hammons, *Injustice Case*, 1970. Mixed-media body print, 63 × 40½ in.

the construction, documentation, publicity, and legal protection of the work could be potentially charged as accomplices. Moreover, if Burden won the case, the jury could become further embroiled in the work, as the presumed illegality of Burden's actions would be unpunished because of their verdict. One of the juror's votes in favor of Burden's conviction for *Deadman* came from a local flight attendant, who was reported as saying afterward "if she ever saw him under a tarp again, she'd run him over herself."[45]

*Deadman* set into motion a relay of ethical involvement that, for the first time in Burden's career, had actual legal consequences for both the artist and his network of accomplices. At its core, the work *Deadman* explores to what extent a person is responsible for another's actions and how much that accountability can be shared with others. Such a sentiment was expressed by Smith, who rhetorically asked, "What is the responsibility of the art gallery to the artist? . . . To what degree should the art community or art establishment come to the support of an artist?"[46]

Similar questions were being probed on social and political levels throughout America in the 1970s. According to historians Laura Kalman and Bruce Schulman, in the wake of the tremendous leftist victories of the 1960s, the following decade was marred by numerous crises that weakened support for liberal agendas, including the US defeat in the Vietnam War, the rise of the religious right, soaring inflation, the deindustrialization of the Rust Belt, and a series of energy crises. This fracturing of the leftist coalition and the disillusionment with the government's ability to effect positive change led to a growing sense of individualism and entrepreneurialism but also disenchantment that set the stage for the conservatism of the 1980s. The sense of community felt by many Americans in the sixties—in both mainstream and countercultural groups—became splintered. Similarly, many "feel-good" or collaborative forms of participation and performance that characterized the late 1950s and 1960s—such as Kaprow's attempts to integrate everyday life into the field of art through his Happenings or Fluxus invitational instructions for audiences to become participants—were ostensibly replaced by body-art practices in the early 1970s, which maintained a distance between the viewing audience and the artist-performer, often through the mediated image. Yet, as I argue throughout *Artist, Audience, Accomplice*, many of these works—such as those by Burden—did in fact continue to explore the role of others in their work, albeit through an alternative model of auxiliary participation that exceeds the current discussions of the participatory art genre.[47]

To extend Anne Wagner's analysis of 1970s art presented in the book's introduction, the role of witnessing that historically had been central to art viewing took on the function of interpretive judgment, which is construed in legal terms in Burden's practice. The expanded circumstances constituting *Deadman* foreground the agency and accountability of Burden's abettors, demonstrating that the role of the witness opens a relay of ethical and legal involvement moving beyond the conventional responsibility of an audience. Yet Burden structures this distribution of potential liability so that the negative costs that might accrue from such actions are transferred to others, thereby mitigating personal risk, while retaining artistic credit for the work's success.[48] That is, to bear witness in Burden's work is to participate and accept complicity in its consequences, thereby assuming the role of an accomplice with all the risks and implications that this produces.

### Private Abettor: Barbara Burden

In *Deadman*, the actual criminal charges that were put forth in a court of law placed the auxiliary participants into the position of accomplices according to its legal definition of "aiding or abetting a crime." However, an expanded sense of the term becomes a useful model for articulating the subject position of other individuals whose visibility within Burden's work has been heretofore ignored or overlooked yet whose agency was strategically exploited by the nominal artist.

Burden's first wife, Barbara, to whom he was married between 1967 and 1977, had been involved with his performances beginning in the early 1970s, photographing projects such as *I Became a Secret Hippy* (1971), *Jaizu* (1972), *Icarus* (1973), and *B.C. Mexico* (1973). Her artistic labor in her husband's work has often been unacknowledged, yet she frequently occupied the role of documenter or unaccredited performer, beginning in Burden's graduate student years at the University of California, Irvine.[49] She was integral to the successful completion of Chris's master's thesis project, *Five Day Locker Piece* (1971), in which he hid himself in a hallway locker rigged with a DIY water system for five days, relying on Barbara to protect him from potential intervention from the authorities and to safeguard his well-being. In a subsequent piece, *Prelude to 220, or 110* (1971), Chris lay between two live 220-volt electric wires that were each dropped into a pail of water. During this performance, she oversaw securing Chris's body to the gallery floor by screwing copper bands serving as metal conductors into the ground that would electrocute the artist if a pail overturned.[50]

Without her, Chris could simply leave the performance site at a time of his choosing; in this way, the ethical and legal consequences of the work were undoubtedly shared. In both *Five Day Locker Piece* and *Prelude to 220*, the prominence of her participation in the performance has been buried—yet Chris had entrusted her with responsibilities on which his life would ultimately depend.

In contrast to those earlier projects in which she remained a covert accomplice, Barbara assumed the prominent role of Burden's co-performer in *Match Piece*, a performance staged on March 20, 1972, that involved her husband launching "match rockets [that were] impossible to control," aimed at her naked body.[51] For the performance *Trans-Fixed* (1974), the roles of giver and receiver of physical abuse were reversed, as was Barbara's willingness to participate. Within an unmarked Venice Beach garage, a car engine hummed. A crowd, consisting of both friends and local bystanders, congregated out front as a gray Volkswagen Beetle was rolled out a few feet onto the driveway. Even the growl of the revved engine could not distract from the spectacle of a shirtless Burden nailed through his hands to the car in a crucifixion gesture. After a few moments, the car was pushed back into the garage and the door shut.

In a 2012 interview, Burden recalled that he had initially asked his then wife to hammer the nails into his palms in *Trans-Fixed*. After going over logistics and advance preparations, on the morning of the performance, Chris awoke to find Barbara had left for the day without saying goodbye. On her pillow was a note: "Took bus to work. Can-*not* do nails. Couldn't sleep."[52] In the end, the gruesome task was given to an "unnamed lawyer friend," potentially James Butler.

Burden's repeated enlistment of Barbara in his artistic projects as co-performer or documenter points to an ongoing interest in testing her boundaries as an abettor against the framework of their shared private life. While she was likely a more willing participant than others because of their romantic relationship, both her reluctance to perform many of the requested tasks and her eventual participation in others must be underscored as a crucial part of these performances. Yet Barbara's entrance into visibility as a key player in an artwork occurs for the viewer only when the physical or psychological pressure staged by her partner calls into question her own complicity.

Reminiscent of the expanded circumstances in *Shoot*—for which Barbara became implicated as a potential accomplice in Chris's actions when he insinuated to hospital staff that she was the perpetrator of the gun violence—Burden's exploitation of his wife exposes how the artist's racial and gender profile plays a significant part in his ability to stage asymmetrical power relationships with his abettors. Even when asked to perform the violence staged on Burden's body, such as hammering nails into his palms, Barbara's actions were undertaken with Chris's directives. While Burden sought the participation of both men and women accomplices in his performance-based work, his own identity as a white man in 1970s America made it possible to pursue exploitative social relations in art practices due to the normativity of such racial and gendered power differentials in society at the time.

The thread of physical violence that reappears throughout Burden's early career is evident on an interpersonal level in these performance pieces from the early 1970s. Another relevant example is *Kunst Kick*, a performance at the public opening of the Basel Art Fair on June 19, 1974. To make a performance befitting the prominent art-world setting, he had asked his then art dealer, Ronald Feldman, to be his assistant and co-performer in the work.[53] Feldman's role involved kicking Burden down two flights of concrete stairs in front of the audience congregating at the opening. After reportedly vomiting in the bathroom at the thought of his role in the piece, Feldman refused to take part. Friend and fellow artist Charles Christopher Hill took his place, willfully sending Burden headfirst down the terrazzo stairs.[54] As one of Burden's main documenters of his early performances, Hill describes Burden's work from this period as having "very little real danger involved. . . . Most of the violence was psychological, attacking the viewer on a painful, subconscious level."[55] Yet the attack was not simply directed at the viewer. Rather, if approached from a legal standpoint, Burden's accomplice would potentially become the individual convicted of the crime (assuming the artist or an eyewitness pressed charges). Ethically, as the action was conducted in an artistically sanctioned space and the artist himself requested this action as a condition of participation in the work, the boundaries were less clear.[56]

In September 1974, Burden performed *Sculpture in Three Parts* at the Hansen-Fuller Gallery in San Francisco, California. For this piece, Burden created a tension between the public viewing space of the gallery and the area he reserved for his performance. In a corner of the gallery, Burden sat on a metal stool positioned on a white pedestal for an unspecified amount of time. Facing the elevator, Burden encountered the audience immediately upon entering the gallery, a confrontation that likely created an element of surprise and wariness beginning with the initial interaction.

As Diane Fuller, co-owner of the gallery, described, "I felt *I* was invading *his* privacy."[57]

For forty-three hours, Burden remained atop this stool without coming down. While fundamentally a durational test—the piece was completed at the moment Burden "failed" and fell to the floor—the work also required the audience not just to view but to become witnesses and documenters. A crucial component of *Sculpture in Three Parts*, which has been often overlooked in most descriptions of the piece, is that a rotating lineup of volunteers from the audience were solicited to photograph the final moment of the work with a 35 mm camera positioned on a tripod in front of the artist. Another volunteer was expected to then attend to Burden's body by producing a typical police crime-scene chalk drawing on the floor with the words "FOREVER" inscribed at the center (fig. 1.11).

The manner in which Burden's body was used to once again simulate a crime scene invites comparison with a piece from Cuban-born artist Ana Mendieta. Beginning in 1973, the artist produced three independent bodies of works—the *Silueta* series in which the artist imprinted or otherwise articulated silhouettes of her body into a landscape; *Rape Scene*, a performance and related suite of photographs depicting the artist re-creating the aftermath of an actual rape and murder of a nursing student at the University of Iowa, where Mendieta completed her MFA one year prior; and the Super 8 film *Moffitt Building Piece* and related slides, which capture passersby as they encounter a substantial pool of what appears to be blood seeping out from the front door of her apartment (fig. 1.12). While her interventionist tactics into public spaces also relate to the conceptual strategy of *Deadman*, Mendieta's work importantly dramatizes the impassive reactions toward violence, particularly the predominantly gendered aspects of domestic violence that occurs against women behind closed doors or otherwise out of sight. Such a perspective provides a critical nuance that exceeded the scope of Burden's more formal investigation, a marker of his white male privilege that is once again worth noting.

More than a dozen different individuals assumed the role of the photographer over the duration of Burden's performance; notably, they became tasked with capturing the work's primary documentation rather than attending to the artist's health or well-being. At various moments of exhaustion, Burden would begin to sway as if about to fall, spurring the volunteer holding the cable release at that moment to jump to attention. Burden described how he deliberately decided against using a mechanical or automatic rig for the camera, instead being interested in how "the guy

**1.11**

Chris Burden, *Sculpture in Three Parts*,
September 10–21, 1974. Hansen-Fuller
Gallery, San Francisco, California.
Photographs by Barbara Burden.

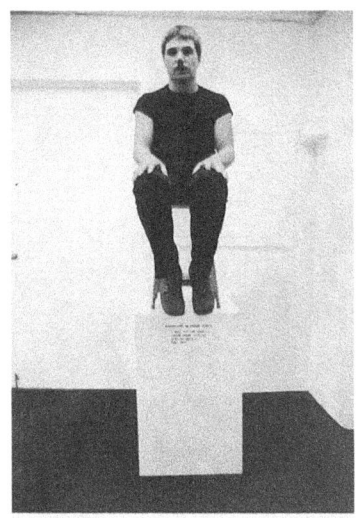
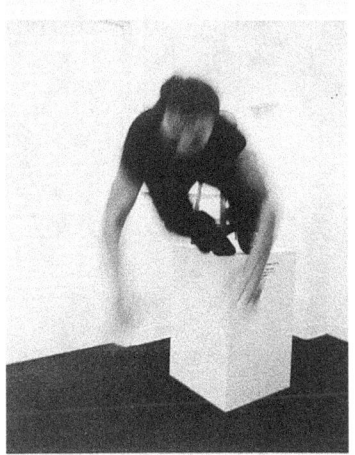
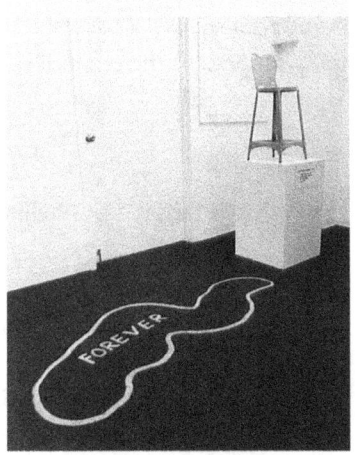

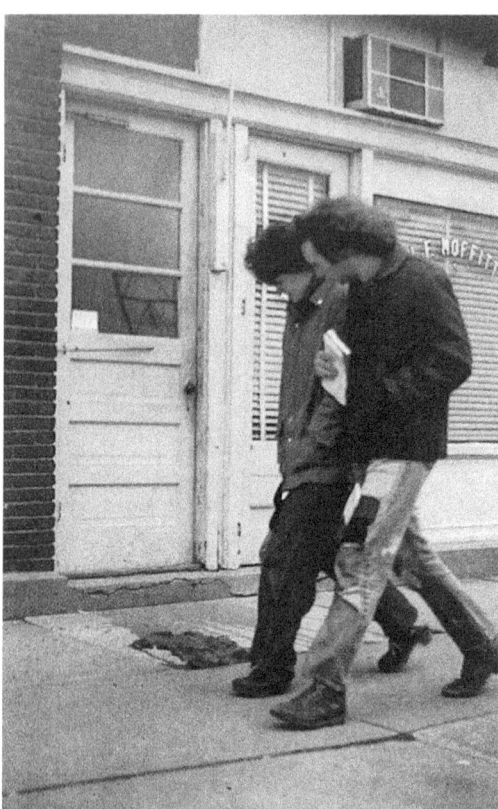

**1.12**

Ana Mendieta, *Untitled (People Looking at Blood, Moffitt)*, 1973. 35 mm color slide.

at the camera was a proxy for me and all the other spectators."[58] In other words, the visibility of these accomplices was predicated upon their constitutive role in the work taking over at the precise moment of Burden's inevitable fall. Following the watchful presence of a dedicated woman who monitored the artist for a six-hour overnight shift, at 5:25 a.m. Burden's body slipped off the metal seat and onto the floor. Barbara was there to capture the shot.

### Public Abettors: Phyllis Lutjeans, Gary Beydler

In contrast to Barbara's witting role as an abettor, Burden also produced a set of works in which he actively sought unwitting participants to assume prominent positions in his performances that would have exceeded those held by a traditional audience. While flipping channels on February 9, 1972, in the Irvine, California, cable TV region, a viewer might have stopped on Channel 3, where Newport Harbor Art Museum curator Phyllis Lutjeans's weekly interview-based live program *All about Art* had Burden on as the show's guest. Lutjeans had known Burden since his graduate school years, when he worked at the museum. She also had uneventfully featured Burden as a guest on her show the year prior, in which she did a segment filmed at his art studio. According to Burden, due to these successful prior collaborations, Lutjeans invited him back to *All about Art* to do an interview and perform a work live on the air. Neither version of his proposed concept—eating the recorded tape of their conversation, either as it was being unrolled or chopping it in a blender to be consumed at a later point—was approved by the station manager.[59] Following some negotiation regarding the content and parameters of what would be permissible, Burden recounts that he "got so frustrated that eventually I said to Phyllis, 'Listen. We're just gonna do a straight interview and talk about all the things that we can't do on live TV.'"[60]

A few days prior, Burden called Lutjeans with a question: "Are you absolutely positive that you want me to do something on the show?"[61] Lutjeans recalled feeling immediately nervous following their conversation, given Burden's reluctance to perform a work after encountering pushback on his initial ideas. Rather presciently, on the day of the taping, she asked her husband, Alfred, to join her in case things got out of hand.

According to Lutjeans's account, she and Alfred arrived at the studio, where Burden and three other individuals with recording equipment were already present. As Alfred took his seat among a small group of audience members in a separate viewing room, Lutjeans attempted to make conversation with her guest. When the taping began, Burden asked the station manager if the interview could be transmitted live, which was agreed to, since there was no broadcast at that time. Lutjeans and Burden began chatting and, noticing a small knife in his belt, Lutjeans jokingly asked, "Are we going to have a bloodletting here today?" In response, Burden swiftly jumped out of his seat, grabbed the knife, and pressed it against her neck, audibly threatening her safety if the station switched off the feed. Held by her hair with a weapon pressed against her throat, Lutjeans was told—as Burden later recounted in an *Avalanche* magazine interview—that he would "make her perform obscene acts" and "threatened her life" if the station manager did not comply with his requests to maintain the live broadcast (fig. 1.13).[62]

Importantly, however, Lutjeans offers a different description of this interaction. In her recollection, Burden had not said (as he himself had

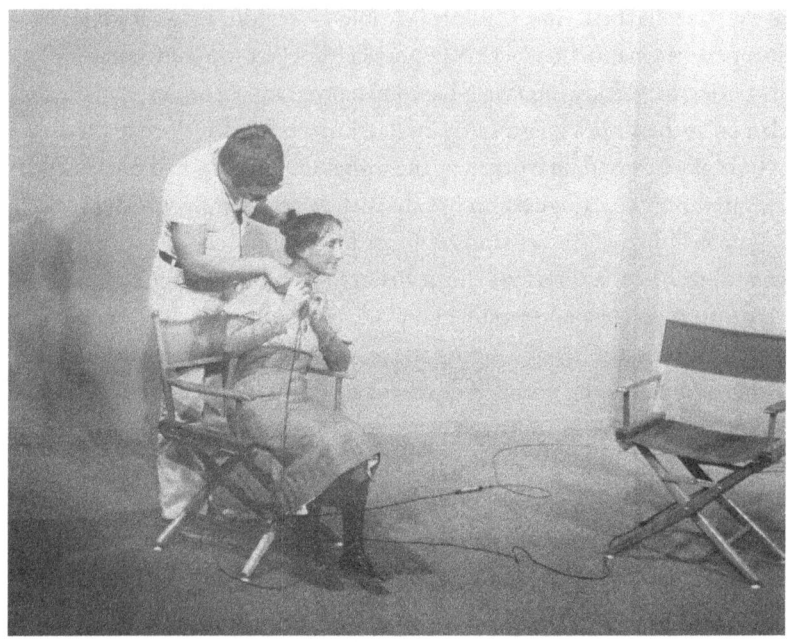

**1.13**     Chris Burden, *TV Hijack*, February 9, 1972. Channel 3 Cablevision, Irvine, California. Photograph by Gary Beydler.

claimed) that he would force her to do obscene things but rather offered assurance of her safety, whispering privately in her ear, "Don't worry, Phyll, I won't hurt you."[63] This divergence of accounts points to the responsibility Burden shared with Lutjeans over the intentionality of his potentially criminal act; culpability would depend on whose version of the story would be believed regarding his intention to do harm. By claiming that he had endangered her life and personal safety, Burden partially shifted agency regarding his legal innocence to Lutjeans as simultaneously his victim and/or coconspiring defendant.

Although statements by Burden and Lutjeans have both stressed the lack of prior knowledge of the piece by Lutjeans or the station, Burden himself has stated that "she knew me, so it was more complicated."[64] As mentioned, Lutjeans was a curator at the Newport Harbor Art Museum, a local art critic, and both familiar with Burden's work and friendly with the artist on a personal level.[65] Moreover, Lutjeans's husband, Alfred, had already taken photographic documentation of the works *Shoot* and *Prelude to 220, or 110*, performances that were notorious for the artist's extreme actions, and even helped set up some of the pieces' most dangerous elements. In a 2016 interview, Lutjeans described the dilemma that she faced as Burden's friend-turned-hostage as to whether she perpetuated Burden's aggrandized account of the event or her own memory of that day, which was less extreme.[66] It is worth noting that while David A. Ross suggests Lutjeans's complicity with the piece must be underscored, as "she was, in a fashion, informed about the piece before the 'crime' took place," neither the scope of her advance knowledge nor her personal and professional relationship with the artist outside the work *TV Hijack* would warrant the violence of Burden's suggested actions.[67]

Interestingly, Burden's expanded accounts of *TV Hijack* seem to modulate his initial claim: he asserts that his intention was never actually to inflict pain on Lutjeans but only to simulate such actions on a live broadcast. For example, later in the same *Avalanche* interview, Burden argues: "I wasn't really putting her life at stake. In my head it was just an example of what I could have done in the TV studio. I had already decided that I wasn't going to slit her throat; I wasn't going to make her do obscene things on live TV, but we were on live, and I was holding a knife at her throat, so they had a flash that I was really doing it."[68] The implications of this statement are crucial to understanding the purpose of Burden's project. If the value of the work was not in fact dependent on the actualization of violence but on its approximation for the audience, then Burden's actions instead function as a test for the network of agents who had to make a judgment call concerning the seriousness of Burden's actions and their personal culpability in aiding a potential crime.

*TV Hijack* (like many of Burden's performances) presented a set of conditions that made it *possible* to commit a crime—one that ultimately did not occur. If the definition of abettors is those who share legal responsibility with a principal offender by offering active support or service in the commission of a crime, the network of agents around Burden would be put into an unsettling position in which distributed legal accountability might be anticipated. On the one hand, those who tried to stop the artist would be admitting that they thought an actual crime was being committed, thereby possibly incriminating themselves. On the other hand, providing aid to Burden on the assumption that a crime was not taking place—but being mistaken—could have equally dire consequences, potentially resulting in abetting a crime anyway.[69]

In works such as *TV Hijack*, Burden probes to what extent a person is responsible for another's actions—a question that assumed a particular urgency in the 1970s, when hijacking and terrorism were notoriously in the public consciousness—not just Burden's. From a spree of global "skyjack-ings" of airplanes in the early 1970s to the Iran hostage crisis—in which fifty-two US citizens were held by Iranian students at the American Embassy for 444 days beginning in November 1979—at the very end of the decade, representations of violence became commonplace in the media and familiar to viewing audiences around the globe. Many of the most high-profile international terrorist actions of the 1970s were televised; three of the most notorious include when terrorists hijacked and diverted five commercial flights carrying 310 hostages to Jordan in 1970, when the Black September organization held and killed eleven Israeli athletes at the Munich Olympics of 1972, and when Ilich Ramírez Sánchez—dubbed "Carlos the Jackal" by the media—took almost seventy OPEC officials hostage in Vienna in 1975. There was significant domestic terrorist activity as well: socialite Patty Hearst's kidnapping by—and subsequent membership in—the Symbionese Liberation Army and the Weather Underground bombings across the United States beginning in 1970 are two notable examples.

Artists in the 1970s frequently responded to the pervasive media representations of violence—whether officially sanctioned, like in Vietnam, or unofficially, with police brutality—circulating in print and on television. For instance, Martha Rosler's photomontage series *House Beautiful: Bringing the War Home* (ca. 1967–72) highlighted the way wartime media images entered American homes by combining documentary *Life* magazine photographs, such as of injured Vietnamese civilians, with bourgeois American domestic interiors reproduced in the publication *House Beautiful*, as a protest against the Vietnam War.

Reflecting the media coverage of extremist acts in the 1970s, artists such as Sarah Charlesworth, Alfredo Jaar, and Gerhard Richter used terroristic events or political operatives as their subjects. For instance, in her 1978 work *April 21, 1978*, Charlesworth removed the text and captions from forty-five international newspaper covers reporting on the abduction (and later assassination) of Italy's former prime minister Aldo Moro by the Red Brigades. Jaar produced a body of works drawing out the then secretary of state Henry Kissinger's connection to the artist's Chilean past—notably his role in the CIA-assisted overthrow of the democratically elected Salvador Allende and the subsequent installation of a dictatorship led by Augusto Pinochet during the 1973 Chilean military coup. Produced in 1988, Richter's fifteen-painting cycle *October 18, 1977* depicts members of the left-wing guerrilla group Red Army Faction, with the title referring to the date when three were found dead in their cells at the Stuttgart-Stammheim prison. In contrast, Burden's mimicking of terroristic strategies himself—rather than representing real-life events—in works like *TV Hijack* were, as I argue, staged to draw out the question of shared responsibility that occurs through the involvement of an expanded network of associates using a visual language familiar to audiences of contemporary media culture.

While the nature of Burden's intentions in *TV Hijack* have been subject to debate, the brutal action of taking Lutjeans hostage has often been the art historical focus of this work.[70] Yet, given that the supporting documentation—which includes ample depictions of Burden's assistants, the station manager, and other individuals present undertaking tasks that extend the temporal and social parameters of the piece—Burden's act of hijacking is only one part of the performative intervention. Considered more broadly, *TV Hijack* incorporates a constellation of other participants who occupy an intermediary space within the artist-audience binary, thereby rupturing the conventional assemblage of discourse, behavior, expectation, and convention that determines such opposing terms.

In *TV Hijack*, Burden also co-opted the media network system and its associates into the position of an abettor to his own ethically and legally suspect actions to test the limits of authority and agency by the nominal artist over another individual. While he had been invited on the show to fill airtime as an interviewee in exchange for free publicity, Burden reversed the relations of power on the day of the taping, making these previously imperceptible figures—such as the assistants, station management, cameramen, and so on—become discernible where they had been otherwise unnoticed. Burden himself described his intention to subvert the typical role of an interviewee that he was expected to perform, stating that *TV Hijack* "was really about who was going to be the paint for whose palette. I was just an act for the station manager's program, but I wanted to use *him* in some way."[71]

After the live segment, Burden asked to see the station's two-inch Quad tape of the interview. He then unrolled the reel so that he and his assistants could douse the entire thing in acetone. The lack of physical documentation after Burden's destruction of the station's copy shifted any potential legal repercussions to be shared by those individuals working at the station, as their testimony would become critical if legal charges were put forward against the artist. By forcing the station staff into the more active and discernible role of accomplices to his act of hijacking, Burden demonstrated that these auxiliary participants are both present and crucial to the work's execution.

Although Burden offered his own video crew's copy of the events (which included both the show and its demolition) to the station manager after destroying the official version, it is significant to note that this documentation was in fact never made. As Burden provocatively explains, extending the blame to his abettors, "My guys forgot to push 'record,' so there is no record of it, unless somebody taped it at home."[72] Whether intentional or not, the lack of video documentation of the piece shifted the responsibility outward to the station manager, his associates, and Burden's camera crew to provide testimony in lieu of actual material evidence. If charges were pressed, the lack of physical records after Burden's destruction of the station's copy would require firsthand witnesses who could speak to the veracity of the events and the nature of the crime committed. Through their participation, albeit entering this responsibility unaware of the legal implications of this engagement, the station manager, crew, and home audience became potential bystanders whose role in convicting Burden of a crime would be essential if legal action was pursued. As he stated in a 1974 Rhode Island School of Design lecture, questions regarding the relative involvement of the auxiliary agents to the work's constitution were at play: "the show only went out once, without a title or anything. In a sense I stole it and destroyed it. So there was really a conflict as to who was the artist."[73]

Lutjeans's role in Burden's performance questions the intentionality necessary for aiding a criminal act, as she was both a potential accomplice *to* and hostage *in* the staging of this "crime." The culpability of Burden's own team, which included friend and fellow UC-Irvine alumnus Gary Beydler, could also be contested, as he continued to (supposedly) record Burden's actions during the armed attack and then willingly allowed Burden to destroy the station's documentation, which could have served as evidence in charging Burden with a crime.

Beydler's role as Burden's accomplice in numerous works from this early period of Burden's practice is significant since he photographed many of the circulated images of Burden's performances, such as *Bed Piece* (1972) and *Deadman*, that perpetuated the oft-rehearsed mythology of the artist as an avant-garde provocateur. The fact that Burden arrived at the TV station with a video crew serves as evidence that he had thought the work *TV Hijack* would include not only his action of taking Lutjeans hostage but also his abettors' actions in filming and then destroying the station's footage.

It is only through an examination of the sequence of the photographs in the contact sheet that Burden included as key documentation for this work published in *Chris Burden 71–73* that one can contest the often retold narrative of the piece regarding the horror and fear on the part of Lutjeans and the staff (fig. 1.14). While this may be true to an extent, what is omitted in these accounts of *TV Hijack* is that after the manager acquiesced to Burden's demands, the interview continued as if nothing had happened. As the contact sheet images indicate, Burden returned to his seat after taking Lutjeans "hostage," while she is shown casually gesturing with her hands as the interview seemingly returned to its original format. A few frames later, Burden is documented walking past Lutjeans while exiting the set as she leans toward him to make eye contact. In the last shot, Lutjeans has her jacket on in preparation to leave the station. However, she is captured speaking informally with a sheepish-looking Burden.

When Burden destroyed evidence that would potentially exonerate him, his careful construction of a "crime" that didn't exist reversed the typical criminal offense in which the perpetrator covers her or his tracks. Burden himself acknowledged that the critical stakes of the work did not reside in the immediate actions of the performance but in the work's consequences. As he noted in a Crown Point Press interview: "A lot of the piece exists after the fact, in the title '*TV Hijack*.'"[74] In other words, the "hijack" that Burden performed was less about his initial actions toward Lutjeans than about the act of commandeering the involvement of a network of associates as critical to this work.[75]

### Mediated Abettors: Home Audiences

Using various conventions of broadcast media—such as the radio interview, television commercial, or newscaster address—Burden created a series of works during the 1970s that explored the consequences of a home audience's involvement by developing methods of disclosure and privacy violations. For instance, at 11:45 a.m. on January 17, 1977, Burden aired prerecorded private telephone conversations with two unsuspecting art dealers on KPFK-FM in Los Angeles. Initially, the station approached him to produce a fourteen-minute audio piece that would run as part of a broadcast series of artists' projects. Burden's submission was an edited track of two separate exchanges: one with his New York dealer at the time, Ronald Feldman; and the second with Anna Canepa, a dealer who wanted to represent Burden's video work and use his name in advertising for her business. Canepa's motivations were to circumvent Feldman's authority as

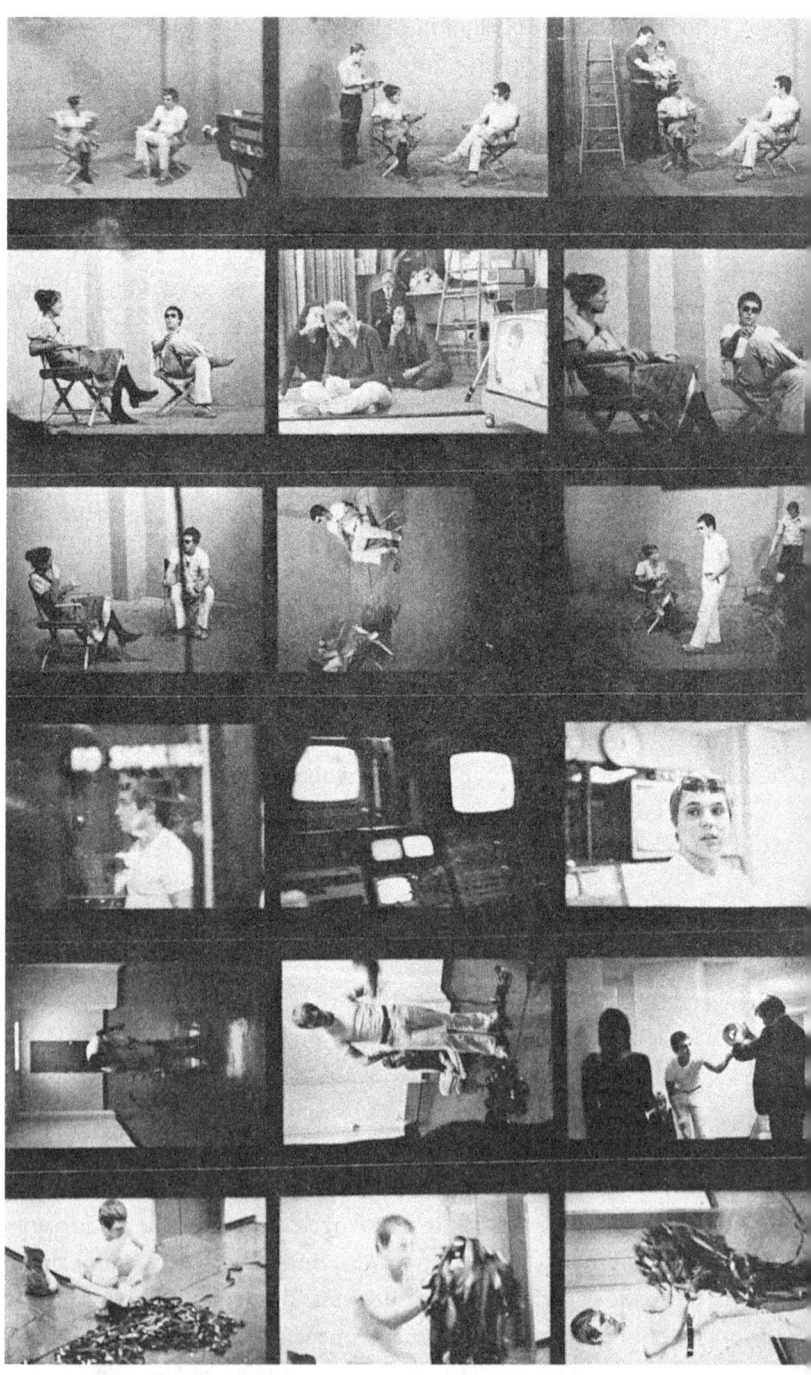

**1.14** Contact sheet for documentation of *TV Hijack*, February 9, 1972. Photographs by Gary Beydler.

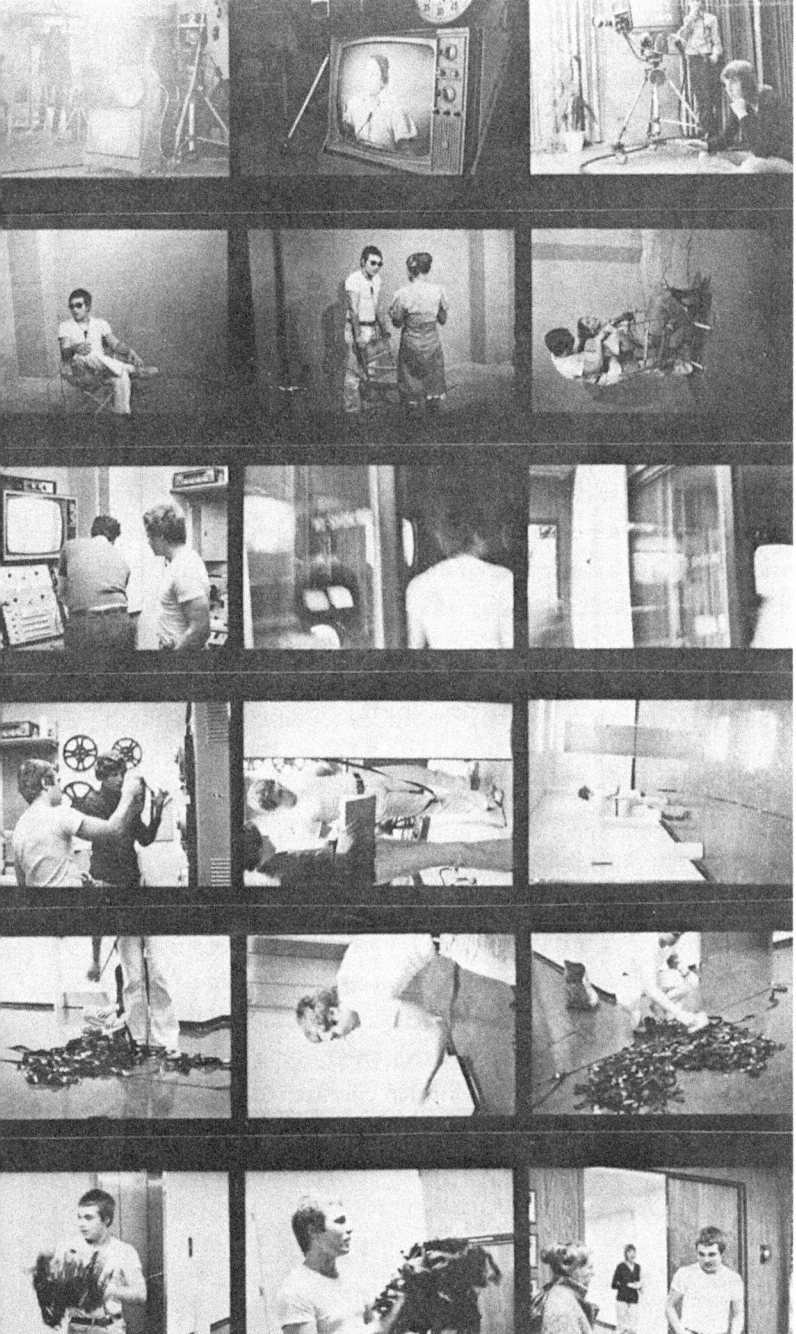

Burden's primary dealer by trying to enlist Burden as her own accomplice in contravening the artist-gallery relationship.

Modifying his home telephone with a wiretapping device, Burden recorded discussions with each party as they both spoke negatively about each other. His decision to edit and broadcast these personal conversations without permission divulged private information that was shared exclusively to him as a recipient; both Feldman and Canepa became his potential accomplices against each other.

While some of Burden's contemporaries also used audio recordings to produce confessional works, pieces like Acconci's *Face-Off* (1972)—in which the artist attempts to shout over a prerecorded monologue divulging his secret sexual deviances—involved personal disclosures rather than surreptitiously recording those of others, thereby remaining on the upside of the law. Given that California is a two-party consent state necessitating joint approval of both parties to be recorded, Burden's broadcast of the unwittingly recorded conversations on public radio in fact implicated *himself* in a crime. The issues that Burden's *Wiretap* makes evident were a visible part of the American cultural consciousness, such as the Watergate scandal, revealing the imbrication between disclosure and the law.

Returning briefly to *TV Hijack*, here Burden transgressed the thresholds of privacy on multiple levels. By hijacking Lutjeans's interview and forcing the television feed to go live, Burden inserted himself into the presumed "private" viewing space of the home television viewer. Those who happened to be watching this particular channel—or listening to the radio at a certain moment—might become inadvertent witnesses to a crime, if one considers whether or not they would report the "hostage situation" or illicit recording to local authorities. Exploiting such mediums' capacity for penetration between the public and private realms, Burden used the television and radio broadcast to entangle those home audiences into a precarious position. In other words, Burden encroached on the private sanctity of his abettors through the potential legal charges that would arise because of their involvement, witting or not, in his work.

### Reciprocal Abettor: Terry McDonnell

Between the performance of *Deadman* and the subsequent trial, Burden staged another work, *747* (1973; fig. 1.15), which reflected his continued interest in testing the limits of individual agency against the legal

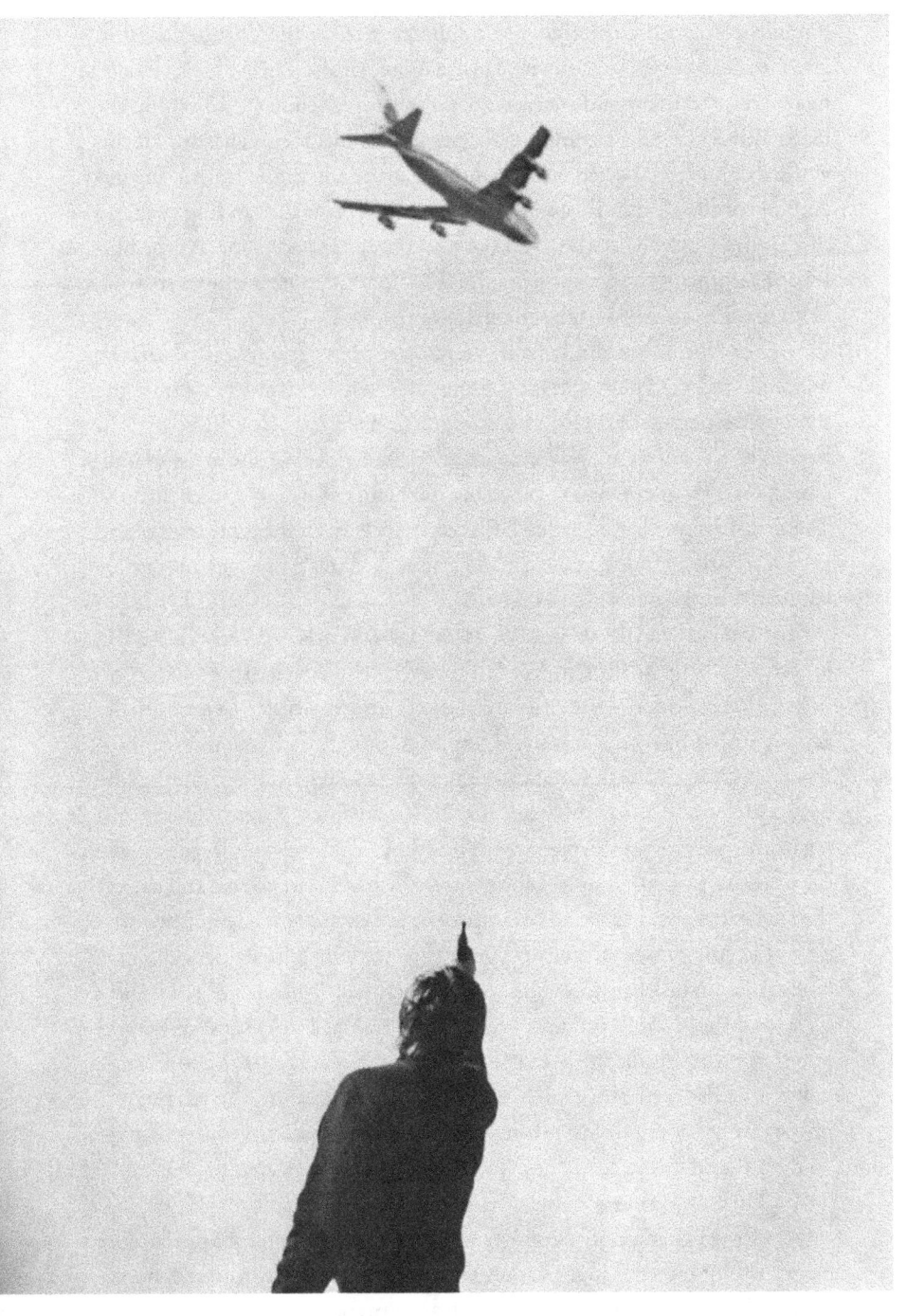

**1.15**　Chris Burden, *747*, January 5, 1973. Photograph by Terry McDonnell.

domain concerning the rights of a subject. Rather than prudently shift away from any associations with lawbreaking while awaiting his trial date, he returned to the pseudo-terroristic tactics deployed in *TV Hijack*. In the black-and-white photograph that serves as the sole documentation of this work, a commercial-sized airplane hovers at the top of the frame. The underbelly of the aircraft is visible, as are details such as the landing gear and tires, indicating the proximity of the photographer and plane. At the bottom of the image, the composition frames the artist in near silhouette from behind as his right arm is raised outstretched.

Given the low angle from which the photograph was taken, the unnamed subject (perhaps recognizable to art-world insiders by Burden's signature haircut) and airplane are set against a vast cloudless sky that heightens the anonymity of the scene. A small gun is in the artist's hand, aimed directly at the passenger plane departing the nearby LAX airport. The actual events that occurred between the release of the gun's trigger and the bullet's trajectory toward the American Airlines passenger aircraft are left unresolved.

After an earlier attempt to stage *747* was preemptively called off, on January 5, 1973, Burden headed down to the beach armed with two boxes of cartridges—one of blank bullets and the other live rounds—accompanied by photographer Terry McDonnell with the intention to shoot a gun at a Boeing plane full of passengers. According to Burden, he began preparations for the work months in advance. After deliberations regarding the use of a silencer, which he eventually forewent, Burden made the decision to shoot a series of the blanks he had in his pocket and collect the shells in a small carrying case that would remain at his feet. The function of keeping these objects in play was to serve as false evidence in case of legal action taken against him. As he described, "After I shot the bullets off I took those shells out and I had a little holder in the sand so I could pop it open and I put the blanks that were shot off . . . so if the cops came down . . . I had a photographer too, right? So I'd say, 'Look, this guy is a photographer, we're doing a thing, the blanks, see these are empty blanks.' So then they'd buy it."[76]

Given the sparse composition in the documentation of *747*, it is easy to forget that a photographer was present and therefore potentially mixed up in any criminal charges that would follow from Burden's actions. While Burden described the advance preparations made to thwart any legal action taken against him following this work, the photographer occupies a complex role that only becomes visible if the illegality of the performance is foregrounded. Not only was the performance composed of a split-second action, but the concise description that accompanies it in *Chris Burden 71–73* and the single photographic documentation of the action itself forces McDonnell, Burden's accomplice, to make up for the artist's reticence.[77]

McDonnell's role in this performance, while officially unacknowledged beyond providing a photographic record of the event, is in fact integral to the work on multiple levels. Although his photograph would undoubtedly serve as evidence in any potential charges brought by authorities, its initial conceit was to strictly serve as the only documentary source of Burden's performance. This evidentiary position would take on various casts depending on the context in which it was used: legal or aesthetic. Moreover, McDonnell himself remained outside the work as an unacknowledged documenter unless required to serve as witness in the case of legal action. In this way, his presence at the performance was also to serve as lookout for the nominal artist, a role that precludes joint authorial recognition but demands legal responsibility that was shared equally.

Burden was not alone in mimicking an aesthetic of conspiratorial surveillance, as seen in *747*. In 1969, Acconci enacted *Following Piece*, a work governed by a similar principle in that the artist selected an individual at random to follow around the streets of New York City. Despite the menacing aspects of such an act, Acconci stated in the written notes for this piece that he used the project to deliberately dispel responsibility to another individual by tacitly granting that person authority over his own actions. While a more extensive analysis of Acconci's work through the accomplice paradigm exceeds the scope of this book, such conceptualization draws important parallels with Burden's practice in the distribution of accountability to operatives who might also be described as abettors.

As was typical in Burden's performances from the early to mid-1970s, *747* was documented in three primary ways: a concise and straightforward descriptive text, a still photograph, and what Burden termed a "relic"—an object featured in the performance, often the locus of the primary "action." For example, *TV Hijack*'s relic was the knife, *Deadman*'s was the canvas tarpaulin, and in *747*, it was the revolver. These were then photographed and often replaced images of Burden himself in supporting documentation of the performances, such as in his self-published artist's books. Significantly, the mode of display—frequently exhibited with the relic placed in a vitrine alongside an accompanying text placard with Burden's description of the related events—is reminiscent of the presentation of crime-scene evidence. This reference to objects playing an evidentiary role in determining the scope of an individual's involvement in certain actions was likely intentional by Burden, as this method of creating a permanent record of his ephemeral performances became a signature feature that has become synonymous with his work.

As detailed in Burden's own description of *747*, he fired several shots at the passenger plane. Based on the photograph's composition, the feasibility of the bullet reaching the aircraft is unclear. However, he explicitly stated that the intention of the gesture was embedded within the contingency of the event as *possible* violence against others rather than actually hurting anyone. Burden noted that a crucial component of the work was the passengers' experience of such a terrifying event, explaining, "If the people in the airplane could see me shooting at them, even if the bullet didn't get to them, they'd just die."[78] Taking Burden at his word that the work would be successful whether or not the bullet reached its intended target, it is possible to imagine McDonnell's position within the work as occupying the role of neither the artist nor the audience. His visibility within the work only becomes legible when the legal pressures of the nominal artist's actions require him to come forward, as either a witness or an accomplice.

As such, *747* marks another example of Burden's work in which documentation is critically important. McDonnell's photograph captures the concept of the piece without incriminating Burden with conclusive evidence of his actions being illicit or not. This ambiguity is crucial—while Burden did shoot actual bullets, his deliberate distance from the aircraft prevented accidental contact. Nonetheless, the potentially illegal nature of such circumstances put McDonnell in the position of an accomplice to either corroborate or disclose Burden's activities.

In *747*, Burden presents yet another work in which the artist set up circumstances for an auxiliary agent, apart from the general audience, to intervene in the constructed circumstances as a way to explore questions concerning responsibility and sovereignty that were integral to both art and law at the time. The preparations and contingency plans notwithstanding, Burden and McDonnell completed the work without outside interruption. As Burden explained in a 1980 interview, "I knew that if I wasn't going to be arrested on the spot that there was no fucking proof that it had happened."[79]

While the two men walked away from the beach that day without any police intervention, four and a half years later, Burden came home to find a business card at his studio imprinted with the Federal Bureau of

Investigation (FBI) logo. The circumstances leading to an FBI investigation began rather innocuously. In April 1975, *Oui*, an American adult men's magazine, published an eight-page article by John Calendo titled "Portrait of the Artist as a Young Sculpture" that was accompanied by a series of photographs depicting the artist's work.[80] Presenting Burden's performance to a mass audience that might otherwise be unaware of current debates in contemporary art, the article consisted of an interview with the artist and his associates in an attempt to clarify the artist's intentions for its readership. According to Burden, the FBI became aware of *747* following the publication of McDonnell's photograph in *Oui*, which caught the attention of one of the magazine's executives.[81] The unnamed informant contacted the FBI with the following complaint: "Who is this Chris Burden? He was shooting at an airplane and he's not in jail? How come?"[82] Shortly thereafter, the FBI dispatched agents to track down the artist.

It is possible that police intervention was Burden's intention for the work all along. After all, his fascination with the FBI was evident during his Pomona College years, as his wife, Barbara, recounted.[83] Furthermore, he had previously impersonated a federal agent in his work *I Became a Secret Hippy* on October 3, 1971, itself a federal offense since 1948.[84] For *Secret Hippy*, Tom Marioni had invited Burden to do a piece at the Museum of Conceptual Art in San Francisco after meeting the artist in Los Angeles through Barbara Smith. For this performance, Burden undressed from his street clothes of jeans and sneakers and had an unnamed friend hammer a star-shaped stud into his chest and shave his head. He then re-dressed in what was described as an FBI uniform, consisting of a nondescript suit and tie. While never prosecuted (likely because FBI agents do not wear official regulation uniforms), Burden certainly would have appreciated the irony of meeting one of these officers in person.[85]

After some negotiations, the meeting with the FBI was conducted at the house of Burden's lawyer since the artist was concerned that the lack of furniture at his own home would be somehow incriminating or insinuate that his character was suspect. During the meeting, Burden wisely left the defense of *747* to his attorney. Having laid out information and images of contemporary art, the lawyer made his rebuttal using other examples of performances from the period and situating Burden's actions within the context of his larger artistic career.[86] The FBI officers ultimately left without further complications.

The delayed response on the part of the FBI, which only became aware of *747* as it appeared in a smutty men's magazine, created a temporal extension of the work that retroactively put further pressure on McDonnell as Burden's abettor. The brevity of Burden's performance reinforced the precarious position in which McDonnell found himself and intensified the necessity to act on Burden's behalf. The brief duration of shooting opened new parameters for the work through reimaginings of temporal and authorial boundaries, which include the legal implications and the social delegation that had been entrenched in the work all along.

## Institutional Abettors: Dennis O'Shea, Ikon Gallery Board of Directors, and Other Museum Support Staff

In the mid-1970s, Burden extended his exploration of the shared responsibility in his performances to include other figures often obscured in an art institutional setting such as a museum or gallery: the security guards and curatorial team. As seen in the photographic documentation of the performance *Doomed* (fig. 1.16), Burden exploited the limits between the authorial role of the artist and the dual authorities of the museum and law. This project expanded the scope of the abettors in Burden's work to include those individuals who might be conceived as institutional accomplices.

In 1975, Burden was invited by curator Ira Licht to exhibit at the Museum of Contemporary Art in Chicago with the specific request that he do a "longer" durational performance to keep the audience's attention. According to film critic Roger Ebert, who was writing an article for the *Chicago Sun-Times*, the exact temporal boundaries of the work would not be disclosed in advance.[87] The artist did, however, request two items for his performance: a wall clock and a large pane of glass.

The work began at 8:20 p.m. when Burden entered the room and slid himself under the thin sheet of glass set at a forty-five-degree angle against a wall, where he lay supine for the remainder of his performance. As the night went on, the approximately four-hundred-person crowd dwindled, leaving only a few loyal viewers who remained throughout the night into the next day. As the performance approached the second-day mark, museum authorities contacted medical specialists out of growing concern over the artist's health. The conflict between aesthetic purity to the artist's intention and the moral obligation on the part of the institution to protect the artist, even from himself, became subject to debate. Ultimately, it was a security guard, Dennis O'Shea, and not the curatorial staff who

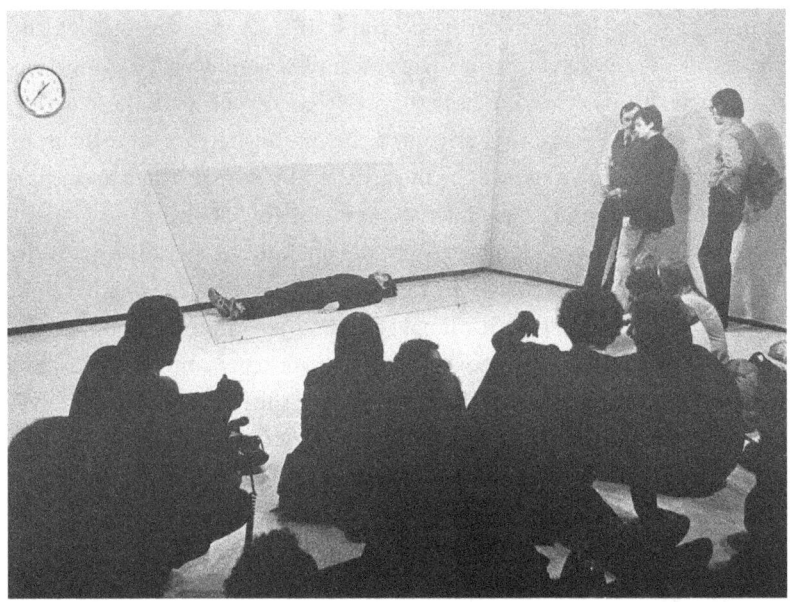

**1.16**    Chris Burden, *Doomed*, April 11, 1975. Museum of
Contemporary Art, Chicago, Illinois.

placed a pitcher of water next to Burden's head almost two days into his
performance. In response to this intervention, the artist immediately got
up and disappeared into another room. He returned with a hammer used
to smash the clock and handed the curator a sealed envelope with a pre-
written statement of intention enclosed.

According to this letter, the work was set in motion by the artist's
initial actions but the responsibility of ending it was left to members of
the museum staff—who were not given instructions in advance. If they
interfered with any of the components of the work—the glass, the clock,
or Burden himself—the performance would be effectively over. This brings
up the complicated issue of cognizance and complicity, in that only those
participants unfamiliar with the work were granted the authority over the
work's scope and parameters. In hearing this statement, the museum's pub-
licist, Alene Valkanas, remarked, "My god, we could have ended it anytime
we wanted to and here we thought we had a contract with him that we
couldn't break unless he died."[88]

In *Doomed*, Burden used the access given to him by the invitation of
the museum to infiltrate the established order of operations and to use its
associates in his performance. In other words, by leaving the responsibility

of his care in the hands of the curatorial staff, operations personnel, and security team, Burden brought these accomplices into view by compelling them to decide whether and how to interfere with the work. In so doing, Burden created a piece that critiqued the established art institution by staging circumstances so that the hierarchies of power and artistic authority entered into visibility in a manner previously overlooked.[89]

While *Doomed* is a prime example of Burden's work in which the outcome would be determined by museum staff, Burden also sought to test the outermost limits of institutional economic responsibility, particularly when such questions were raised in the face of legal complications. For instance, in *Diecimila* (1977), Burden solicited the help of Kathan Brown, the owner of Crown Point Press in San Francisco, to reproduce fake Italian currency, effectively creating an institutionally sanctioned counterfeit operation. In advance of Crown Point's participation in a 1977 art fair held in Bologna, Burden worked directly with the press's staff. While he gave direction to his artistic aims, he left the actual act of creation to the printers, who hand-made the plates and paper, re-created watermarks, and produced the set of editioned prints on larger sheets of paper that Burden signed. According to artist Tom Marioni, Burden cut out at least one of the bills and passed it off as authentic in a commercial purchase.[90] When this work was sent to the Italian art fair, local police were notified about the counterfeit bills and came to the Crown Point Booth in search of the culprit. As Marioni recounts, after having learned the radically inflated prices of the art prints (selling the equivalent of $10 bills for $1,000 apiece), "they threw up their hands and left."[91] Since Burden did not attend, Crown Point Press ostensibly took on accountability for the work in the face of legal retribution by local authorities, indicating yet another example of Burden's strategic tactics of distributing responsibility among institutional agents while maintaining nominal authority over a given work.

Continuing the theme of financial falsifications and institutional involvement, in 1981 Burden manipulated the presumed financial value of an object positioned within an art institution. Burden convinced the Ikon Gallery's board of directors to finance the purchase of a diamond, which he then replaced with a cubic zirconia replica, pocketing the original. While the audience in Birmingham, England, was not aware of the switch, instead marveling at the suspended "diamond" gleaming under a makeshift spotlight in an entirely black room, news of the performative aspect of Burden's installation *Diamonds Are Forever* reached various board members, who began discussing pressing charges of fraud, embezzlement, or theft against the artist. The question of legal or ethical culpability rested on the initial guidelines presented by the gallery, which gave Burden a $500 budget to acquire materials with the stipulation that whatever was purchased would become his property to keep.

Burden's actions expanded the work to a legal domain as the board of directors discussed the status of their financial support and whether the artist could be sued for defrauding the publicly funded exhibition space. As Howard Singerman points out, "The board, it seems, expected Burden to purchase materials that would be worthless until he transformed them."[92] However, the liability of their case was likely determined to be inconclusive as the curator had "received special permission to issue a check to a local jeweler; no such permission would have been necessary for the local lumberyard"; this indicates prior knowledge of the diamond purchase that would presumably absolve Burden of legal responsibility to the board members.[93]

While *Diamonds Are Forever* is most often described as comprising the installation and relics, I contend that the potential charges of illegality discussed by the board of directors expanded the parameters of the work in important and deliberate ways. Burden breached the contractual agreement between artist and institution to involve the Ikon Gallery's curators, board of directors, and administrative staff as institutional accomplices in his work through the illegal or unethical transgressions that he deliberately put forward as tests. In *Diamonds Are Forever* and the related 1981 project *Napoleon d'Or*—in which Burden purchased a small amount of gold with the Centre Pompidou's funding that he then melted with a blowtorch to create a replica of a cheap Napoleon figurine—Burden brought the gallery and museum's administration into the foreground of the work because of his actions; their roles and responsibilities must then also be considered as part of the piece. Turning those people involved into accomplices to his ethical violations, Burden once again manipulated the social relationship between artist and auxiliary agents to investigate the scope of an individual's authority over another. Perhaps unsurprisingly, the real diamond remained in Burden's possession when he returned home to Los Angeles at the close of the exhibition.

### Abettors on Record

Over the course of a ten-year period—from his first live performances such as *Shoot* staged in 1971 through his 1981 institutional interventions—Burden explored ways of putting pressure on a network of individuals who functioned as proxies for the artist, sharing in the accountability for artworks that often involved ethical transgressions as a key component. In the earliest performance examples, these abettors remained largely in the background, their presence hardly noticed in scholarly or critical accounts of the work. Yet by the early 1980s, as Burden moved further away from performance projects in his practice in favor of large-format sculptures and installations, the abettors became a more obvious component of the artwork, as seen in the manipulation of various institutional representatives as the central artistic act in *Diamonds Are Forever*.

Burden's initial testing of the threshold of individual rights belonging to his immediate circle of auxiliary participants expanded in his later pieces to include wider networks of potential accomplices. Yet despite the shifting types of abettors, he maintained an ongoing interrogation of the scope of agency for those not typically registered as participants in a performance. In the pieces discussed, Burden's body was obscured (*Deadman*), his identity used as bait (*Wiretap*), or his presence ambiguously sidelined (*747*). These examples demonstrate how Burden's work often involves more than the artist's apparent physical actions—whether getting shot in the arm or simulating a hostage situation—but rather a whole set of consequences and a network of implicated players crucial to the work's construction.

This chapter conceptualizes the "abettor" as a type of accomplice that emerges in Burden's work whose largely unacknowledged role in artistic works becomes visible through their involvement in ethical and legal disobedience enacted under the authority of the titular artist. The implications of such a claim undermine the dominant focus on Burden's early performances such as *Shoot* that featured the artist's body, which is at the center of his contextualization within the critical category of "body art." If one instead considers such projects more broadly to include the range of assistants, romantic partners, legal representatives, documenters, and others who were called on by the nominal artist to act in a potentially illegal way, then Burden's work redefines the boundaries of a given piece not as a set limit but as a network that extends temporally, socially, and ethically.

Burden's constellation of abettors became the intermediaries between the artist and the audience by documenting, witnessing, or otherwise aiding in the work itself. Those who are conceived as accomplices in Burden's work—even when they initially encountered the performance or intervention as a typical audience member—were used in such a way that their own privacy, agency, and sovereignty were exploited and tested.

Rather than being considered as a masculinist glorification of violence, a position that the artist himself disavowed repeatedly, these illicit actions that Burden staged in his 1970s performance-based work constituted a new way of exploring questions of accountability and agency among a network of associates, who would otherwise not be visible, using ethical and legal stakes.

This book opens with Burden's abettors because they serve as the clearest example of the accomplice model, featuring actual illicit transgressions and a social structure that is clearly networked yet hierarchical. The following chapters chart the evolution of the accomplice as it assumes other forms, eventually feeding back in/to the artist. Under Burden's nominal authorship, the accomplices became extensions of his public artistic identity in a manner proportionate to their compromised individual private agency as legal subjects. In short, to conceive of Burden's performances as simply having staged exaggerated provocations is to ignore the vast social, legal, and institutional networks that were in fact integral to his work and that demand representation on their own fugitive terms.

# Partners

**In September 1989,** New York–based attorney Tim Cone published a brief two-page article as part of his "Art and the Law" series in *Arts Magazine* that offered a legal perspective on emerging debates regarding intellectual property, art, and architecture. In "Life over Art: Oldenburg's Privacy, Wilke's Publicity," Cone unpacked an important case brought forward by Claes Oldenburg against fellow artist Hannah Wilke over the use of his likeness and their shared personal history. The legal contestation focused on Wilke's right to exhibit and reproduce images for three of her artworks—which prominently included photographs of Oldenburg made during the height of their romantic relationship that occurred between 1969 and 1977—in the exhibition catalog for her first major retrospective at the University of Missouri that year. As Cone explains, Oldenburg's reasons for refusal were twofold and, in many ways, contradictory in his claims of authority over his image: (1) despite giving Wilke approval when the photographs were initially taken, Oldenburg asserted his right to privacy over the public disclosure of his personal entity in perpetuity; and (2) his right of publicity meant that as a public art-world figure, he retained ownership over his personal image for economic gain.[1]

Following the sudden demise of their relationship in 1977, Wilke's role as Oldenburg's artistic collaborator was almost entirely expunged from his personal and professional history.[2] Moreover, as articulated by Cone, Oldenburg also sought to block Wilke from using his image through both official and unofficial channels. This presented a tremendous problem for Wilke, a younger woman whose artwork was centered on intimate explorations of herself, her personal life, and those with whom she socialized—both during and after her relationship with Oldenburg, who was a highly successful white male artist. While the legal debate between Wilke and Oldenburg resulted in the omission of images depicting his likeness in her 1989 exhibition catalog and any projects going forward, these circumstances have relevance for Wilke's artistic practice more generally.

Set within the context of 1970s second-wave white feminism, intellectual property and privacy laws, and emerging artistic critiques concerning the politics of representation, this chapter develops and interrogates key issues introduced in Cone's 1989 article to offer an alternative narrative through Wilke's career as she negotiated various rights over her personal agency. I first take a brief look at key works by Wilke produced before 1977, while in a relationship with Oldenburg, that centered on the exposure of details from her personal life. This establishes the driving concept of disclosure as critical to Wilke's practice—an approach that was conceptually in line with the second-wave feminist slogan "the personal is political"—which would be a necessary point to distinguish her later work from possible accusations of vengeful retribution. Then, I consider the case and circumstances around *Advertisements for Living*, the work upon which Oldenburg's legal action was primarily based. The chapter lastly presents examples of artworks made by Wilke beginning in 1977 that were motivated by Oldenburg's ongoing obstruction of her work in the years after their relationship, until her death in 1993.

Wilke's unacknowledged labor for projects attributed solely to Oldenburg as well as his legal petitions against using his likeness in her projects were transformed into the subject of her own artistic practice as she sought recognition for her contributions and equal ownership of their shared personal history. The legal framework of publicity and privacy law is used in this chapter because viewing art through this lens provides a potential means of exposing those who have been previously written out of history, thereby taking the first steps to reestablish parity. Through her work, Wilke sought to rebalance the unequal scales of agency, recognition, and responsibility she believed were meant to be shared.

The previous chapter examined Chris Burden's deployment of a broad network of abettors in the form of assistants, romantic partners, and legal representatives; here, I contend that Wilke was herself a former "accomplice" to Oldenburg, whose experience of deliberate exclusions from public recognition for her labor in his works—and her comparatively limited professional success—spurred a set of projects undertaken to recalibrate the discrepancies in stereotypically gendered conventions of authorship and agency. Reappropriating what she saw as prior arrogations by Oldenburg and developing countertechniques based on principles of disclosure, Wilke strategically revealed the role of auxiliary participants in her work while also retroactively calling attention to her unattributed labor in Oldenburg's artistic practice.

On February 5, 1991, less than two years before her death, Wilke sketched a proposed museum exhibition design composed of her and Oldenburg's works. Created on a thin sheet of torn semitransparent paper, the drawing—now stained in spots—provides a detailed layout of the show, with handwritten annotations about some of her curatorial decisions. While the checklist of included works primarily consisted of Wilke's sculptures, photographs, and installations, it also featured artworks that had been historically attributed to Oldenburg alone. For example, Wilke's mixed-media work *Even-tu-ally* (1969–91) and Oldenburg's lithograph *Alphabet in the Form of a Good Humor Bar* (1970) flank opposite sides of the exhibition's entrance, while a multicolored set of Oldenburg's *Fireplug* multiples, which Wilke claimed to have painted, are installed along an outer wall of her *Proposed I-Museum in the Form of an H Series* (1991). This enigmatic drawing therefore describes a plan for an ultimately unrealized exhibition that would bring attention to her artistic career—as well as specify works typically ascribed exclusively to Oldenburg for which she believed she was due shared credit—to uncover sexist hierarchies of authorial recognition and artistic labor embedded in much of the American art world at the time.

Wilke's proposed exhibition drawing serves as a blueprint for retracing the networks between her and Oldenburg's shared history, artistic agendas, and legal battles that are essential to her work. That is, I believe that the artist used this private document as a way to map the interconnections of her and Oldenburg's personal and professional lives after a series of intertangled events: she was cut off romantically from her former partner, blocked from showing artwork featuring Oldenburg that was previously approved, legally refused permission by Oldenburg to exhibit or reproduce her works that included his likeness, received no public credit for her artistic labor in his works, and described merely as an artistic assistant in legal documents produced by his lawyers to refute her claims to health and life insurance policies that were to be given through Oldenburg's Store Days corporation. This chapter asks a key question about the nature of the "crime" itself: was it Wilke invading his privacy or in fact Oldenburg's manipulation that violated her rights to publicity over their shared personal history in her art?

Although Wilke's unpublished 1991 exhibition drawing has heretofore not been discussed in the scholarship on her work, it is in fact crucial in mapping many of the artist's central concerns and artistic strategies that she explored throughout her career.[3] The role of this drawing, I argue, has as much to do with recovering acknowledgment of her unattributed labor in Oldenburg's practice as it does with establishing a feminist model for demanding representation and agency based on principles of disclosure.

The 1970s marked a moment of substantial revisions to privacy and publicity laws in the United States. Concerning women's rights, in the 1965 case *Griswold v. Connecticut*, the Supreme Court ruled that the right to purchase contraception was a privacy right for married couples, which helped lay the groundwork for the landmark 1973 *Roe v. Wade* case over women's abortion rights. The Privacy Act of 1974 changed legislative policy around data privacy, greatly restricting the federal government's ability to collect, share, and use details that might disclose personal information. Over the course of its history, the Supreme Court has only once—in 1977—ruled on a case concerning publicity rights; five years prior, the "human cannonball" Hugo Zacchini sued Scripps-Howard Broadcasting for filming his act without his consent, arguing that broadcasting it would infringe on his ability to monetize his performance. The case ultimately went to the US Supreme Court, where the court decided in Zacchini's favor regarding this infraction on his self-image as "professional property."

Wilke's tactic of making her private life publicly visible through her art was a strategic gesture that forced various individuals in her life to come forward—an effort to use her personal experiences to tell a larger narrative regarding the marginalized position and inadequate agency felt by women during this period more generally. In contrast, Burden often used his network of abettors as proxies in undertaking legal or ethical indiscretions, yet access to this model was not widely available to women artists at the time. Instead, Wilke offers an alternative conception of the accomplice figure, in which she develops strategic techniques to recalibrate authorship by staking a claim for others to recognize her as an equal *partner*. Despite the fact that the term *partnership* was not widely integrated into the discourse as a means of describing personal relationships until the 1980s, the particular formulation of partners used in this chapter specifically refers to the equitable types of relationships with men—both personally and professionally—to which Wilke aspired.[4] Therefore, its usage here is consciously anachronistic and is meant to draw out the ways in which such equality was frustrated and often refused to women artists at the time.

With Wilke as my primary case study, chapter 2 focuses attention on how the figure of the accomplice became a useful tool for reversing the

unidirectional trajectory of power structured according to gender disparities. Therefore, while Burden demonstrated that his performances—which
often prominently featured his physical presence—were not simply about
him but crucially involved the integral participation of others in the work's
execution, Wilke sought to gain power by moving outside the auxiliary
position she previously occupied as an accomplice. Therefore, the term
*partner* speaks to her desires as a woman to receive recognition for her
artistic and personal contributions in a manner that suggests parity across
genders, a key point for white feminism of the 1970s. This ambition for
retroactive partnership haunts her work, visibly and conceptually, speaking
to the numerous longings by other women artists who never emerged from
the specter of being a man's accomplice.

### Oldenburg Portfolio

One of the first pieces that a viewer would have encountered upon entering Wilke's imagined exhibition would be an untitled portfolio of twenty
black-and-white photographs taken of Oldenburg between 1970 and 1975,
known as the *Oldenburg Portfolio*. According to her notation in the proposed exhibition drawing, Wilke wished to enlarge the prints and arrange
them in five tight rows in a separate viewing room alongside the 8 mm film
*Erasers, Snails, and a Couple of Towels* (1970), which featured Wilke undertaking various performances while Oldenburg served as her cameraman. The
reasons for installing these two projects together perhaps seem, at first, unclear, yet both were specifically contested after the official end of the couple's
romantic relationship in 1977.

Although the legal demands set by Oldenburg in his official lawsuit
against Wilke focused on works that will be discussed later in this chapter,
there were also critical points of contention between the artists that were
not ultimately resolved through legal means. One of these was Wilke's claim
that thousands of photographs she had taken during their relationship had
disappeared or remained in his possession following his sudden marriage
to curator Coosje van Bruggen that same year.[5] In an undated letter to her
lawyer Barbara Hoffman, Wilke wrote, "Claes did show me a file of photographs when I picked up my clothes and other possessions at his house after
his marriage in 1977. He first offered it to me and then took it back saying that we would work something out later about the return of my nega-
tives and slides."[6] While Oldenburg later returned to Wilke a total of 997

photographs following legal action, he claimed that *Erasers, Snails, and a Couple of Towels* and many additional works had been permanently lost.

Although photographs in Wilke's *Oldenburg Portfolio* were initially made to capture their life together, they would have taken on an evidentiary role testifying to an artistic as well as romantic partnership when blown up and set off in Wilke's planned exhibition. The *Oldenburg Portfolio* depicts the lovers in various moments of intimate sexual play, revealing the pleasure of their relations. In contrast to the standoffish and macho public art-world image of Oldenburg, in Wilke's photographs he is shown in private moments of vulnerability. In one such image, Oldenburg lightheartedly holds an object across his upper lip as if a moustache, mugging for Wilke's camera. In another, she catches him shaving in a bathroom mirror with a Mickey Mouse toy on his sink.

Many of the photographs portray Oldenburg nude: on the toilet, in bed, or working bottomless in his art studio. In multiple images, Oldenburg poses for Wilke, using various props to convey a spirited and imaginative sexual life. For example, Oldenburg sits comfortably on an overstuffed chair with a wine glass in one hand and the other gently touching his face. A knit mask, pulled over his head so that his entire face is covered, disrupts the semblance of suburban domesticity, giving an element of bondage or sadomasochistic undertones to the otherwise tame scene. In another, Oldenburg assumes a position directly on the carpeted floor. Wilke's image captures him on all fours, fully clothed in everyday trousers, shirt, and leather belt, looking straight ahead. An element of sexual submission is present, which hints at a role reversal of the typical artist-model relationship that recurs in their joint projects. This is also captured in another work from the series, in which Oldenburg lies face down on a couch, completely nude save for an undershirt. His face is turned toward Wilke's camera and his acknowledgment of the camera is clear. His position and the patterning throughout the domestic setting recall the reclining nude odalisque tradition in painting, effecting a further inversion of conventional gender roles.

One of the most striking photographs from the *Oldenburg Portfolio* was included as one half of the large black-and-white photographic diptych *Dear Claes* (1970–76) (fig. 2.1). The work consists of two seemingly unrelated images that are reconciled by the verbal pun of the title. The photograph on the left is focused on a tightly framed image of a deer looking up at the camera. The fawn's eyes are in clear focus, as are the delicate hairs on its face. The background is blurred, underscoring the tenderness of the encounter. This intimacy connects to the right image, which depicts the

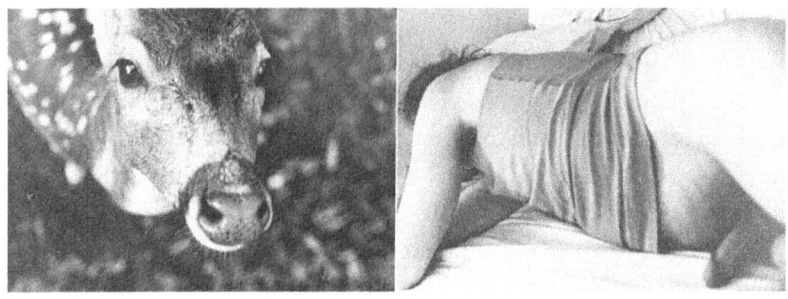

**2.01**  Hannah Wilke, *Dear Claes*, 1970–76. Gelatin silver photograph, 28 × 81 in.

partially nude Oldenburg lying on his side. Taken by Wilke while they were in bed together, the photograph frames her lover's torso and upper thigh. His face is blocked by the position of his raised arms while she crops the image strategically to include his erect penis resting against the bedsheet.

While this specific work, and the *Oldenburg Portfolio* more generally, has largely been excluded from the scholarly literature on Wilke's work—as well as from major museum shows—*Dear Claes* did appear in both the exhibition and the catalog for Elisa Decker's *The Male Nude: Women Regard Men* at the Hudson Center Galleries in 1986. Alongside artists including Carolee Schneemann, Alice Neel, and Joan Semmel, Wilke's photographic diptych provided a candid glimpse of a private relationship. Yet in contrast to many of the explicitly sexualized or objectifying male nudes on view, Wilke defied the typically heroic depiction of the male body.

It is likely for this reason—showing an intimate side to an art "celebrity" that went against the highly controlled public images of Oldenburg—that Wilke was unsuccessful in exhibiting the *Oldenburg Portfolio*. This exceeded Oldenburg's own actions; it seems that he directed his gallery representatives—either explicitly or tacitly—to block Wilke's attempts at showing this work. For instance, Wilke gave Oldenburg's then gallerist Marian Goodman a set of the *Portfolio* prints around 1978–79 "for the stated purpose of showing them at the Basel Art Fair" and even wrote again to Goodman in 1989 asking her to consider these images "for possible exhibition or publication."[7] According to the Wilke family, however, these photographs were never returned to the artist. This caused multiple affronts, as Wilke could not make future work using the missing photographs as source material, nor could she exhibit work previously produced with Oldenburg's apparent approval.

By recasting these private images as her artistic work, Wilke sought to use her access to Oldenburg's personal life at a time when his artistic successes and institutional support outperformed hers. It is significant to note, however, that Oldenburg himself had shown the *Portfolio* to gallerists Sidney Janis and Virginia Zabriskie in the hopes of publicly exhibiting the works.[8] Therefore, against the notion that these photographs were intended to serve only as private snapshots to be shared among Oldenburg and Wilke alone, both parties pursued—at some point—circulating the images in a public context. As a result, Wilke considered the status of the missing photographs to be relevant to her ongoing legal debates with Oldenburg, particularly since he attempted to restrict her usage of his image in other projects and these photographs were of an especially personal nature. His actions taken to hinder her ability to exhibit and sell her completed artwork, which may or may not have officially violated her own right to privacy, inadvertently thrust the imbalanced nature of power that characterized the terms of labor in their relationship prominently into visibility.

Against the backdrop of second-wave white feminism, many women artists in America during the mid-1970s were actively seeking means of gaining agency and recognition within the art world. Yet their ability to achieve such goals and receive more widespread public attention was often based on their proximity to prominent male art-world figures. One tactic that women artists used to counteract this imbalance was to reclaim authority over images: both their own and that of their romantic partners in a reversal of male-generated objectification. While this was often the impetus for women artists to present themselves outside the perspective of the male gaze, staging independent and self-generated portraits that asserted women's experiences as their own, certain artists—like Wilke—created works that instead recalibrated the typically gendered artist-model relationship, turning the camera around onto male subjects.

One prominent example of this tendency is Schneemann's contemporaneous representations of the male nude and the disclosure of her private life in her work. In *ABC—We Print Anything—In the Cards* (1976–77), Schneemann mined the intimate history of her overlapping romantic relationships at the time. The piece comprised a set of cardboard cards (that could be shown as an artist's book as well as a projected slideshow), each featuring a typewritten text that recounted advice the artist received about her personal relationships, proffered recollections of the artist's dreams, and/or reproduced quotations from the three intertangled lovers. While only using the first letter of their names (A. for her soon-to-be former lover, Anthony McCall; B. for Bruce McPherson, her burgeoning romantic interest; and C. for herself), the level of specificity of the printed text details private exchanges concerning sexuality, fidelity, and happiness, among other topics. Such cards were also accompanied by a single, unrelated snapshot attached to the verso, which included depictions of pets, the artist's travels, and the three central parties—A., B., and C.—in various scenarios, ranging from the quotidian to the erotic. Schneemann's impulse to disclose such encounters— and the nonhierarchical presentation of female and male nudes—connects to Wilke's pursuit of recalibrating the conventions of depicting men's and women's bodies. Both artists offered nuance to the representation of nude subjects by offering a woman's perspective.

By the late 1970s, other women artists sought means of exploiting the presumed "privacy" of others, testing the scope of legal and ethical culpability for such actions. For instance, in 1980 French artist Sophie Calle began a project that reversed the typical structure of the voyeuristic male gaze on women subjects. In *Suite Vénitienne*, the artist began performing extensive surveillance of a man, known only as "Henri B.," while in disguise, even following him from Paris to Venice. Two years later, as part of her work *The Hotel* (1981), Calle assumed a job as a hotel chambermaid, where she studied and photographed the guests' personal belongings without consent. As Yve-Alain Bois has noted, here "the artist could have found herself in real trouble" since her project "flirted much more openly with criminal activity."[9]

In 1983, Calle published a series of articles in the French newspaper *Libération* in which she disclosed personal details and created an imagined "portrait" of an anonymous man that led to actual threats of lawsuits and retaliatory actions. In this work, titled *The Address Book* (1983), Calle had used the contents of a real address book found on the street to contact its owner's acquaintances and learn more about this unspecified subject. She then created a body of photographs that offered projected insights about this man, which were reproduced alongside transcripts of her phone conversations. While Calle never disclosed his identity, the owner of the address book—Pierre Baudry, a French documentary filmmaker—came forward and accused Calle of staging an illicit invasion of privacy. Seeking revenge, Baudry then sought retribution by demanding that *Libération* publish a nude photograph of Calle taken when she worked as a model. In seeking to publicly humiliate Calle through the disclosure of private images, there is a gendered aspect of Baudry's punitive response that relates to Oldenburg's desire to control Wilke's photographs, to the point of condoning his gallery's embezzlement of them, presumably under his orders.

During the course of their relationship, besides contributing conceptually to his work, Wilke photographed Oldenburg in a professional role for which she was included on the company payroll.[10] This formed the basis for the artist's later lawsuit against Oldenburg for a breach of an "oral lifetime employment contract" following the end of their eight-year romantic partnership, when Wilke received word in 1977 that he had suddenly married van Bruggen in Europe while they were still involved in a relationship.[11] While the timeline for such entanglements problematically overlap—Oldenburg first met van Bruggen in 1970, worked together on an exhibition in 1976, and then married in 1977—Wilke had also been involved with other men during this period, indicating a potentially open relationship between the two parties.[12]

The *Oldenburg Portfolio* was not the only example of a body of work that Wilke made exposing intimate moments typically viewed solely by romantic companions, a point that underscores the significance of these unreturned photographs for Wilke's work. She had shot hundreds of photographs taken of various male lovers, friends, and associates during the 1970s and early 1980s that she categorized in her archive as the "Men" file. Adopting a format similar to the *Oldenburg Portfolio*, Wilke featured a variety of male subjects—ranging from well-known figures such as artist John Chamberlain and filmmaker Christopher Giercke to the anonymous "Blond Boy Lugas"—in private contexts. The photographs range in composition, yet they all share a glimpse into an innermost personal life: some depict the subjects in domestic roles, while others focus explicitly on sexual interactions between the men and Wilke.[13] Her subjects are often documented fully naked and captured in conjugal circumstances: bathing nude, in various stages of undress, or in the aftermath, rather than height, of sexual relations.

By sharing moments of vulnerability and intimacy in her male subjects, Wilke presents a model of masculinity like that of Peter Hujar, whose pioneering depictions of the male nude uncovered the personal, spontaneous selves of male sexuality. In this manner, she takes advantage of her role as sexual partner rather than being limited by it. Using photographic modes of exposure as an operative strategy, Wilke quite literally adopts what Margaret Iversen has called the "deflationary impulse" in presenting her male subjects through a postcoital perspective, potentially recovering a sense of agency for herself as a result.[14]

Although some of these images were used in other projects, such as her photographic diptychs, postcards, and installations, Wilke's archival notes and documentation seem to show that she had initially intended to exhibit them collectively as an independent series. According to her sister, Wilke approached gallerist Ronald Feldman about showing the "Men"

# RONALD FELDMAN FINE ARTS INC

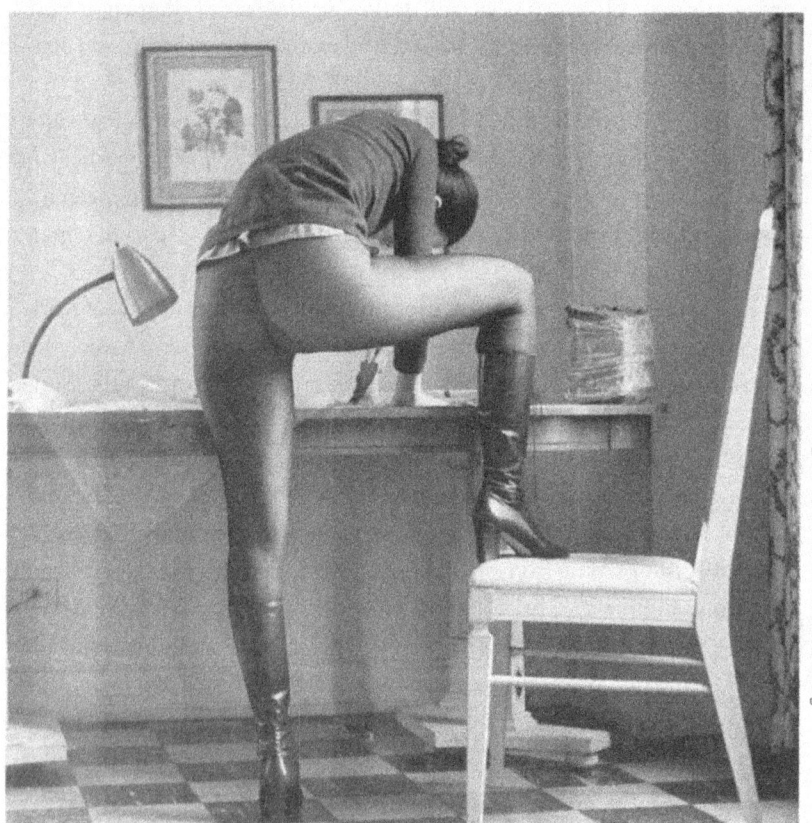

The artist in her studio, Chateau Marmont, Los Angeles, August 1970. Photo: Claes Oldenburg

# HANNAH WILKE

**2.02** Advertisement for Hannah Wilke exhibition at Ronald Feldman Fine Arts, New York. Photograph by Claes Oldenburg, August 1970.

photographs, but he refused. Wilke regarded this as an example of the double standard regarding public depictions of male and female nudity, particularly concerning images that went against conventions of dominant masculinity.

Notably, Feldman used a provocative photograph of Wilke for advertisements published in *Avalanche* magazine promoting her first exhibition at his gallery in 1972 (fig. 2.2). Taken at the Chateau Marmont in Los Angeles by Oldenburg, who is prominently credited as the photographer, the photograph captures Wilke from behind wearing sheer tights and knee-high heeled boots. Her right leg is raised, perched atop a chair, as she bends forward provocatively, writing on the desk in front of her. Feldman's (and Wilke's own) willingness to exploit a female artist's sexuality to publicize an exhibition was in direct contrast to his response to the photographs of Oldenburg nude, which read as gently intimate and affectionately playful rather than explicitly sexual or titillating.

Art historian Anna Chave has emphasized the inequalities in opportunities and recognition felt by female artists in the 1970s who may have felt it necessary to exploit their personal relationships to achieve success in the commercial art world.[15] For example, she cites Harmony Hammond, who wrote in a 1977 issue of *Heresies*: "For women, the economic class system is largely determined by their relationship to men. The higher up the man she relates to, the more she benefits from the system."[16] The prominent attribution of Oldenburg's name on Wilke's solo exhibition advertisement as well as Feldman's reluctance to upset Oldenburg by exhibiting Wilke's photographs only emphasize such a point.

While this photographic series of male nudes and the *Oldenburg Portfolio* have received little scholarly attention, art historian Richard Meyer's discussion of Wilke's 1960s phallic drawings and 1970s "Men" photographs is a notable exception.[17] Pointing out the complicated status of these photographs, Meyer writes: "the 'men' slides, for example, are at once private images (taken in the context of intimate sexual relationships) and professional source material (Wilke saved and filed them, at least in part, for possible use in later artworks)."[18] Meyer contextualizes Wilke's photographs of men within her association with the East Coast–based "Fight Censorship" (FC) group that sought to develop an affirmative visual language depicting sexual intercourse, and, in turn, the sexualized male body, from a female point of view. Meyer argues that, in contrast to the CalArts-based Feminist Art Program, which focused on producing imagery of women's bodies in an effort to express an essential female experience, the FC members, which included Louise Bourgeois and Joan Semmel, "responded to the broader social conditions that render men the primary agents and women the objects of both sexual and artistic authority."[19] Moreover, they explicitly used phallic imagery as "a means to both critique male supremacy and to claim the male body as a site of female fantasy and desire."[20]

Notably, there was a tremendous level of censorship imposed on art featuring the male nude produced by Fight Censorship associates. This was experienced in the form of formal legal threats, such as the investigation directed by the Rockland County district attorney regarding Anita Steckel's violation of New York State obscenity laws in her photomontages, as well as off-the-record verbal pressure. As Meyer writes:

> The censorship of sexual imagery by female artists in the 1970s cannot be limited to moments of overt suppression and public controversy. It also entailed far less visible forms of restriction such as the warning relayed to Steckel before her show at Rockland Community College ("if you bring anything erotic, you can forget about getting a job") or the response of Wilke's dealer to her proposal for an artwork ("Hannah, why don't you come up to my hotel instead?").[21]

Although these photographs by Wilke have been neither exhibited nor published due to potential legal claims, the *Oldenburg Portfolio* and "Men" photographs are central to understanding Wilke's larger artistic project.[22] Here, she tactically moved from the typical position of a woman playing a supporting, domestic, or behind-the-scenes role to one that claims authorial recognition by turning private intimacy into the very subject of her work.

### Laundry Lint (C.O.'s)

Returning to the 1991 proposed exhibition layout, Wilke also included a loose sketch in the upper-left register of the drawing depicting a cluster of forms best described as two ovals conjoined at the uppermost point. While this abstract shape appeared in many artworks over the course of her career, in one example here, the top-right side of the first oval opens up, which shifts the appearance of the object's shape to appear as two letters—"CO"—written in cursive script. Given that these symbols likely served as visual shorthand for Wilke's folded sculptures, in which she gathered and doubled over various materials to create organic, labia-shaped forms, the allusive reference to Oldenburg draws out his shadowy presence in another important body of Wilke's artwork.

Introduced in the mid-1960s, Wilke's "vaginal" sculptures underwent material transformations over time. While the earliest incarnations of these were made in porcelain, ceramic, or terracotta, by the mid-1970s she had added kneaded erasers, chewing gum, lint, and latex to her expanding sculptural practice, which now included monumental wall sculptures and installations. While often exhibited as a series, the sculptures were also incorporated into other projects such as performances, mixed-media photographs, or large-scale installations.

*Laundry Lint (C.O.'s)* (1971–73) is an installation comprising twelve vagina-shaped sculptures—arranged in three gridded rows set on a low floor platform—that were composed of the accumulation of lint collected over a two-year span from Oldenburg's laundry dryer. Acting as a physical record of her shared intimacy with another individual, *Laundry Lint (C.O.'s)* condenses many of the key issues Wilke negotiated in her work: producing a feminist commentary on her role—here performing domestic upkeep as primary housekeeper—in her and Oldenburg's shared home, developing a sculptural investigation of vaginal imagery, and testing the thresholds regarding the authority of an artist through her use of materials acquired through private means.

Wilke's shift to exploring materials that were by-products of other objects, processes, or actions reflected a broader tendency in art practices of this period (Eva Hesse and Robert Morris stand as notable examples). Moreover, the desire to expose the forms of invisible labor performed by women was shared by fellow artist Mierle Laderman Ukeles, whose "Manifesto for Maintenance Art 1969!" articulated the profound gender discrepancies between the types of labor performed to sustain the myths of the autonomous artistic genius that were central to the white-male-dominated art world. Explicating the distinctions between the valorization of creative innovation by men (what Ukeles calls "development") and its reliance on the performance of private, domestic ("maintenance") tasks typically enacted by women, Ukeles conceptualizes alternative forms of typically unacknowledged work and workers as valid artistic subjects and creators. As artists like Ukeles, Lucinda Childs, and Alison Knowles working in the 1960s understood, the avant-garde concept of bringing "everyday life" into the field of art or redefining everyday actions as art only really applied to men's activities and lives, which were largely unfettered by the particularities of domesticity.[23]

In Wilke's case, by reclaiming the laundry lint that served as a physical record of her domestic labor, she sought to combat the disposability of such contributions and to affirm her right to present her everyday domestic existence within Oldenburg's orbit as her intervention in the avant-garde tradition of dissolving the art-life divide. Therefore, while *Laundry Lint (C.O.'s)* was created while the partners were romantically involved, Wilke's decision to use such objects as material in her work indicates her ongoing thinking about exposing her private, auxiliary role in the perpetuation of Oldenburg's public success as an artist. In a discussion about her sculptural practice using another discarded material, chewing gum, Wilke explains: "In this society we use people up the way we use up chewing gum. I chose gum because it's the perfect metaphor for the American woman—chew her up, get what you want out of her, throw her out and pop in a new piece."[24] By presenting her household work performed in the direct service of Oldenburg and the maintenance of his artistic practice, Wilke threatened the illusory optics of such invisible everyday labor that bolsters the myth of the solitary male creator.

While the specificity of the laundry's reference to domestic household labor connects with 1970s white feminist interrogations of sexism and the role of women in the home, the bodily source of the materials—her romantic partner—also complicated and expanded such critical claims. In the case of *Laundry Lint (C.O.'s)*, Oldenburg's identity was quite prominent, presumably with his approval. The inclusion of his initials, along with the possessive apostrophe to signify his ownership over the material used in her work's title, was a deliberate gesture by Wilke intended to make visible their affiliation and to call to mind the expanded set of exchanges between them in the field of art making. Once again, she brought her intimate relationship with Oldenburg into focus by breaking the veneer of his public persona and offering something more personal, bodily, domestic, and partnered that was otherwise eradicated from his practice.

Interpreting Wilke's work through the accomplice paradigm crucially provides a way to reveal the exclusions of networks of undisclosed female labor within established formulations of male artistic authorship. In her quest to be seen as an equal partner as well as a successful artist within the still-sexist art world of the 1970s, Wilke created a body of artworks that acts as a silent record to her unaccredited role in the creation or maintenance of Oldenburg's artistic celebrity. These objects, such as *Laundry Lint (C.O.'s)*, bear witness to these metaphorical crimes against women and other unacknowledged individuals with whom a male artist often shared responsibility and labor—but not official accreditation—for the public and private tasks required to be an artist.

### Intercourse with . . .

In his lithograph *Alphabet in the Form of a Good Humor Bar*, which appeared in Wilke's 1991 drawing of her proposed museum exhibition, Oldenburg had sketched out his ideas for what would later become a sculpture in the shape of a Good Humor brand ice cream bar on a stick. In his account, the concept for the work was generated in part by Wilke, which he acknowledged in the 1975 essay "History of the Alphabet / Good Humor." He wrote: "I had a commission for a poster/print, to be circulated mainly to students, for which the alphabet seemed a perfect subject. The original conception used a grid similar to the calendars of 1963 and included numbers but, at the suggestion of Hannah Wilke, in whose studio the drawing was made, the letters were recomposed in the format of the Good Humor Bar."[25] Still, Wilke's reasoning for the prominent inclusion of this work in her 1991 proposed museum exhibition initially seems ambiguous.

In a later document made by Wilke for legal proceedings, she cited this work as evidence of Oldenburg acknowledging her contributions, writing: "In this work, the letter H in the initials AHB—for my original name, Arlene Hannah Butter, touches the O in the center, which seems an acknowledgement by Claes that I was AHB Oldenburg. Claes partially recognizes my collaboration in his history of the monument which appears in the catalogue for the Margo Leavin show."[26] Drawing attention to the significance of what she read as coded messages embedded in the lettering in *Alphabet in the Form of a Good Humor Bar*, Wilke deployed this tactic in her own installation and later video performance known collectively as *Intercourse with* . . . .

Wilke's mixed-media installation *Intercourse with* . . . was shown in 1975 at one of gallerist Jeffrey Deitch's first exhibitions, *Lives: Artists Who Deal with Peoples' Lives (Including Their Own) as the Subject and/or the Medium of Their Work.*[27] The piece comprised a metal-bound binder, a framed poster, and a two-hour-long audio playback featuring an edited selection of telephone answering machine messages from friends, romantic partners, family, and work associates who had contacted Wilke between 1973 and 1975.[28] Directly above the recorder, which was placed on a small white table, Wilke hung a poster with an edited list of selected callers, divided into the dates of their recording. A binder contained a transcript of the audio recordings and a typewritten list of original callers with handwritten annotation regarding who would be used in the final tape.

For the *Lives* exhibition catalog, each artist was given a single page to present an image or text of their choosing.[29] Wilke used a full-page, black-and-white photograph that depicts her sitting on a couch in Oldenburg's Broome Street studio cradling a phone under her ear (fig. 2.3). Wilke's stereotypically flirtatious gestures—playing with her hair and suggestively placing a pen in her mouth—are heightened by her provocative

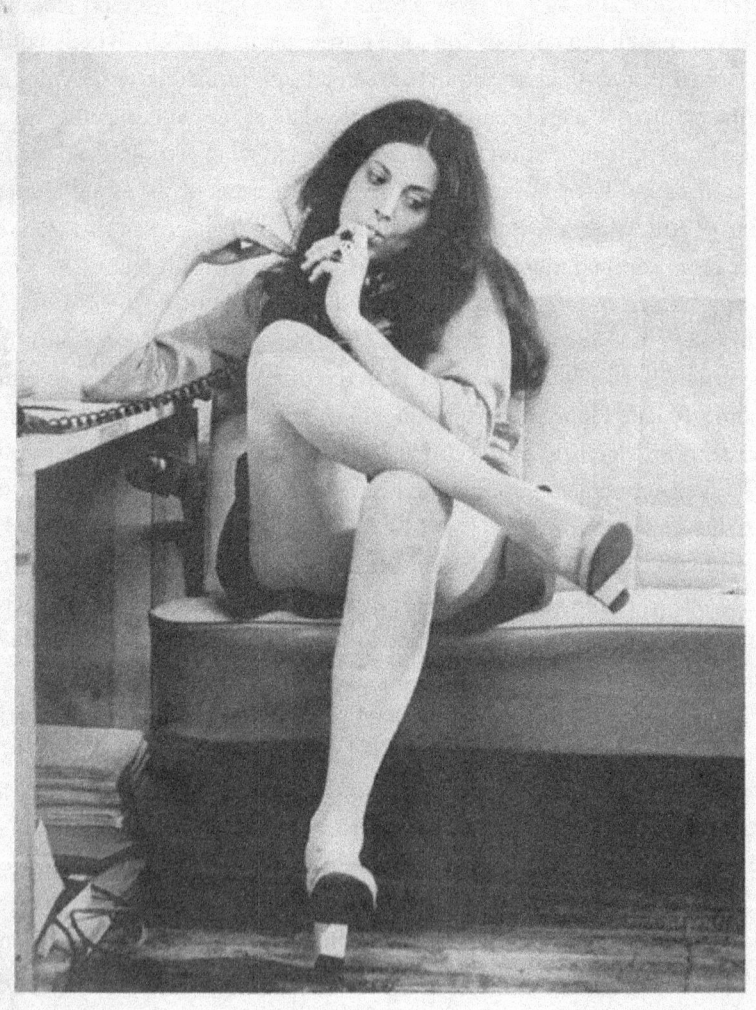

INTERCOURSE WITH –

SEPT 2 1973 – NOV 25 1975

**2.03**   Hannah Wilke, *Intercourse with . . .* ,
September 2, 1973–November 25, 1975.

calf-on-knee cross-legged position in which her modesty is precariously dependent on the angle of her left leg. Along the bottom of the page is the work's typed title as well as the date range of the recorded messages (September 2, 1973–November 25, 1975), in addition to the artist's signature.

As can be determined from an unmarked contact sheet in her archive, Oldenburg was likely Wilke's uncredited photographer for this image—which also appeared on the cover of the binder in the *Intercourse with . . .* installation. Based on the other images from the film roll, the photo shoot began with Wilke seated on a couch dialing a call and then listening intently. While the first images capture her behaving naturally, unaware of the camera, Wilke then shifts her attention to her photographer. She glances seductively at the camera and raises her leg in an act of sexual titillation for its operator. This flirtation with Oldenburg as cameraman is suddenly broken as she leans forward, focused on her telephone conversation again while scribbling something in a notebook. A poster for Oldenburg's *Mouse Museum* is visible above the couch, just outside the cropped frame of the final photograph.

While Oldenburg was a critical but spectral figure in Wilke's mixed-media installation from 1975, his presence assumed a greater—yet still coded—prominence in the conceptually related, twenty-seven-minute videotaped performance that Wilke made in 1977, shortly after she and Oldenburg split for the final time. For this version of *Intercourse with . . .* , Wilke used her nude body as the literal ground for various performative actions that were then recorded at the London Art Gallery and Museum in Ontario, Canada. The work comprises Wilke sitting in an otherwise empty room listening to an audio loop playing various answering machine messages left for her. Early in the performance video, her facial reactions to the callers vary based on their communications: at times, she reacts by shaking her head, at other points she giggles at a man's voice as he expresses impassioned pleas for her to call him back. While often the callers do not state their names, assuming familiarity with Wilke, she identifies them collectively by performing a striptease that reveals the names or initials of her callers, which had been marked on her body with black peel-off letter stickers (fig. 2.4). Notably, two variations on Oldenburg's name appear conspicuously near the center of the frame on each of her breasts; his initials are featured multiple times across her body.

About halfway through the video, the callers begin checking in on her well-being and warning her to stay away from someone or something, the specifics lost in the muffled recording. Immediately, Oldenburg's voice

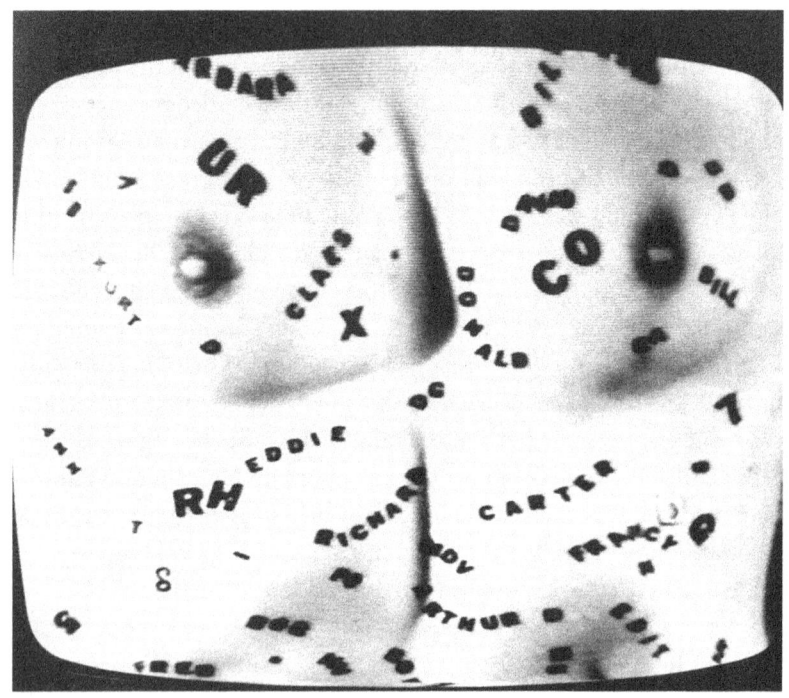

**2.04**    Hannah Wilke, *Intercourse with . . .* , 1977. Video still of performance at the London Art Gallery and Museum, London, Ontario. Black and white, sound, 30 minutes.

comes on, announcing himself with a stilted formality seemingly uncommon for a lover, whether former or current: "This is Claes Oldenburg speaking. This is a message. I am at home and perhaps you'd like to call me up. So maybe I'll be hearing from you. Goodbye." By the end of his brief message, her mood has decidedly shifted. Oldenburg's voice returns, alluding to the return of undefined belongings: "Anyway I wanted to say that the stuff's coming back from the Clocktower on Monday. And I'll give you a call tomorrow. Have a good evening. This is Claes, by the way." Following his message, the classical music that had been in the background throughout the performance abruptly stops. At that moment, she is bent forward with her bare back exposed as the camera zooms in on an empty chair.

When the music resumes, this time without the telephone recordings, Wilke sits upright, pulling a sweater over her head. On her nude torso are the names and lettered initials of men: Kurt, Claes, Bill, Donald, RH, UR, CO. With her face still covered by her sweater, Wilke begins using her hands to trace the letters on her body, as if they are in braille. She begins peeling them off blindly; her voice-over begins: "Since 1960, I have been consumed with the creation of a formal imagery that is specifically female. . . . To make objects instead of being one. The way my smile just gleams, the way I sip my tea, to be a sugar giver instead of a salt-seller. To not sell out. The memory of all that. . . . No, they can't take that away from me."[30] With the end of her recorded monologue, Wilke finishes pulling the letters off her body, leaving herself completely exposed. Leaning back in the chair, she smiles self-confidently into the camera as her body is freed from male associations.

Produced shortly after her and Oldenburg's breakup, the video work *Intercourse with . . .* demonstrates an evolution of concepts first developed in the 1975 version of the piece. Staging the central artistic strategy of exposure, *Intercourse with . . .* interpellates gender in various ways: from the auditory directives of the answering machine messages to the textual encoding of names and initials in the form of stickers placed onto Wilke's bare body as a kind of imprint. Her decision to include what were intended to be private messages in a videotaped artwork that would feature such recordings demonstrates how Wilke sought to harness the evidentiary power of language (recalling Burden's work *Wiretap*).

Here, Wilke flirted with the limits of her artistic authority to make public what others had assumed to be private by also exposing herself. By performing a striptease that unfolds against the audio of various recorded messages left for the artist, Wilke serves as the physical center to the centrifugal constellation of friends, lovers, family members, and work colleagues. Yet Wilke's strategy—upending the power differential by turning those who might have previously used *her* as an accomplice into her own—also importantly revealed how the use of others is fundamentally based in privilege. While she sought recognition as a viable "partner" or equal via forms of retroactive exposure of certain discriminatory exclusions, the gendered components of her predicament are laid bare.

By including the specific individuals on her body, Wilke suggests that she has been marked by them, either as a kind of emotional scar that remains private long after a relationship has ended or as a more public stain that haunts women in their relationships with men, particularly in the case of well-known art-world figures.[31] As Roberta Smith articulates in a review of a 1996 exhibition of Wilke's work at Ronald Feldman Fine Arts, "Wilke rebelled against her further objectification as a woman by taking matters into her own hands, objectifying herself even more blatantly, while taking on the male artists who piqued her interest or her ire."[32] In this manner, *Intercourse with . . .* reinforces and yet complicates some of the more prominent critiques of her work.

Wilke occupies an important position in relation to two central feminist artistic debates in the 1970s, as she was one of the earliest examples of a female artist presenting explicitly vaginal or vulvar imagery in the early 1960s while also creating works that actively staged the objectification of her own body. For example, critics such as Lucy Lippard leveled the following attack:

> Hannah Wilke, a glamor girl in her own right who sees her art as "seduction," is considered a little too good to be true when she flaunts her body in parody of the role she actually plays in real life. She has been making erotic art with vaginal imagery for over a decade, and, since the women's movement, has begun to do performances in conjunction with her sculpture, but her own confusion of her roles as beautiful woman and artist, as flirt and feminist, has resulted at times in politically ambiguous manifestations which have exposed her to criticism on a personal as well as on an artistic level.[33]

Taking issue with Wilke's practice of using her sexuality and personal relationships as artistic subject matter, Lippard questioned whether this conflation was deliberate or indeed parodic, as Wilke at times claimed. Yet as Anna Chave argues, although Wilke can be said to have achieved the feminist goal of "the advent of an authentically different art, marked by women's experience," much of Wilke's work oscillated at the limit point between collusion and critique.[34] She points out:

> Lippard was completely justified, of course, in charging that Wilke wanted to have it both ways: she did want to be both agent and object. . . . At a time when foiling the indiscriminately objectifying male gaze seemed an overriding goal—and when feminists were widely policing each other over the cosmetic use of razors, tweezers and the like—Wilke's efforts to mime, and send up, the role of the sex object tended to be viewed as complicit (a view likely cemented by the fact that *Oui, Penthouse* and *Playboy* all ran stories about her during the '70s).[35]

The social, economic, and political advantage of Wilke's decision to make her private life public was a tactical gesture used to gain leverage by exploiting the interest in viewing her often-nude body as a sexual commodity by viewers and intimate partners alike.

The critical reception of body art and women's art movements in the early 1970s illuminates the complicated position of women artists such as Wilke who specifically created imagery that placed the female body at the center. This was succinctly summarized by Esther Adler in the exhibition catalog for *WACK! Art and the Feminist Revolution* (2007). Adler points out that "Wilke's physical beauty, her romantic and sexual relationships with established figures in the art world (which she did not shy away from incorporating within her work), and the consistent nudity in her performances made her a target of feminist disapproval."[36] While 1970s male "body artists" such as Vito Acconci, Chris Burden, and Paul McCarthy were understood to present their nude bodies as a neutral background for experimentations in repetitive actions, ritualized processes, and other task-based actions that tested the limits of the corporeal in a variety of forms, the use of the female body by women performance artists at this time took on a social and political manifestation. Wilke herself summarized the discrepancy between representations of the female body: "Female nudity painted by men gets documented and when women create this ideology as their own it gets obliterated."[37]

The actions of Wilke, assuming the roles of both subject and object, became a political gesture, one that recast her sexual encounters and personal details as tools to circumvent the unilateral authority placed on her own means of expression. For example, in a 1985 interview with Marvin Jones, Wilke explicitly adopted the second-wave feminist slogan in pointing out that "people have denied the importance of women for thousands of years. We have to start with the personal. The personal, the value of individual lives, really is the politics."[38] It is worth noting, however, that Wilke's intimate interpretation of "the personal is political" was radically distinct from many of her artistic contemporaries: while she used material in her work that contained highly specific "evidence" of relations others wished to keep private, the "personal" issues taken up by other women artists were typically more generalized experiences, such as household work (Ukeles), motherhood (Mary Kelly), sexuality (Lynda Benglis), and race (Adrian Piper).

As Oldenburg sought to maintain the existing Romantic model of the artist-genius as the sole source of artistic creativity, agency, and production, Wilke attempted to break open such narratives and undermine hierarchies of value through strategic disclosures that made public the multiple lives and labor that were collapsed or compressed into a singular model of the nominal author. It is noteworthy then that, as Nancy Princenthal points out, "it is perhaps not a coincidence that Wilke's relationship with Oldenburg ended in 1977, the year the *Intercourse with . . .* performance appeared. Their mutual professional support was significant to both Oldenburg and Wilke, but only she was willing to make it a matter of public record."[39]

The tactic of exposure running throughout Wilke's practice breaks with the tacit understanding of discretion and privacy within a partnership, in which the members' needs and rights are distributed equally. Employing the few possible tools at her disposal, Wilke includes private material—an action that would likely be unconscionable if performed by a man—to identify those who refused to treat her as a true partner and expose the truth of relationships from a woman's perspective. Therefore, the ethics of her approach must be understood as a potential recourse to reestablish parity, using Oldenburg to rebalance the uneven distribution of power through the limited means available to her—namely, her art.

### Proposed I-Museum in the Form of an H Series

In 1959, Oldenburg created the first of what would later become an ongoing series of "ray guns," both created and found. The prototype for the concept was derived from 1930s science fiction comic books such as *Flash Gordon*; it was conceived as a gun that "shoots but doesn't kill," akin to a camera.[40] The first ray gun piece, *"Empire" ("Papa") Ray Gun*, was made from papier-mâché newspaper set in layers on a wire frame and was included as part of Oldenburg's installation *The Street* (1960) in the basement of the Judson Memorial Church in New York. That same year, he initiated his practice of collecting ray guns based on morphological approximations to an abstracted gun shape.

The ray gun became a conceptual designation for found or handmade objects that would be amassed according to two criteria: (1) being in the shape of a right angle and (2) receiving Oldenburg's approval. The phrase "ray gun" was also the name of an alter ego; Oldenburg and artist Jim Dine collaboratively worked under the pseudonym Mr. Ray Gun. The ray gun also took other forms: it appeared as currency (ray gun money that was distributed to audience members at the *Snapshots from the City* performance), as theater (Ray Gun Theater), and as a commercial operation (Ray Gun Manufacturing Corporation), among others.

The ray gun was a critical component of Oldenburg's *Ray Gun Wing*, a 1977 addition to his earlier *Mouse Museum*, which was a small-scale museum installation originally built in 1972 for Documenta 5 in Kassel, Germany. The initial incarnation of the *Mouse Museum* comprised a room in the shape of Oldenburg's "Geometric Mouse," described as a "combination of the early film camera and a stereotypical cartoon mouse" that was itself set within a gallery.[41] Inside the cartoon mouse "head" were glass vitrines that lined the perimeter of the space, in which 367 found and studio-made objects were placed on display.

For his exhibition at the Museum of Contemporary Art in Chicago in 1977, Oldenburg conceived of an updated design for the *Mouse Museum* featuring an addition: the *Ray Gun Wing*, a distinct yet conceptually related pseudo-museum that would be used to house and display his now extensive collection of ray guns. Collecting objects over the years, Oldenburg eventually exhibited 258 found objects as approved "authentic" ray guns. Itself made to resemble a schematized and geometric articulation of a handgun (fig. 2.5), the phallic architectural space of the *Ray Gun Wing* exemplified male machismo through Oldenburg's invocation of weaponry and the authoritative taxonomy of its contents. The objects were collected by a variety of individuals, yet Oldenburg claimed credit for all of them.

Such working methods were not new for Oldenburg. In fact, evidence of him not acknowledging the collaborative labor of others can be traced to the early 1960s, when Oldenburg started rendering objects from daily life as sculptures created from soft, fabric-like materials, such as vinyl or cloth. In 1960, Oldenburg had married Patricia Muschinski, later known as Patty Mucha, who had trained as an artist at the University of Wisconsin–Milwaukee and was pursuing a career in art when they first met. It was she who sewed Oldenburg's soft sculptures, including the works *Floor Cake*, *Floor Cone*, and *Floor Burger* (all 1962), which were the centerpieces of Oldenburg's celebrated Green Gallery exhibition. Given that Mucha's technical abilities comprised the production of patterns, construction of muslin samples, and finishing details—and since Oldenburg himself did not know how to sew—it is significant to note that her labor in these works went almost entirely unrecognized for decades, despite documentation of her contributions, as seen in the photograph of preparations for Oldenburg's 1966 survey exhibition at the Moderna Museet (fig. 2.6). Like Wilke, Mucha also provided integral labor for pieces that Oldenburg included in his *Mouse Museum* and *Ray Gun Wing* yet was not credited with coauthorship or mentioned by name.

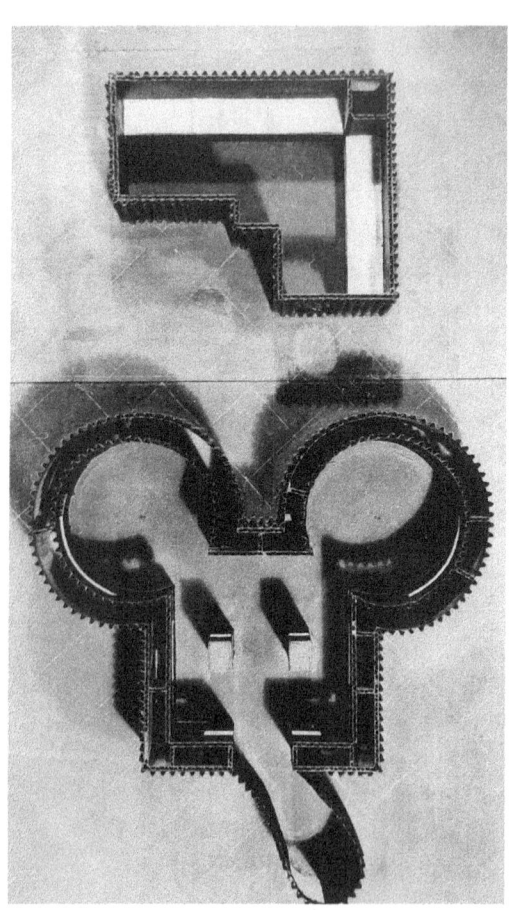

**2.05**

Claes Oldenburg, *Model of the Ray Gun Wing* and *Model of the Mouse Museum*, 1977. Cardboard and wood painted with tempera and spray enamel, pencil, 6⅛ × 12⅞ × 18⅞ in.; 6⅞ × 18⅞ × 18⅞ in.

**2.06**

Claes Oldenburg and Patricia Muschinski constructing *Soft Giant Light Switch (Ghost Version)* for Oldenburg's retrospective at the Moderna Museet, Stockholm, 1966. Photograph by Hans Hammarskiöld.

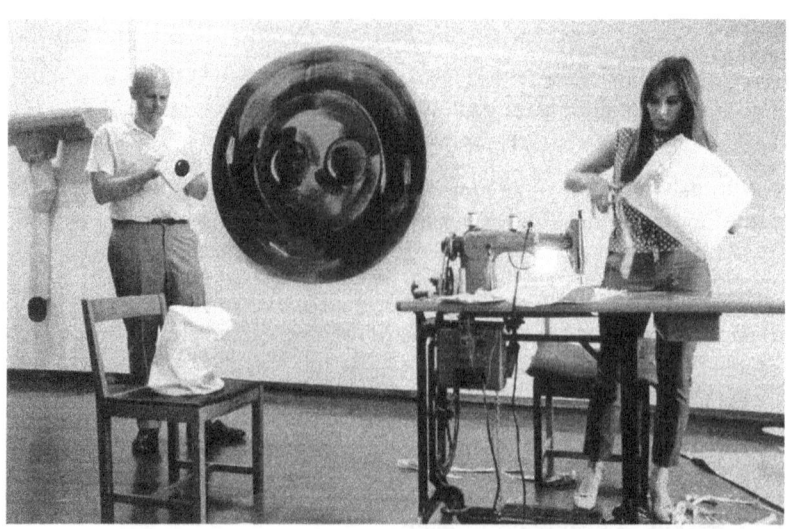

This deliberate oversight on Oldenburg's part has only recently begun to be addressed. In 2017, Genevieve Waller published an essay that charts the history of Oldenburg's three female partners with whom he collaborated on the making of the *Mouse Museum / Ray Gun Wing*: Mucha, Wilke, and van Bruggen.[42] While van Bruggen received explicit coauthorship on all of Oldenburg's works beginning at the time of their marriage in 1977—even receiving public credit for an updated design of the *Mouse Museum* in 1978—both Mucha and Wilke only had a limited presence, frequently appearing in coded or otherwise covert forms.[43] This is particularly striking when compared to the 1979 *Ray Gun Wing* exhibition catalog, in which Oldenburg gives Dine and other friends coauthorial credit (e.g., "Ray Guns by Jim Dine," 1960).[44] Even photographers such as Nathan Rabin and Ad Petersen were noted as making "Certified Ray Guns," objects that were site-specific or too fragile to be transported, instead having been photographed, collected into binders, and placed on shelves. The discrepancies of attribution were split down gendered lines: men were credited, and (most) women were not.

Oldenburg's attempts to limit the visibility of his personal relationships had a long-standing precedent that was only undone following his marriage to van Bruggen.[45] In the case of Mucha and Wilke, what little recognition they received came in the form of diminutive nicknames or abbreviations: Mucha was referred to in presumably affectionate yet ultimately dismissive terms such as "Poopy" in the 1976 book *Store Days: Documents from "The Store" (1961) and "Ray Gun Theater" (1962)*, while Wilke was called "Stinky" and only given credit for her collection of ray guns given to Oldenburg for exhibition in *Ray Gun Wing* with the cryptic name "Performance Group H."[46] While Mucha was acknowledged in a 1962 Green Gallery exhibition poster for Oldenburg, her name appeared upside down, a mode of co-billing that suggests unequal decision-making and disproportionate—albeit shared—recognition. His omissions of the proper names of two of his long-term female partners—while making a point to cite the names of the architects for the *Mouse Museum* and *Ray Gun Wing*, his furniture makers, industrial fabricators, and even "guards at the Venice Biennale"—suggests that there was an underlying sexism in his system of attribution that disregarded his romantic partners as authorial agents in their own right.[47]

In a likely effort to disclose the coded recognition she received from Oldenburg for his ray guns in the form of the first letter of her name, Wilke developed another unrealized project, known as *Proposed I-Museum in the Form of an H Series*, which was related to—but distinct from—her planned retrospective drawing. Wilke, mimicking the form and concept of

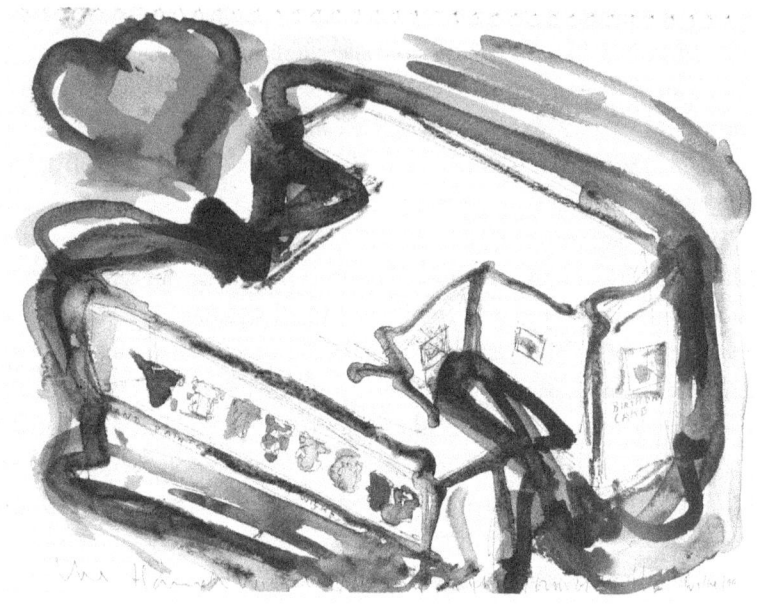

**2.07**  Hannah Wilke, *Proposed I-Museum in the Form of an H Series (Museum in the Form of an H)*, 1991. Watercolor and ink on paper, 9 × 12 in.

Oldenburg's novelty architecture, created five watercolor and ink sketches depicting variations on her own interpretation of a personal museum that made direct reference to Oldenburg's *Mouse Museum* and *Ray Gun Wing* as well as to the way in which he had credited her. Following a similar format as Oldenburg's museum designs, Wilke's versions would be made in the shape of the letter *H*, which could also be interpreted as a letter *I*, depending on one's position when viewing (fig. 2.7). Since the drawings were produced when she was entering her final battle with lymphoma, Wilke was likely considering them as a tool for evaluating her artistic legacy, as the *I-Museum* title would suggest.[48] These drawings would also serve as one of Wilke's most explicit attempts to appropriate Oldenburg's own imagery in an effort to highlight the interconnectedness of their work and life that he actively sought to bury, since all the objects she planned to install in this mini-museum would be artwork previously attributed to Oldenburg alone.[49]

Wilke's decision to use specific alphabetical letters for the design of her museums had a precedent in other examples of Oldenburg's work. For example, in 1976 Oldenburg cast an edition of four inverted letter *Q* sculptures in concrete, after having explored the form in rubber in a commission for the Akron Public Library garden in Ohio a few years earlier.[50]

Furthermore, her written notations on the drawings, such as her proposed title "I-Museum in the *Form* of an H Series," offered explicit reference to Oldenburg's phrasing used in the titles of his sculptures, such as *Sculpture in the Form of a Fried Egg* (1966–71).[51]

In one of the five *Proposed I-Museum* watercolors, Wilke depicts vividly painted objects set in vitrines. On the right side is a dab of red paint with the words "Birthday Cake" written below, which references a sculptural gift from Oldenburg that she maintained in her collection. On the other side is a row of eight multicolored T-shaped forms, a reference to Oldenburg's fireplug sculptures that Wilke claimed co-credit for making. Peeking out from a semiopaque outline that forms the architectural walls in the drawing is a faint phrase: "Hand Painted by Hannah Wilke 1970 New Haven." Referring to Oldenburg's 1969 studio move to Connecticut, this assertion of her artistic contribution and labor in the multicolored fireplugs (Oldenburg's were typically uniformly painted red) had already been expressed publicly in a January 1973 interview with Lil Picard for *Interview* magazine in which Wilke had gone on record saying that she had taken the rejected plaster cast hydrants that he had made for an exhibition and formulated them into her own distinct works: "I liked them and wanted to save them and painted them in the bright colors, red, green, yellow, silver, gold."[52]

In another drawing of the *I-Museum* from this series, Wilke includes approximately twenty smaller objects in a vitrine with the accompanying phrase: "Ray Guns Collected as Gifts for Claes Oldenburg 1969–1977." These were not examples of work she produced herself but rather were intended to substantiate her claims of unrecognized artistic labor in the creation of his *Ray Gun* series.[53] Wilke went on record about this too: in a 1989 interview, she succinctly declared, "I reappropriated back 'ray guns' that were gifts to Oldenburg from 1969–1978."[54] These "reappropriated" objects would appear as a central and evidentiary component in one of Wilke's best-known series, *So Help Me Hannah: Snatch-Shots with Ray Guns*, when interpreted through the accomplice model.

### So Help Me Hannah: Snatch-Shots with Ray Guns

In the fall of 1978, both Wilke and Oldenburg had large-scale solo exhibitions that were on view concurrently within three miles of each other. The *Mouse Museum* and *Ray Gun Wing* were shown at the Whitney

Museum of American Art from September 28 to November 26, while Wilke's show, titled *So Help Me Hannah: Snatch-Shots with Ray Guns*, was staged through the Institute for Art and Urban Resources (IAUR) at PS1 in Long Island City, New York (now MoMA PS1), as part of a special projects series that ran between October 1 and November 19, 1978. Wilke's PS1 installation featured a complex body of work comprising forty-eight black-and-white photographs, a collection of her own ray guns, and one hundred postcards printed with quotations from prominent male thinkers or writers and attached to a chalkboard.

The concept for the project *So Help Me Hannah: Snatch-Shots with Ray Guns* (1978) emerged during the summer of 1978. On the invitation of PS1 director and founder Alanna Heiss, Wilke drew inspiration from the former public school building's derelict roof and basement as the location for a photographic series featuring herself as a model. This included a set of images in which she posed nude—save for a pair of heels—wielding a small toy gun as she moved throughout her industrial setting as if amid a chase.

According to Waller, there is no definitive record of Oldenburg's attendance at the PS1 exhibition, yet Wilke's decision to exhibit such work at the same time as his show at the Whitney Museum suggests that her desired audience wouldn't fail to make the connection between these exhibitions. Such a reference to Oldenburg was indeed made explicit: the first of one hundred postcards she exhibited states: "with thanks to P.S.1 . . . —and of course to Claes Oldenburg without whose indifference this show would not have been possible."[55]

Considered together, the photographs depict Wilke as she navigates her dilapidated environment. Some of them have a sultry undertone, presenting Wilke as a dangerous seductress whose body would serve as "bait" for her pursuer as she bravely fought back (fig. 2.8). In others, she is unequivocally a victim, lying limply on a filthy staircase and giving the camera an expressionless stare. Yet her adversary is undefined: while her attention is often directed toward the camera and the presumed viewer of the resulting photographs, the threat of pursuit suggests other significant parties lurking, although not explicitly shown, outside the frame of these images.

The subtitle "Snatch-Shots *with* Ray Guns" alludes to the confrontation Wilke sought to provoke by introducing her photographic "snatch-shots" (a play on the term *snapshots*, acknowledging her pronounced nudity) as a mechanism to oppose—or shoot back at—Oldenburg's "ray guns." While the production or collection of "ray guns" could be enacted by anyone adhering to Oldenburg's criteria, the need for the artist's autho-

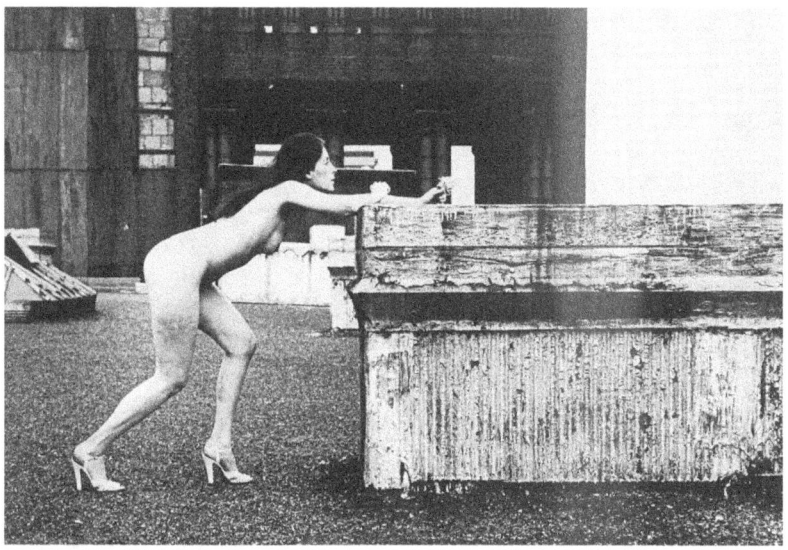

**2.08**   Hannah Wilke, *So Help Me Hannah*, 1978. Performalist self-portrait with Donald Goddard, MoMA PS1, New York. One of forty-eight black-and-white photographs, 11×14 in.

rization protected it against threats to the value of his work and authorial presence. In contrast, Wilke's terminology describes a conceptual operation of exposure, particularly using the camera as a tool for "snatching" evidence of previously undisclosed forms of labor.

Against the typical objectification by which a subject is made into an object and captured through the camera's lens, Wilke developed an alternative model of photography in which she appropriated and exposed key images, artworks, and tactics used by men in her work to create feminist counterstrategies of representation. To expand on Wilke's term, the "snatch-shot" offers a conceptual framework for approaching her diverse practice that uses artistic procedures of disclosure to show how women's work is devalued in both personal and professional contexts. While Wilke specifically coined the phrase for her *So Help Me Hannah* installation using a pun on the word *snatch*, which was a vulgar term for vagina at the time and referred to the prominence of female anatomy throughout that project, "snatch-shot" becomes useful as a theoretical approach to describe works in which one's own sexuality was strategically embraced as a means of recovering agency.

Wilke exhibited these photographs at her PS1 exhibition along with a set of ray gun–shaped objects arranged grid-like on the floor, emphasizing

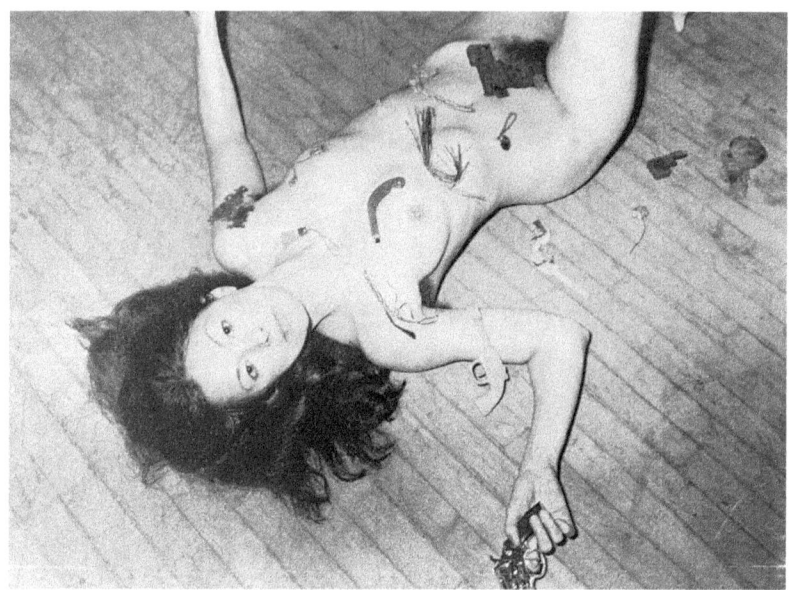

**2.09**    Hannah Wilke, *Snatch-Shot with Ray Guns Collected from 1969–1978*,
1978. Offset printed double-sided postcard, 5¼ × 7¼ in.

the connection to Oldenburg more explicitly. Found after the end of her
relationship to Oldenburg, the displayed objects ranged from actual toy
guns, whistles, broken lighters, and cassette tapes to wire and electrical
cords bent in the shape of a right angle. Such a selection mimicked the vast
range of ray gun possibilities put forward by Oldenburg and demonstrated
Wilke's intimate knowledge of the stipulations for "authenticating" a ray
gun. While the size of the objects varied, they could all be described as
handheld, which was useful when Wilke conceptually wrested them from
their context in Oldenburg's *Ray Gun Wing* as found objects by including
them in her self-portraits as performative props.

In one of her postcards, titled *Snatch-Shot with Ray Guns Collected
from 1969–1978*, Wilke created a remapping of the body that reversed the
typical figure-ground relationship by using her exposed figure as the sculptural ground for her "ray guns" (fig. 2.9). The specificity of such objects
and the solicitation of attention through the sensational gesture of presenting her nude body was done to bring visibility to the interconnections between herself and Oldenburg that she felt were obscured. For example, in
one such photograph, Wilke is depicted lying directly on the floor with her
entire body and the surrounding floor covered by various ray guns. While

she still wields her handgun, her arm is limp as she looks neutrally toward the camera. The image reads as though the emotional weight of the ray guns has overtaken her; she resigns to the fact that her singular handheld weapon is rendered useless against the multitude of other ray guns that surround her, literally and metaphorically.

On the verso of another *So Help Me Hannah* postcard found in her archive, Wilke points to Oldenburg's knowing omission of her participation, writing: "RE:Guns, Ray:Guns, Rea:Guns. Innovation before imitation—why am I not invited to be in your show." The multiplicity of the word *ray*—here used to suggest a direct response (in re:), a directional spread (to spread rays), and a legal cast (*mens rea*)—is combined with her pointed remarks regarding her exclusion from the *Mouse Museum / Ray Gun Wing* exhibition taking place at the Whitney Museum. Using the "ray gun" name for the title of her exhibition and photographic series while also literally bringing Oldenburg's signature ray gun motif into her own photographic work, Wilke presented the image as impotent, a toy rather than a weapon but also one that she could use against him on multiple levels. As Waller articulates: "She [Wilke] called attention in this body of work to contributions to the *Ray Gun Wing* and Oldenburg's oeuvre that were erased from the exhibition and documentation, but also made fun of and exposed the Ray Gun—Oldenburg's beloved emblem with which he identified for years—as a phallic macho symbol, despite all its pretensions to mere childishness."[56] Such a point was reiterated in another work from this series, in which Wilke presented the ray guns alongside Mickey Mouse figurines.[57]

Wilke's tactic of deploying sexual desire as a trap to solicit and subsequently capture evidence of male objectification was also implemented as an operative strategy by other women artists of the period. For instance, in Laurie Anderson's *Fully Automated Nikon (Object/Objection/Objectivity)* (1973), the artist documented various men who made inappropriate comments to her on the street. She then blocked out her subjects' eyes in her series of prints, using a nondescript white bar to reclaim control and permanently refuse their gaze. Anderson alluded to the violent operations at play in such a viewing exchange in her title, which equates the camera to an automatic weapon. Such an allusion was made explicit by Austrian artist VALIE EXPORT's performative intervention *Aktionshose: Genitalpanik (Action Pants: Genital Panic,* 1969), which purportedly involved the artist entering a pornographic movie theater in Munich wielding a Thompson submachine gun and clad in crotchless pants, presenting her exposed genitalia to the seated audience to challenge the scopophilic objectification of the women on screen.[58]

The *So Help Me Hannah: Snatch-Shots with Ray Guns* photographs are a central example of Wilke's "performalist self-portraits," a term that Wilke created to describe works in which she directed an outside cameraperson to document her performances. The images were produced through a particular form of hierarchical delegation among close associates, as she frequently worked with her then partner Donald Goddard, whom she met in 1975 and later married. Explicitly naming her photographer in the credit of these works by using the phrase "Performalist Self-Portrait with [photographer]," Wilke adopted this terminology to assert her artistic control while acknowledging the delegation of labor, a means of reconfiguring the conventionally gendered distribution of power awarded to the male photographer. The designation served to reinforce the concept of authorial ownership over the work as her own, notably by delineating the role of her hired photographer as distinct from the nominal author. At the same time, the neologism "performalist self-portrait" was an example of one of Wilke's beloved puns, playing on art historical formalist analysis, which focuses on the purely visual attributes found in a work of art.

In contrast to previously discussed works that were produced during the time of her and Oldenburg's relationship, in which her role as a former accomplice was only evident with hindsight, the *So Help Me Hannah* project signaled a transition in Wilke's work on two levels. First, she explicitly made Oldenburg's misconduct around the ray guns the subject of her work to expose her erstwhile accomplice role. Second, she tried to avoid the exploitative aspects of this role in her own working relationships, creating a more equitable form of artistic partnership, as seen in her formulation of a different type of attribution with Goddard.

Whereas Oldenburg represented the preexisting and long-standing hierarchical male perspective on women's viable positions within the photographic medium as a "captured" subject (i.e., the "ray gun" model of photography that arrests subjects, turning them into objects), the working relationship between Wilke and Goddard represents an alternative model of collaboration in line with Wilke's vision for feminist equality. Goddard photographed two works—*Intra Venus* and *So Help Me Hannah*—under Wilke's direction, and she gave Goddard credit but had him sign an agreement stating that she held all rights to any photographs he made of her during their relationship.

The introduction of a formal legal document delineating the official scope of Goddard's role signals an alternative method of exposure through the identification of ownership over labor. When Wilke described the *So Help Me Hannah* series as one of her earliest collaborative works in a 1989 interview, she was likely referring not only to her equitable personal relationship with Goddard but also the way that her pieces cunningly appropriated key motifs and phrases from Oldenburg as a means of recalibrating what she considered an imbalanced distribution of power and recognition through surreptitious means.[59] In this manner, her acts of exposure in this series showed the "criminal" aspects of Oldenburg's ray guns—in only acknowledging the male contributors—but also presented a countermodel for authorial attribution that would rectify the types of omissions that she experienced as Oldenburg's accomplice.

Wilke's direction of Goddard focused his labor on becoming an extension of the artist, managing the camera according to her orders. In a 2008 interview in *Art Journal*, Goddard described how he fulfilled a role that had been delegated to him by Wilke, who maintained power over the finished image: "I was the one taking the pictures, but I always felt like I was looking through her eyes at herself. . . . I saw it as Hannah's work, and I felt wonderful to be a part of it."[60] By assigning the camera's operation to Goddard but maintaining a directorial role, Wilke attempted to recalibrate the hierarchies in the representation of the female nude. With Goddard's assistance and that of the other photographers she worked with, Wilke developed a feminist model of photography in which she used her physicality to present men as subordinate to her authorship, a marked contrast to Oldenburg's photographs of Wilke. At the same time, Goddard's comment about "looking through her eyes" indicates that they acted as a team in their partnership, with Wilke at the helm.

### *So Help Me Hannah* Performances

In 1982, Wilke performed and videotaped a version of *So Help Me Hannah* at the A.I.R. Gallery in New York, a live extension of her posed photographs at PS1. According to video documentation of the piece, the performance began when Wilke entered the gallery through a door, once again fully nude except for two props: a pair of white heels and a small handgun. Throughout the twenty-nine-minute video, Wilke moves fluidly between prowling through the space and breaking into various poses directed at the camera; the visual result is a performance that is less narrative and more of a formal experimentation in gesture. In the audio component, a man's voice is heard repeating the words "I'm sorry," which alternates with the artist's voice on themes of gender and power, such as the phrase "Society is indeed a contract. A partnership." Her careful yet swift movements suggest a desire to track down an unnamed entity, yet at the same time she is followed by her two cameramen, Robert Rubin and Bill Dolson, turning the huntress into the hunted.

The construction of the performance and the forms of its documentation are significant in terms of explicating Wilke's multifaceted feminist tactic of artistic exposure that assumes a range of possible meanings: at once physical nakedness, self-revelation, a means of seeking revenge, and a truth-telling disclosure. For example, the fact that Wilke frequently disrobes in her work to publicly solicit and redirect attention toward her exclusions that had been experienced privately suggests a secondary layer of meaning (as a disrobing, a "dis-clothes-ure") to the concept of disclosure that would function in line with her ongoing verbal and linguistic punning that runs throughout her work. Disclosure also extends to the construction of her image, as seen in the 1985 version at the Art Gallery of Windsor in Ontario, Canada. In this piece, the video component of the *So Help Me Hannah* performance began with Wilke alone. Yet the subsequent shot revealed a second camera operator filming Wilke at closer proximity.

The gallery audience would thus have experienced *So Help Me Hannah* in two ways: as a live performance and through the television screen, which played the live feed of her cameramen's views. Photographic documentation of the work indicates that Wilke also had Goddard serve as still photographer, whose images capture all three individuals—the two cameramen (Mark Sikich and Paul Vandeborne) and Wilke—as performers (fig. 2.10). As she begins a dance-like performance directly for the second cameraman that is captured by the first, Wilke's voice-over (using a critique of her own work taken from Lucy Lippard) declares: "A woman using her own face and body has a right to do what she will with it. But it is a subtle abyss between what separates men's use of women for sexual titillation from women's use of women to expose that insult."[61]

The double act of filming recurs throughout the video documentation, as glimpses of the second male camera operator come in and out of view. The fact that the first cameraman—following the nude Wilke in close proximity—is being documented by the second cameraman demonstrates how these roles operate in conjunction: the second cameraman captures

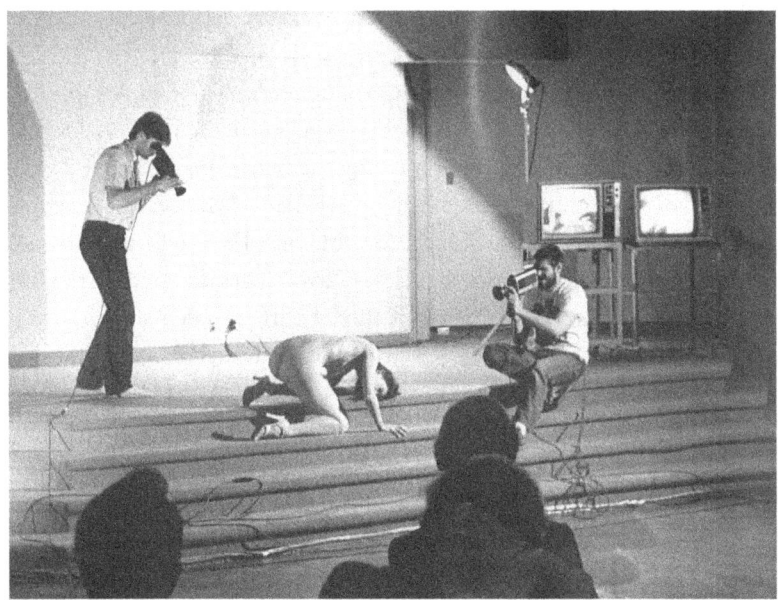

**2.10**    Hannah Wilke performing *So Help Me Hannah* at the Art Gallery of
Windsor in Ontario, Canada, 1985. Photograph by Donald Goddard.

and exposes the first's invasive practice in line with Wilke's broader artistic project. The inclusion of the cameraman coming between her and the "primary" camera exposes how men typically mediate the image of women and how Wilke's agency resides in the exposure of such power differentials.

At the same time, it is significant that the cameramen were operating under her direction and therefore, like Goddard, were "seeing through her eyes." Rerouting their perspective through a female one, Wilke hijacked the "ray gun" model of visual representation and used it against its intended purposes of arresting the female subject. Therefore, Wilke's performalist actions of posing for the camera while directing her cameramen under her artistic authority dramatizes the ways in which she both assumed the role of the male perspective by integrating it into her own position and reclaimed authority over it by mobilizing a second cameraman who became an extension of her own female viewpoint.

In *So Help Me Hannah*, the "victim" assumes a position of power by documenting such hierarchical inequities and presenting them as a central feature of the work. This reading of Wilke's work is supported by the artist's voice-over at a later point in the video, when audio of the words "Annihilate Illuminate," taken from Oldenburg's proverbial phrasebook, is followed by the sound of gunshots as Wilke-as-performer falls to the floor. In Wilke's use of Oldenburg's phrase (it later appeared as the text printed on a 1984 poster-sized image of a *So Help Me Hannah* photograph), she expresses the reciprocity between violence and representation at the core of feminist debates regarding the female image in the 1970s. For Wilke, it seems, the phrase had a particular relevance: the attempts at annihilation that she was subject to could only be counteracted by her attempts not only to illuminate such erasure and gender inequalities but also to create a counterphotographic model of the "snatch-shot" that aggressively deploys her body to solicit attention to such ends.[62] Whether naming photographers in the credits of her "performalist self-portraits," using visual iconographic citations to draw out adversaries, or positioning typically unseen cameramen as central players in her performances, Wilke sought new avenues for exposing the networked model of social relations embedded but often overlooked in artistic production while also asserting her authorial role as a woman artist at a time when feminist cries for agency and recognition often went unheard.

### Advertisements for Living

On the far side of the 1991 exhibition drawing, Wilke situated two photo-based works—*I Object: Memoirs of a Sugar Giver* and *Advertisements for Living*—on adjoining walls in the far corner of the room. In the diptych *I Object*, Wilke combines two mirror-like, reversed images depicting her nude body set in a rocky landscape: she is both the seductive provocateur who put herself at the center of the voyeuristic male gaze as an "eye-object" and yet she declares, as if refuting false statements made in a court of law, "I object." Given that Oldenburg went on to legally censor Wilke's use of his image in *Advertisements* as well as the reproduction of their love letters in her possession in the related book project *I Object*, it seems that her point in connecting these works in the exhibition space was not simply an attempt at revenge on account of a spurned lover but rather a statement on the scope of her limitations with regard to artistic agency and authorship.[63]

In *Advertisements for Living*, Wilke created a work composed of nine vibrant Cibachrome photographic diptychs arranged in three rows. On the left panel of each diptych, Wilke combined the printed name of a famous male historical figure—such as artists David Smith and Henri

Matisse, or philosopher Friedrich Nietzsche—superimposed on Wilke's own abstract photographs. On the right panels of the diptychs, Wilke selected photographic portraits of individuals with whom she shared a relationship, often including herself in the chosen image. The final composition, seen cohesively, offers a sarcastic take on commercial advertising conventions. As her original working title "Name Brands" suggests, in *Advertisements for Living*, Wilke presented a feminist critique of the public-private divide by revealing the personal lives of men that were often obscured and deemed inappropriate to their proprietary professional image.

Wilke included Oldenburg twice in the *Advertisements* diptychs: in both print and image. In the former, Wilke includes Oldenburg's surname in a diptych containing a photograph of Wilke sunbathing with her Russian lover, Vanya. Clad in swimsuits, the two recline on a towel, gazing adoringly at each other. Reversing the pairing of text and image, a photograph of Oldenburg with Wilke's niece Emanuelle is conjoined with the boldfaced name *Marx*. Here, Wilke captures Oldenburg as extended family (of which he was considered a member at the time) who visited the Art and Technology exhibition in Los Angeles. He leans forward on a wood counter, peering toward a window for a telephone booth–type machine exhibit. On the other side of the glass pane is Wilke's niece, looking out in a floral dress, while the reflection of Oldenburg's image is overlaid onto her body.

This specific photograph was one of three images by Wilke that Oldenburg blocked from publication in the exhibition catalog for her retrospective at the University of Missouri. Oldenburg's lawyers also restricted access to images documenting the work's installation at the university museum with the following stipulation: if *Advertisements* were to be reproduced, there would have to be an object or individual placed in front of Oldenburg's likeness to block it entirely from view. The composition of the work—more specifically, the arrangement of the order of the diptychs—was accordingly altered to accommodate the demands of Oldenburg's lawyers. Therefore, while Oldenburg could not ultimately restrict Wilke from exhibiting an image of her work, he could arrange that any institution with which she worked would be required to make complicated provisions for accommodating such legal limitations.

While the University of Missouri Press ultimately decided to follow Oldenburg's request for excluding images of *What'll I Do*, *Artists Make Toys*, and *Advertisements for Living* on the grounds of a violation of his right to privacy, the debate opened significant questions regarding the limits of authority over another's personal information. Moreover, although the press largely acquiesced to removing photographs that depicted Oldenburg's likeness, it is worth mentioning that reproductions of *Advertisements for Living* retained the prominent inclusion of his last name. As with his self-proclaimed alter ego of the ray gun and his signature Mickey Mouse figure, Oldenburg had no problem with his brand as artist being promulgated textually, particularly alongside such art-world luminaries as Sol LeWitt, Carl Andre, and Matisse. Rather, his concern was the distribution of photographs that broke with his highly controlled self-image: specifically, those that made visible his personal relationship with Wilke and showed him within the context of a family day trip.

In this manner, one can conceive of Wilke's strategy in this work to reverse previous exploitations by "advertising" that wrongdoing had been performed against her. While not the initial intention of Wilke's work, these legal restrictions became a crucial aspect as they intensified her investigation of the thresholds of privacy over which an artist or other authorial figure has control.[64] That is, Oldenburg's legal attacks ultimately worked against him, in that Wilke tactically turned Oldenburg's actions around to reveal her role as an accomplice within his work that would have otherwise remained hidden. Inverting the operations invoked by Burden, who deliberately mined the occluded spaces occupied by his abettors, Wilke provoked Oldenburg by testing the limits of his privacy rights in works such as *Advertisements for Living* in a deliberate effort to make him, and therefore his exclusion of her, become visible.

### Even-tu-ally / Artist's Proof

In 1991, Wilke began a body of mixed-media works comprising documents—including actual legal files and personal letters from former romantic partners—printed in Mylar over photographic self-portraits that were used to bolster her claims of artistic ownership for specific works and concepts. Although *Even-tu-ally* (1969–91; fig. 2.11) is the only example of these works ever publicly exhibited, archival research shows that Wilke also used this compositional format in a series of heretofore unknown pieces, such as *Artist's Proof* (1991). Taken as a whole, these works demonstrate how Wilke tested the thresholds of privacy by making juridical documents enter the public domain as a tactic for substantiating her demands for representation and agency.

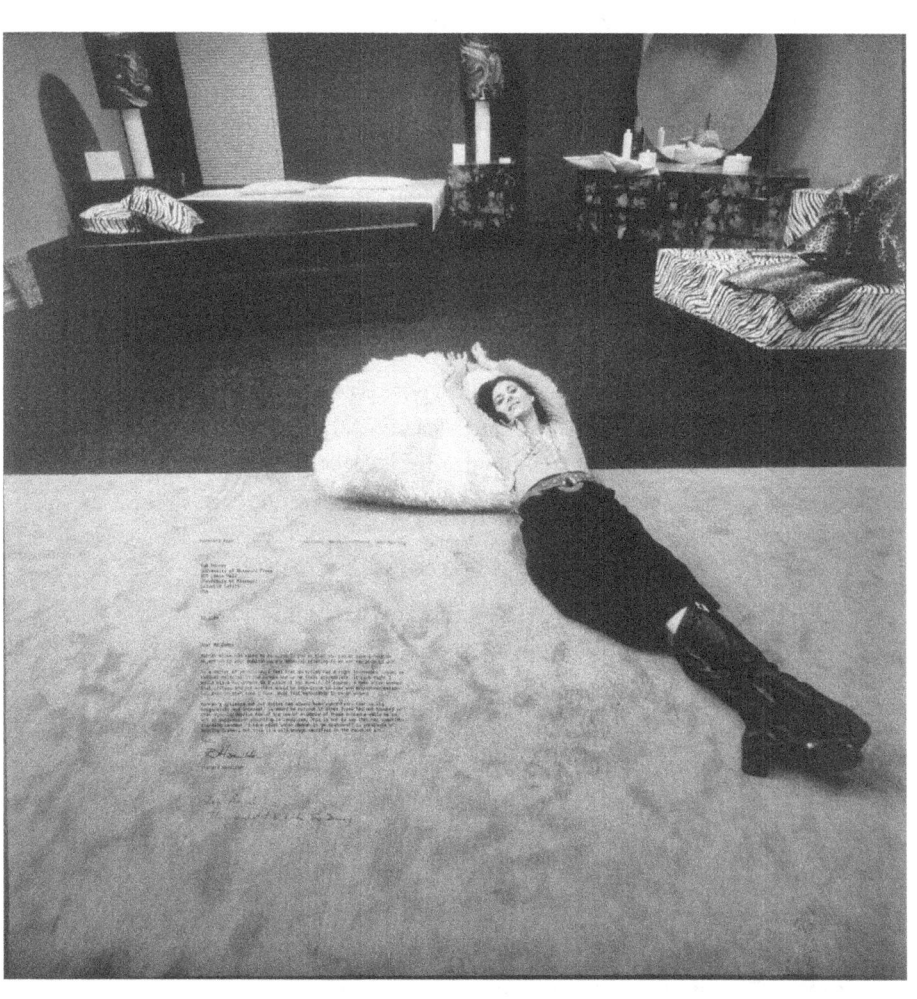

**2.11** Hannah Wilke, *Even-tu-ally*, 1969–91. Cibachrome with silkscreen imprinting of text, 21 × 21 in.

*Even-tu-ally* is composed of a 1969 photograph of Wilke reclining on a rug in the foreground within Oldenburg's *Bedroom Ensemble I* (1963). In this tableau, Oldenburg replicated a seedy midcentury California motel room, complete with a zebra-print couch and glossy faux-marble furniture.[65] Yet the contents of the room were not as straightforward as they initially seemed: Oldenburg sought to augment the artificiality of the space using nontraditional materials and deliberately nonfunctional bedroom furniture, such as white patent leather sheets that were sewn together to prevent the possibility of using the bed. The objects in the installation were also rendered strange by their proportions, emphasizing the inhospitality of the room; for example, Oldenburg altered the sizes of two bedside tables to correspond with conflicting perspectives and designed the bed to take a trapezoidal form that mimicked the visual technique of foreshortening.

In the 1969 photograph, Wilke's pose is playful and seductive, as she leans back against a fluffy white ottoman with her arms raised overhead. She comfortably inhabits the pseudo-domestic environment in a manner that would only be available to a close associate of Oldenburg's. Importantly, the final date listed for Wilke's *Even-tu-ally*—1991—marks the artistic intervention that transformed the work from a personal snapshot reflective of the intimacy shared by the two artists into a work of art that served as a public contestation of Oldenburg's attempts to silence her.[66]

The finished version of *Even-tu-ally*, published by Juni Verlag, was composed of two parts: the original photograph taken of Wilke and a letter from another former romantic partner, Richard Hamilton, printed alongside her image on the bottom left side of the work.[67] In the letter, dated February 22, 1989, and addressed to the editor of Wilke's exhibition catalog for her University of Missouri retrospective, Hamilton asserts his complete backing regarding Wilke's usage of "any material relating to me."[68] Writing in direct response to Oldenburg's refusal, Hamilton offered not only his support against what he saw as artistic suppression but also suggested that Oldenburg's actions may themselves have been considered illegal:

> As a matter of principle, I feel that an artist has a right to present visual or textual material in the manner she or he feels appropriate. It is a right I would claim for others as I claim it for myself. . . . Hannah's artistic subject matter has always been egocentric, that is its originality and interest. It would be curious if other lives had not touched on that ego: to deprive her of the use of evidence of those contacts would be an act of suppression amounting to vandalism.[69]

Like Julius Caesar's last words ("et tu, Brute?"), the title of *Even-tu-ally* then must be understood as taking on an accusatory cast, a play on both the French and the Latin word for *you* that was directed at Oldenburg. Read as both a resigned acknowledgment of facts and a rhetorical question (even *you*, [my former] ally?), the title chosen by Wilke suggests a betrayal that is reinforced by the contrast to Hamilton's warm letter of support.

*Even-tu-ally* was not the only work by Wilke that combined documents of a legal nature with photographs. Taken at the time of Wilke's *Intra Venus* series, which documented her aggressive cancer treatment, *Artist's Proof* captures a sullen yet defiant-looking Wilke at the end of her life. While her posture recalls a criminal mug shot, the work's title asserts a call for artistic authority and legal restitution. Printed atop one image is a letter, dated December 7, 1989, in which Oldenburg's lawyer, Lawrence M. Phillips, responded to Wilke's lawyer, Barbara Hoffman. In it, Phillips attacks Wilke's character, adopts a patronizing tone with her female legal representative, and even accuses the artist of harassing and threatening Oldenburg by using his image in her work:

> While it expresses fully the position of your client and her rationale to justify her invasion of my client's right to privacy, in my opinion it totally lacks legal and factual merit. There is no valid claim for injury to her property or career simply because my client took proper steps to protect his private life; a constitutionally protected right I might add, not easily overcome by your client's spurious argument that her right to "Artistic expression" is above anyone's individual right to privacy. . . . The point is clear, my client will not submit to your client's continued harassment or threats akin to blackmail to obtain money from him by the use of private material, nor suffer her compulsive need to exploit his name or likeness to further her career.

Other Xerox prototypes exist in her archive as well. In one, Wilke superimposed a Certificate of Information letter from the Union Central Life Insurance Company of Cincinnati that she had signed to receive health and life insurance under Oldenburg's Store Days corporation. Dated July 28, 1976, the policy was put in effect shortly before he married van Bruggen and its coverage was one of the main points of contention in the years to follow. In another example, she published a romantic letter from Oldenburg from 1975 that offered an intimate perspective on Oldenburg's daily activities as well as their shared life together. She also printed a formal document shared with her lawyer outlining the scope of her labor in various "Art Collaborations," including key works that have been attributed entirely to Oldenburg (such as a work referred to as "*Marble Bicycle Seat*").[70]

Rather than shrinking from legal debates, Wilke exploited the private nature of these documents and brought them into prominence through her artwork. By doing so, she was able to circumvent the restrictions imposed on her and her practice by Oldenburg's legal team by making such conditions public through the inclusion of those documents in the very work they aimed to suppress. Part of her intention in including these documents was likely because—while her own work was restricted owing to Oldenburg's legal injunction—Wilke claimed that he was continuing to use photographs taken by her and was exhibiting other works in which she performed various labor without attribution. In her archive, there are numerous photocopies of various Oldenburg catalogs annotated by Wilke in which her photographs are used, such as *Notes in Hand* (1971). These images, in Wilke's estimation, were her own photographic works of Oldenburg performing for her camera or thousands of documentary photographs that she had taken and he had used for his books despite her retaining sole authorship and presumed copyright.[71]

In a particularly revealing document in her archive titled "Relationship between Hannah Wilke and Claes Oldenburg 1967–1978," Wilke offered a poignant defense of her position in her former partner's life. Shifting her focus away from shared artistic projects, Wilke pointed to the multifaceted roles that she adopted, which reflected the enormity of women's responsibilities for which credit is still withheld: "During the years of our relationship, I lived with Claes as a wife, collaborator, photographer, and business advisor, helping not only to further his career but also stabilize his emotional condition. . . . Service as a wife included shopping for food and his clothing, cleaning, buying furniture, haircutting, etc. which enabled him to devote himself to his work as an artist. During this time his prices rose." Wilke's articulation of her domestic, business, and other typically private roles demonstrated a feminist position calling for acknowledgment of forms of responsibility that have typically been overlooked as labor. Yet this document reveals a desire on the part of Wilke to seek reparations for her contributions. Given Oldenburg's dismissal of her demands, Wilke found restitution by transposing the "evidence" of such obfuscations into her art, allowing the redress to come in the form of publicity for her work.

Considered together, *Even-tu-ally* and *Artist's Proof* demonstrate that Wilke's invocation of the ongoing legal battles was a strategic tactic used to bring these otherwise private and nondisclosed issues into the public record by the act of including them in her art.[72] Through the physical inclusion of actual legal texts, Wilke undermined Oldenburg's attempts to assert legal threats by revealing how his claims to certain privacy rights violated her own right of publicity. It was only by exposing his actions as unethical and potentially illicit that Wilke was able to show her role as a potential accomplice within his crimes against her.

### Retribution

At its core, the term *partner* describes a relationship in which the constituent members have each been allocated an equally distributed share, for better or for worse. While partnerships can occupy public space, as in the case of working relationships, or take a private form, such as personal liaisons, such affiliations assume equivalent responsibility, agency, and recognition. In line with certain feminist calls for representation in the 1970s, Wilke strategically used her artworks to bring forward evidence of the responsibility of others—whether her unrecognized labor in Oldenburg's works as an uncredited former accomplice or those associates embedded (willingly or unwillingly) in her own artistic endeavors. Rather than reinforcing the divide between the public image of the artist and the private forms of support that bolster it, Wilke exploited such details and made them fundamental to her work in reconstituting personal and professional relationships on her terms. Harnessing the nominalist authority held by the artist handed down through Marcel Duchamp's readymade—but redirecting it toward artistic subjects rather than objects—Wilke, like the other artists in this book, discloses a set of unrecognized auxiliary participants whose presence reshapes our comprehension of authorship and agency in well-known artworks.

While the first chapter addressed Burden's testing of distributed accountability by enacting illicit transgressions that brought into visibility previously unacknowledged figures that I term *abettors*, here Wilke transformed her role as Oldenburg's disregarded and unattributed former accomplice into a generative artistic position that was weaponized to redress the inequality of women as artistic and romantic *partners*. Whereas Burden (and Oldenburg) was happy to distribute authorship if it shifted legal and ethical responsibility to others, not when it threatened the value of the artwork or the artist's public image, Wilke cannily inverted such a position to reveal her role as a former accomplice to crimes of erasure. To state plainly, Wilke recognized that she didn't have a partner in Oldenburg, but through her tactics of exposure she made him into one and exposed her as his accomplice, against his wishes.

Seeking public retribution and acknowledgment from Oldenburg and the patriarchal art world for neglecting to interrogate existing models of singular authorship, Wilke sought to recalibrate the agency and attention afforded to a network of significant yet unacknowledged participants, notably romantic partners. While this critique was largely leveled at Oldenburg specifically, she simultaneously sought to present alternative models of authorship that would account for distributed labor while retaining nominal control. For example, her development of the phrase "performalist self-portraits" to address the contributions of photographers under her direction, her notable inclusion of cameramen in the *So Help Me Hannah* performances, and her use of a wide network of individuals in *Intercourse with . . .* point to her interest in highlighting the role of others in artwork while developing the visual and conceptual language to maintain her authority as an artist. In the case of *Laundry Lint (C.O.'s)* or the *Oldenburg Portfolio*, Wilke transformed the residual markers of domestic and intimate life into artworks that both foregrounded the traditionally female role as homemaker as well as offered specificity regarding her own relationship with Oldenburg by prominently including signs of his identity. In *Proposed I-Museum in the Form of an H Series*, Wilke deployed artworks to gain visibility so that hidden attributions and artistic contributions would be made public. In works such as *Artist's Proof* and *Even-tu-ally*, Wilke reversed the power relations between these former partners by using Oldenburg's private actions in public artworks that undermined his initial aims of silencing her.

As for the enigmatic 1991 untitled drawing, never exhibited despite— or perhaps because of—the breadth of coded information embedded on the page, it has since been returned to the archive, awaiting a future recovery. But perhaps that's the point. In proposing this exhibition, Wilke sought a different future for these objects than her own. Much like the accomplices themselves, this drawing uncovers a narrative running between artworks that surges through epistemological cracks for brief moments, only to return to obscurity.

# Assistants

**In a 1990 essay titled** "I Was an Assistant (to Kippenberger, Büttner, and Oehlen)" published in the inaugural issue of *Texte zur Kunst*, artist Merlin Carpenter offered a firsthand account of the interdependent relationship between assistant and nominal artist he experienced while working in Martin Kippenberger's studio beginning in November 1989.[1] Although the majority of Carpenter's text recounts the process by which his personal creativity was brought under the direction of the more established artist, in an important passage near the conclusion of the essay, he provides a brief characterization of the poststructuralist "death of the author" logic promulgated by Roland Barthes and Michel Foucault in the late 1960s as it applied to his own experience, noting: "French philosophers might say it is good to make oneself 'we' instead of 'I,' as this more accurately reflects the fact that the 'I' can be maintained as a device, so that it is really someone else who is 'I,' and who is forever wrong. There are other forms of responsibility than that of the enlightened subject."[2] Although this formulation of the authorial subject as a "device" that was outwardly cohesive and singular—while in fact masking multiple unrecognized agents who share in the accountability for a given work—is an applicable model for all the artist case studies analyzed thus far, Carpenter's mention of intentional failure through the delegation of labor ("someone else who is 'I,' and who is forever wrong") is significant for understanding the complex network of social dynamics that operate in Kippenberger's artistic practice. This introduction of "wrongdoing" as a deliberate feature within distributed authorship demonstrates a savvy comprehension of the role that he played under Kippenberger's authority—distinct from that of a traditional studio assistant who is directed to execute tasks successfully for the nominal artist.

The initial motivation behind Carpenter's essay was to explain his involvement in Kippenberger's 1989/90 installation *Heavy Burschi* (*Heavy Guy*), for which he was the artist's primary assistant (fig. 3.1). Shortly after Carpenter was hired, one of his first tasks was to create a body of fifty-one

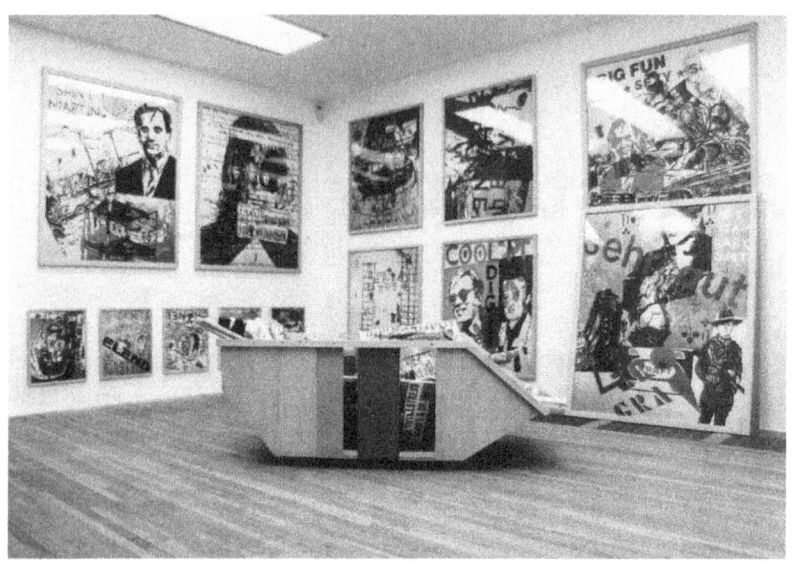

**3.01** Martin Kippenberger, *Heavy Burschi*, 1989/90.
Installation view, Tate Modern, London, 2006.

unique paintings. According to the artist's directions, these were to be based on collages composed of recycled motifs taken from Kippenberger's earlier catalog of artworks, which appeared expressionistic but were in fact derivative of other works, as well as commercial logos of well-known brands, in-jokes, made-up slogans, and other self-referential gestures. However, the collages on which the paintings were based were not made by Kippenberger, as might be assumed. As Carpenter expressed in his exposé of assistant life: "The myth was that I worked from collages. Partly true—but they were my own collages!"[3] The result was a series of "Kippenberger" paintings that appeared to be produced directly from the nominal artist's hand but were in fact realized through dual tactics of appropriation—in terms of both the reuse of existing images and the annexation of Carpenter's intellectual labor in rendering those images as distinctive paintings.

Despite conceiving of the compositions and performing the manual labor for both the collages and subsequent paintings, Carpenter did not receive credit for his contributions. This might seem typical of the long-standing hierarchical working relationships between artists and assistants going back to the Renaissance atelier, in which a work of art has been historically attributed to the nominal artist exclusively. Yet in such precedents the original idea for the work—the scope of creative labor that would

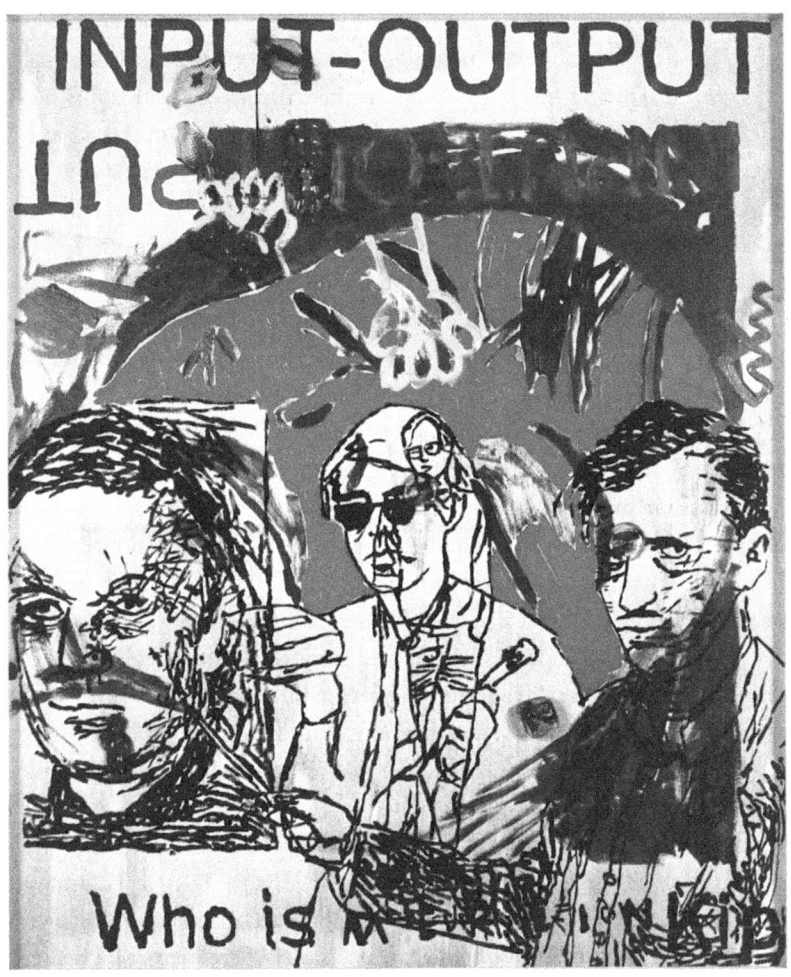

**3.02**  Photograph of an untitled painting from the *Heavy Burschi* series, 1989/90, 47¼ × 39⅜ in., before it was destroyed.

theoretically be protected by intellectual property law—was created by the nominal artist, with a network of hired laborers performing the physical execution of the artist's conceptual vision. While Carpenter performed such tasks as an employee of Kippenberger, thereby renouncing certain rights over his artistic undertakings, the extent of his contributions—as well as the ways Kippenberger interfered with such endeavors—brings up a set of legal issues that will be the subject of this chapter.

In an untitled painting from the *Heavy Burschi* series (1989/90; fig. 3.2), Carpenter created a densely multilayered composition that combines references to Kippenberger's signature iconography (an outstretched fist), other artists (including Albert Oehlen and Andy Warhol), and even Carpenter himself (as seen in the truncated question "Who is Merlin Kip" that links Carpenter and Kippenberger's names to create a fictitious hybrid authorial identity). The phrase "INPUT-OUTPUT," which is printed twice across the top of the composition—once forward and once in reverse and upside down—refers to the 1989 artist's book of the same name. Yet it also concisely describes the unique procedures by which Kippenberger created a singular model of authorship while distributing the labor for the artistic production to a network of assistants who themselves functioned in accordance with processes of reuse and delegation.

These *Heavy Burschi* paintings—made by Carpenter but attributed to Kippenberger—underwent two further operations that introduced an important element of strategic interference into the working process. First, Kippenberger directed the art collector and photography aficionado Wilhelm Schürmann to photograph each individual work and turn them into prints matching the exact size of the source paintings. In this state, the images had undergone at least three medial transformations: beginning with collaged compositions (themselves borrowing visual motifs from other artworks), they were made into paintings, and then reproduced as photographs that were hung on the wall—all labor performed by others under Kippenberger's direction.

Second, in contrast to those generative actions, Kippenberger also enacted a series of negative tactics—he deemed the paintings by Carpenter "too good" and ordered the series to undergo various destructive procedures such as slashing, cutting, and puncturing, effectively reducing Carpenter's production to waste.[4] This was then literalized in the work as the detritus was thrown in a modified garbage dumpster with Plexiglas siding for gallery viewers to see inside. Instead of seamlessly transferring the responsibility for artistic labor to his assistant, Kippenberger introduced a critical component—that of disruption—to the typically smooth process of delegation.

In this manner, the *Heavy Burschi* photographs undermined the status of the image according to a neat binary of either original or reproduction by staging what can be characterized as a feedback loop of remediation, defined by Jay David Bolter and Richard Grusin as "the representation of one medium in another."[5] For Bolter and Grusin, there are two primary logics of remediation that can be deployed either singularly or in conjunction with each other: *immediacy* and *hypermediacy*. Immediacy is evidenced in forms of media that attempt to achieve complete transparency into representation so that the medium itself disappears. In contrast, hypermediacy attempts to make the viewer aware of the medium rather than the represented content. In *Heavy Burschi*, the positioning of the photographic reproductions, installed on the wall in the exact dimensions of the source paintings, demonstrates an adherence to the logic of immediacy. Yet the prominence of the garbage container, holding its painterly remains, breaks open the seamlessness of the medial transformation, as through its hypermediated instantiation it "acknowledges multiple acts of representation and makes them visible."[6] These interconnected processes can be seen to produce a kind of closed system centered on the reuse of images, thereby undermining the hierarchies of an original and a reproduction. Yet Kippenberger also introduces a strategic application of delegated labor in *Heavy Burschi* that consciously works *against* the concurrent feedback loop of remediation, setting the two cycles into opposition. Through this gesture, Kippenberger reformulates an alternative model of artistic authorship that paradoxically reaffirms his own role in the work.

Drawing upon his assistants to create different modes of "noise" within extant cycles of remediation—as (1) irregular disturbances that obscure the original signal or (2) the dissemination of information, publicity, and rumors ("to make noise")—Kippenberger shifts the locus of artistic agency and authorship to the site of *interference* between these two feedback loops. This empties the author of an internally generated expressive or subjective function to instead establish a model of authorship as a kind of interruptive mechanism that can be inhabited by a variety of subjects while maintaining nominal authority. In this way, one can see how Kippenberger's formulation of this authorial role establishes a kind of dynamic equilibrium in which the contributions made by other agents are nested within his public authorial identity.

In what follows, I present a third accomplice paradigm that assumes the form of studio assistants whose intellectual labor and authorial rights were deliberately manipulated in Kippenberger's practice as a performative gesture. While these assistants were hired by the artist and therefore ostensibly gave consent to Kippenberger's role as the primary controlling actor of the artistic output created within the studio setting, I argue that Kippenberger purposely sought ways of testing the limits of the rights of his assistants and the ethics of his relationship with them within the framework of intellectual property law that was in effect during the 1980s.

The *Heavy Burschi* project introduces potential violations of three critical components of intellectual property law that will be elaborated on in this chapter. Similar to the modern legal protections granted in other Western countries, Germany's 1965 Act on Copyright and Related Rights (UrhG) protects not only the economic interests of a work of art but also three types of moral rights, which are granted to creators of original content and seen as intrinsic to their person.[7] These inalienable and nontransferable rights include the recognition of authorship (Section 13 UrhG, otherwise known as the right of paternity), which oversees the right to be correctly identified as the author; the right of publication (Section 12 UrhG), which grants a creator protections in determining whether a work or its production process can be made public; and the right to integrity (Section 14 UrhG), which guards against alterations or the destruction of a work of art by others.

Moral rights are inalienable, cannot be transferred or waived, and remain indefinitely with the author—the only exception being hired labor. While in most cases the distinctions between work created while under employment (in which the employer would be entitled to the copyright ownership over output) and creative work belonging to an artist (falling under the domain of moral rights) are quite clear, the conventional assumptions around aura, authenticity, and originality in an artist's studio present a unique set of opportunities to blur such defined boundaries.[8] By taking control of Carpenter's contributions, refusing to publicly give acknowledgment of his labor, and destroying his artistic efforts—all conceivable moral rights violations—Kippenberger explores an alternative authorial model based on networked yet hierarchical social relations using art studio assistants.

I argue that Kippenberger introduced three forms of interference— what I term *error, residual individuality,* and *waste*—into the circuits of delegated labor performed under his authority as the nominal artist. These interruptive tactics—which exposed the typically obscured system of labor in behind-the-scenes operations—were meant as a critique of the sovereign image of celebrity that was pervasive during the 1980s, while also harnessing such image power to serve his own desire for greater notoriety. The works analyzed in this chapter chart Kippenberger's deliberate attempts at putting pressure on the legal protections of intellectual property as a means of making the assistant visible by transforming their role into that of an accomplice to potential transgressions of moral rights. In my estimation, this represents another way that artists explored the extent of authorial control over another individual in the context of art. While I am not claiming that Kippenberger (or his associates) actively sought to or indeed did commit any illegal acts, the types of inquiries that can be probed by viewing his works through the accomplice paradigm open onto interrelated issues of delegation, celebrity, and authorship that were at the core of his artistic practice as well as the new image economy of the 1980s.

### Social Beginnings: Celebrity Value

In 1976, Kippenberger left West Germany, where he had studied with Sigmar Polke at the Hamburg Art Academy, in pursuit of an acting career in Florence, Italy. When he returned two short years later, his ambition was galvanized by the fleeting experience of celebrity, having been frequently mistaken for the young Austrian film star Helmut Berger by unwitting fans. Settling in West Berlin, Kippenberger sought to make a name for himself. Despite his disenchantment with conventional art training and practices, Kippenberger shrewdly understood that art could be a vehicle for generating a public persona as well as a tool for commenting on the growing adjacencies between art, entertainment, and commercialization.

In the late 1970s and early to mid-1980s, Kippenberger developed various tactics for cultivating his image and expanding his audience, both within and outside the art world. Modeling himself in a manner akin to the social hierarchies of celebrity, in which a famous "star" is supported by an unseen team of background players playing critical roles in the promulgation of one's public image, Kippenberger became involved with projects that allowed him to explore the creation of extrapainterly social networks as a mode of collaborative production while remaining at the public helm. This can be connected to two related endeavors at the outset of his career: the development of "Kippenberger's Büro" in 1978 and his short-lived management of the punk and new-wave club Süd Ost 36 (S.O. 36) in 1979.

Kippenberger's Büro, based in the Segitzdamm neighborhood of West Berlin, hosted a revolving lineup of activities, including serving as an exhibition space, roller-skating rink, editorial headquarters, fashion studio, print shop, and design lab. Consciously modeled on the collaborative creative structure of Andy Warhol's Factory in New York, the six-hundred-meter industrial loft—also known simply as "the Office"—was conceived by Kippenberger and gallerist Gisela Capitain as a site to bridge the divide between social conviviality and artistic experimentation.[9] In existence for two years, Kippenberger's Büro hosted regular art exhibitions by a rotating cast of friends and associates, printed a massive amount of ephemera (such as invitation cards, posters, and flyers), and served as the unofficial center for new-wave and punk music in Berlin, which was bolstered by Kippenberger's concurrent position as manager of the nearby S.O. 36 music club, where he featured bands such as Red Krayola, Scritti Politti, and Throbbing Gristle.[10]

Warhol became an important point of reference for Kippenberger, one that he returned to throughout his career. During the Factory's first four years (1964–68), Warhol opened the singularity of an artist's output—defined by one's signature medium and style—to include silkscreens, photography, films, musical albums, and even a novel, all of which were produced in conjunction with participants whose skill level, professional status, and formal association with the Factory varied widely.[11] Despite shifting roles and degrees of collaboration between Warhol and his "employees," nominal authorship remained in the hands of one—a formulation akin to corporate models in which a worker's labor becomes the exclusive property of the company.

By the mid-1970s, Warhol took measures that further articulated this transformation of his art practice into a corporate entity—what he called his "business art"—including rebranding his Factory as "Andy Warhol Enterprises, Inc."[12] According to Vincent Fremont, a longtime employee, 1974 marked the consolidation of the various film production companies and artistic projects (the Andy Warhol Studio, Factory Films, *Interview* magazine) into one corporate identity, which corresponded with the creation of official-sounding job titles and an increased emphasis on employees procuring corporate art and portrait commissions, often flouting the political and social allegiances that characterized the liberal-minded art world.[13] *Interview* magazine became *Andy Warhol's Interview*, his cinematic services were sold in a department store catalog for $150,000, and he personally began appearing in print advertisements, including one for the Drexel Burnham Lambert investment bank (fig. 3.3).

Warhol was certainly not alone in this strategic surrender to the world of rampant commerce and self-promotion. His transformation of the image of the artist into a business was increasingly in step with the accelerated commercialization of art during this time.[14] The 1980s marked a moment of transition for the art world, as the global network of art fairs, biennials, galleries, and institutions exploded the business side of contemporary art. Moreover, interest in the art world grew in more mainstream

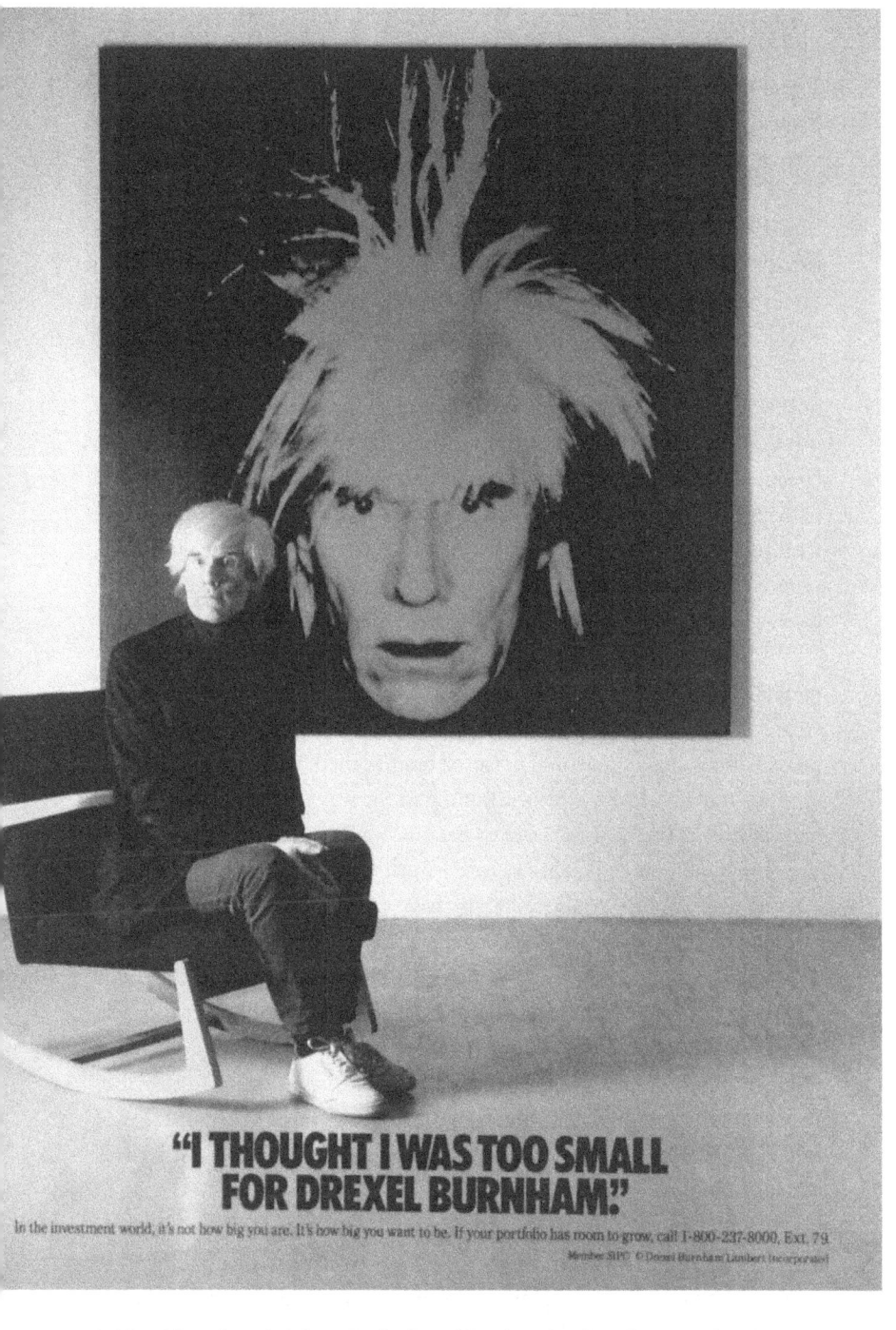

**3.03**  Magazine advertisement for Drexel Burnham Lambert featuring Andy Warhol, 1986. Published in *New York Times Magazine*, November 23, 1986.

circles in the United States and Western Europe. This is perhaps best exemplified by a television program launched in 1985 by MTV titled *Art Breaks*, a series of promotional video art pieces—with appearances by Richard Prince, Keith Haring, Dara Birnbaum, and Warhol—meant to generate interest in contemporary art from a music video–watching viewership.

Kippenberger's desire, as a young German artist seeking an international audience, to expand his celebrity during the 1980s was in line with broader shifts in the status of the artist as a public figure in the United States and Western Europe. Artists such as Jean-Michel Basquiat, Anselm Kiefer, David Salle, and Julian Schnabel gained recognition as "art stars," whose personalities and public images became fodder for publications both within and beyond the art world. This moment of the celebrity artist was notably tied up with valuations of singularity and personal expression (particularly in the Neo-Expressionist camp of highly subjective gestural painting), with artists presenting clearly articulated "signature styles" that were readily consumed by the booming 1980s art market. At the same time, such visual branding of artists aligned with the practices of global expansion and increased notoriety of corporate trademarks and brand identities.

Some of Kippenberger's contemporaries began to parody this commercialization and self-promotion of art and its makers. Ashley Bickerton created a series of tongue-in-cheek self-portraits using an amalgam of commercial logos and an invented personal brand called "Susie," which he then used to "trademark" his work—alluding to the way in which corporations had infiltrated the private realm to become an integral part of one's identity. The same year as Warhol's Drexel Burnham Lambert advertisement, artist David Robbins produced an incisive work that articulated this ambition for celebrity as part of a new approach to creative production.[15] In *Talent* (1986; fig. 3.4), Robbins depicts eighteen young stars of the 1980s American art world—including Jeff Koons, Cindy Sherman, and Robert Longo—in individual black-and-white headshots, taken by a famous entertainment photographer. This representation of artists as pseudo-celebrities slyly expressed the polarities between the rarefied world of art and that of celebrity culture and alluded to the ways in which the artists themselves had become market commodities.[16]

Kippenberger's own relationship to self-branding was complex. Understanding that publicity is built on the dissemination of a cohesive external persona, he began exploring alternative production and circulation models in the early 1980s that would augment his self-image. But instead of cultivating his own artistic "signature," he worked prolifically across medi-

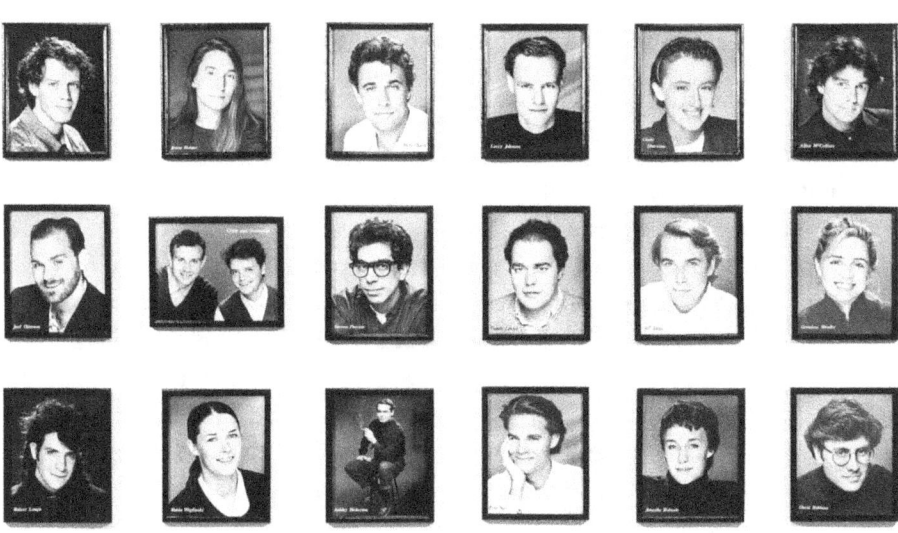

**3.04**    David Robbins, *Talent*, 1986. Eighteen gelatin silver prints, each 10 × 8 or 8 × 10 in.

ums and styles; the only constant was the promotion of himself. In notable contrast to other artists working at the time, however, Kippenberger's self-presentations were often scrambled, distorted, or presented in an unflattering light.[17]

This was evident in the development of various alter egos that would appear throughout his paintings and sculptures, such as a cartoon amphibian called "Fred the Frog," a wire sculpture of the well-known Marvel character "Spider-Man," and "Kippenblinky," his trademark curved lampposts made to appear inebriated. On the level of production, these alter egos were often generated by appropriating extant imagery from popular culture, such as animated cartoons, which he then hyperpersonalized by emphasizing his own shortcomings as emblematic characteristics. Rather than amplifying a positive public image of the artist, these works presented symbols of failure: depicting solitary, lonely figures, often shown in a state of drunkenness—in reference to the artist's ongoing struggles with alcoholism.

Another technique that Kippenberger used to augment his celebrity was to invoke collaboration, effectively growing his presence by becoming tangentially involved with projects that would gain momentum outside his own active labor. For instance, Kippenberger made his oatmeal-covered car sculpture *Capri by Night* (1982) with his frequent collaborator Oehlen and cofounded a secret society known as the Lord Jim Lodge with

Oehlen, Jörg Schlick, and Wolfgang Bauer in 1985. Kippenberger also developed a practice of producing branded multiples featuring a signature trademark to help build his public persona. Using low-cost and readily available materials, Kippenberger distributed prints, commodity objects, and other ephemera through his expanding network of galleries, publishers, and business associates.

Straddling the threshold between pure publicity stunts within the Kippenberger "brand" and high-art production, Kippenberger exploited the presumed hierarchies among art objects in which multiples and commercial merchandise occupy a secondary position in relation to the value of a "master" medium, like painting. For example, Kippenberger produced an extensive set of large-scale imitation Alka-Seltzer tablets carved from wood and imprinted with various fabricated logos, such as "Castelli Seltzer" (in reference to Leo Castelli's influential art gallery) and "Kippen Seltzer." These works, along with the vast output of objects such as bath mats, T-shirts, and household games trademarked under the Kippenberger name, worked in conjunction with the massive dissemination of promotional materials such as catalogs, books, and posters to expand the "Kippenberger" visibility.

The introduction of disruption into his artistic practice can be seen in one of Kippenberger's first major painting series, *Lieber Maler, male mir* (*Dear Painter, Paint for Me*) (1981), in which he sought new avenues for delegating labor and authorship while still maintaining authority. This series comprised twelve representational paintings that were exhibited at Berlin's neue Gesellschaft für bildende Kunst (nGbK, New Society for Visual Arts) under the title *Werner Kippenberger: "Lieber Maler, male mir."*[18] This suite of works ranged in content from portraits to still lifes, resembling both photorealism and commercial advertisements. The source material for many of the paintings featured the artist: touristic photographs taken of Kippenberger during a visit across the United States by his friend and co-owner of S.O. 36, Achim Schächtele.

Kippenberger's working process for the *Lieber Maler, male mir* series can be broken down into a set of three operations. First, he assigned the task of taking photographs to Schächtele but then reasserted his authority by selecting certain images to be given as a commission to Hans Siebert, a commercial sign painter who, through his association with Kippenberger, became publicly known only as "Werner."[19] Second, Siebert, whose background was in making film posters and billboard advertisements, was directed to transfer the photographic images to a set of large-scale paintings.[20] Finally, Kippenberger took the completed works produced by Werner and exhibited them collectively as the series *Werner Kippenberger: Lieber Maler, male mir*, using a title that both declares a hybridized authorial identity and issues an ambiguous request: "Dear Painter, Paint for Me." By recasting the anonymous individual under his own surname, Kippenberger points to the singular recognition received by the nominal artist despite the accountability for the physical labor—both photographic and painterly—being distributed among other agents.

Combining the contributions of Schächtele, Werner, and himself into an independent authorial entity, Kippenberger folded their respective labor into the finished paintings in a way that reaffirmed the legitimation of his sole position as the conceptual artistic authority while also opening the possibilities of an authorial subject that is generated from multiple sources. This tactical strategy of mining the strengths of other individuals (such as Siebert's background in commercial billboards and photorealist painting)—and combining their labor within his output—is a model in which auxiliary agents are sought out for certain features that are valued and then exploited by the artist.[21] These arrangements would be further developed in more official relationships with hired assistants in the years to come.

The *Lieber Maler* paintings exemplify one of Kippenberger's early attempts to generate notoriety through the development of a public persona that had been networked among multiple parties. In *Lieber Maler*, Siebert and Schächtele were able to effectively execute Kippenberger's direction, yet they seemingly lacked two interconnected principles that would later become central to his practice. The first was that at the time of their work for Kippenberger, they both had career profiles outside his studio, as they were hired for a limited period to participate in the direct translation of images from photographs to paintings. Second, their status as temporary laborers rather than formal assistants meant that Kippenberger would direct Siebert and Schächtele's contributions only toward productive ends, thereby furthering the feedback loops of remediation rather than fully producing modes of interruption.

Kippenberger's development of these various self-branding techniques in the early to mid-1980s suggests a canny exploration of the multiple ways that intellectual property could be articulated—a point that would be pursued more fully through his subsequent work with assistants. The formulation of copyright and author's rights arose in the eighteenth century in response to issues of exploitation by publishers and the changing market for published books; this was later codified in 1886 through the

Berne Convention for the Protection of Literary and Artistic Works, which formally mandated an international agreement over the basic framework of copyright law as it is known today.[22] In the United States, both copyright law and trademark law—concerning individual and corporate intellectual property, respectively—underwent significant changes during the 1970s and 1980s. Many of the laws governing such areas had been unmodified for decades, despite technological, social, and conceptual transformations in types of objects and ideas that could fall under the domain of intellectual property; for instance, according to economic theorists Patricio Sáiz and Rafael Castro, intellectual property rights were rarely given attention by economists or business scholars until the 1980s.[23] One of the biggest legislative changes to American intellectual property law was the US Copyright Act of 1976, which articulated the legal protection for "original forms of expression" across a variety of art forms—the first time such concepts had been amended since 1909. However, in distinction from European intellectual property laws, the US Copyright Act strictly protected economic interests, such as an unauthorized commercial exploitation of a work of art; this was only amended to include moral rights with the passage of the Visual Artists Rights Act of 1990.

The concept of moral rights originated in nineteenth-century France, as part of the *droit d'auteur* (author's right); its basic principles have subsequently been adopted across Europe.[24] Seen as an inalienable natural right, moral rights determine that an individual has exclusive entitlements over their creation, as such endeavors are considered an extension of the self. Martha Buskirk has noted that moral rights (also known as "personality rights") attribute ownership of intellectual property to the artist exclusively—therefore, despite its commercially traded status in the art market, an artwork is understood as something for which certain authorial rights could not be transferred or exploited based on a work's ownership.[25] Notably, this power granted to the author as an individual person is not reflected in copyright law, which considers the author as a producer; for instance, such moral rights would consider various contributors to a collaborative work such as a film as joint authors, whereas copyright law in the United States would consider such endeavors as hired labor, with the final work attributed to the producer or production company—which would allow for transferals of ownership if the corporation shifted hands.

It is these moral rights that dovetail with Kippenberger's artistic activities. As briefly outlined in the introduction, German moral rights have three general components: (1) the recognition of authorship secures legal protection over attribution—both to be rightly credited as the author over creative endeavors and to prevent others from falsely claiming credit for a given work; (2) the right of publication concerns the artist's intentionality over the completion of a work of art, awarding the author rights over whether and how to make a work public; (3) the right to integrity ensures that the work is not subject to misrepresentation, mutilation, or destruction in a manner that would harm the work or the creator's reputation.[26] In what follows, I argue that Kippenberger introduced three forms of interference into his relationship with his studio assistants to test the limits of each of these intellectual property rights, an approach that represents the third accomplice paradigm of this book.

### Error and the Recognition of Authorship

Beginning in 1987, Kippenberger adopted a new mode of social relations with auxiliary agents who worked exclusively within the Kippenberger studio. Yet their role was untraditional; instead of employing them as conventional art studio assistants, Kippenberger sought methods of enacting stoppages, exploitation, and missteps that would bring their presence into visibility. In this manner, failure was used by Kippenberger as an operative strategy for the squandered delegation of labor as well as a visual motif seen in his various forms of self-presentation. By dissipating or otherwise thwarting the efforts of his assistants through transgressions of their own intellectual contributions—in addition to his parodic embrace of the commercialization of art—Kippenberger's forms of enacted failure can be understood as a means of circumventing such mechanisms of celebrity while nonetheless becoming its beneficiary.

In 1987, Kippenberger showed more than forty-five sculptures together in an exhibition titled *Peter: Die russische Stellung* (*Peter: The Russian Position*), held at the Max Hetzler Gallery in Cologne (fig. 3.5). Most of the individual works consisted of various combinations of found and built elements that referenced at once industrial furniture, Minimalist objects, and workplace equipment such as filing cabinets, briefcases, shelving, and storage containers. Rather than organizing these hybrid structures according to conventional exhibition practices—in which they would be evenly spaced across a white cube gallery or within an architectural setting where they would be functionally oriented in relation to each other—here

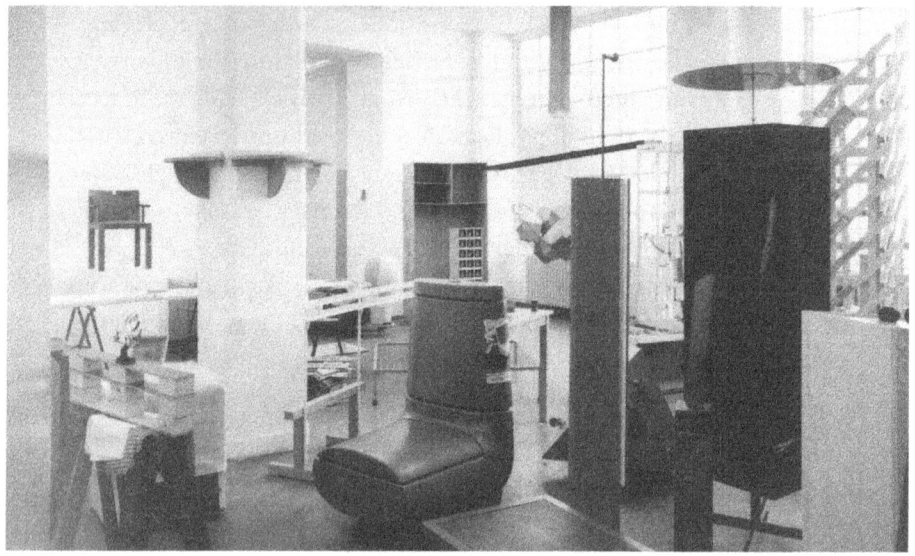

**3.05** Martin Kippenberger, *Peter: Die russische Stellung* (*Peter: The Russian Position*). Installation view, Galerie Max Hetzler, Cologne, Germany, 1987.

the objects appear haphazardly accumulated over the years, as if stumbled upon in a basement or attic.

Kippenberger conceived and produced the *Peter* works—his first major series of sculpture and the related corpus of drawings—primarily with his then assistant Michael Krebber. But the artistic labor in making the *Peter* sculptures was also shared among a wider network of associates: Kippenberger's other assistant, the lesser-known Barbara Schüttpelz; industrial and commercial fabricators, such as the Cologne-based Kunstgießerei Schweitzer; and an array of art and design luminaries such as Gerhard Richter, Aldo Rossi, and Walter De Maria.[27]

This project was significant in that it was the first example of Kippenberger's conceptual strategy in which he hired other individuals as paid studio assistants, in contrast to his more informal collaborations that occurred before 1987. Yet these assistants performed an atypical role: to independently generate and take responsibility for artwork that Kippenberger would ultimately claim exclusive ownership over—which was produced through various processes of error, stagnation, or failure. The determination of failure here is grounded in legal theory; I argue that Kippenberger sought to set his pseudo-corporate persona's trademark rights into direct opposition to his assistants' authorial rights in a deliberate attempt to stage violations that would rupture the cohesion of artistic celebrity and singular authorship as propagated in the 1980s commercial art market.

Much as Burden and Wilke predominantly developed structural circumstances to invoke the engagement of unwitting or unwilling participants in their performance-related practices, Kippenberger looked to his own network of associates in shifting their prescribed roles and functions. In contrast to art practices in which an artist instructs or hires other individuals to perform aspects of artistic labor under their exclusive direction (which includes Yoko Ono's *Instructions*, a set of directions by the artist that may be uniquely interpreted and executed by viewers; Christopher Williams's photographic outsourcing, resulting in the production of images for which he plays only a directorial role; and Félix González-Torres's sculptures, in which both audience and institutional participation are key in maintaining endless cycles of depletion and replenishment), Kippenberger developed strategies for undermining the efforts of those who were hired to assist him. This differed from his earlier projects that were not solely attributed to the artist (such as his collaborative work with Krebber, Oehlen, and Schlick) or those in which auxiliary agents were hired to execute specific tasks under direction from the artist. Instead, as Diedrich Diederichsen explains, Schüttpelz and Krebber had the job to "produce insufficiencies and obstacles, to make mistakes, to misunderstand and sidetrack the boss," in addition to traditionally productive contributions.[28]

Krebber and Kippenberger's working relationship began in 1987 when they were based for a period in Tenerife, Spain. During this time, the two developed a symbiotic practice, taking turns napping while the other produced sculptures. However, Krebber's role was not meant solely to fulfill Kippenberger's needs in the studio. Rather, as will be demonstrated in the following examples, Kippenberger deployed Krebber strategically by staging destructive or pseudo-accidental circumstances that would interrupt the planned execution of said projects. These interventions would arrest a given work within ongoing feedback loops as an "original" despite its networked authorial sources. In contrast to seamless transfers of manual labor to assistants, as in conventional studio practices, the manufacture of a unique creative act—through deliberate forms of error enacted by Kippenberger—wrests the work from the domain of straightforward intellectual property rights and into a potential transgression of what is known as the "recognition of authorship," governing a creator's right to be credited for their creative contributions.

The premeditated harnessing of chance, error, and manipulation was applied to strategic formulations of violence and demolition in the *Peter* sculptures. At times, Kippenberger directed his assistants to deliberately act on the artworks in ways that would augment the possibility of accident. A prime example of this can be found in the *Peter* sculpture titled *Worktimer* (1987; fig. 3.6), which comprised a turquoise modified industrial dolly with two leather school satchels attached to the front bars. Embedded into *Worktimer* was an element of humiliation, intended to demonstrate Kippenberger's authorial control over his assistants like Krebber. According to Carpenter, who humorously narrates many accounts of the Kippenberger assistants' experiences, in advance of the opening of the *Peter* exhibition Krebber was directed to

> go and meet the funfair scrap-metal collector guys who also helped with *Peter* and get laughed at. Then on the day of the opening . . . Kippenberger disappeared to the pub. So when the *Worktimer* piece didn't fit through the door and had to be sawed in half, it was Krebber who had to deal with the crisis and those horrible funfair guys, get it welded back together, then solemnly hang his own school satchels on the front. Then he would have to explain the meaning of the work to Diedrich Diederichsen for the catalogue essay. Kippenberger had somehow delegated both the conceptualizing and making of this work to Krebber, all he retained for himself was the name, the controller standing in the background, laughing.[29]

While Carpenter's account likely exaggerates the informality of Kippenberger's instructions, the accidental yet presumed result was an artwork that underwent a transformation from an object in which the artist's single subjective expression was articulated by a dutiful assistant to a process of splitting and resuturing that cleared away subjective associations to stage the manipulative social relations underlying its making.

Joshua Decter has described one of Kippenberger's primary operating philosophies of self-promotion as "frame yourself before you yourself are framed."[30] This concept of framing becomes an important part of Kippenberger's working procedure, as he actively sought to "frame" others in terms of transferring responsibility or legal accountability for their own experience of exploitation in not being credited for their work or failing

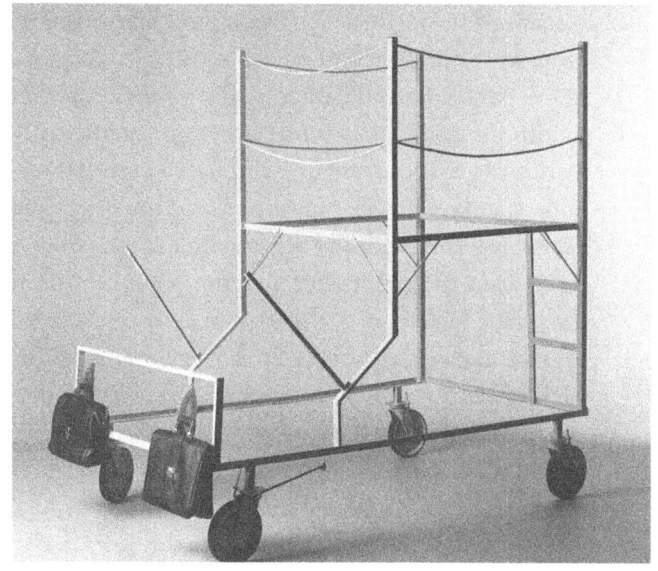

to perform their hired role, while "framing" or shaping the positive outcome of the completed artwork by his assistants as his own. As such, the way in which Krebber assumed all constitutive tasks in the conception and production of *Worktimer*—including explaining the meaning of the work to Diederichsen as if his own—calls into question his recourse to protections over his moral rights, particularly the recognition of authorship. Moreover, the questionable responsibility over one's intellectual property rights potentially shifts Krebber's role from that of a conventional studio assistant into that of Kippenberger's accomplice. While Krebber gave consent to Kippenberger for actions performed in the service of his work as an assistant, the deliberately exploitative components of Kippenberger's directives put the ethics of such actions in conflict with the rights of his assistants within the framework of continental intellectual property law that was in effect during the 1980s.

Kippenberger's introduction of strategic forms of error into the delegation of labor marks an evolution of the inquiries into issues around aesthetic ownership that emerged in late 1960s Conceptual art. Just as Conceptual art issued certificates, contracts, signatures, instructions, and other legal directives to guide the physical labor of others and affirm the authenticity of the art object, Kippenberger also sought legal recourse in determining the potential scope of his power as the nominal author. Like Burden and Wilke, however, Kippenberger belongs to a genealogy of artists who invert the logic of Conceptual art's interrogation of *objects* as artistic property to consider the limits of authorial agency over *subjects*.

Art dealer and Conceptualist impresario Seth Siegelaub played a significant role in presciently bringing together the previously distinct worlds of art and commerce through a legal framework. With a canny understanding of the implications for the often immaterial art that he dealt, Siegelaub skillfully began molding the public image of his artists, recognizing the importance of not only legalistic documentation but also the auratic "presence" of the artist in determining a work's authenticity. In 1971, he and lawyer Robert Projansky developed "The Artist's Reserved Rights Transfer and Sale Agreement," a legal contract meant to be used by artists to protect their economic rights, particularly over issues of the reproduction or resale of an artwork. Yet Siegelaub also looked toward possible alliances with commercial industry; he had developed in 1967 what was effectively a public relations company that would liaise between corporations and contemporary art in creating synergistic co-branding opportunities.[31] The connection between the legal and the commercial, which Siegelaub understood was mutually based on the artist's authority, expanded in subsequent decades, with artists like Kippenberger exploring its implications in their work.

In other *Peter* sculptures, Kippenberger ordered the unauthorized appropriation of works made by notable artists such as Gerhard Richter and Aldo Rossi. The best-known example of this is Kippenberger's *Model Interconti* (1987), an artwork that thwarted conventions of nominal authorship.[32] At first glance, the work appears to fit within the model of the generic, office-furniture style used throughout the installation. Yet this work has an important feature. Kippenberger purchased a 1972 *Grey* painting by Richter and transformed it into a functional component in one of his own *Peter* sculptures by adding metal legs and a wood frame. By wresting Richter's work from its existing circulation as a painting and refashioning it as the surface of a coffee table in a sculptural assemblage, the work (as it had been conceived by Richter) was effectively destroyed.

Through the procedure of *détournement*, Kippenberger's double appropriation (his appropriation of Krebber's appropriation of Richter) calls into question the singular valuation of the nominal artist, instead positing the authorial role to operate according to a process in which agents could enter in and out of the work while nominally remaining under Kippenberger's authority. Such a formulation recalls that of a corporate employer, which assumes copyright ownership of its workers' labor—a model that had been followed for celebrity branding. Given Richter's level of fame at the time, Kippenberger sought to both capitalize on the more famous artist's commodity status and explore a means of folding it into himself as a kind of devaluation of his "brand." Seen in this way, such a gesture—delegated to Krebber to execute as his accomplice—reveals Kippenberger's interest in testing the parameters of intellectual property rights, particularly concerning authorial attribution for Richter and Krebber's creative contributions.

In the *Peter* sculptures, Kippenberger directed Krebber to create artworks that used various appropriative procedures to scramble a direct line of accreditation, while adopting certain procedures of failure in the production process that would make his own presence visible. This was achieved by staging intentional accidents: distributing certain letters and notes to his assistants regarding alterations of details in the work without further communication, forcing them to translate Kippenberger's deliberately ambiguous concepts to third parties such as printers or fabricators, and rapidly executing directives through Kippenberger's accelerated mode of production. These circumstances were then accepted and readily incorporated into the work even when the artist did not preemptively plan for them. By stripping his assistants of agency, Kippenberger simulated a corporate model by which individual responsibility and intellectual labor become subsumed under the public image of the company.

Kippenberger's aesthetic strategy invites comparison with the changes to workplace structures that occurred during the 1980s, particularly concerning corporate leadership roles. Despite increased regulations of wages and time in newly enacted labor laws that preserved the postwar social contract in both the United States and West Germany, the confluence of "trickle-down" economic policies, increased globalization, outsourced manufacturing, changing education requirements, erosions of union bargaining power, and the advancement of digital technologies resulted in broad transformations of the workforce that were in favor of the private-sector corporation above all else. The younger generation of CEOs and corporate managers broke from the existing model of leadership, in which profit maximization and short-term earning potentials were balanced with social responsibilities for worker and community relations. Unlike the more equitable approach of many postwar-era managers, who sought to balance the interests of multiple stakeholders beyond only investors, CEOs in the 1980s assumed a more exploitative, rather than supportive, role, using managerial militancy to support the greatest financialization of corporations. It might then be said that Kippenberger internalized and parodied such a model of corporate power through his broader explorations of the limits around authorship, authority, and intellectual property.

Elaborating on Kippenberger's own formulation of himself as a "living vehicle," an animate machine through which input and output processes produced paintings, art historian Michael Sanchez describes how Kippenberger subsumed Krebber's identity under his own: "In place of a human machine and painting as its double, Kippenberger and Krebber constituted a system of two machines: MK1 (as Kippenberger called Krebber) and MK2 (as Kippenberger called himself)."[33] Using their shared initials as a way to blur the sovereign boundaries of artistic production while bringing the artistic output under a single designation associated with Kippenberger ("MK"), Kippenberger used the hierarchical numerical ordering strategically, with himself placed second behind Krebber as MK1 to express his role as recipient of another's labor.

Like a game of telephone, the relay of information staged by Kippenberger deliberately introduced error within a given artwork through the multiplication of authors and objects. In the *Peter* sculptures, the actions performed by Krebber inverted the typical role of the assistant, in which one alleviates the workload of the nominal artist while remaining subsumed under that authorial designation. Krebber was hired to complicate Kippenberger's artistic production processes, whether conceptually or physically. Diederichsen points out how, during the development stage of the *Peter* project—which was characterized by intense discussion and experimentation by the individuals involved in the piece—Krebber was specifically tasked with recalling information that Kippenberger had been told but since forgotten.[34] This, coupled with Kippenberger's deliberate attempts to divert, thwart, or muddle communication, marks a shift away from the efficient execution more typical of artist's assistants.

The *Peter* sculptures build upon earlier experimental projects developed in the 1980s that were centered on principles of value and waste, in that "successful" individual contributions were deliberately squandered to make visible Kippenberger's redefined authorial role as a ringleader of interruptive actions. This formulation of hierarchical yet ineffective artistic production can be productively compared to Gregory H. Williams's analysis of humor in West German art during the 1980s. In *Permission to Laugh*, Williams argues that Kippenberger, along with his contemporaries Oehlen and Büttner, adopted the logic and structure of the commonplace, quick-fire joke in their work to allow for a broad range of interpretive possibilities, whether through the prioritization of the speed of execution, the production of peripheral artistic media, or the emphasis on deliberate conflicts of meaning. While Williams locates such tendencies in Kippenberger's work, the specific configuration of the disjointed and unresolved joke setup that refuses clear meaning might also be found in Kippenberger's working procedures, in which he set up his assistant's *actions* to be at odds with one another. Williams points out how such humor "was more often than not tinged with a note of aggression"; indeed, the underlying nastiness of Kippenberger's enlistment of his assistants to enact forms of error and failure shares the mean-spirited form of a joke played at another's expense.[35] It is worth pausing at this point to note that the ease with which Kippenberger was able to assume a position of authoritative power—even when parodied through the guise of failure and performed delinquency—to enact strategic manipulations of others was only even possible on account of his privilege as a white middle-class German man, which mirrored the typical socioeconomic paradigm for corporate white-collar workers (and that of many of the Minimalist and Conceptual artists who adopted similar roles of outsourced labor in an art context).

Usurping Krebber's artistic labor by deliberate miscommunication, Kippenberger ostensibly reordered the hierarchies among Krebber, various fabricators, other contributors, and himself, creating an external stasis that masked the process of internal recycling that occurred among agents within the authorial field. Offering an insider's perspective as a fellow former assistant, Carpenter characterizes Krebber's experience as one of deliberate exploitation and mired with complications: "For example: go to the flea market outside Cologne, buy a table, some chairs and two suitcases full of junk and carry it all back into Cologne, not being able to afford any other transportation. And then do everything else, such as assist the photographer or the silk-screen guy all day, then come up with more ideas in the bar at night."[36] The result was that Krebber's artistic hand became dispersed among a variety of artworks and procedures that were considered "Kippenberger's," a distribution that would only become visible through mistakes or accidents that broke open the seamlessness of Kippenberger's authorial image. In addition to the darkness of the humor underlying this exploitation, such behaviors by Kippenberger also emphasized a particular form of masculinism found in models of artistic authority. Williams points out that Kippenberger presented an ambiguity toward the very notion of artistic creativity, writing that "if great artists of the past have often been singled out partly due to their abundant output and fertile imagination, Kippenberger's project was simultaneously to rival and lampoon these qualities."[37] In the *Peter* works, Krebber became the conduit for such output under the nominal artist's authority, yet both the very procedure of delegation and the deliberate staging of circumstances to provoke interruptions ultimately mocked such models of the male artist while further reaffirming Kippenberger's ultimate control.

This intentional staging of circumstances in which the assistants would produce (un)expected inaccuracies also appeared in other works. For example, Kippenberger hired Brian Tucker, an American who had no knowledge of the German language, to assist on his series of *Fred the Frog* paintings (1988–90). These works feature a cartoonish amphibian in various states of crucifixion, often holding a mug of beer amid fragments of text and recognizable visual motifs such as a fried egg or Coca-Cola bottle. The phrases had been preselected by Kippenberger and Oehlen, often banal single-word descriptors such as "understand" or technical terms referring to aspects of a painting, such as "color" or "background." Tucker's task was to transcribe these German phrases onto the canvases, which themselves were often made by another individual. As was expected, this resulted in numerous misspellings or nonsensical grammatical errors due to Tucker's lack of German comprehension (for example, the word *Doppeldeutich* has no translation in either language). As Kirsty Bell points out, Kippenberger knowingly invited the prospect of failure at this task: "the words were chosen from a scrawled list and set in different typefaces, sometimes misspelt . . . thus creating a layer of chance and embedded mistakes like those that came to animate the *Peter* sculptures."[38] The likelihood of failure was laid bare in Kippenberger's direction, as he tasked the assistant who would be the least, rather than the most, successful at transcribing German. This intended malfunctioning of communication removed any notion of the words serving an expressive or subjective purpose; rather, like the painting itself, they become hollow.

In the *Peter* sculptures and *Fred the Frog* paintings, Kippenberger adopted the externalized distribution of labor that he first developed in the 1980s and applied it to those working within his own studio. Although he expanded the constellation of participatory agents through the incorporation of works made by well-known artists, he also included references within the *Peter* sculptures that opened the series to a self-referential feedback loop, one purposely situated within the closed constellation of assistants. As noted by Bell, Kippenberger and his assistants "developed an obscure, bastardized form of DIY, whereby many of the works were derived from a conscious cultivation of mistakes that occurred in communications between each other and the various fabricators."[39] In other words, when Kippenberger deliberately created circumstances that resulted in his assistants failing to execute his stated artistic intentions, he exposed their role as accomplices to his potential exploitation of the moral rights governing authorial recognition of others.

If the recognition of authorship was meant to protect the intellectual property rights of those who make creative contributions to an artwork, the way in which Kippenberger staged error and claimed authorship over the unique contributions of his assistants tested the limits of these legal rights within the framework of the artist as a corporate brand, in which all labor performed within the scope of one's job becomes subsumed under the company's output. By enacting consciously interruptive actions, Kippenberger consolidated authorial intentionality (rather than offering a distributed and open-ended working model in which new work is collaboratively generated), thereby thrusting his influence as the "master" nominal artist back into the spotlight.

## Residual Individuality and the Right of Publication

Beyond the principle of error as a critical strategy to interrupt the typically closed system of authorship, Kippenberger also explored a tactic of outsourcing highly individual and subjective features—such as gestural brushwork, personal memories, or handwritten text—to complicate the seamless transfer of responsibility in each work as well as the self-contained nature of the authorial subject. In contrast to the *Peter* sculptures, the projects discussed in this section demonstrate Kippenberger's use of distributed labor in other ways, particularly how he exploited aspects of others' individual identities, thereby complicating conventions of personal expression and potentially violating their ability to manage their own subjective output. The two main examples are representative of how Kippenberger developed various forms of what I term residual individuality—his own, those belonging to well-known artists, and unknown "assistants"—to interrupt the remediation and delegation processes by exposing the network of authors embedded in artworks through legal transgressions of the moral right of publication in German intellectual property law.

In his "Picasso" self-portraits (1988), which were notably produced without an assistant, Kippenberger integrated the public image of a canonical artist into his own self-presentation to disrupt the presumption of interiority and personal expression embedded in the genre of self-portraiture. In the *Weisse Bilder* (*White Paintings*) (1991), Kippenberger reversed the typical hierarchy of assignments by personally adopting the assistant role himself and conferring creative authority on a second individual, notably a small child who was thoroughly removed from the artistic process in a conventional sense. Together these works demonstrate how Kippenberger sought means of evacuating his own interiority and subjectivity by exploiting the "residual individuality" of others in the service of his own artistic aims.

As much as he sought to propagate his persona, Kippenberger notably often cultivated it in negative terms—a marked contrast from his contemporaries that signaled an underlying critical approach within his outward willingness to promote himself at all costs. The artist developed alter egos whose images were largely based on failure; this undesirable perspective figured prominently in his painting practice in particular. His earliest self-portraits assumed nonheroic representations of the artist, couched in painterly tropes of Neo-Expressionism such as thickly layered impasto and dramatic compositions that purportedly expressed the artist's subjective experience. For instance, Kippenberger produced a body of self-portraits in the early 1980s, such as *Alcohol Torture* (1981–82) and *Dialogue with the Youth of Today* (1981), that depicted him inebriated and handcuffed by the plastic packaging rings of beer cans, or badly beaten and bandaged, presumably due to drunken antics gone wrong.

In 1988, Kippenberger took a slightly different tactic, creating a body of self-portraits that play on the public image of artist Pablo Picasso—whom David W. Galenson suggests is likely the first artist of the twentieth century to actively promote and embrace his own celebrity.[40] While in Vienna for an exhibition at the Wiener Festwochen in the spring of 1988, Kippenberger took a series of photographic self-portraits in his low-budget Pension Elite hotel room that became the source material for a wide range of interrelated projects, including a painting series and a set of handmade drawings, which were further reproduced and circulated as posters and invitation cards for exhibitions. Working from a famous set of photographs of Picasso in his studio taken by David Douglas Duncan, an American photojournalist and war photographer who documented the final two decades of Picasso's life in the south of France beginning in 1956, Kippenberger improvised means of modeling himself after Picasso, adopting similar poses and wardrobe so that the source material would be made evident to the viewer. Yet Kippenberger also presented key visual differences that created an imprecise mapping of himself onto the authorial persona of the influential artist.

Kippenberger's performative photographs first appeared as ELITE '88, a dual-sided spiral-bound calendar that had been produced for the 1988 calendar year in an edition of twenty-seven with five artist's proofs. The pages alternated between these representations of the artist adopting unremarkable and rather sad poses among dilapidated hotel room furniture paired with small white lettering marking the various months and full-page images of unpopulated buildings. Kippenberger had already used exact copies of Duncan's original 1962 photographs of Picasso in promotional material for his own exhibitions, such as those advertising his 1985 show at the Galería Leyendecker in Tenerife. The irony that Duncan's photographs were initially taken in Tenerife prompted Kippenberger to collapse the identities between the two artists, at once exploiting the celebrity of the modernist hero while positioning his own name alongside the reproduced image.

While these 1988 photographs were distributed independently, they became best known for being used as the source material for ten untitled painted self-portraits. The paintings are characterized by a reduced color palette, minimal compositional elements, and three recurring motifs: the depiction of Kippenberger clad only in underwear (in accordance with Picasso's self-presentation in the source photographs), painted reproductions of four of his *Peter* sculptures (*Wittgenstein*, *Worktimer*, *Hausbar Simone de*, and *Peterkasten*), and the presence of a multivalent balloon-mirror hybrid, which was often used in these paintings to allude to the authorial doubling that occurs on the levels of both intellectual and physical production.[41]

Kippenberger's interest in generating his personal celebrity coincided with the explosion of branding that emerged in the art and commercial worlds during the 1980s. As noted by curator Gianni Jetzer, whose 2018 exhibition *Brand New: Art and Commodity in the 1980s* at the Hirshhorn Museum and Sculpture Garden explored such themes, the connection between branding and identity "developed most rapidly in the 1980s, when contemporary art, once a hermeneutic circle, became big business, and artists came not just to accept but to revel in the commerce of art."[42] Artists and corporations alike sought means of fashioning memorable—and marketable—public identities that could capitalize on the economic boom of the so-called Greed decade, during which Wall Street traders often spent their new fortunes on contemporary art. In contrast to the Conceptualist legacy of "dematerialized" art in the 1970s, demand for saleable artworks grew in the subsequent decade—and the market responded in kind.

A set of artists whose work fit such capitalist demands—being immediately recognizable with an obvious signature style or familiar "trademark," using traditional mediums like painting or sculpture that were easily marketable for domestic settings, and a return of markers denoting the "hand" of the artist—were catapulted into art stars. So-called Neo-Expressionist artists such as Francesco Clemente, Anselm Kiefer, David Salle, and Julian Schnabel—as well as Jeff Koons, Cindy Sherman, and Jean-Michel Basquiat—became celebrities, both within and beyond the art world.[43] Public interest in these artists' lives was intertwined with interest in their art, with their activities profiled in magazines ranging from *Vanity Fair* to *Interview* and their likenesses used in mainstream advertisements or fashion spreads to sell nonart products. As John A. Walker points out in his 2003 examination of art and celebrity, even the promotion of art openings, exhibitions, and related events became part of the broader category of "entertainment," further linking the image of the artist with traditional formulations of mainstream celebrity culture.[44]

At the same time, interest in the artists themselves expanded in accordance with the rising prices and demands for contemporary art. This was perpetuated by an increasing number of appearances by the artists in culture and lifestyle magazines such as *Interview*, which presented such individuals as "personalities" much like film and television stars. In a 1985 article in *ARTnews*, Deborah Phillips astutely noted: "As artists become the subjects of increasing media hype, high visibility and upward mobility are defining their lives. What they wear and where they eat, live and play, as much as the art they make, are topics that attract the seemingly insatiable curiosity of a starstruck public."[45] Returning to notions of artistic "aura," the artist's presence regained value for the art market. For instance, collectors began specifically requesting to only purchase photographs that featured Sherman as sitter; in response, the artist decided not to reveal—even to her longtime gallery representatives at Metro Pictures—in which images she was physically present.[46]

This focus on artistic branding and developing signature trademarks can be contextualized within the recent history concerning transformations of authorial property. Both Buskirk and Alexander Alberro have convincingly articulated how the shift away from the art object and the corresponding removal of the artist's visible "hand" in late 1960s Conceptual art did not result in diminishing authorial power or creating a more democratic, decommodified form of creative expression, as might be assumed.[47] Rather, Buskirk argues that the delegation of labor and other administrative processes for what she calls "contingent objects" in fact *reaffirmed* the need for the artist's presence, whereas Alberro identifies how such "dematerialization" in fact allowed for a more seamless assimilation into the art market. The implications of this transformation in the status of the art object can be taken one step further, however; as can be seen in the rise of the celebrity artist in the 1980s, the absence of a physical entity in creative production meant that artists *themselves* might assume such a role in becoming commodified subjects.

Kippenberger understood the implications of this transformation. He took the reaffirmation of authorial power and administrative logic of Conceptual art—a point made by art historian Benjamin H. D. Buchloh, who pronounced Conceptual art an "aesthetics of administration"—to outsource much of his intellectual or creative contributions to assistants as if a corporate company, then fed its output through the contemporary market demands for Expressionistic art.[48] Yet, by structuring such a paradigm on deliberately *unsuccessful* forms of delegated labor, Kippenberger parodied the way in which the artists' public artistic personas became treated as corporate entities during this period, while also using it to achieve his own celebrity.

For instance, *Untitled* (1988; fig. 3.7) features an unflattering portrait of the artist—overweight, disproportioned, and rendered in a sickly blue-hued skin tone—on the right side of the composition. His left hand holds a string attached to the bottom of an oversized gray balloon, which dominates the center background of the image. His right hand is placed on the side of the *Peter* sculpture *Worktimer*, a modified industrial dolly with two of Krebber's leather school satchels attached to the front bars. Within the sculpture's frame is the "Sun-Breasts-Hammer" logo of the Lord Jim Lodge, the trademark of the art collaborative cofounded by Kippenberger and used by many of its members.

While this work features multiple references to other artworks, social networks, and individuals, the most distinctive feature is the representation of the artist in the image of Picasso, mediated by Kippenberger's performative photographs. Working from the well-known images of the artist taken at Villa La Californie in 1957, Kippenberger adopted key details yet resisted a cohesive self-presentation, as suggested by the genre of

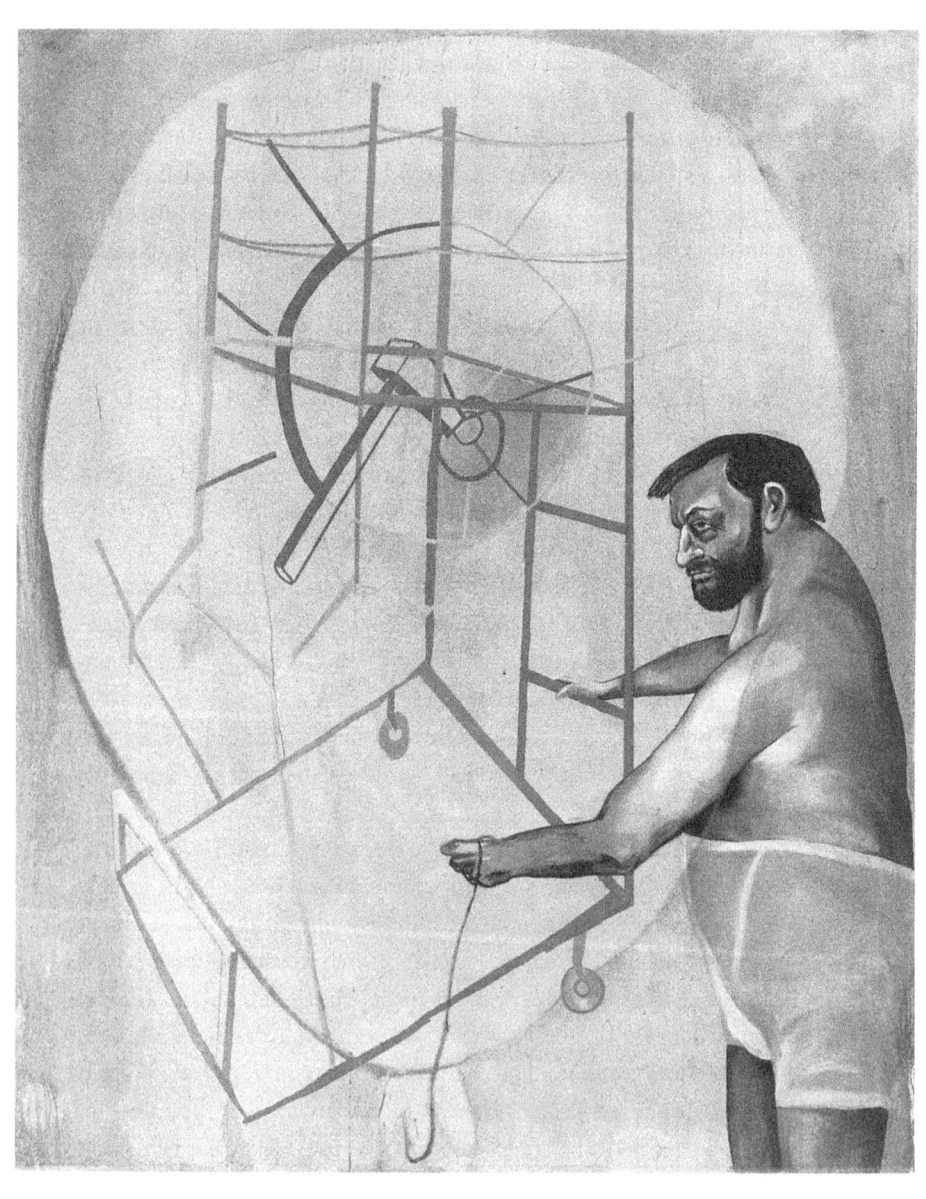

**3.07**  Martin Kippenberger, *Untitled*, 1988. Oil on canvas, 94½ × 78¾ in.

self-portraiture. For example, in contrast to the seventy-five-year-old Picasso's virility, physical prowess, and seemingly innate confidence, Kippenberger offers an unabashed depiction of a relatively young thirty-five-year-old artist whose battle with alcoholism and itinerant, freewheeling lifestyle had taken its obvious toll. Picasso's underwear-cum-bathing suit reflects carefree days spent along the Mediterranean coast in Cannes, while Kippenberger's adoption of such attire within the context of his dingy hotel room presents a more tragic figure. Here, the artist's grotesque self-presentation within the guise of Picasso displayed an ambiguity between self-deprecation and self-aggrandizement, often in equal yet contradictory measures. For Williams, this was a conscious decision, as he writes: "Kippenberger could depict the overweight, feeble-looking body of the male artist in his self-portraits as a means toward exploring the traditional link between masculinity and authenticity."[49]

This element of failure recurs in Kippenberger's work, both in the artist's unflattering self-representations and in terms of how he used others, notably his assistants, by exploiting their deliberate malfunctions. In the "Picasso" paintings, Kippenberger models himself after an artist who achieved the pinnacle of critical and commercial success, yet his self-negation of such empowerment, seen in his own puerile representation, probes an alternative model of "success" based on failure and exploitation. While curator Ann Goldstein has interpreted Kippenberger's actions as having "mastered the act of 'failing up' not through this own incompetence, or even that of others, but through a savvy and strategic application of the oppositional and incongruous," the role that failure plays within tasks performed by other individuals—notably his assistants—is critical to understanding the structures and aims of his work.[50] Adopting failure as an alternative working strategy for labor performed within an artist's studio offers a mechanism for altogether evading conventional and largely pretentious forms of valuation and success, which had been glorified in the 1980s; as Ralph Rugoff noted in the catalog essay for the 1990 group show *Just Pathetic* (which featured the work of Burden, John Miller, Mike Kelley, Raymond Pettibon, and others), "To be pathetic, in other words, is to be a loser, haplessly falling short of the idealized norm."[51] According to Kelley, this embrace of ineptitude was integral to Kippenberger's work and practice, as he "was not much interested in producing works of 'quality.' In fact, he strove to create works that had an aura of failure about them."[52]

This can be seen structurally in *Untitled*, where Kippenberger presents appropriated imagery that refers to himself, his assistants, and his sculpture, creating a system of representations that does not serve to depict an external reality that is being transcribed within the field of painting but rather a network of references to be understood within and through each other. In 1980, Craig Owens offered an important theorization of what he termed the "allegorical impulse" in art, in which "one text is *read through* another, however fragmentary, intermittent, or chaotic their relationship may be; the paradigm for the allegorical work is thus the palimpsest."[53] For Owens, the return to allegorical imagery seen in appropriation practices signaled a shift from the modernist notion of the artwork as universal and expressive to the postmodern, in which visual art is immersed within a network of intertextuality and multiple meanings. He defines allegory in contemporary art as an image that carries a second narrative or meaning within its outward appearance; he writes about the work of Troy Brauntuch, Sherrie Levine, and other artists for whom "the appropriated image may be a film still, a photograph, a drawing; it is often itself already a reproduction. However, the manipulations to which these artists subject such images work to empty them of their resonance, their significance, their authoritative claim to meaning."[54]

Kippenberger's self-portraits such as *Untitled* operate according to the logic of a failed allegory, as he created an image in which his public persona was "read through" Picasso by incorporating key attributes of his predecessor—but he notably combined them in a nonintegrated manner so that such references piled up as fragments without resolution.[55] That is, the differences between the "model" and "artist" are accentuated more than the correspondence between them. Therefore, the model of appropriation found in Kippenberger's work in exploiting Picasso's residual individuality operates according to far more cynical, desperate, and ironic principles than those found in the work described by Owens. By casting himself in the mythologized persona of Picasso, Kippenberger both upgraded his image by associating with a leading art-world celebrity and downgraded himself by presenting his body in an unbecoming light with a worn-down physicality and saggy underpants. In so doing, he offered a failed allegory in which the layered effect that typically coalesces in an image remains disjointed and insufficient so that the various components can't be readily read through each other. For Kippenberger, then, the genre of self-portraiture became a vehicle through which he was best able to imprecisely superimpose his own authorial identity onto that of a successfully famous artist while destabilizing the expressionistic and subjective associations of his paintings.

Kippenberger's sustained focus on extending his self-presentation through what might be perceived as personal gestures or details by viewers that were in fact appropriated presents a radically different model of authorship from that of other contemporary artists for whom assistants also play a critical role in the art production process. For instance, in 1996 Takashi Murakami launched his Hiropon Factory, which was based on an atelier model that has roots in traditional Japanese art-making practices as well as animation (anime) and comic (manga) studios. In 2001, he expanded by formally incorporating his studio enterprise as Kaikai Kiki Co. Ltd. in Japan and New York (with a branch later established in Los Angeles in 2010) and opening the scope of his endeavors to include promotional offices, galleries, merchandise production, and offices for the management of emerging artists. Murakami's establishment of an art corporation that employs hundreds of studio assistants (around three hundred globally is a recent estimate) and fabricators serves the needs of his large-scale and highly detailed work. Following duties listed on dry-erase boards and retiring to formal break rooms when not working, Murakami's assistants perform highly specific tasks that seamlessly blend into the artist's signature "Superflat" style.

In contrast, Kippenberger consciously selected certain figures as his formal (or, at times, informal) assistants and maintained a much tighter studio enterprise. Unlike Murakami (and other artists using similar working models, such as Koons), Kippenberger was particularly interested in using the intellectual labor of his assistants and testing the lengths to which they would go in their employment. While these artists shared a similar celebrity status that was deliberately cultivated, Kippenberger maintained a distinct interest in how subjects working under his nominal authority could be manipulated as an alternative form of aesthetic property or material. Notably, this antagonistic position was practiced by a white male artist, whose identity closely mirrored established models of corporate authority such as CEOs in Western Europe and the United States during this time.

In his *Weisse Bilder* series, Kippenberger recalibrated the process of appropriation by transforming an unofficial "assistant" into a source of content for the work while also restricting the expressive components of the contributions to be obtained from his own previous actions. As with many of Kippenberger's projects, the labor for this series of paintings shuttled between himself and an auxiliary agent, in this case, a nine-year-old child. According to Manfred Hermes, the work was formulated when Kippenberger had shown some of his own exhibition catalogs to a neighbor's son in Graz, where he was visiting in the winter of 1990–91.[56] He asked the boy to describe the reproduced artworks in his own words and then transcribe his responses onto graph paper used for school exercises. These included a range of descriptive yet superficial phrases such as "A beautiful house by the sea" or "A poor boy being happy finally being allowed to drink a Coca-Cola." Each was followed by the simple exclamation "Sehr Gut," often concluding with an exclamation mark. This phrase was already familiar within Kippenberger's practice as it was the driving principle behind the destruction of the *Heavy Burschi* paintings that Kippenberger found to be "too good" as replicas of his own image back catalog. He then projected the boy's writing onto white canvases, using glossy matching paint to execute the handwritten notes. Depending on their dimensions, many of these paintings did not accommodate the entire projected text and therefore words and phrases were often cut off midway, suggesting a spontaneously generated rendering on the canvas that masks the preplanned process of its production.

This project is notable because Kippenberger gave existing artworks to the child as the foundation to create personal responses that would then be mobilized in the production of more artwork under the Kippenberger name. Yet this series also marked a shift in the artist-assistant relationship from Krebber's aesthetic freedom hijacked by Kippenberger to a production model closer to the *Lieber Maler* paintings, in which he limited and predefined the parameters within which an auxiliary agent could creatively act. The outsourcing of artistic labor to a small child is a strategy of deskilling to create a kind of ersatz manual virtuosity and authenticity through the inclusion of personalized messages and gestural brushwork suggestive of a unique artistic hand. Moreover, the relations of authorship are further scrambled: the boy's commentary is based on paintings listed in the exhibition catalog made by Kippenberger or his assistants, some of which offered a standard model of painterly subjectivity through the gestural brushstroke and others that extended the relay of distributed responsibility.

By copying the boy's handwriting, itself a social marker of individuality, Kippenberger shuttles "ownership" of the painting's presumed subjectivity both toward and against himself. As noted by Hermes, "the technique of appropriation and associatively condensed cross-linkages, references, and connotations is applied in this work no less intensively than in his others, it is only better concealed."[57] In every painting, the prescribed phrase runs counter to the appearance of individual expression and spontaneity expressed by the personalized handwriting and descriptive yet vacant phrases. The inauthenticity of the remarks—made by a child who gives a nondifferentiated evaluation of all the works by repeating the "very good" designation for each one—interrupts the appearance of the painting as a pure and unmediated interface between the viewer and the artist's subjectivity. Given that the boy was a minor and did not work for Kippenberger, pressure was provocatively placed on his moral rights—which cannot be transferred or waived, and indefinitely remain with the creator for the scope of their contributions—governing the agency over his performed labor.

In many artworks made at the end of the 1980s and early 1990s, Kippenberger consciously appropriated features of residual individuality from a variety of sources that appeared to reveal the expression of his own interiority but in fact parodied the performativity of artistic identity in the creation of a mythologized artistic persona. Yet this process of appropriation on the level of both authors and images in fact emptied out artistic subjectivity from such works, resulting in an externalized public identity for the artist that became effectively excavated and aggrandized. Given the predilection for economically valuing the uniqueness of painting over reproducible media such as photography, particularly in the historical context of the Neo-Expressionist-driven 1980s and early 1990s art market, Kippenberger adapted painting as a medium to be divested of its associations with the projection of subjectivity or interiority and to instead serve as a site to test the outermost limits of others' performed labor that could be folded within an authorial position.

### Waste and the Right to Integrity

Following Krebber's departure to pursue his own artistic career in 1989, Kippenberger hired Merlin Carpenter as his new assistant. He sought to find someone who could work according to the previously used principles of delegation and remediation but also wanted to introduce new processes of creative production that could further test the scope of his authority as the nominal artist. As described at the outset of this chapter, one of Carpenter's first tasks was to work on the *Heavy Burschi* collages and subsequent paintings—generating new compositions mimicking his employer's artistic style, which were produced from extant materials sourced from both within and outside Kippenberger's studio. In perhaps the most memorable component of the multifaceted work, Carpenter's paintings were exhibited only as photographic reproductions and in battered or otherwise mutilated form contained in a dumpster.

As Sanchez explains, Carpenter's position in the chain of production was quite different from Krebber's. In contrast to Krebber's assignments to produce his own independent creations, which the nominal artist then appropriated and subsumed under his authority, Carpenter instead received Kippenberger's artistic output as the source material from which to generate further works under the Kippenberger name.[58] Such efforts were, at times, deliberately squandered by overcomplicated and thwarted executions enacted by a secondary set of subassistants, generating a nonproductivity defined here as "waste." "I couldn't give Kippenberger my ideas fast enough," Carpenter recalled. "I needed his assistance to dispose of them."[59] As such, Kippenberger's unproductive interventions into the delegation of creative tasks infringed on a specific legal concern of his assistants like Carpenter: that of the right to integrity, which protects against intentional distortions of one's creative endeavors in an artwork.

Waste was a recurring theme throughout Kippenberger's career, even outside his use of assistants. For instance, in his first painting series begun in 1976, *Uno di voi, un tedesco in Firenze* (*One of You, a German in Florence*), Kippenberger planned to present his eighty-four grisaille painted canvases as a 189-centimeter-high stack, thereby "wasting" the compositional details of the work to instead function as sculptural components. Similarly, the METRO-net World Connection project that he began in 1993 comprised a series of full-scale subway entrances—produced both as portable renditions and site-specific works installed at locations across the globe, including Dawson City, Canada, and Syros, Greece— that led nowhere. Deliberate formulations of waste also appeared in many of his *Peter* sculptures. One such example of the reuse of Kippenberger's earlier projects in the *Peter* works is found in *Hinten ist noch ein Loch frei* (*There's Still an Empty Hole at the Back*) (1987), a mixed-media sculpture in which a standard gray school locker underwent a series of modifications that rendered it unusable, such as the removal of three circular portions of the back end of the structure so that objects placed inside could be readily taken off the interior shelves. In *Not to Be the Second Winner* (1987), Kippenberger wrested Aldo Rossi's famed "Teatro Chair" from its circulation as a functional design object, directed his assistants to place it on a white pedestal, and drilled a series of holes into its wooden frame, rendering the chair's legs and back support weak and unstable. This delegation of labor produced a dynamic in which nonproductive or strategically ineffective elements (such as adding holes to weaken the strength of the chair) were used and reformulated as constructive within Kippenberger's authorial identity, while violating the original creators' inherent moral right to have their works remain intact.

Such a counterintuitive representation of the assistant is similarly explored by philosopher Giorgio Agamben in his essay "The Assistants." For Agamben, the role of the assistant represents "the measure of oblivion and ruin, the ontological waste that we carry within ourselves."[60] Looking to Franz Kafka's novels, children's fairy tales, and Sufi *wuzara'* (helpers), Agamben articulates the incomplete and displaced subjects of the assistants, who exist relationally to a primary subject—much like Kippenberger's assistants, who become exploited and subsumed into his authorial identity. As Agamben points out, the assistants might be expected to provide assistance, yet "help seems to be the last thing they are able to give."[61] The nonproductive nature of their labor, then, allows for their obsolescence: "These figures are forgotten by the narrator by the end of the story when the protagonists go on to live happily ever after. We learn nothing more about them, this unclassifiable 'crew' to whom, at bottom, the main characters owe everything."[62]

This formulation can be compared to Kippenberger's dissipation of his assistants' energies, yet the accomplice paradigm presents a formulation of assistants that does not ultimately result in neglect or desertion. The assistants-turned-accomplices become visible because of the ethical or legal disobedience conducted under Kippenberger's direction; this interference into the flow of labor delegation shifts their role into a new space beyond that of a subordinate helper. In the case of Carpenter, whose right to integrity was repeatedly broken as a governing principle of his wasted labor in Kippenberger's studio—one may immediately think of the destruction of his paintings in *Heavy Burschi*—the record of his squandered work became dependent on his own articulation of the circumstances, as seen in his *Texte zur Kunst* essay, which opened this chapter.

While living in Los Angeles between 1989 and 1990, Kippenberger commissioned the California-based artist Mikel Alatza to create a series of paintings. For $500, Alatza created a large-scale portrait of Kippenberger, rendered in a moody dark-greenish tone that permeates the entirety of the canvas. The sitter is depicted in three-quarter profile against an abstract background of red and green swaths of paint. While his head is oriented toward the viewer, his eyes are cast to the side. Yet rather than being adopted by Kippenberger, this work was ultimately used only as an underpainting. It subsequently endured a series of modifications, including alterations to the color palette, the addition of phrases rendered in varying fonts, and the insertion of a large green depiction of "Fred the Frog" with his signature beer can, likely made by Kippenberger's assistant Tucker. The multiple levels of image appropriation and shared labor in this series—whether in terms of the reuse of images or the deliberate squandering of the work solicited from Alatza by directing an assistant to paint over it—resulted in paintings that foreground the social relations of their making as purposely wasteful.[63] By delegating forms of labor to his network of associates, including Tucker and Alatza, Kippenberger redefined his artistic role as one based on forms of interruption rather than pure propagation, forcing each assistant to violate another's integrity rights over their creative contributions.

During the time of Kippenberger's move from Los Angeles back to Germany in 1990, he produced a set of sixty works known as the *Latex Paintings* (1989–90), which introduced a more complex application of delegated labor than had been previously seen in his work. Kippenberger hired multiple individuals to share in the responsibility for the production, yet this dispersal broke the direct one-to-one relations between assistant and artist, often impeding the successful execution of a given work. This problematized any notion of individuality since each contributor undermined the other's input. By multiplying assistants, Kippenberger exacerbated an ineffectual process of inertia in which one person's inputs were undermined by those made by others. It was precisely this formulation of wasted labor—exploiting one another's right to integrity under direction from Kippenberger—that turned such assistants into potential accomplices.

The paintings themselves were executed according to a decentralized process of production. First, Kippenberger adopted a familiar model of labor in which works were generated by directing his assistants Tucker and Jory Felice, who were based in Los Angeles with Carpenter, to work collaboratively on creating a set of paintings with subject matter taken from Kippenberger's past exhibition catalogs, such as his "Picasso" self-portraits, *Fred the Frog*, and *Preis* paintings. The resulting paintings were then sent to Germany, where another Kippenberger assistant, Ulrich Strothjohann, was instructed to cover them with latex skins over the entirety of their surfaces, creating a protective sheath that obstructed visual access to the compositions below. Effectively pitting assistants against each other, Kippenberger broke the artistic labor into two temporal and material halves that resulted in a stalemate: rather than creating a hierarchy, the relationship between these assistants was organized so that everyone's labor canceled out what came prior while perpetuating the forward momentum of Kip-

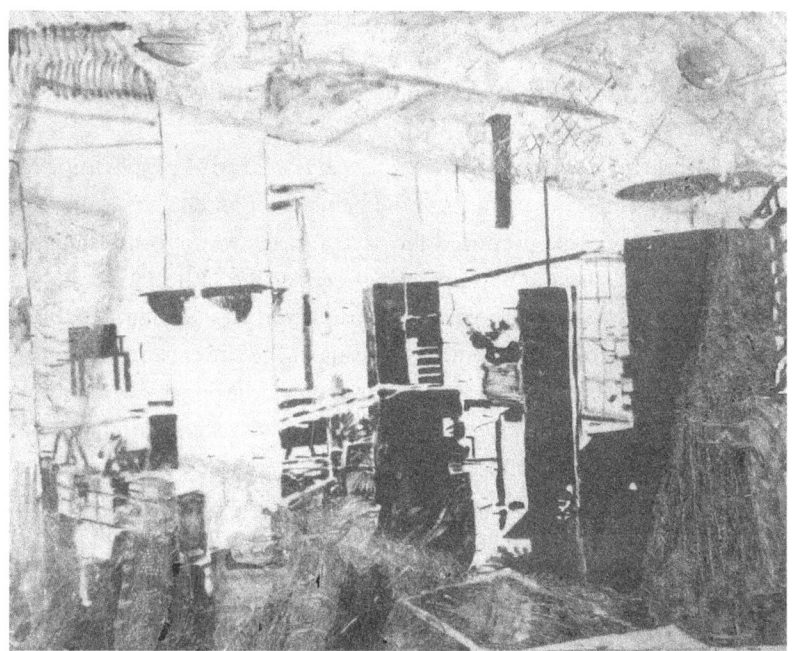

**3.08**   Martin Kippenberger, *Peter*, 1990. Oil, acrylic, and latex on canvas, 94½ × 78¾ in.

penberger's outward persona. The result can be characterized as a dynamic equilibrium of nominal authorship perpetually reinforced by disjunction in the production processes and images themselves.

Largely self-referential, *Peter* (1990; fig. 3.8) comprises a painting by Carpenter that was itself based on a 1987 installation photograph of *Peter: The Russian Exhibition*. Here, Carpenter transferred the image to a painting, yet this underlying illustration was obscured through the addition of the latex sheath by Strothjohann. Rather than achieving the high-gloss texture most typically associated with the material, here the latex took on a textured, yellowed cast that gave the surface a weathered appearance. Such a gesture transformed Krebber's initial labor in conceiving of and creating the *Peter* sculptures as well as Carpenter's contributions in creating the underpainting. Given that it is unlikely either assistant gave their explicit approval for such distortions to their creative endeavors, such actions suggest a possible violation of the moral right to integrity. Yet as this labor was conducted while working within the studio of the artist, such actions remained lawfully permissible, if not ethically suspect. By using his assistants in this way, Kippenberger sought to bring the network of his accomplices into visibility, thereby dismantling the illusion of the sovereign, independent creator in art while nonetheless internalizing such a model for his own desire for fame and fortune.

While for Kirsty Bell the latex serves as a "kind of prophylactic for the audience, shielding them from the paintings' content," it also reveals the social network that produced the paintings as a way of controlling the visibility of the assistants' underpaintings, reasserting authorial hierarchies by stymieing their work through a semiopaque surface.[64] Along these lines, Manfred Hermes offers a significant reading of the latex coatings as metaphorical condoms, used by Kippenberger to block the possibility of unique reproduction by his assistants.[65] Here, Kippenberger's manipulation of "paternity" rights over authorial recognition is literalized in the latex painting *Sperm* (1990), in which "sperm cells" are painted on top of the phrase "FALSARETESTESSO" (Italian for "Fake Yourself") in white lettering on a red background; a coating of latex covers the entire surface of the composition, leaving a yellowish cast. Here, Kippenberger's reference to sperm, a bodily fluid that carries the singular genetic material of men, parodies the overtly masculine displays of painting as seen in the work of Jackson Pollock, whose heroic, virile image was tied to the dramatic ejaculatory applications of dripped or splattered paint—which was also wittily satirized by Warhol in his semen-covered canvases known as the *Cum* paintings from 1977 to 1978. Despite the fact that Warhol outsourced obtaining his chosen material of bodily fluid—one of Warhol's employees, Victor Hugo, reportedly hired "assistants" by the hour at various bathhouses in downtown New York for such a task—Kippenberger's approach was once again based on the squandered waste of his assistants' energies. He used latex to impede the visual transmission of the assistants' underpaintings, rendering them artistically impotent, while he "successfully" produced the finished *Latex Paintings*.

In the *Latex Paintings*, Kippenberger sets up a relay of production centered on principles of rejection and dissipation. In creating a chain of labor among his multiple assistants in which each works against each other's prior contributions, paintings undergo various transformations that split the "authenticity" of the finished artwork as the product of Kippenberger. The phrase "fake yourself"—which appears as a running theme throughout many of the *Latex Paintings*—announces this calculated disruption of authorial identity. Bell describes the logic of this terminology: "A compressed tautology is at work here, as Kippenberger reproduces a version of his own work—fakes himself—while revealing this fact at the same time. But beyond this literal interpretation is the fact that this exhortation—to fake yourself—is what drives his reach for posterity: a continual reassertion and reinvention of his artistic persona, aimed at guaranteeing himself a legacy that can exist independently of his work."[66] For Sanchez, this question of authenticity is directed toward the assistants, which resulted in an artwork with an indeterminate status: "a fake is an unauthorized reproduction of another artist's work. By ordering his assistants to fake themselves, Kippenberger confronted them with a double bind: neither authorized nor unauthorized, neither their own work nor a reproduction of Kippenberger's."[67] This feedback loop of seemingly forward motion becomes perpetually co-opted, exemplifying waste as one of three tactics used strategically to disrupt the cycle of remediation while also redirecting it toward the expansion of his artistic identity in the public sphere.

The doubling of assistants in the *Latex Paintings* established a paradoxically prolific stalemate. This created a system in which one assistant's output became another's waste, transforming it back into a productive substance only to be devalued and subsequently recycled once again. This dispersed mode of production operated in accordance with the double and triple exhibition format that he adopted in which several shows would be staged simultaneously. By generating new work across continents and sending art objects onto perpetual tour like a publicity circuit, Kippenberger developed circulation models that mirrored his own peripatetic lifestyle. More significantly, this rootless nomadism performed a specific function: it doubled down on the central authority of the artist as vital despite the delegation of labor. In other words, as can be seen in the hiring of assistants' assistants for the *Latex Paintings*, this centripetal production made Kippenberger's nominal presence even more critical to the work, repositioning him at the center of social gravity.[68] After having asserted his role as a "master" artist through the three forms of disruption, Kippenberger was free to channel the feedback loops to serve his own ends, exploiting them to perpetuate the dissemination of his own infamy.

### Proliferation

Less than two years after the work's ostensible completion, Kippenberger revisited his *Heavy Burschi* installation—both extending the conceptual logic behind its initial manifestation and reengaging with the material objects themselves. The two segments of the installation described in the introduction to this chapter—the photographic copies of paintings and the dumpster filled with the destroyed remains—became further subsumed within ongoing feedback processes that resulted in the production of two bodies of related artworks: a series of drawings titled *Heavy Mädel* (1991) and a set of serigraphs on wood known as *Inhalt auf Reisen* (*Content on Tour*) (1992). The ongoing transformation of the "INPUT-OUTPUT" painting in these later two bodies of work exemplifies how Kippenberger's proliferation of images attached to his authorial identity generated a mechanism of celebrity that allowed his physical presence to become redundant while simultaneously inhabited by others in the service of the artist's proper name. Given that moral rights in intellectual property law fundamentally protect authorial attribution and the unique creative act, Kippenberger's violation of all three constitutive elements—the recognition of authorship, the right of publication, and the right to integrity—in *Heavy Mädel* and *Inhalt auf Reisen* shows how the valuation of singular authorship and expressive creative production that had returned in the 1980s art world was simulated and ultimately precarious.

In *Heavy Mädel*, Kippenberger produced a set of hand-copied pencil drawings on hotel stationery that exploited the intimate associations of the medium while using processes of image remediation on the levels of content, production, and circulation.[69] For example, in *Untitled* (1991), Kippenberger rendered a copy of the "INPUT-OUTPUT" *Heavy Burschi* painting, which had been created manually by Carpenter under Kippenberger's direction. Working from the photographic reproductions of the paintings and using a mirror to transcribe the image in reverse, Kippenberger manipulated any residual individuality by reformulating Carpenter's work—itself having undergone multiple levels of recycling through Kippenberger's own image bank—as remade by the nominal artist's own "hand." The drawings were then reproduced in the exhibition catalog *Heavy Mädel*. That same year, the "INPUT-OUTPUT" image underwent further processes of remediation and delegation as Kippenberger directed his then assistant, Adam Kuczynski, to create a series of watercolors that depicted each of Kippenberger's own publications, including *Heavy Mädel*, with a magnifying glass. The sweeping relay of remediation charted through this "INPUT-OUTPUT" image scrambled the typical chain of image production by which reproductions are generated from a primary original creation, releasing the artwork from a stable expression of meaning. Moreover, it set up the assistants as potential accomplices in contravening the

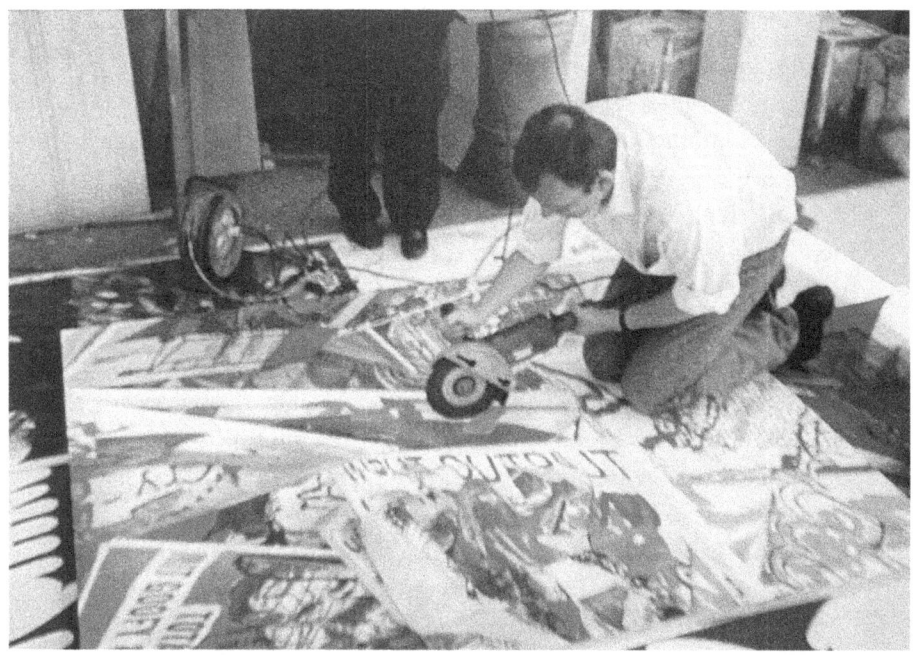

**3.09**   Martin Kippenberger working on *Inhalt auf Reisen* (*Content on Tour*), Edition Artelier, Graz, Austria, 1992.

moral rights of an author in deciding when and how a work can be used in a different context.

In 1992, Kippenberger embarked on a second trajectory of artwork generated from the *Heavy Burschi* installation. For *Inhalt auf Reisen*, a photograph taken of the interior of the garbage container filled with destroyed paintings were given to the Austrian publishing house Edition Artelier in Graz to reproduce as a set of silkscreens. As noted by Christophe Cherix, there were four main variations: a direct reproduction of the photograph and three cropped versions of the same image—which notably featured the "INPUT-OUTPUT" painting.[70] Each of these were then mounted on plywood and subjected to a further round of manual destruction, in which Kippenberger (or his assistant) cut and slashed into the surfaces with the use of a handheld saw (fig. 3.9). Yet rather than destroying the original paintings, as was the case with Carpenter's compositions for *Heavy Burschi*, the destructive actions performed on the *Inhalt auf Reisen* silkscreens paradoxically recast these works as exclusive iterations—in their wasted form—rather than merely printed multiples.[71]

The silkscreen process in *Inhalt auf Reisen* changes the *Heavy Burschi* images from photographs back to painting while also reiterating the possibilities for the generation of multiples. The selection of this medium continues the disassociation of the artwork as *either* a singular object or a copy of an indeterminate number, instead allowing the image to be materialized in paint that is at once both an original and a reproduction. This point was underscored by Kippenberger's use of the handsaw to make individualized cuts to the works' surfaces. Such a gesture pitted his assistants-turned-accomplices' protections over altering a work's content (right to integrity) against the creative interventions that would be safeguarded through paternity and publication rights. Considered together, the chain of images becomes a loop rather than unidirectional, as the output becomes the input that becomes output once again. As such, the phrase "INPUT-OUTPUT" aptly describes the actions of remediation and delegation that are processed and directed by the artist's authorial role as a kind of mechanism for generating his personal celebrity.

By proliferating these interrelated feedback loops of images and delegated labor, Kippenberger—with the assistance of his accomplices—both internalized and satirized the art world's commercialization of art and its artists. At once serious and sarcastic, Kippenberger generated a network of images and distributed labor to help expand his celebrity persona within the context of the 1980s image economy in which the branded identity reigned supreme both within and outside the art world. Adopting a parodic pseudo-corporate persona as a commentary on the growing commercialization of the art market and its workers in the 1980s, Kippenberger sought ways of generating himself as a celebrity brand based on principles of failure. At the same time, however, he sought to interrogate the imbrications between the rise of art commerce, celebrity, and the valorized return of Expressionism, aura, and subjectivity in Neo-Expressionist painting during this decade. Recognizing the contradictions in such a paradigm of 1980s artists simulating authenticity when they in fact often operated according to a corporate model of marketing, Kippenberger attempted to make the presence of his assistants visible to critique the fantasy of the sovereign artist.

Using the framework of intellectual property law, I argue that Kippenberger explored how the simulation of singular, expressive subjectivity and the exploitation of unacknowledged networks of delegated labor nested into an authorial identity are mutually behind the mechanism of celebrity that became pervasive in the worlds of art and entertainment in the 1980s. Put differently, the two main points of protection in moral rights—autonomous authorial "input" and distinctive creative "output"— were precisely what was valued in celebrity and therefore undermined by Kippenberger's assistants-turned-accomplices. Like his artistic peers probing the growing proximity between art and commerce, Kippenberger sought to break open the seamless veneer of singular authorship that had become a lucrative commodity in the 1980s art market—using it affirmatively to hyperactively propagate his own celebrity as much as derisively mock its artificiality through his persona based on failure. Ironically, these interlocking feedback loops of remediation and labor delegation that were interrupted by potential legal violations might be said to have become Kippenberger's signature, despite his attempts to evade any such characterization through his profligate deployment of mediums, styles, and assistants.

The extensive relay of authorship and the dissemination of aggregated artworks generated from the *Heavy Burschi* project exemplify the procedures that characterize Kippenberger's practice more generally. Kippenberger established an authorial model in which he was physically dispossessed from the proliferation of images he orchestrated while aggrandizing his personal celebrity using his auxiliary agents as accomplices to suggested transgressions of the moral rights protected by IP law. That is, Kippenberger created images that were emptied as they were set in transit, moving beyond the physical and impermanent limits of a particular producer to instead become self-generating, while feeding back into the authorial identity of the single artist.

Kippenberger's model of the accomplice differs from those of the abettors and partners put forth in the previous two chapters. While Burden explored the thresholds of power and control over auxiliary agents who did not formally work for him or have explicit involvement in his work's production, Wilke not only sought retribution for her unacknowledged labor as a former accomplice to Claes Oldenburg but also explored the possibilities of equitable partnerships—both personally and professionally—with figures such as Donald Goddard. Kippenberger, in contrast, incorporates elements taken from both of those accomplice models. He staged deliberate dispossession onto others in a manner similar to Burden, yet he integrated the accomplices into himself by hiring them to work in his studio under his artistic authority, using a model that is reminiscent of Wilke's more formal roles for her photographers who operated under her purview and direction. Whereas the previous chapters look at criminal law (Burden) and rights of publicity or privacy (Wilke), this chapter instead focused on how Kippenberger strategically set up his assistants to become his accomplices on account of their role in exploiting or violating the moral rights—the recognition of authorship, right of publication, and right to integrity—that characterize the fundamental questions at stake in the 1980s art world of branded celebrity and marketed forms of authentic expressivity.

The continuous circuit of reuse and interference that is dramatized in the expanded *Heavy Burschi* project through material and social means—recycled images, objects, and people—presents an alternative model of the accomplice that captures the ways individual workers experienced an accelerated devaluation of their intellectual property or personal identities within the explosion of corporate branding and commercialization during the 1980s. Through his deliberate manipulations of those assistants hired to (ostensibly) help him produce art that performed potentially illicit acts against their own moral authorial rights, Kippenberger tested the limits of the ways in which one's intellectual labor and personal identity become subsumed as property of the entity for which they work. While this played out most explicitly in terms of public corporate identities, Kippenberger drew inspiration from this business model of collective authorship under a single branded identity to show its proximity to the celebrity culture that was predominant during this period as well.

In the case of Kippenberger, his attempts at staging failure—within his public persona and through his networked yet hierarchical social working relationships—might present a means of evading the conventional valuation of the successful artist as autonomous, expressive, and authentic. By setting up his trademark rights—over the creative contributions and labor performed by others as his own aesthetic property owned by his artistic brand—in opposition to his assistants' authorial rights, Kippenberger used these potential violations of intellectual property to break open the seamlessness of the celebrity image. Refusing productivity and pragmatics, Kippenberger developed a new way of showing the network of unrecognized labor operating beneath the surface of artistic "success" without granting agency to such operatives. Therefore, Kippenberger did not put forth an ameliorative resolution—power is not redistributed to his hired assistants, nor equitable practices restored—but rather imitated the cycles of manipulation on the level of both images and subjects that became pervasive in art of the 1980s.

# Preservers

**On January 2, 1983,** artist Lorraine O'Grady wrote a letter to her friend Tony Whitfield that expressed her ambitions in finding an audience for her work that did not presently exist: "Right now, my goal is to discover and create the true audience, and something tells me that, for a black performance artist of my ilk, this will take a many-sided approach. Because I sense that the true audience may be *coming*, not here now."[1] This prophetic statement—made shortly before the artist took a five-year hiatus (1983–88) from art making to assume primary care for her mother, who was diagnosed with Alzheimer's disease in June of that year—succinctly articulates the artist's palpable longing for viewers who understood and appreciated her work. Yet it also poetically expresses O'Grady's recognition of her own role in bringing this ideal audience into existence. Her objective, then, was twofold: to find contemporary allies and to seek ways of protecting her work for audiences yet-to-come.

Over a brief, three-year period in the early 1980s, O'Grady produced a multifaceted body of groundbreaking works—including guerrilla performances, curatorial endeavors, and text-based interventions—frequently staged in public spaces that dealt with issues of race, gender, and class. While her own projects explored Black female subjectivity through what we have come to know as intersectionality, she found that the New York–based art-world context in which her work was produced—both white-dominated art institutions and the Black creative community—remained conservative in terms of racial and gender diversity.[2] As such, she felt her work rarely achieved its desired effects at the time, a stark reminder of the realities of being a Black woman artist in America during the early 1980s, because it required a certain type of audience, one "who, whether or not they are *like me*, can see what I see."[3]

Directly invoking Martin Heidegger's aesthetic theory in her letter to Whitfield, O'Grady found faith in the philosopher's notion of "preservers." This auxiliary role, according to Heidegger, is performed by a set of individuals that he describes as "presenters, critics, and audiences," whose proper comprehension of an artwork becomes a critical act of conservation or stewardship in bringing a piece fully into existence. As O'Grady explained: "There's a wonderful passage in Heidegger where he speaks of the need for 'preservers,' that combination of presenters, critics, and audience required for the work to come into *existence*, into *being*, after it has been created by the artist. . . . I take that to mean that it's a matter of who understands the work, who needs the work in order to *be* themselves."[4]

While preservers, according to Heidegger, are essential, their presence in O'Grady's case was often speculative. There were real, tangible risks involved in the act of preservation for Black artists and audiences: not only livelihoods that could be lost if overly critical of the white-run institutions that dominated the reception and circulation of art during this time but also potential legal repercussions in making or supporting artworks that disturbed the public status quo. What O'Grady intuits in her letter to Whitfield is the need for help—as the mere attempt by Black artists to locate gallerists, critics, or audiences to exhibit, analyze, and view their work was itself a radical act in the 1980s New York art world, despite its progressive pretenses.

Her "many-sided approach" in actively seeking out these preservers, I argue in this chapter, was the central motivating factor of O'Grady's live performative interventions from the early 1980s—one that can be productively analyzed through the accomplice paradigm. Focusing on O'Grady as my central case study, I consider how certain marginalized artists—predominantly women, particularly those of color—during the mid-1970s and 1980s began seeking alternative ways to achieve agency through the creation of self-enacted performance characters that allowed for a circumvention of the "legal" ways of exhibiting or documenting their work. In my estimation, it became an especially useful tool for O'Grady as she sought out potential preservers who would help her effectively infiltrate the social circles and institutions safeguarding the establishment that could otherwise not be breached on account of her race and gender.

This fourth model of the accomplice, as a preserver, notably exceeds the definition offered by Heidegger to serve as neutral presenters, critics, and audiences; in the context of O'Grady's work, one assumes the increased risks related to job security, social standing, potential retaliation, and even possible police intervention that might arise. Given that the "lawful" avenues for finding preservers, whether formally or informally, were largely closed to her as a Black woman artist, I position her performances as conceptual or even potentially literal forms of "trespassing," intended to breach the law governing certain spaces and discourses that were otherwise not possible given the gendered and racially segregated climate of the 1980s art world. In an important contrast to other forms of the accomplice described in previous chapters, however, it was O'Grady herself who, perhaps surprisingly, assumed the role of her own accomplice as she developed a performance-based character to act in her place until other preservers could be found.

Approximately three years earlier, on the evening of June 5, 1980, the Just Above Midtown (JAM) gallery held the opening reception for *Outlaw Aesthetics*, a group exhibition of contemporary art. For many audience members, the title of the show signaled the outsider status of the exhibiting artists within the predominantly white mainstream art world at the time— the artwork was made exclusively by Black artists and shown in a Black-run independent art space. The prominence of the term *outlaw* was provocative, formally defined as someone who has broken the law and remains at large, like a wanted fugitive. For one viewer in attendance, however, the connotation of illicit rule breaking that was suggested by the show's title failed to materialize, an unfulfilled promise that stoked her ire. Mlle Bourgeoise Noire, as she was known, was determined to change all that.

JAM's opening night festivities were well attended; the reception featured edible art, "experiential happenings," and even a disco to celebrate the gallery's recent relocation from Midtown Manhattan, the city's mainstream commercial art hub, to Tribeca, the burgeoning downtown art-world enclave. Like the other fashionable attendees, Mlle Bourgeoise Noire (also known as MBN) appeared in an outfit selected with considerable care. Her floor-length gown was constructed from 180 pairs of white gloves, sewn flat in a pattern of successive tiers to create a fringe-like texture, and was complemented by a dramatic cape created from white lace and gloves. Held by thin shoulder straps, the sleeveless dress was accessorized with elbow-length white gloves, which drew attention to MBN's other eye-catching accessories: a sash, a rhinestone and seed pearl crown, and a bouquet of white chrysanthemums.

As seen in the photographic documentation of the construction of her costume (fig. 4.1), these details were intended to broadcast Mlle Bourgeoise Noire's background. As O'Grady's alter ego, MBN shared a similar biography to the artist, who grew up in a Black middle-class household in

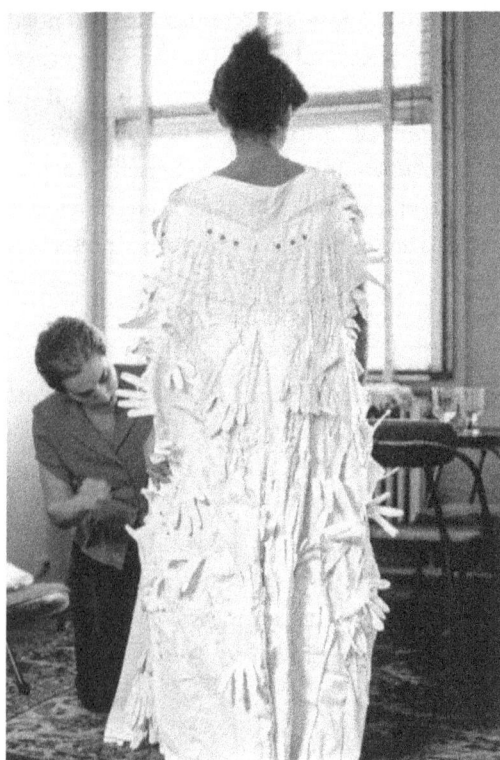

**4.01**

Lorraine O'Grady
dresses for her
performance as Mlle
Bourgeoise Noire at
Just Above Midtown,
New York, 1980.

Boston, Massachusetts, with Caribbean immigrant parents. The character of MBN was partially based on O'Grady's experiences as a young woman; Mlle Bourgeoise Noire—Miss Black Middle Class—was a former beauty queen from Boston who adopted as her moniker the pageant title she had won in Cayenne, the capital city of French Guiana, on June 5, 1955. According to MBN's backstory, the opening of *Outlaw Aesthetics* coincided with the twenty-five-year anniversary of her coronation known as the Silver Jubilee—a fortuitous confluence of events that warranted commemoration.

Mlle Bourgeoise Noire was accompanied by the pageant's "Master of Ceremonies" (MC); the pair arrived for their debut at Just Above Midtown at exactly 9:00 p.m. After encountering difficulties at the entrance door—they were not found on the gallery's official guest list—the duo quickly made their way inside to greet their unwitting audience-to-be. Mlle Bourgeoise Noire began the evening in a jovial mood. An ever-consummate hostess, she chatted with guests and handed out flowers with a warm, welcoming smile reminiscent of her pageant days. Pulling off the chrysanthemums one at a time, MBN posed a seemingly playful question that carried more serious historical undertones concerning the weight of past violence against Black women: "Won't you help me lighten my heavy bouquet?"

As the night went on, Mlle Bourgeoise Noire's true intentions were revealed. As Mlle Bourgeoise Noire distributed the flowers to her fellow attendees, her bouquet transformed, revealing its underlying structure to be a cat-o'-nine-tails whip, which had barbed tips hidden beneath the delicate petals. With her bouquet bare and the gallery's disco band on break, she removed her cape and signaled to her MC with a predetermined code; he responded by handing her a pair of long gloves. According to O'Grady, something had shifted for MBN in the time since her coronation: "Mlle Bourgeoise Noire has had a change of heart between 1955 and 1980. . . . All these years she has been waiting for this 25th Anniversary to give her subjects her final conclusion."[5] Given that 1955 marked a significant year in the civil rights movement and coincided with O'Grady's projected graduation from Wellesley College—the epitome of her middle-class upbringing— the occasion of MBN's Silver Jubilee offered an opportunity for reflection on the societal and personal growth that occurred over the past quarter century.[6]

Much to the surprise of the gallerygoers, Mlle Bourgeoise Noire dropped the veneer of social propriety that she had maintained until that point in the evening. She began hitting herself with "the-whip-that-made-the-plantations-move" in an act of self-flagellation, performed with ever-accelerating rhythm. Then, laying down her weapon, she began shouting an amended verse of "Trève" (Enough) (1937), a poem about refusing assimilation and Black bourgeois identity written by the French Guianese poet and cofounder of the Négritude movement Léon-Gontran Damas.[7]

With her targeted audience rapt, Mlle Bourgeoise Noire demanded accountability from both the art gallery and individual artists, calling on them to refuse existing paradigms of aesthetic value based on white ideals:

That's ENOUGH!
No more boot-licking . . .
No more ass-kissing . . .
No more buttering-up . . .
No more pos . . . turing
of super ass . . . imilates . . .
BLACK ART MUST
TAKE MORE RISKS!!![8]

Then, as quickly as she came, Mlle Bourgeoise Noire disappeared into the night.

Mlle Bourgeoise Noire's arrival at JAM was a conceptual as well as literal one; it marked her first introduction to the public after being conceived as a performance character by O'Grady a few months prior. As a forty-five-year-old mixed-race, middle-class Black woman who was newly pursuing an art career, O'Grady encountered profound racism, sexism, ageism, and classism that frequently rendered her invisible in the contemporary art world.[9] The reception of O'Grady's works—which addressed, at varying moments, the conservatism within the Black avant-garde, the narrow definition of "inclusion" or the outright lack of Black representation in white art museums and galleries, and the ignorance of second-wave white feminists for the more complex intersections of race and gender—was mixed, with reactions at times resembling dismissal or even offense. Mlle Bourgeoise Noire was created from this lack of understanding for O'Grady and her work. The MBN persona, which was performed exclusively by O'Grady, was given primary agency and responsibility for a flurry of projects made between 1980 and 1983 that fall under the conceptual purview of what is called the *Mlle Bourgeoise Noire* project.

Mlle Bourgeoise Noire became O'Grady's central operative, performing an integral role in a body of performative interventions that were staged as strategic disruptions into various institutions and discourses of the early 1980s New York art world. Thinking of such actions as forms of illicit "trespassing" into the established order, as I do here, allows us to more fully see the circumstances in which the repressive forces of sexism and racism persisted in the art world despite the advancements made by the 1960s women's and civil rights movements. Moreover, it shows how O'Grady's tactic of deploying an alternate persona attempted to disrupt the perpetuation of such mechanisms and to seek out "preservers" for her work and ideas.

Building upon the important recent scholarship published on O'Grady's work—most notably by Aruna D'Souza, Catherine Morris, and Stephanie Sparling Williams—I examine how the artist's early performance-based projects undertaken with the Mlle Bourgeoise Noire character can be productively analyzed through the accomplice paradigm that connects to the other three artists featured in this book.[10] I draw from O'Grady's own language found in her letter to Whitfield to show how the accomplice analyzed in this chapter assumes the form of a preserver. Yet

Chapter Four

rather than conceiving of Mlle Bourgeoise Noire as O'Grady's accomplice (as might be the case in the models developed in prior chapters), I situate the artist-accomplice model inversely following O'Grady's own attribution of artworks to Mlle Bourgeoise Noire rather than herself. Given the ongoing surveillance and regulation of Black bodies, I understand O'Grady to have developed this performance character to conceal and protect her personal identity, much like a feminine suit of armor, while also drawing attention to herself to amplify her message. Put differently, it was by communicating through MBN that O'Grady's voice was finally—and more so retroactively—heard within the noise of racism and sexism that permeated the early 1980s art world as she awaited her ideal future audience.

Many of the projects that fall under the purview of MBN are guided by three fundamental questions that O'Grady had herself articulated. The first was about evaluating the situation at hand—what are the present circumstances vis-à-vis the ongoing issue of segregation in the art world? The second concerned authorship: which artists deserved recognition? Finally, the last inquiry advanced the question of reception: who should make up the audience for this work?[11] I contend that each of these inquiries can be at least partially answered by exploring the three major components of the *Mlle Bourgeoise Noire* project: her performative intervention at Just Above Midtown in 1980, the reprisal of this project at the New Museum in 1981, and *Art Is . . .* , a participatory work staged at a Harlem parade in 1983.

Deliberately invoking the militaristic terminology O'Grady used when describing her work as an "invasion" of the contemporary art world, I argue that the artist developed her MBN persona as distinct from her personal identity to more effectively breach the properties, territories, and rights that belong—both conceptually and physically—to other subjects in the name of art. In this chapter I use the term *trespassing*, drawing from tort law, in place of O'Grady's *invasion* to draw out expanded forms of "unlawful" intrusions that O'Grady pursued using her MBN character, which exceeded visibly hostile entries into established institutions to include undetected operations in pursuing her goal of finding preservers for her work.[12] That is, her work surpasses attempts to merely invade and disrupt institutions by seeking representation and inclusion; as this chapter will demonstrate, O'Grady ultimately found solutions to her inquiries by bypassing the institutions altogether.

Unlike the artists in previous chapters, who mobilized other people to act on their behalf, O'Grady ran up against substantial limitations in finding outside agents who could act as her accomplices. It was this circumstance that ended up being a motivating factor in her development of a networked yet hierarchical mode of artistic authorship within herself using a performance character who would assume risk on her behalf but also remain under her conceptual control. This was a necessary formulation; not only would it have been likely impossible due to social power imbalances as a Black woman for her to take an accomplice through exploitation of another individual, as was readily available to white male artists such as Chris Burden and Martin Kippenberger, but O'Grady had to make herself her own accomplice to her invented persona due to the persistent racism and sexism that rendered her own voice as a Black woman unheard without the framing of her critiques as "art." Expanding on Uri McMillan's argument that Black women performance artists such as Adrian Piper and Howardena Pindell often developed techniques of using their bodies like objects that were granted "human-like agency" (what he calls "avatars") as a tool for gaining forms of power and control, I contend that O'Grady created her Mlle Bourgeoise Noire persona to act as a primary operative in place of the nominal artist, thereby relegating O'Grady to the position of the accomplice in order to infiltrate spaces that had traditionally excluded Black women artists.[13]

In further distinction from Burden and Kippenberger—whose work received immediate public attention—the dearth of press coverage, retaliatory institutional responses (for instance, rescinding invitations), and the absence of found accomplices on account of O'Grady's performance work as MBN indicate how her gender and racial identity positioned her outside the scope of agential possibility. In other words, despite O'Grady using strategies of tactical disruption successfully undertaken by white male artists, the stark differences in the reception of O'Grady's work at the time can be attributed, in large part, to the widespread erasure and systemic exclusions of Black women in the art world, rendering her gestures invisible. Mlle Bourgeoise Noire certainly had her work cut out for her.

### Presenters

The initial impetus for O'Grady's development of the Mlle Bourgeoise Noire persona first arose on February 17, 1980, at the opening for the *Afro-American Abstraction* exhibition at PS1 in New York. She had come across a newspaper advertisement for the show, which seemed fortuitous as it arrived at a time when O'Grady—who was teaching at the School of

Visual Arts at the time, having taken over a course from a friend—began developing nascent ideas about more fully establishing her own art practice. Guest curated by April Kingsley, the exhibition included works by Ed Clark, Melvin Edwards, David Hammons, James Little, Howardena Pindell, Martin Puryear, and Senga Nengudi—a lineup that thrilled and inspired O'Grady in concept.

With many of the artists in attendance at the opening, O'Grady felt initial enthusiasm for the stylish crowd of Black intellectuals and the possibility to create a creative community among them. It was exhilarating to see a convergence of work by leading Black artists and their inclusion in a white-run art institution. Yet her hopes for stumbling upon a Black avant-garde art community as her first potential "preservers" were quickly dissolved. In her opinion, the artwork on view was too safe, caving to the unspoken rules and opinions of the white art world. Explicating the connection to her MBN costume, she later expressed: "I felt that the art on exhibit, as opposed to the people, had been too cautious—that it had been art with white gloves on."[14]

For Black artists working in the early 1980s, there were two conventional paths of making art that would be accepted into the white art museums and galleries. As Sparling Williams succinctly explains, "mainstream audiences largely expected to see either visual culture that bespoke of struggle and self-determination, as with folk art, or art that was familiar, nonconfrontational, and palatable—as O'Grady's critique of the PS1 show highlighted."[15] And yet, even when making work that adhered to such designations approved by white audiences, many Black artists *still* experienced significant limitations regarding the possible avenues for, and the cultural expectations around, creative expression. For O'Grady, the implication seemed to be that if Black artists were to remain marginalized within white-run institutions regardless, they should pursue creating art that felt authentic to their values, outside the dictates of establishment tastes or expectations. Even progressive, Black-run institutions like the Studio Museum had a specific focus at the time; for instance, it frequently eschewed showing abstract or Conceptual art by Black artists, instead focusing on representational works or pieces that foregrounded artists' African heritage (reflecting the influence of Amiri Baraka and the Black Arts Movement [BAM]).[16]

Several of the artists whose work was shown in *Afro-American Abstraction* were also informally affiliated with the pioneering Just Above Midtown gallery, where MBN made her first appearance. Founded by Linda Goode Bryant in 1974, JAM functioned as a social space for Black community building as much as a formal gallery where contemporary Black artists could show and sell their work—at a time when both were rare in New York. As Goode Bryant saw firsthand, the largely segregated commercial art world of the mid-1970s also fell into prescribed categories. There was a limited set of gallerists who dominated the mainstream, white-run commercial art spaces—including Leo Castelli, Paula Cooper, André Emmerich, Sidney Janis, Ronald Feldman, and Ileana Sonnabend—whose stable of artists were almost exclusively white. While artists of color were at times included in group exhibitions, solo shows by Black artists at such galleries were extremely rare. Furthermore, many of the alternative New York art spaces that opened in the 1970s and '80s—like ABC No Rio, White Columns, and PS1—rarely showed work by Black artists. With JAM, Goode Bryant hoped to address this issue by providing a space dedicated to fostering a Black artistic community.

Goode Bryant was not alone in noticing the limited spaces for Black artists to exhibit their work. On September 11, 1978, the *Village Voice* published an article by Kingsley titled "Black Artists: Up against the Wall," in which she addressed the difficulties for Black artists negotiating the contemporary art world. As Kingsley points out, by the end of the 1970s there were disparate levels of support for Black and white artists—an issue that she noted had gotten dramatically worse following the comparative outpouring of institutional support for Black artists in the wake of the civil rights movement during the late 1960s and early 1970s.[17] In response to the widespread economic decline that characterized the decade, institutions such as the Studio Museum—which focused on Black art—began receiving a substantial reduction in their public funding, and mainstream galleries began cutting back on the number of Black artists they represented as they felt the market was not there (Kingsley noted fewer than six Black artists had representation in the top twelve New York galleries at the time of publication, for instance).

While the 1980s marked a moment of economic rebound from the precipitous market fall of the 1970s, ongoing economic instability persisted for Black communities. This discrepancy was noted by O'Grady, as she succinctly expressed that "only black people were getting poorer, only black artists seemed to worry about the price of paint."[18] According to Kingsley, this contributed to the growing conservatism in the Black art world among galleries and artists alike. The economic pressures were tangibly felt, as Black artists sought practical ways to continue their art careers and support themselves. By tempering their work to suit the demands of the white art market, artists thought that they stood a chance at receiving mainstream recognition.

Yet this often required reframing their social identities, particularly those concerning class. As O'Grady explained, Black artists seeking acceptance in the white art world needed to appear avant-garde—however, this was often at odds with the preconceptions of Black "authenticity" dictated by the mainstream institutions and audiences. For while the avant-garde was largely the purview of the middle class—made possible by the education, financial support, and access granted with such social status—Black creative production that was being shown in the white-run galleries or museums frequently presented an image of, in her words, "the glamour of the Street."[19] This lack of representation of the Black middle and upper classes went beyond the art world, as the Black bourgeoisie were rarely seen in popular culture. As such, many artists tried to downplay their affluent backgrounds: "You had this weird spectacle of middle-class adult artists trying to pass as street kids. And always the pressure, that mainstream artists don't have to feel, to be 'relevant' to the 'community,' whatever that is. . . . No wonder, too, that so much of the work was cautious and fearful."[20]

Beyond racial segregation, there was also the issue of gender disparities regarding the already inadequate recognition for Black artists. As is perhaps unsurprising, the most successful Black artists were predominantly men. Kingsley drew attention to the plight of Black women artists, writing: "If black men of such high caliber have had difficulty getting their work viewed in proper settings . . . imagine the problems black women artists face. Finding no solace within the heavily macho black-art movement, most of them identify and associate with the women's art movement instead; but to a large extent they are disenfranchised from both."[21]

It was amid the complexities of such a context that inspired Goode Bryant to open JAM at 50 West Fifty-Seventh Street, in a locale befitting the gallery's name bordering Midtown and Uptown Manhattan. This location was strategic—situated near many of the white-run galleries—as Goode Bryant sought to position contemporary Black avant-garde art so that it could enter conversations happening within the mainstream art world (Kingsley noted that JAM had "made a valiant effort to correct common errors of omission").[22] In a 1994 interview, Goode Bryant stated that "primarily it was about allowing African American artists to function on the same platform equal to their white counterparts. To have been in Harlem or Bedford-Stuyvesant would not have afforded that. It was to get consideration in the context of the larger art world."[23]

Four years into its existence, in 1978, JAM moved downtown to Tribeca, where it remained until closing in 1986. Located near Artists Space, JAM quickly became the epicenter of Black artistic activities in New York, exceeding its role as an exhibition space to become a vital platform for experimentation and social exchange. The gallery hosted a variety of creative activities, including performances by dancer Bill T. Jones, visits by musicians Roberta Flack and Stevie Wonder, and the formation of *Black Currant*, a journal edited by musician and critic Greg Tate.

According to O'Grady, Just Above Midtown was a world unto itself, a space for Black artists, thinkers, and writers to engage in dialogue.[24] Art historians Kellie Jones and Judith Wilson were honing their critical eyes; curator Lowery Stokes Sims had a firsthand look at work by emerging artists; and artists such as Nengudi, Hassinger, and Hammons refined their nascent practices. Certainly this could be O'Grady's audience, where her preservers might be found.

Two months after seeing the *Afro-American Abstraction* show, O'Grady began volunteering at JAM, in April 1980, working on mailers, performing media outreach, and writing the gallery's press releases. Many of the JAM-associated artists were helping Goode Bryant open the gallery's new location, and O'Grady recalled wanting to express her feelings to them about the current state of Black avant-garde art. Yet she remained silent, working in the background, until one day she had a vision while walking across Union Square Park of seeing herself "completely covered in white gloves."[25]

The visualization of the Mlle Bourgeoise Noire persona came rapidly and cohesively; O'Grady said it was complete by the time she had crossed the park. Only the whip was a later addition: "I understood that the gloves were a symbol of internalized oppression, but knew I needed a symbol of the external oppression, which was equally real."[26] O'Grady sourced her materials strategically: the backless polyester gown was made in Miami; the white gloves were found in thrift shops around Manhattan. It was vital "that the gloves should have been worn by women who had actually believed in them" as symbolic markers of bourgeois respectability, which governed the social thinking behind the white art-world establishment.[27] Once the character was formulated, the question became where she should make her debut for greatest impact. O'Grady decided to introduce Mlle Bourgeoise Noire at the *Outlaw Aesthetics* show at JAM, where her calls for a Black artistic avant-garde would be heard by a predominantly Black art audience.

As the unofficial PR representative for JAM, O'Grady likely had a significant hand in the press materials for the show. This included the exhibition's promotional pamphlet—which forecasted "beguiling sensations and electrifying encounters" through elaborate, experiential components requiring viewer participation, including a "spectacular medicine show benefit," culinary experiences, disco and blues music, and "visual voodoo for video villains."[28] Perhaps most aptly, the brochure promised performances that would present "haunting, sometimes amusing visions of alternative futures in the present"—a description that certainly foreshadowed MBN's forthcoming intervention.

The extravagance of the show opening, coupled with the optional dress code, meant that MBN's initial presence might not have been questioned or noticed. Yet, as indicated by later comments from O'Grady regarding the responses to her work by those in attendance at the opening, it was the frankness of her critiques expressed by her recitation of the poem—as well as her decision to direct such points publicly to her fellow Black artists rather than the white art world—that was most surprising for the audiences present that evening. After all, she had introduced herself at JAM as an administrative volunteer with no artistic aspirations; upon her debut two months later came the collective audience realization that "the strange lady licking envelopes was an artist!"[29] Such a transformation was a shock; as Goode Bryant later noted upon hearing O'Grady's plans, "I wondered to myself, 'Will she take creative risk?' That night answered it. That took so much courage. . . . I don't know that I expected she would be so stark in her reveal of the layers and contradictions."[30]

Mlle Bourgeoise Noire's intention at Just Above Midtown was to create a situation in which she could both serve as O'Grady's proxy in communicating her critique of the perceived artistic conservatism of her peers and—in so doing in front of a live audience—identify potential preservers in the Heideggerian sense who were sympathetic to her aims of creating a progressive Black avant-garde independent of market trends or white institutional demands. Through her provocative performance, which called out aesthetic timidity, MBN asked her audience to do more than witness from a distance. She hoped it would serve as a rallying call for a new kind of community of outsiders, who would reject the options presented to them and forge an alternative path governed by their own rules and values.

Based on O'Grady's recollections of the events that transpired, it seems that nearly no one in the audience (apart from Goode Bryant and Hammons, as well as her Master of Ceremonies) was willing to join her cause. She had gone to JAM because she thought its progressive program and leadership might harbor a network of associates who could be united together under a shared vision for the future. Yet the urgency with which MBN worked was not readily met. However, this did not mean her audience was against her cause; as she would later find out, the preservers might need more time. Instead of inciting support in the form of a newly minted army of allies willing to assume risk on her behalf, Mlle Bourgeoise Noire was on her own—for now.

## Fugitives

For O'Grady, the promise of a Black avant-garde—independent of white determinations of value—was found neither in the *Afro-American Abstraction* exhibition nor in *Outlaw Aesthetics*. In a 1998 email interview, O'Grady explained her reasoning behind creating an alternate persona with whom she shared characteristics to stage her multipronged critiques rather than doing so as herself. While she expressed a desire to heighten the "irony of the hyper-bourgeois black woman (the infinitely silent and compliant figure in art and Western civilization) making radical demands," a point that was readily apparent in her MBN beauty pageant costume, there was a more telling motive as well. As O'Grady confessed: "Of course I needed someone to blame it on. I didn't do it, SHE did it."[31]

Such a statement is critical to understanding the relationship between O'Grady and MBN as well as the application of the accomplice paradigm in this chapter. Given the legal dimension of using accomplices to analyze art practices, looking at O'Grady's work through such a model as various acts of trespassing offers an opportunity to examine more closely the limiting circumstances in which she was working as a Black woman. As seen at JAM, Black artists and audiences didn't necessarily want to hear critiques of the art they supported as being, in O'Grady's mind, overly timid and deferential to white tastes, nor were they willing to undertake actions that might threaten the support, however limited, they had personally gained.

O'Grady's decision to create an alter ego in the form of her Mlle Bourgeoise Noire character was a practical solution to the problem of subjectivity and expression. Embodied in her performative interventions, the formation of another character—who was similar to the artist in most obvious ways, including class, racial background, gender, ethnicity—offered a means of shifting accountability while also gaining access to certain spaces and personal recognition that was otherwise not readily available to O'Grady herself. As seen at JAM, her act of trespassing into the Black art community circumvented the standards dictating what Black art was supposed to look like—and critique—at the time. Yet by creating MBN to question the work made by her fellow Black artists, O'Grady thoroughly rejected the "legal" ways in which she believed the Black art community was attempting to gain agency in the contemporary art world by adhering to the unspoken laws of parity and representation established by those in power. Instead, she sought an alternative realm of possibility, one that could be forged by her MBN performance character as she waited for other preservers to make themselves evident.

Such an approach can be productively thought of in terms of Fred Moten and Stefano Harney's provocative concept of fugitivity.[32] For Moten and Harney, the term *fugitive* describes an individual who escapes the customary or proposed standards of freedom, instead enacting a lawlessness in which one does not simply violate the rules of the law but rather rejects them altogether to seek alternative sites of possibility. Instead of staging an engaged critique, this fugitivity—which is integrally tied for Harney and Moten to the very notion of Blackness—produces an outlaw subject, who takes flight from regulative forces and operates in spaces existing outside the logical order of the "law." As this chapter will demonstrate, O'Grady—by way of MBN—developed techniques that increasingly refused to behave "lawfully": first seeking out fellow accomplices to help fight such battles for developing a true Black avant-garde art and then, in realizing her outlaw status, going at it alone. It wasn't until she left the art world behind altogether that she would achieve her mission of finding preservers.

Although notable efforts to create racial equality had been legally codified in the United States by the 1980s, less obvious forms of racism and bigotry were perpetuated in the institutions and policies that structured American life. Black women in the 1980s were legally protected against discrimination in certain spaces, yet the underlying prejudice that persisted through institutionalized racism and sexism meant that such safeguards were precariously upheld and under constant embattlement. Both Black Americans and women had something to fear from the law and its defenders; Black women felt this perhaps most urgently.

The period in the early 1980s in which O'Grady was working coincided with the beginning of Ronald Reagan's presidency, in which he pursued an aggressive neoliberal agenda that dismantled many of the advances made by the progressive activists of the 1960s. For instance, among his efforts were appointing William Rehnquist (who expressed in a 1951 memo that *Plessy v. Ferguson* "was right and should be re-affirmed") to the position of Chief Justice of the Supreme Court; removing support for the Equal Rights Amendment (which maintained women's constitutional equality); pursuing antiabortion and antiwelfare policies; and limiting funding for or closing government departments such as the Equal Employment Opportunity Commission, which investigated workplace sex discrimination, and the Office on Domestic Violence.[33] Reagan, of course, was not alone in this agenda; the tremendous victories of the 1960s civil and women's rights movements incited a widespread and powerful "New Right" grassroots conservative countermovement in the 1970s that rallied behind Reagan as a protector against what were seen as assaults on "traditional" American values. Despite the abolition of legally sanctioned racial discrimination, restrictions and prejudices motivated by race persisted throughout the United States, as they continue to do so today.[34]

Deliberately dispossessing herself through her performance character, O'Grady decentered understandings of authorship that were either fully sovereign or relational, refusing to be objectified, reduced, or controlled. The act of creating an accomplice within oneself opens up O'Grady's subjectivity in radical ways. Moten and Harney describe of the fugitive: "it's about allowing subjectivity to be unlawfully overcome by others, a radical passion and passivity such that one becomes unfit for subjection, because one does not possess the kind of agency that can hold the regulatory forces of subjecthood, and one cannot initiate the auto-interpellative torque that biopower subjection requires and rewards."[35] To put it another way, the accomplice can be thought of as a means of distracting attention from O'Grady, dispersing agency so that she could move and act in ways that would avoid conscription into the status quo. Therefore, the "Outlaw Aesthetics" proclaimed by the exhibition title at JAM may have been realized only in retrospect, with the unanticipated addition of Mlle Bourgeoise Noire's performance.

As D'Souza points out in her introduction to *Writing in Space, 1973–2019*, O'Grady's insistence on exploring "black female subjectivity as both the expression of the most intimate and personal aspects of selfhood *and* a function of larger cultural and historical forces" occurred at a moment when the very notion of the subject was under considerable pressure in American academia influenced by postmodernist theory.[36] Against the backdrop of deconstructive dissolutions of categorical oppositions like male/female and Black/white that dominated the 1980s, the urgent question became how to assume a position of agential power through the particularities of her subject position. O'Grady recalls asking herself rhetorically at the time: "God, will it never end? Will they never stop taking up all the room, stop speaking for themselves as though speaking for everyone? The death of the author? The total construction of subjectivity? Sexual liberation as a prime victory of feminism? For you, perhaps. But for others, there was more."[37]

### Seeking Allies

While MBN's main target at JAM was the perceived conservatism of Black artists who O'Grady believed modified their work to achieve inclusion in white-run art spaces, she also sought to dismantle the considerable sexism she personally experienced from male artists in this community. The gendered aspects of MBN's critique are evidenced by her costume—the gown, gloves, and tiara unequivocally symbolize the forms of socially acceptable middle-class femininity, as exemplified by the beauty pageant queen. Herself familiar with such bourgeois values (as a young woman she had refused invitations to join prestigious Black social clubs and college sororities), she innately understood how such accessories carried with them the performative veneer of female respectability by their wearers.

While the cultural climate at Just Above Midtown was progressive, it harbored certain reactionary sentiments over the position of the Black female voice in both white and Black art worlds. As O'Grady has recounted, despite being founded by a woman, JAM was predominantly made up of a group of male artists—Houston Conwill, David Hammons, Noah Jemison, George Mingo, and Lorenzo Pace—who dictated much of the agenda and conversations at the gallery. According to O'Grady, the attitudes of these "locker room boys," as the women artists at JAM called them, were "like those in the civil rights movement: women's place was prone or, at least, not talking too much, and if possible, typing out grant applications for them. Above all, women artists weren't supposed to be too successful, too good."[38]

In the early 1980s, performance art was largely considered an outlier in the commercial art world as it was difficult to market and sell such works. Yet it was due, in part, to its decentered position that it was a particularly intriguing medium for women artists, providing space to experiment outside the long-harbored dictates and traditions of the male-dominated mediums of painting and sculpture. Whereas in the 1970s, photography often offered this respite for women artists, at times seen in so-called body art staged for the camera, by the 1980s photography had been largely re-cuperated into the mainstream art world, while performance remained on the relative periphery.[39]

In her important essay "Aspects of Performance in the Work of Black American Women Artists," art historian and curator Lowery Stokes Sims explains how the Black art community's hostility toward performance art was attributable, in part, to the noncommercial nature of the medium.[40] Yet such disinclination was gendered as well, something she attributes to the fact that "the overwhelmingly male focus of black American art might not be able to accommodate an expressive form that is dominated by women." She went on, "the peculiar machismo of the civil rights and black-power movements were definitely at odds with the goals and aspirations of the concurrent women's movement. And, as Michele Wallace has eloquently shown, not a few black women of that generation got caught at cross purposes."[41]

O'Grady's decision to stage her critique using an alternate persona was derived from her own marginality in the art world; MBN was to be a confrontational, demanding, and politically engaged character that could undermine the image of a deferential or submissive Black middle-class fe-male subject in Western culture. At the same time, as Sims explains, "the act of performing also plays provocatively into certain stereotypes about women, black women in particular. 'Acting out' was the exclusive province of black American women long before it was accepted as a creative strategy for women as a whole." She continues, "The suitability of 'acting out' as an expressive strategy for a class of individuals who have few accepted or sanctioned means of self-expression—and women of color in this society are particularly stymied in this regard—also comes into consideration here."[42]

Speaking on behalf of her MBN character, O'Grady exclaimed in 2007, "Drop that lady-like mask! Forget that self-controlled abstract art! Stop trying to be acceptable so you'll get an invitation to the party!"[43] MBN's—and by proxy O'Grady's—intention with the JAM "invasion" was, at its core, to jolt Black artists from their perceived complicity in making art for white audiences in the hopes of being accepted by the establish-ment institutions of the American art world. Given that her first attempt at trespassing as MBN—surreptitiously infiltrating the Black art world to call forth hidden preservers—did not incite her desired support, MBN sought another approach. This time, she would specifically contact Black artists and solicit their help for her cause.

## Solicitation

In 1982, a letter appeared in the mailboxes of thirty-six leading Black artists, including Frank Bowling, Ed Clark, Ray Grist, David Hammons, Maren Hassinger, Sandra Payne, Adrian Piper, Howardena Pindell, Martin Puryear, and Betye Saar. Addressed to "Advanced Black Artists," the dispatch issued a warning: "MLLE BOURGEOISE NOIRE is about to strike again." What followed was an ambiguous explanation of her plans: to pose a series of questions to Black artists about her or his personal experience in the art world and to compile the answers to help her stage another attack that would occur "this time between the covers (of a book)."[44]

She demanded truthful feedback, even threatening violence for noncompliance: "Please feel free to get angry, but don't feel free not to tell the whole truth and nothing but the truth, unless you want MLLE BOURGEOISE NOIRE to lay her whip on you!" The questions included "Who buys, looks at, cares about your work: i.e., who is its actual current audience?" "If there is a future, what might it hold for you and your work?" "Do you think advanced black art is permanently consigned to both the ivory tower and the ghetto? What would it need to become a vital factor in black life? A force in the white art world?" It was signed MLLE BOURGEOISE NOIRE, c/o Lorraine O'Grady.

What was Mlle Bourgeoise Noire's motivation behind sending this letter? Certainly, some of her inquiries sought to gauge the metaphorical temperature of the creation—and reception—of Black art circa 1982 in New York. But there was a deeper purpose, found in the leading nature of her questions. Transferring her tactical trespassing from physical to more conceptual intrusions undertaken through the postal service into artists' homes and studios, MBN intended this letter to serve as a new way of finding preservers. By soliciting her fellow Black artists' unfiltered honesty to provocative questions and for their utopian aspirations typically kept under wraps, MBN sought private disclosures that would reveal potential allies, those who shared her frustrations regarding the institutional racism that was pervasive in the art world.

The replies to MBN's questionnaire were largely disappointing, as only six artists are known to have taken her up on the task—an experience familiar to her previous attempts at engaging the Black artistic community to date. The returned letters speak of experiences of racism by white curators (Pindell), offer practical suggestions like recruiting larger numbers of

Black art students (Payne), and express hopes for Black art achieving equal recognition with that produced by white artists (Grist). Yet many other artists seemingly did not respond. Perhaps this disengagement indicated tacit disapproval for MBN's provocation in stirring up sentiments and reflection about the status of Black art and its future possibilities. Or perhaps it was fear of going on the record with said critiques, given the limited possibilities for Black artists at the time. Such an ambiguous position might be gleaned from a terse response from Janet Henry, who wrote pointedly: "Lorraine, you're asking a lot and frankly most of the questions concern topics I could give two shits about. Sorry but I can't do this. Sincerely, Janet."[45]

From her incursion at JAM to her mailed letters, Mlle Bourgeoise Noire staged two divergent tactics of trespassing in seeking out potential accomplices: undertaking performative actions within public Black art communities and privately soliciting support for her cause through critical engagement in the form of a questionnaire. Despite the distinctions in strategy, the artist's motivation in both cases was to locate preservers in her fellow Black artists, whom she admired but thought did not fully develop their potential in creating an independent Black avant-garde. As O'Grady's work with Mlle Bourgeoise Noire shows, the accomplice as a preserver—conceived both as a self-generated proxy for the artist and a potential auxiliary ally—introduces a new model for marginalized or dispossessed subjects like Black women artists in the 1980s to gain a kind of fugitive agency within a system that precluded lawful attempts at engendering parity.

### Critics

While her own experience was one in which she—as a bourgeois Bostonian with a stellar educational record and employment history—moved within white society with little difficulty, O'Grady has noted that she experienced overwhelming racism when she entered the art world in the early 1980s. As she explained at a 2018 lecture given at the Crystal Bridges Museum of American Art for the opening of the *Soul of a Nation: Art in the Age of Black Power* exhibition, when compared with the "equitable" assessments of achievement in standardized tests (like the SATs, GREs, and Federal Service Exams) that O'Grady excelled at, the arbitrary and highly subjective nature of the art world's determination of value was shocking.[46] She claimed she "had never encountered a world as absolutely segregated as the art world—where the segregation wasn't simply social, it was also an intellectual and cultural form of segregation justified under the rubric of 'quality.'"[47] Her point was supported by statistical evidence; in 1987, Pindell produced an important study on racial diversity in mainstream New York galleries, finding that a staggering 95 percent of represented artists at the time were white.

The latent conservatism behind what was presumed to be a liberal art world surprised O'Grady and galvanized her thinking about her racial identity. Early on in her career, as exemplified by her poetry-collages made from found newspaper clippings titled *Cutting Out the New York Times* (1977), O'Grady had produced work largely exploring universal themes of human subjectivity (an approach similar to what Thelma Golden has described as "postblack," as seen in work by artists during the 1990s such as Glenn Ligon, Kara Walker, and Hank Willis Thomas, who "were adamant about not being labeled as 'black' artists, though their work was steeped . . . in redefining complex notions of blackness").[48] However, a single phone conversation with an editor at the *New Yorker* made while conducting press outreach for the *Outlaw Aesthetics* show as a JAM volunteer drastically changed her perspective. With a snide comment about Goode Bryant's preference for titling exhibitions ("Oh, they always put titles on shows there, don't they?"), the editor of the "Goings on about Town" section made it clear that JAM was not going to receive coverage in the *New Yorker* and, presumably, the mainstream press more generally.[49] It was this very call in which O'Grady realized that she needed to more fully express her Black identity as a crucial part of her work if her aims of fostering an independent Black avant-garde might ever be achieved.[50]

Her activism had also been roused by another, unrelated experience the prior year. In 1979, O'Grady had attended artist Eleanor Antin's performance *Before the Revolution*, which was staged at 80 Langton Street in San Francisco. This work marked the debut of Antin's fictional character "Eleanora Antinova," an African American ballet dancer who would make recurring appearances in later plays, films, and still photographs as well as a series of drawings and texts. The darkly comedic narrative in *Before the Revolution* explored Antinova's promising career with Sergei Diaghilev's famed *Ballets Russes* and her experiences with racial profiling in the dance world. As her story goes, despite her talent, she was overlooked for leading roles on account of her race and age in a white- and youth-dominated institution. While Antinova's plight rang true to O'Grady, she felt that Antin's performances as the ballerina—which were problematically conducted by a white woman in blackface makeup—were emblematic of the ways in which some white artists were speaking on behalf of Black artists about their experience at the time.[51] O'Grady later recalled her impression of this work:

> The problem I had was that, as I was looking at Eleanor Antin in blackface with a tutu, I kept thinking of my mother: what she was like as a young woman in the early '20s and what would have happened to her had she gone to audition for Diaghilev. Antin didn't have the answers, and neither did I, but the show I was seeing in my head was more interesting than the one Antin was presenting. I thought, "I can speak for this black ballerina better than she can. It's time to speak for my own black self."[52]

Between Antin's performance and the *New Yorker*'s dismissal, Mlle Bourgeoisie Noire's next incursion became urgently clear. She needed to address the limited representation of Black artists in white art institutions—which she predicted would prefer to maintain the status quo. Cynicism aside, might *they* be her preservers-in-waiting? It was unlikely, as O'Grady presumably knew. But maybe, she seems to have surmised, by making visible the experience of racial segregation that precluded her inclusion, new preservers might paradoxically be forged from somewhere within the mainstream art museum. As she would soon declare to an unassuming audience, perhaps *now* was the time for an invasion—to probe the critical question of which artists deserve recognition.

On the evening of September 18, 1981, the New Museum held the opening reception for its *Persona* exhibition. According to curators Lynn Gumpert and Ned Rifkin, the show's concept "originated in response to the increasing number of artists that we have seen who use specific characters and alter egos in their art," with a focus on those who "have sustained this interest by integrating themselves directly into their personae."[53] The nine artists selected to exhibit their work were Antin (presenting her male character as *The King of Solana Beach*), Colin Campbell, Bruce Charlesworth, Colette, Redd Ekks, James Hill, Lynn Hershman Leeson, Mr. Apology, and Martial Westburg. Despite the curators' insistence on the pervasiveness of this tendency across art practices, not one Black artist was included.

Mlle Bourgeoise Noire arrived at the New Museum to rectify this oversight. Certainly, she assumed, her presence would be welcomed—as she would be not only the lone example of a live enactment of a persona but also the only persona created by an artist of color. Yet O'Grady had not been entirely overlooked, as one might assume; the New Museum's education department had in fact reached out to inquire about having her participate in a series of *Persona*-related outreach events for local schoolchildren—in place of the actual exhibition—sidelining her artistic labor by only offering an auxiliary role apart from actual inclusion in the show. Without committing either way, O'Grady responded by suggesting that she and the education department revisit their conversation after the opening.

Many of the details of Mlle Bourgeoise Noire's 1981 intervention at the white-run New Museum recall that of her JAM performance the year prior. First making a self-described "tournée" around the exhibition space, MBN initially charmed her unwitting audience; she distributed flowers until her bouquet was bare, exposing the whip below. The next segment of the performance was notably longer in this instance; the artist recalls repeatedly whipping herself for approximately five to ten minutes "until there were practically welts on my back."[54] The extended length of this gesture was likely a deliberate attempt to grow MBN's audience in this significantly larger museum setting. As predicted, bystanders began gathering to see what was going on and "after she [threw] the whip down because she has had enough and all eyes are on her, she [shouted] out the poem."[55]

In contrast to the modified Damas poem "Trève" performed at JAM, here MBN had written an original verse expressing her feelings. It read:

WAIT
wait in your alternate/alternate spaces
spitted on fish hooks of hope
be polite
wait to be discovered
be proud
be independent
tongues cauterized at openings no one attends
stay in your place
after all, art is only for art's sake
THAT'S ENOUGH
don't you know
sleeping beauty needs more than a kiss to awake
now is the time for an INVASION![56]

The language of both performances by MBN was directed to an audience of Black artists (despite the predominantly white spectators in attendance at the New Museum); however, while the first version called out the actions commonly undertaken to gain acceptance ("boot-licking, ass-kissing") to inspire risk taking in Black art, the second was more antagonistic, taking a mocking approach toward the reasons she believed Black artists often accepted their exclusions and demanding militant action instead. While both poems end with a directive for Black artists, the one written for the New Museum demands greater activity than simply changing one's art; rather, it solicits a full-on invasion to rouse the "sleeping beauties," presumably referring to the white art institutional workers and audiences who remained willfully unaware of ongoing racism in the museum setting.

Such distinctions in the performance scripts clarify the goals of each of MBN's respective interventions. At JAM she hoped her actions would bring forth a network of Black artists who sought to pursue a freer aesthetic agenda, no longer beholden to the existing system of aesthetic value based on outside perspectives of Black creative expression. Whereas at the New Museum she sought radical transformations from white audiences and art workers, she used MBN to call on potential preservers from within to dismantle or radically reform the art institution altogether.

The differences between these two interventions continued in the structure of the performance itself. As noted in the performance script, she was accompanied at the New Museum by four other individuals, two of whom were new additions since the JAM staging. Jeffrey Scott, a hired actor, reprised the role of tuxedo-clad "Master of Ceremonies" that had been previously played by O'Grady's brother-in-law; Richard DeGussi, an erstwhile art director and frequent collaborator in O'Grady's performances (he would also appear in *Rivers, First Draft*), assumed the role of "Art Critic"; and photographer Coreen Simpson was cited as the "Paparazza." Additionally, a second photographer, Salima Ali, was brought on to document the performance. Even though this expanded lineup of performers is cited in the cast list as well as featured prominently in the photographic documentation of the performance, their role in MBN's intervention at the New Museum has received less attention than seems warranted.

In particular, the Art Critic and Paparazza did not appear alongside MBN at JAM; their addition invites closer analysis. In one particularly telling image (fig. 4.2), the distinct roles of each character can be surmised. MBN stands just right of center in the composition; she is closely shadowed by her Master of Ceremonies as she gives an interview to the notepad-wielding white "Art Critic," who metaphorically acts as the gatekeeper to mainstream audiences and critical reception. At left is Simpson,

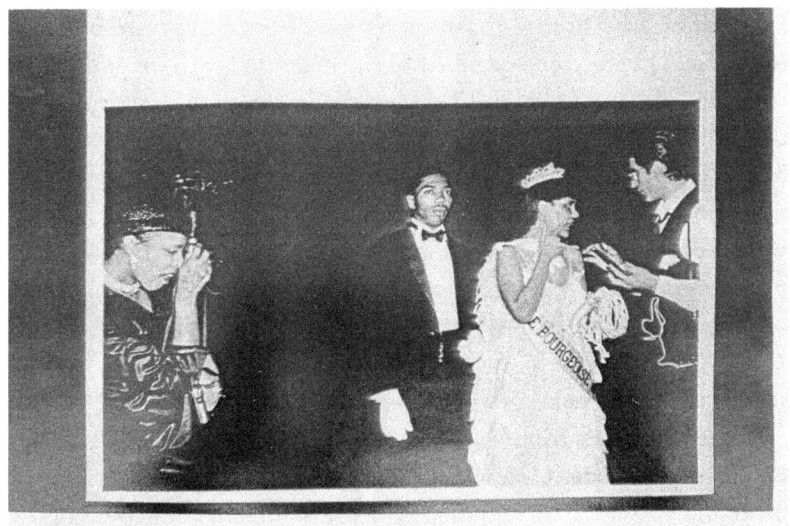

As the astonished crowd buzzes furiously, Mlle Bourgeoise Noire gives an interview.

**4.02** Annotated photocopy of photograph by Salima Ali for Lorraine O'Grady's performance *Mlle Bourgeoise Noire Goes to the New Museum*, 1981. Box 10, folder 9, Papers of Lorraine O'Grady, MSS.3, Wellesley College Archives, Wellesley, MA.

whose chic, all-black satin jumpsuit provides a contrast to O'Grady's stylized white gown. Depicted in Ali's photograph with her camera raised, Simpson's presence signals to the viewer that MBN's actions were worthy of being recorded for both the live and secondary viewers—recalling the structure of dual cameramen operating in Hannah Wilke's performances of *Intercourse with . . .* described in chapter 2. Here, however, MBN notably chose that her image be made through the eyes of other Black women, who acted as proxies for the artist in presenting her perspective and potentially preserving it for future audiences.

In the years since, O'Grady has repeatedly pointed out that many of the reductive misunderstandings about this piece generated from the circulation of only two photographs—out of a total of twenty-seven that constitute the full documentation of the work—as being representative of her larger, and decidedly more complex, performance. These images—one of MBN taken midshout and the other of MBN performing self-flagellation—were often presented without verbal or visual contextualization, resulting in misapprehensions about her agenda. O'Grady has described this situation as the performance being "captured or rather imprisoned by the empty signifier of the image[s]," with "no indication of an audience. . . . An oddly distilled anger had been the only quality of the performance the art world would know."[57] Notably, there exists an extensive body of celebratory images that depict MBN cheering and toasting with her collaborators in the aftermath of her invasion. Just as with Burden's performative interventions, the fact that the artist included such photographs as integral parts of the work's documentation indicates that a substantial portion of the piece occurred after leaving the New Museum and involved the contributions of those who invaded with her, thereby sharing in the potential consequences.[58]

Isolating this complex work to one or two images had significant effects on its reception. As noted by Sparling Williams, the circulation of incomplete visual documentation resulted in limited evaluations of the wide variety of firsthand responses that were experienced when the piece was staged at the New Museum: "Popular interpretations of the work alienate the work itself, obscuring the possibility of complex and diverse reactions from the crowd. While many white mainstream audiences may have been shocked and irritated, the Black middle-class subjects to which her enactment was actually directed reacted with humor, awe, delight, and anxiety."[59] To Sparling Williams's point, in contrast to the responses to her JAM performance, which might have felt like a personal attack against those grappling with similar frustrations, a portion of the Black audience members likely appreciated the boldness of MBN's attacks taken on the "home turf" of the white viewer over the racial discrepancies of accreditation, recognition, and representation that were being unquestioned in art institutions such as the New Museum. And yet O'Grady privately expressed recognition that her piece would likely be controversial for both white and Black audiences, as she wrote shortly after the New Museum performance: "I expect that a great deal of my work, in general, is going to be misunderstood. I'm going against all the stereotypes in a way that most whites, and blacks, find frightening."[60]

While O'Grady has voiced frustration with the limited focus on one particular photograph of Mlle Bourgeoise Noire shouting as definitive of the project more generally, it is significant that the artist in fact selected this exact image as the background for a text-based collage that appeared in issue 14 of the feminist journal *Heresies* (fig. 4.3).[61] Titled in all-caps, "MLLE BOURGEOISE NOIRE GOES TO THE NEW MUSEUM TO REMEDY BEING OMITTED FROM THE NINE-WHITE-PERSONAE SHOW," the photograph

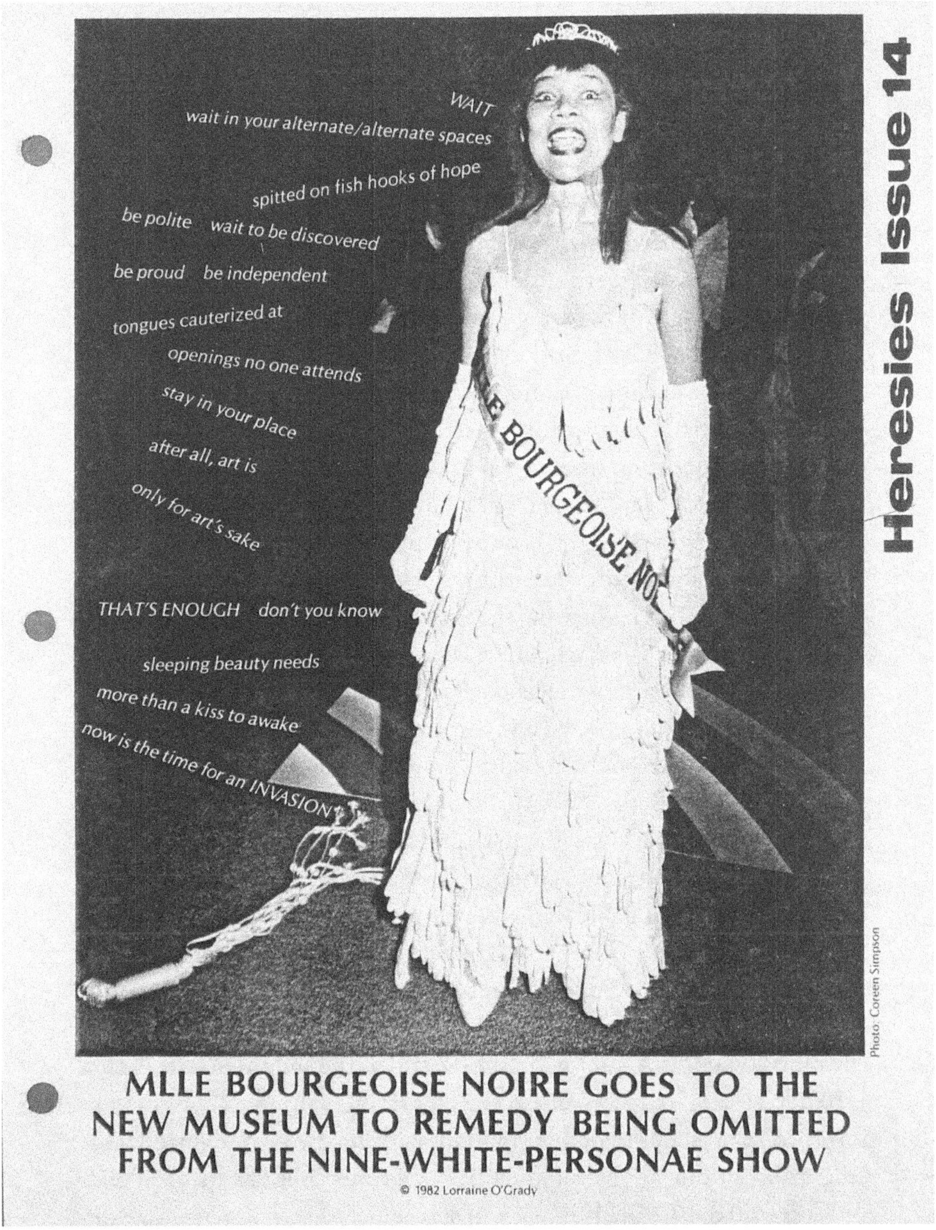

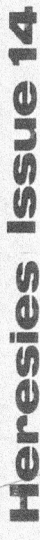

WAIT
wait in your alternate/alternate spaces
spitted on fish hooks of hope
be polite wait to be discovered
be proud be independent
tongues cauterized at
openings no one attends
stay in your place
after all, art is
only for art's sake
THAT'S ENOUGH don't you know
sleeping beauty needs
more than a kiss to awake
now is the time for an INVASION
BOURGEOISE NO
Heresies Issue 14
Photo: Coreen Simpson
MLLE BOURGEOISE NOIRE GOES TO THE NEW MUSEUM TO REMEDY BEING OMITTED FROM THE NINE-WHITE-PERSONAE SHOW
© 1982 Lorraine O'Grady


**4.03** Lorraine O'Grady, *Mlle Bourgeoise Noire Goes to the New Museum to Remedy Being Omitted from the Nine-White-Personae Show*, 1982. Published as an artist's page in *Heresies* 4, no. 2, issue 14, "The Women's Pages" (1982). Photograph by Coreen Simpson.

captures O'Grady addressing the camera with her whip laying limply on the floor and her mouth agape.[62] Her verbalized poem is printed here alongside her image; the text is positioned at various diagonals, with the first three lines appearing as if coming from her own lips like a live utterance.

This photograph also ran in the October 7, 1981, issue of the *Village Voice*; it accompanied an article by critic Lucy Lippard titled "Open Season," about the current activities of the art world. As it was the only image in the article, readers were undoubtedly drawn to the powerful and provocative appearance of its protagonist. The accompanying caption—which reads "Lorraine O'Grady at the New Museum: Surprise!"—augmented this sensationalized interpretation of the work centered on O'Grady's embodiment of MBN alone, while also troubling the distance that O'Grady seemingly sought to create between herself and her alter ego.

The crux of Lippard's text did, however, provide contextualization for MBN's trespassing at the New Museum; it elaborated on the concept of an invasion and reprinted the artist's poem in full. Lippard drew attention to O'Grady's exclusion from the *Persona* show and called out an important element of the work's afterlife: that the offer from the New Museum to participate in its auxiliary educational outreach programming was abruptly rescinded after her unexpected invasion. Lippard writes, "There are no third-world artists in 'Persona.' O'Grady, who works like this [using a persona] herself, was only asked to do a workshop for schoolchildren on the subject, though the invitation was withdrawn after she had performed uninvited."[63]

By prominently publicizing the disinvitation of O'Grady, which the New Museum presumably wanted to keep quiet, Lippard—and by proxy, MBN—soon received a response. On behalf of the New Museum, Special Projects Coordinator Ed Jones penned an unprinted "Letter to the Editor" that countered Lippard's tacit accusations of retaliation and racism-by-omission. He first asserted in the letter that the educational invitation extended to O'Grady was an esteemed position, writing: "I consider our artist-led workshops to be an important and effective way of introducing the art of our time to the community."[64] Of course, the fact that this offer was presented to O'Grady in place of actual inclusion in the *Persona* exhibition only reaffirmed O'Grady's point. As she sarcastically wrote in a letter the following month to art critic John Perrault: "I wasn't really accusing the New Museum of racism (heavens forbid! We all know they're far too evolved for that sort of thing), but just of the same old bullshit—not feeling the need to look beyond a 'small circle of friends.'"[65]

Lorraine O'Grady,
"Mlle Bourgeoise Noire
begins to concentrate,"
from *Mlle Bourgeoise
Noire Goes to the
New Museum*, 1981.
Gelatin silver fiber
print, 10 × 7¾ in. (Note:
Redd Ekks, *Retnec*,
1980, in foreground.)

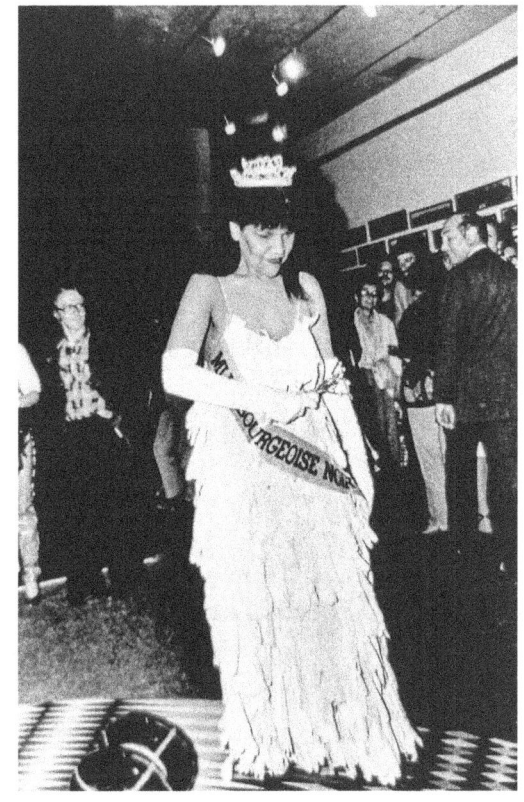

Second, Jones claimed that the reason for retracting the previous offer was on moral and ethical grounds. He pointed out that, as could be seen in the documentary images of the New Museum performance (fig. 4.4), Mlle Bourgeoise Noire had staged her actions within the physical bounds of a work in the *Persona* show: Robert Rasmussen's (also known as Redd Ekks) sculptural installation *Retnec* (1980), which featured a component situated directly on the gallery floor. This, according to Jones, was a crime worthy of substantial punishment and an indication of moral ineptitude, particularly as an acting representative to children on behalf of the *Persona* artists and the sanctity of the museum. He explained, "I could not in good conscience ask someone to interpret an exhibition to children when that person had violated the integrity of the same exhibition by performing literally inside another artist's piece."[66]

As a representative of the New Museum, Jones therefore took issue with multiple aspects of Mlle Bourgeoise Noire's performance.

First, her intervention—and its resulting publicity—encroached on the unquestioned inviolability of the museum as art institution, exposing its conservatism. Moreover, by bringing the MBN persona to the museum itself, O'Grady overturned the presumption that a lack of racial diversity could be explained away as simply being part of different social circles. Her staging of a live-action piece—the only event-based work seen at a show about alter egos—using a persona that was both Black and middle class also violated the ongoing perpetuation, glamorization, and commercialization of "authentic" Blackness as lower class. As O'Grady explained to Perrault: "I'm really tired of bourgeois black artists playing out the roles that white people have unconsciously assigned to them, and pretending to be experts on rats and roaches and the mores of the street. One of the efforts I'm making in my work is to try to wake minority artists up to the kinds of attitudes they will have to take if they want to be accepted without condescension."[67]

As this work exemplifies, O'Grady's Mlle Bourgeoise Noire character pushed the nominal artist into the role of the accomplice to operate within new modes of exclusion in which intersectional questions of race and gender could be forged. Her act of conceptual trespassing into the spaces run by the hegemonic white art world required the contextualization of this being a staged performance—it was not the actions of O'Grady herself, who maintained her social acceptability, but rather a character playing a role of provocateur that was more palatable when conducted in the name of art. And yet, by employing performative interventionist tactics that were readily accepted by prominent art institutions when performed by white artists—as exemplified by Burden, for instance—O'Grady exposed the racialized discrepancies in reception by white-run museums such as the New Museum.

The perceived antagonism of her actions was possibly meant to reveal such covert allegiances, exposing those who would protect the institutions by accusing her of being a trespasser. Yet it also uncovered potential preservers such as Lippard, who went on the record in publicly defending O'Grady in print. This indicated that her tactics were working in getting closer to creating or finding the audience she urgently sought out. If her "lawbreaking" was explicitly drawing attention to the unofficial yet ongoing segregations of the art world in a post–civil rights era, those who saw her point became potential accomplices in breaching her outsider status within the art world and its institutions.

## Trespassers

O'Grady's development of the Mlle Bourgeoise Noire persona can be contextualized within a broader tendency in American art during the mid-1970s to early 1980s in which artists explored other identities through the formation of third-party characters. While this tradition traces back to Marcel Duchamp's gender-bending alter ego Rrose Sélavy at the beginning of the twentieth century, there was a notable resurgence of performance personas created by women artists around this time, including those by Antin, Judy Chicago, VALIE EXPORT, Joan Jonas, Lynn Hershman Leeson, Linda Montano, Pindell, Piper, and Martha Wilson. Many instances of such practices were pursued under the influence of second-wave feminism: Chicago famously renounced her birth name—Judy Gerowitz—and assumed her art persona as "Judy Chicago" to divest herself of patriarchal markers of ownership and social property, whereas Joan Jonas created her alter ego Organic Honey in front of the video camera, performing in a bejeweled and feathered headdress and a mask of a doll's face to explore ideas around female archetypes, masquerade, and subjectivity.

Such practices invite comparison with male artists who experimented with different personas around the same time. The creation of alter egos appeared in various performance projects by men in the 1970s and early 1980s, yet these often assumed more playful undertones, as exemplified by Mike Smith's "Baby Ikki" character, in which he performed as a diaper- and sunglasses-clad infant in a grown man's body. In marked contrast, women artists frequently used impersonation and role-playing to act out fantasies of power and witness firsthand the discrepancies in admission, security, and authority that are normalized and readily accessed by men. Whether or not their disguises achieved successful concealment of their gender, they often adopted performance practices to effectively see what they were missing as motivation for their ongoing feminist demands for equal rights. Yet by maintaining similarities in terms of race, gender, biographical backstory, and physical appearance, O'Grady's creation of MBN based on her own personal identity represents a marked difference from the performative personas created by many of her fellow women artists at the time.[68]

In 1978, O'Grady began regularly attending events at Franklin Furnace—one of the leading experimental performance spaces in New York—where she became acquainted with the types of works being made by fellow artists, including Laurie Anderson, Dara Birnbaum, and Jenny Holzer.[69] While women artists in this circle were producing pieces that O'Grady found inspiring, those using performance or creating alternate personas to explore other identities were predominantly white. Part of the issue behind this racial discrepancy concerned the nature of performance art itself.[70] In the context of the contemporary art world, it was Black women artists for whom using performance personas to act out scenarios that were otherwise not available to them assumed a particular urgency, especially as they negotiated the intersectional dynamics of gender and race that were being overlooked in much of mainstream second-wave white feminist art.

Piper is a notable example of a Black woman artist who was producing alter egos at the time. She occupied a place of considerable significance in O'Grady's life, as a personal ally and ongoing creative interlocutor, and her position in the art world was significant; in the 1980s, she was often the only Black woman artist to be included in white-run exhibitions and was certainly one of few who made performance-based work using alternate personas.[71] Piper had introduced her alter ego, The Mythic Being, much earlier than MBN; in 1973, she placed a set of newspaper advertisements in the gallery listings section of the *Village Voice*, featuring herself in drag accompanied by text taken from the artist's personal teenage journals, melding a fictional male alter ego with her own identity. She subsequently followed this up with a body of legendary performances enacted on the streets of New York in which she investigated public perceptions of racial and gender identities by altering her outward appearance through a short, Afro-style wig, fake moustache, and mirrored sunglasses as she assumed certain stereotypically masculine behaviors in her enactment of a Black man.[72] Yet there are significant distinctions between Piper's and O'Grady's personas; Piper performed a male character in public that was vastly different from her own identity as a mixed-race woman, whereas Mlle Bourgeoise Noire shared much of O'Grady's personal attributes.

As O'Grady knew from personal experience, Black bourgeois women in America—particularly in the 1940s and 1950s, when she was growing up—were commonly expected to conduct themselves in a manner thought to be suitable in the eyes of the white population. She explained: "It's not so much a desire to be part of, to actually socialize in the white world—most blacks would find that quite boring, dead, not fun—but to be acknowledged as really equal."[73] Much of Black middle-class identity continued to be tied up in this pursuit of parity and recognition in subsequent decades—as power was still held by white individuals who determined cultural value—which, in O'Grady's estimation, led many to minimize their own identities, styles, and cultural backgrounds to gain acceptance within white determinations of worth. "Measures of success are defined by the white world, and styles of being and behavior are inept adaptations of white styles instead of developments of original black personal and cultural modes," she noted in 1986.[74]

These forms of staging acceptable sociability were ingrained in her as a young girl. While O'Grady was born and raised in New England, her parents emigrated from the Caribbean, where they played an intermediary role within the history of British colonialism and American identity. As she explains, their own biracial background was entrenched in their self-image even after moving to Boston:

> They came from the mulatto class that was employed by the British to help rule those islands: the British couldn't rule those islands themselves; they had to have help, and they had this ready-made caste of mixed-bloods who could be used to control the blacks on the island. To use this class effectively they had to make allies of them, let them feel they were superior to the blacks. My parents brought that feeling of social superiority inherent in light skin coloring with them to this country. That is what I have been rebelling against all of my life.[75]

It was this desire for social ascendency by her parents that shaped O'Grady's formative years: "I'd had an exceptionally traditional and elitist education, which I had to work hard to rid myself of in order to become an artist. I went to Girls Latin School in Boston . . . then to Wellesley College, where I majored in economics."[76]

And yet it was this familiarity with such expectations that enabled O'Grady to so readily assume Mlle Bourgeoise Noire's affectation and character. In her costume and social references, MBN prominently parodied the bourgeois values that O'Grady had seen from her upbringing as a young woman. Moreover, it was this awareness that refined her critiques against Black artists trying to gain acceptance within the white-dominated art world.

At the time of MBN's creation, social politics were largely partisan and unwilling to account for multiple coexisting identities. Critiques were presented universally, without nuance for the varied subjects affected by intersectional issues of race, class, and gender. This often played out with

Black male artists concerning themselves with the issue of race and white second-wave feminist women interpellating gender, with little discussion from either camp about class (unsurprisingly, white male artists largely absolved themselves from any discussions of identity altogether; instead, such "universal subjects" frequently focused on formalist aesthetic concerns). O'Grady recounts:

> In 1980, when I created it, there were no role models in white feminist art for a tri-partite critique, or at least none that I was aware of. That era's feminism seemed concerned strictly with gender. Second-wave feminism was basically a white bourgeois construction that seemed to operate as though unconscious that it was white or that it was middle-class. It was a time when white feminists could still believe that their definitions of sexual liberation and professional advancement applied identically to all women . . . and that they could speak for all women.[77]

While maintaining a long-standing engagement with white feminist initiatives throughout her career, O'Grady has been consistently vocal about her feelings of exclusion from established categorical binaries. In 2015, O'Grady appeared at the National Museum of Women in the Arts clad in a gorilla mask as part of the feminist activist group Guerrilla Girls. There she pointed out the typical distinction between "women artists" and "artists of color," leaving behind those who identify with both, as she does. Yet this intersectional position—never finding full articulation of her subjecthood within the strict parameters of either social group—recalls the agential possibilities described in Harney and Moten's fugitive subjects who exist as outlaws, beyond what can be defined within or against the law.

Whether on account of her gender, class, or race, O'Grady recognized that she effectively *had* to trespass to enter the art world, resulting in the development of Mlle Bourgeoise Noire as a kind of proxy who could move through covert routes and behave in ways that defied the established rules. For Harney and Moten, the way that the fugitive doesn't violate the established laws but refuses them outright opens up an alternative operating model that evades the limitations of such externally imposed standards altogether. Within the context of the 1980s art world, O'Grady's identification between and across such social groups greatly informed her self-generated MBN persona as a subject that could assume a public role in her place, allowing O'Grady to operate largely undetected.

While O'Grady certainly believed that a critique of gender disparities was necessary, she was critical of the narrow agenda and focus that constituted second-wave white middle-class feminism. While the primary goals for this circle of women were the right to pursue a career and the right to sexual freedom, this was not a universally held position. O'Grady expressed: "If you asked what those goals might mean to black women who'd never had the right not to work, never had the right not to be considered sexual objects, you could see the goals might need calibrating."[78] This opinion was shared by Pindell, who pointedly stated that "what the white male's voice was to the white female's voice, the white female's voice was to the woman of color's voice. The dominant voice was usually limited to the middle- and upper-class white women, but all classes of white women participated consciously or unconsciously in racism."[79]

Similarly, the very form of performance art looked quite different for Black and white women artists. For instance, nudity and the freedom to present one's body assumed importance for many white women artists in the 1970s; one might only think of Wilke's attempts to deliberately solicit attention to her cause of omission using her exposed body. Yet for Black women artists, nudity was historically forced on them, and therefore, as O'Grady expresses, "freedom may be the ability to keep our clothes on if we want."[80]

O'Grady's development of the MBN persona allowed her to enter the rarefied spaces of the white-dominated art world without formal invitation while also mounting an attack on said institutions. Since the rare works by Black artists that were included in white galleries and museums were considered "well-behaved" and seen to have tempered their criticality, the solution was not, in O'Grady's eyes, mere inclusion. Moreover, it was the very notion that the presence of a single Black artist could be representative of the goals and aesthetic program of Black artists more generally that often allowed for the widespread occlusions of other voices. Even the growing visibility of Black artists was motivated by white institutional needs, with artists of color being featured only when it served the art world's public image of being inclusive. Therefore, the Mlle Bourgeoise Noire character served as a way of gaining attention and interrupting the circuits of exclusion at the same time—marking MBN's trespassing as perhaps the only possible avenue to get O'Grady's point across to her desired audience.

First at Just Above Midtown in 1980 and then at the New Museum the following year, O'Grady developed a tactic of using disruptive actions that would equally enact critiques against the closed-off white institutional art community as well as that of the Black art world. As she explains, these two interventions were similar in that "they were guerrilla actions in which, uninvited and unexpected, she invaded a space to give a message that presumably would be painful to hear."[81] As seen at the New Museum, her hopes for creating preservers by exposing the exclusionary politics of white institutions did not work out as intended, although it got her closer to locating the preservers she so desired. The answer to her question regarding which artists deserved mainstream recognition had not changed—it still lingered provocatively in the air, like a challenge for MBN to continue carrying on through alternative means.

## Alternate Tactics

After her performative intervention at the New Museum, Mlle Bourgeoise Noire tried a radically different approach in soliciting the attention of the white-dominated art world. In April 1983, she curated *The Black and White Show*, an art exhibition staged at the Kenkeleba Gallery on East Second Street in New York's East Village. Described as a "conceptual art piece employing other artists' work to make its point" and, at another time, "a Mlle Bourgeoise Noire performance," *The Black and White Show* signaled a new direction in MBN's tactical strategy.[82]

While O'Grady had worked as a curator for the Black-owned Independence Bank in Chicago that same year, *The Black and White Show* fell under the purview of Mlle Bourgeoise Noire, making it a project headed by the invented persona rather than O'Grady herself. The exhibition featured a body of exclusively monochromatic work made by twenty-eight artists—fourteen Black and fourteen white. Given that she did not use labels or other didactic texts articulating this precise balance of racial representation, MBN sought to focus attention on the formal relationships between artworks. Such a clear visual representation of the equal number of compelling artworks by artists identifying as both Black and white would, she hoped, counter the tokenism that was frequently used to maintain disparities in racial representation within mainstream, white-run art institutions. For instance, in a 1993 article for *Artforum*, O'Grady recounted a telling conversation with a white curator at a major museum who said about patrons: "For many of them, every black artist is a black artist by definition. . . . They're looking for the one typical, quintessential black artist, so then they can say, 'I've done it,' and not do any more."[83]

In contrast to the still predominantly segregated New York art world—perhaps no more clearly expressed than at the New Museum's "all-white Persona show"—MBN's selection of artists included in *The Black and White Show* was a stark reminder of the profound lack of diversity seen in other art galleries and museums at the time. This aim was fully intentional; in the project proposal, MBN situated her curatorial endeavor as a conceptual continuation of concerns introduced at the New Museum intervention about segregation in the art world. Instead of trespassing in front of an unwitting live audience, MBN here pursued a different method in setting a counterexample to serve as a potential paradigm for other institutions. The resulting show, O'Grady explained, would be "the first I'd seen in the still segregated art world with enough black presence to create dialogue."[84]

Despite the achromatic color scheme, the works on view revealed a considerable variety of styles. In contrast to the art seen at the *Afro-American Abstraction*, *Outlaw Aesthetics*, or *Persona* shows, MBN selected work by artists that she felt represented a true Black avant-garde. Mlle Bourgeoise Noire had two aims in *The Black and White Show*. First, she sought to show strong examples of art produced without those trappings of Black identity dictated by white audiences. Second, she wanted to present an exhibition model in which there was equitable racial representation without explicitly stating such a curatorial strategy, allowing the audience to first examine the works qualitatively before potentially discovering details about the artists' racial identities.

Contributing artists to *The Black and White Show* included Piper, Nancy Spero, and Jack Whitten. Jean-Michel Basquiat had promised Mlle Bourgeoise Noire that he would participate; however, he pulled out at the last minute. Numerous abstract works were featured, many of which indirectly explored the influence of Black culture. For instance, Tyrone Mitchell's sculpture was influenced by his experience living with the Dogon, an indigenous ethnic group from Mali, in his choice of materials and form. Whitten found a more contemporary source of inspiration in free jazz, performed by musicians such as Ornette Coleman.

Yet at least two of the works in the show explicitly addressed the racial tensions that spurred the curatorial agenda. For instance, Randy Williams's sculptural installation, *Between the White Man and the Land There Was Thus Interposed the Shadow of the Black Man* (1983), mined the artist's experience of using segregated bathrooms while growing up in the South. Stephen Lack's drawing depicted an actual event experienced by Basquiat and his fellow graffiti artists; it shows four Black men being violently accosted by two white police officers. Given the dearth of reporting on such racially motivated examples of police brutality, Lack's work assumed an evidentiary role in documenting this act, all too common in New York during the early 1980s.

Despite the interest of the curatorial concept and the strong roster of participating artists, visitor attendance was low at *The Black and White Show*. While this was in part due to Kenkeleba's location amid the drug markets and high crime that dominated the East Village at the time, the lack of press coverage—while not unexpected, given the Black ownership of the gallery—contributed to the limited viewership. This factor inspired O'Grady to reach out to media outlets, even after the official temporal parameters of the MBN project ended.

In October 1984, O'Grady wrote to Elizabeth Baker, the editor of *Art in America*, through the voice of Mlle Bourgeoise Noire to counter many of Baker's claims written about the East Village art scene in the summer 1984 issue of the magazine. In this correspondence, O'Grady-as-MBN returns to the problem of the absent media coverage about *The Black and White Show* and its host gallery, Kenkeleba, despite some of its artists and site-specific artworks made for the show—such as John Fekner's *Toxic Junkie* mural—gaining considerable notoriety.[85] Pointing out this oversight, she writes: "By any standard, 'The Black and White Show' was a major event. . . . Perhaps I should say, it was a major show by any other standard other than the curator and gallery owners were black."[86] Explicitly stating the racial motivations behind such coverage, MBN goes on to say: "I do think your editorial decision not to discuss Kenkeleba Gallery in East Village Report 84, as well as your original decision not to send a critic to look at 'The Black and White Show,' raises questions both about your attitude toward black curators and gallery owners, and toward not-for-profit art spaces."[87]

*The Black and White Show* was a continuation of MBN's significant and vocal interrogation of race in contemporary art as well as a new attempt at creating preservers for her work. Yet in following the unspoken rules of the art world to attempt to gain visibility, MBN failed to make an impact. The outcome was familiar to O'Grady from her time working to publicize *Outlaw Aesthetics* a few years prior; according to her, the show was not reviewed by any art publications, only mentioned briefly in the local downtown newspaper, the *East Village Eye*.[88] Its audience ended up being mostly limited to East Village residents and friends of the artists. As O'Grady explained, "In the end, its 'appeal to reason' had as little effect as Mlle Bourgeoise Noire's 'joyous anger.' The art world's complexion was the same" and "it was another shout that disappeared without being heard."[89]

Being a law-abiding citizen under such circumstances, it seemed, wouldn't get her very far.

## Audiences

In the typewritten project description for *Art Is . . .* , the final endeavor undertaken as Mlle Bourgeoise Noire, O'Grady posed the following rhetorical question: "Can art compete with floats sponsored by music stations and beer companies to reach half a million people?" Fed up with her experience of the conservative art world, she began pursuing a new audience by reconfiguring her focus toward a Black public found in extrainstitutional spaces. After unsuccessfully looking for preservers in her fellow artists, gallerists, critics, and art institutions, MBN's performative intervention *Art Is . . .* , staged at the 1983 African American Day Parade in Harlem, was an attempt to find out whether a nonart audience might finally fulfill her quest for locating accomplices.

The origins of this project arose in 1982 when O'Grady was invited to work on an upcoming issue of *Heresies*.[90] The primary editorial collective had contacted O'Grady as well as various artists and intellectuals of color about contributing content for an issue titled "Racism Is the Issue"—a temporary amelioration of the editorial board's general lack of racial diversity. During one of the editorial meetings, a colleague on this project—a Black female social worker—dismissed art's ability to effect change, declaring: "avant-garde art doesn't have anything to do with black people!" O'Grady later recalled that this comment stung deeply, yet she wasn't convinced of its truth; she began asking herself, "Where would I find the 'black people' to answer her?"[91]

Such a remark was problematic for O'Grady on multiple fronts: in her art and writing, she railed against the systemic racism that perpetuated inequalities in the creation and reception of art; she articulated a nonbinary form of subjectivity that complicated racial and gender polarities; and she believed in art's potential power to transform its viewers. In this manner, she engaged with the historical avant-garde pursuit of dissolving the distinctions between the rarefied world of art and everyday life—and began thinking of ways to introduce untraditional audiences to art on a large scale using her MBN persona.

In *Art Is . . .* , O'Grady built an actual parade float with interactive and participatory elements that would be inserted within the public

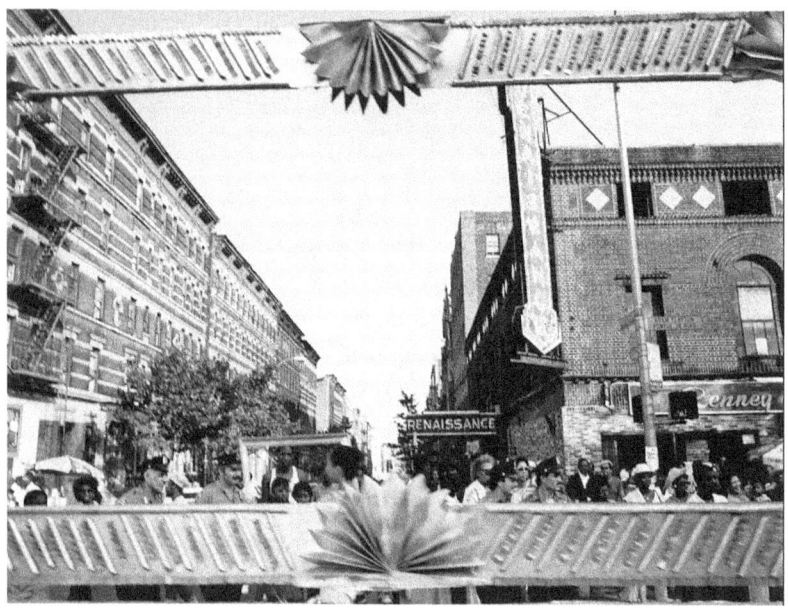

**4.05**    Lorraine O'Grady, *Art Is . . . (Faded Renaissance)*, 1983.
Chromogenic print, 16 × 20 in.

context of the African American Day Parade. Early logistical concerns involved the content of her float; as can be seen in archival material for *Art Is . . .* , O'Grady originally considered having artists make artworks in real time while riding atop the flatbed truck, which would be effectively transformed into a moving art studio. She later revised her concept after speaking with the truck rental company, which pointed out the relatively brief audience viewing time in the parade format. As O'Grady noted, "So I switched, from putting art into the parade to trying to create an art experience for the viewers."[92]

Explicitly conceived as a project directed by Mlle Bourgeoise Noire, *Art Is . . .* was composed of two main elements. The first was the float itself; O'Grady enlisted the help of artists George Mingo and Richard DeGussi in building a vintage-style gold picture frame—spanning nine by fifteen feet—that was mounted atop a flatbed truck base. This was then decorated with a matching golden skirt featuring the work's title printed on either side. O'Grady oriented the empty frame laterally, so that audiences located on either side of the street along the parade route could see and be seen through it. This would create the first of her desired effects: whether in motion or at moments of pause along the parade route, the unfilled picture

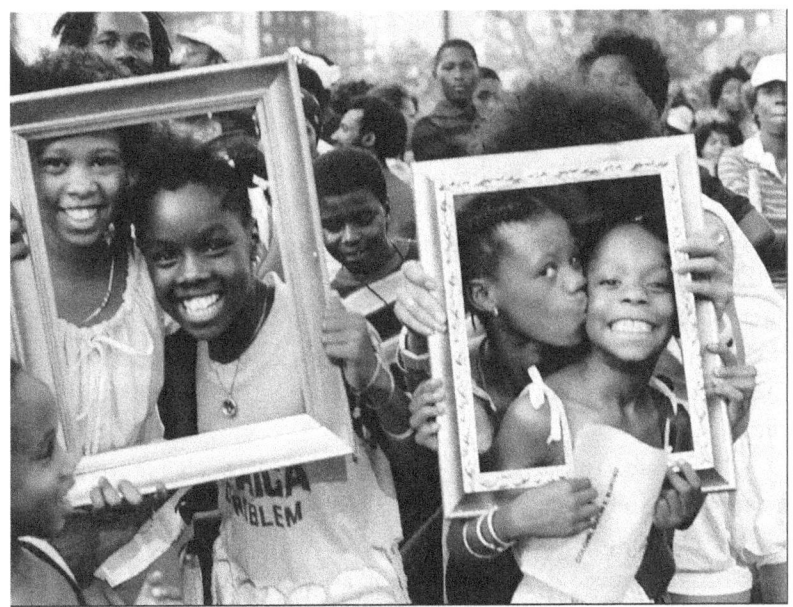

**4.06**    Lorraine O'Grady, *Art Is . . . (Girlfriends Times Two)*, 1983.
Chromogenic print, 16 × 20 in.

would act as a framing device, capturing wide-shot images of the Harlem neighborhood and its inhabitants (fig. 4.5). As O'Grady articulated in her project proposal, this would constitute "a performance in '3-minute parade viewing time,'" recognizing the typically brief period that each parade float would be in front of any given spectator. In this manner, the mounted frame functioned like a stationary film camera, defining what the artist has described as a "moving proscenium" with staccato starts and stops to the parade flow "as if it were in an old Moviola editing machine."[93]

The second component of *Art Is . . .* involved a collection of smaller, handheld versions of empty gilded frames, which were carried by fifteen performers. Clad in white clothing (a feature harkening back to MBN's own sartorial color palette), the all-Black lineup of professional dancers and actors—who were hired from an ad O'Grady placed in *Billboard*—joyously interacted with the parade's spectators. Serving as proxies for Mlle Bourgeoise Noire, they were directed to "frame viewers along the parade route" as if captured in a photographic snapshot (fig. 4.6).[94] As the parade forged ahead, with intermittent delays, they moved to the margins of the street, using their props to highlight the numerous individuals watching along Adam Clayton Powell Jr. Boulevard.

Over the course of five hours, the performers—which included Mlle Bourgeoise Noire, wearing her white "karate uniform"—approached old and young alike, defying the long-standing racist history of Western portraiture by holding up their picture frames to define these Black individuals as "worthy" subjects of high art. The responses by the unassuming audiences varied; some nervously smiled, while others mugged for the camera. The performers even framed themselves at times, coming together in groups within the picture frames to model the behaviors sought after by the audience. In creating a sequence of ephemeral "snapshots" of the onlookers, MBN made it possible for Black nonart spectators to see themselves as the subjects of art while becoming audiences for the work at the same time.

O'Grady's role in *Art Is . . .* notably differed from her previous Mlle Bourgeoise Noire interventions. In earlier projects, MBN assumed primary responsibilities as the operative agent in undertaking various transgressions or "invasions" into established art-world discourses and spaces. However, here, in front of a Black audience that was not involved with the downtown New York art world, the two identities became increasingly synthesized. Put differently, as O'Grady got closer to finding her sought-after preservers, the accomplice-artist formulation became less necessary, allowing MBN to shift into the background of the work while O'Grady began to take her place.

The growing overlap between MBN and O'Grady was symbolized by the presence of a single pair of white gloves, which were prominently pinned to the front of Mlle Bourgeoise Noire's shirt. In contrast to the unspecified gloves used for MBN's gown and cape, which were sourced from thrift stores, the gloves pinned to O'Grady-as-MBN's white T-shirt in *Art Is . . .* were her own personal pair of debutante gloves, which she wore as a young Wellesley student. O'Grady had carried this particular pair with her for the past twenty-seven years, without concrete plans for their use—until this performance.

The significance of this gesture was critical to the artist, who remarked, "By not wearing my own gloves [in previous performance outings], by some measure I was resisting that I was part of the system I was critiquing. It wasn't until *Art Is . . .* that I pinned my own gloves to my chest."[95] This act of taking the "white glove," an object associated with bourgeois ideals of social propriety—which in turn O'Grady appropriated for her MBN persona, shifting the aspirational associations of the glove within upwardly mobile social circles to that of a criminal tool used by someone attempting to obscure their felonious tracks—and proudly wearing it as a marker of MBN's presence signaled a growth in O'Grady's personal agency. In 2012, using the third person, O'Grady described herself in this performance: "Perhaps she was getting stronger."[96]

By staging *Art Is . . .* in Harlem, O'Grady was unsure of what the audience's reception to the work would be. In contrast to Brooklyn, where she first thought of presenting a float in the annual West Indian Day Parade due to her cultural familiarity with other diasporic Caribbean people and the West Indian community who lived in the area, O'Grady chose to go to Upper Manhattan, which was historically populated by African Americans whose heritage can be traced to the southern United States. She has described this decision as entering "alien territory," with unforeseen outcomes, thereby marking the piece as another form of trespassing: "I mean, the only instructions I could give people on the parade route were the words on the sides of the float—'Art Is . . .' . . . Would they get it? Would they do anything? It could have been something or it could have been nothing, and I had no idea which."[97] Yet, as bystanders began calling for the performers to frame them and be photographed, "It was like 'Wow!' They wanted to be on camera! Everybody wanted to be on camera."[98]

*Art Is . . .* brought Black life into focus for Black audiences. Based on the bystanders' participation, O'Grady's intentions for the work were seemingly understood and embraced by many of the parade-goers, despite their outsider status vis-à-vis the art world: "Everywhere there were shouts of: 'That's right. That's what art is. WE're the art!'"[99] At another point, O'Grady recalled that "the people on the parade route got it. . . . 'Frame ME, make ME art!'"[100] In this instance, O'Grady once again adopted fugitive tactics in completely sidestepping the mainstream art world, refusing its unofficial laws governing the types of art and artists deemed acceptable. In its place, she found an alternative that exceeded her expectations in her quest for locating those individuals willing to assume risks on her behalf in the preservation of her work.

Given that O'Grady did not formally announce *Art Is . . .* , only informing a select group of friends at JAM and the women in the *Heresies* collective, the documentation of the work was integral. Yet O'Grady had only hired a few photographer friends to take a couple of rolls of film each, instead primarily relying on sourcing photographs from the parade-goers—by asking for people's phone numbers when she saw them taking pictures of her float and later connecting with them to acquire extra slides. This element of informal documentation produced by the audiences of *Art Is . . .* , who became crucial contributors to the project's success and longevity, demonstrates the ways in which Mlle Bourgeoise Noire sought to create—and was relatively successful in creating—preservers. Taking matters into her own hands after the disappointments of previous *Mlle Bourgeoise Noire* projects, she quite literally outsourced the role of producing a record of the work for the future to individuals who did not necessarily consider themselves artists nor did they adhere to the rules and laws determined by the art world. In one particularly compelling photograph, a young woman uses her moment within the frame to both smile at the camera and point directly at it; it is as if she recognizes the reflexivity of becoming both subject and audience of O'Grady's art experiment, while pointing out the creative role inadvertently assumed by the anonymous cameraperson in contributing to the legacy of *Art Is*. . . . As subjects of both the momentary act of physical framing and the permanent capture by the camera's lens, the Black audience reveled in this declaration of long-overdue subjecthood in multiple contexts.

Expanding her signature interventionist strategy outside the art world, in *Art Is* . . . MBN sought to bypass the conventional art institutional circuits, rejecting their unspoken laws altogether. Yet, as O'Grady has explained, her Caribbean background meant that she felt like an outsider to the local Harlem community and therefore still required the bracketing of her goals as "art" to trespass effectively. This metacommentary of using the pictorial framing device of the camera lens to capture other acts of framing and documentation that were executed by her hired performers in the context of a historically African American neighborhood alludes to the contradictions of visibility as a form of control as well as agency, or to be framed as a means of gaining representation or becoming unjustly blamed for a crime.

The complex message of *Art Is* . . . is reflected in the diverse responses to the work; while the spectators largely embraced its call for focusing attention onto typically underrepresented subjects, others present at the parade didn't share this enthusiasm. For instance, O'Grady has recounted that the parade announcer made jokes about not understanding how her float could be art, while individual police officers conveyed visible unease regarding the outpouring of excitement over representational agency.

As the audiences of *Art Is* . . . were likely aware, becoming O'Grady's preserver involved a level of risk. At least five of the photographs include depictions of white police officers; blue NYPD police barricades are present in the background of several more. In one notable image (fig. 4.7), one of

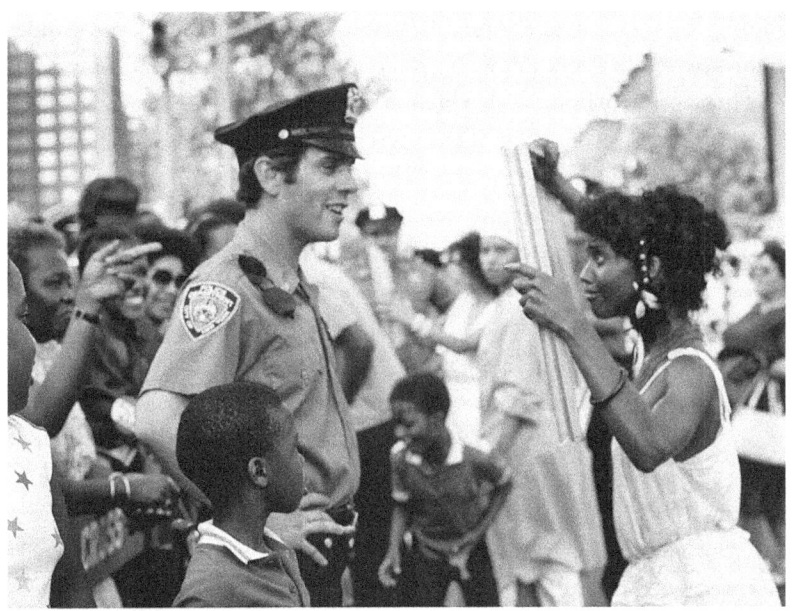

**4.07**  Lorraine O'Grady, *Art Is . . . (Framing Cop)*, 1983.
Chromogenic print, 16 × 20 in.

the *Art Is . . .* performers is captured holding up a frame in front of her face within a few feet of a white New York Police Department officer. Her expression is defiant and bemused, with a closed-mouth smile; meanwhile, the police officer places his hands on his hips to appear larger, even though he was already markedly taller than the woman. This condescending and authoritative stance—staged in response to the woman's self-fashioning within a gilded frame that had been historically used to feature white subjects—impresses the seriousness of circumstances in which O'Grady's art practice operated as well as the potential radicality of the work's central gesture. The ostensibly innocuous act of approaching a police officer with an empty picture frame and holding it near his face as a Black woman in Harlem circa 1983 was to undertake profound and possibly life-threatening danger, one that these accomplice-preservers assumed in support of O'Grady's work. The confrontation of police, however playfully framed, had conceivable repercussions that were certainly as scary, if not more so, than Burden lying in a Los Angeles street amid nighttime traffic.

The prominence of law enforcement depicted in these images also makes visible the issue of policing tactics that were present in the 1980s—notably that of unjust framing for a crime that one has not committed.[101]

In the aforementioned *Art Is . . . (Framing Cop)* photograph, the woman frames herself in a standoff with a police officer; her almost mocking smile and the close proximity with which she holds the frame to her face convey to the officer a recognition of the ways in which the police conduct their own crimes against the innocent. This act of illicit framing for criminal actions is provocatively mentioned in O'Grady's subtitles for the *Art Is . . .* photographs; the captions accompanying the images of police officers ("Cop Framed" and "Framing Cop") mockingly reverse the accusation of entrapment typically experienced by Black populations, a point shared by art historian Catherine Damman.[102]

Throughout the series, the joyous elation of the work's participants is undeniable. Some individuals were captured by the cameras of their peers as photographic subjects—in addition to being the imaginary and fleeting subjects of the roving empty picture frames. Others were brought into the project as participants in the work's documentation as retroactively enlisted photographers, while others served as audiences for those posing for the cameras or carried the frames themselves. *Art Is . . .* therefore engendered peer-to-peer art making—producing Black creators, subjects, and audiences—MBN's long sought-after accomplices.[103]

However, this willingness of the Harlem community to participate in the work would soon devolve. In a 2015 interview with Amanda Hunt, O'Grady pointed out that, given the impending crack cocaine epidemic—which would radically transform policing policies across the United States, particularly in the form of mass incarceration in historically African American neighborhoods such as Harlem—"1983 was really one of the last moments that these photographs could have been taken, with a whole population so open to the camera. The business of framing is really problematic now, as you know."[104] In one photograph, subtitled *Cop Eyeing Young Man*, a white police officer is shown trailing a Black man who seems unaware of the former's presence (fig. 4.8). This discriminatory profiling is not only captured in the photograph; one of MBN's performers positions her frame around the police officer, further emphasizing and exposing these policing tactics.

Indicating her frustration with the art establishment, O'Grady deliberately chose not to situate *Art Is . . .* within the context of either the Black or white art world. With few exceptions, she neither notified her art-world associates nor sought to publicize her intervention as an "art piece." Her reasoning behind this decision was calculated, likely motivated by the anticipation of misunderstandings, apathy, or antagonistic responses to her work. As O'Grady has herself explained, "Unlike the disappointment she'd

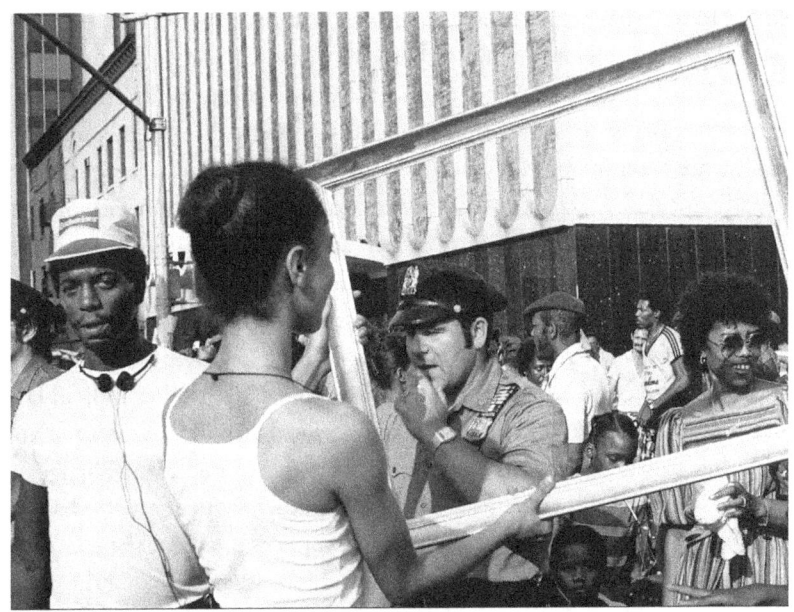

**4.08**   Lorraine O'Grady, *Art Is . . . (Cop Eyeing Young Man)*, 1983.
Chromogenic print, 16 × 20 in.

felt with Mlle Bourgeoise Noire and The Black and White Show, this piece was to be about art, not about the art world . . . rather than an invasion, it was more a crashing of the party."[105] Such a comment regarding her desire to present *Art Is* . . . within a nonart context to preserve the essential nature of aesthetic experience ("to be about art, not about the art world") indicates a different perception of the parade as a potential site of preservers, wherein the impenetrable walls that fortified the art institutions that refused her entry were laid flat onto the streets of the parade route in Harlem.

Despite *Art Is* . . . being funded by a New York State Council on the Arts grant, O'Grady conceived of it as a project that could sidestep the art institutional power in communicating directly to a public audience. Through its successful formation of engaged art makers and viewers outside the strictures of the still white-dominated art world, *Art Is* . . . arguably came closest to MBN's goal of developing Black avant-garde work that took risks and evaded conscription into white aesthetic ideals. By granting this unwitting audience agency in their own image making, within the context of a parade in Harlem celebrating Black life, O'Grady no longer needed MBN as her mercenary-by-proxy to gain entry. While in previous interventions O'Grady felt that she required the character of

MBN to stage her critiques bracketed as an "art piece," here MBN only appeared symbolically through the gloves pinned to O'Grady's shirt.

Until this point, MBN had tried various means of finding allies: looking to Black artists, white-run institutions, critics, and the public—each time attempting new tactical approaches to combatting the art world's unacknowledged conservatism. Nothing seemed to have worked: not performative interventions (as seen at Just Above Midtown and the New Museum), nor conceptual solicitations of artists (in the form of letters to "Advanced Black Artists"), nor the creation of alternative modes of art exhibition (*The Black and White Show*). Whereas white male artists such as Burden and Kippenberger could readily exploit other individuals in the name of art, and Wilke could use her own visibility as a former accomplice to a more famous white male artist to expose her experience of occlusion as a white woman, O'Grady—as a Black woman artist—had to seek out and ultimately create her own accomplices to expose the complicity of those involved with the crimes of exclusion that pervaded the early 1980s art world. In *Art Is . . .*, MBN's potential accomplices-as-preservers revealed themselves in multiple guises: as the subjects of the framing, the photographic documenters, and the audiences.

And yet this wasn't enough. Although O'Grady had collected the photographs for *Art Is . . .* in the months following the parade events, the piece remained a largely forgotten performance within the artist's oeuvre for almost twenty-five years. It wasn't until 2009 that O'Grady revisited these saved images, tucked away in her archive; they ultimately resurfaced as material for a photographic installation that O'Grady presented at the Alexander Gray Gallery in New York. Therefore, even though Mlle Bourgeoise Noire might have finally found her desired accomplices in *Art Is . . .*, during the extensive time that the work was lost to history, O'Grady was once again relegated to the role of her own preserver. That is, the Harlem audiences got the message—but perhaps they just didn't know how fragile it was, how urgently it needed to be protected.

### Invited Guest

O'Grady has repeatedly insisted that she intended for the *Mlle Bourgeoise Noire* project to continue; it was strictly circumstantial that it ended. Yet perhaps anticipating both the need to wait for future preservers and the impending problem of her mother's deteriorating health, between 1981 and 1983, O'Grady took three private letters—the first written to Lippard, the second to Judson Memorial Church, and the third to Whitfield (which opens this chapter)—and made them into formal performance statements that addressed different aspects of her recent work. On the recommendation of a friend, shortly after finishing her last one, O'Grady mailed copies of the letters to the editor of *Artforum* in the hopes of having them published.

After waiting several weeks with no response, O'Grady assumed her texts were rejected outright. As she recounts, "I had not heard back and didn't follow up, assuming I had landed in the slush pile." In a poignantly tragic turn of events, her statements were, in fact, never received. She continues, "A few months later, there was a small manila envelope in my mailbox. It was unopened. It had been returned to me as 'undelivered' by the post office. By then, I was already in Boston, taking care of my mother. It was not the right time."[106]

She was not alone in this feeling of wrong timing. Many Black American artists spent the remainder of the decade in relative obscurity. Although this took a sudden turn by the late 1980s, when discussions of multiculturalism, diversity, and the crisis of representation began to enter mainstream institutions and discourses, O'Grady has astutely pointed out that this "emergence" was strategic, "brought to light by the needs of the white art world."[107]

Since the early 1980s, O'Grady has carefully documented her work. While there is a tradition of documentation in body-art practices, which was often done without a live audience and therefore necessitated these supplemental materials to experience the work secondhand, O'Grady's commitment to recording and archiving her pieces—now found online in her prolific and comprehensive website that she began in 2007 to coincide with her recent inclusion in the groundbreaking exhibition *WACK! Art and the Feminist Revolution*—reflects a different agenda. Her process of documentation indicates a speculative dimension in which she developed a system to both await and create her anticipated viewer. Projecting into the future, O'Grady sensed that her careful records would one day find their intended audience.

In 2020, exactly forty years since the first appearance of Mlle Bourgeoise Noire, the right time eventually came. On the occasion of *Lorraine O'Grady: Both/And*, her first career retrospective, held at the Brooklyn Museum in 2021, O'Grady created the first new performance persona since Mlle Bourgeoise Noire: a figure known as the Knight. While the Knight had been in development privately since 2013, she was debuted in two main forms: in a set of life-size photographic *carte de visite* from 2020 titled

*Announcement of a New Persona (Performances to Come!)*, and in a video based on the documentation of a live performance staged at the Brooklyn Museum titled *Greetings and Theses*.[108]

When performing as the Knight, O'Grady wore a customized plated-steel suit of armor, which covered her body from head to toe. The design was initially based on a boy's suit on view at the Art Institute of Chicago; O'Grady adapted it for a female wearer to accommodate the hefty metal. Historically used as a tool to protect medieval soldiers in battle, the suit of armor takes on a particularly charged meaning when worn by O'Grady, whose performative aesthetic agenda was marked by militaristic invasions of the established order. This costume was designed specifically to conceal identifying characteristics and direct attention away from her race, gender, and age.[109] Much like her pageant gown donned as Mlle Bourgeoise Noire, the Knight's costume offered protection from the ways in which Black bodies are surveilled and drew attention to the artist's message by delineating the performance character from everyday life.

In *Family Portrait 1 (Formal, Composed)* (2020; fig. 4.9), the Knight sits frontally on a dark box, facing the viewer. Flanked by Rociavant and the Courtier—two additional characters who coexist in the Knight's world—she leans forward with hands placed lightly on her knees, a gesture that suggests she might spring to an offensive stance at any moment while currently sizing up her viewer as a potential adversary. By her side is a large silver lance, held by the Courtier. Typically used in mounted combat, this weapon remains close at hand, a constant reminder of possible threats. The Knight, it seems, will be going into combat alone.

In the third-floor halls of the Brooklyn Museum's Elizabeth A. Sackler Center for Feminist Art, shortly before the opening of *Both/And*, Mlle Bourgeoise Noire and the Knight finally met. As documented in the performance video *Greetings and Theses*, the Knight—accompanied by the Courtier—enacted a dramatic procession through the museum leading to the room in which Mlle Bourgeoise Noire's costume was situated on a pedestal. After engaging in a silent greeting of reverence, the Knight ceremoniously gifted MBN her sword, a wordless acknowledgment of the battles she undertook in the early 1980s without the proper weaponry, defense, or allies.

The Knight accompanied her performance with a set of nine written propositions, which she tacked to the wall near the end of *Greetings and Theses*.[110] Reminiscent of Martin Luther's sixteenth-century critique of the religious establishment, these "theses" were declarative statements directed toward what D'Souza describes as "mainstream feminism, the movement for

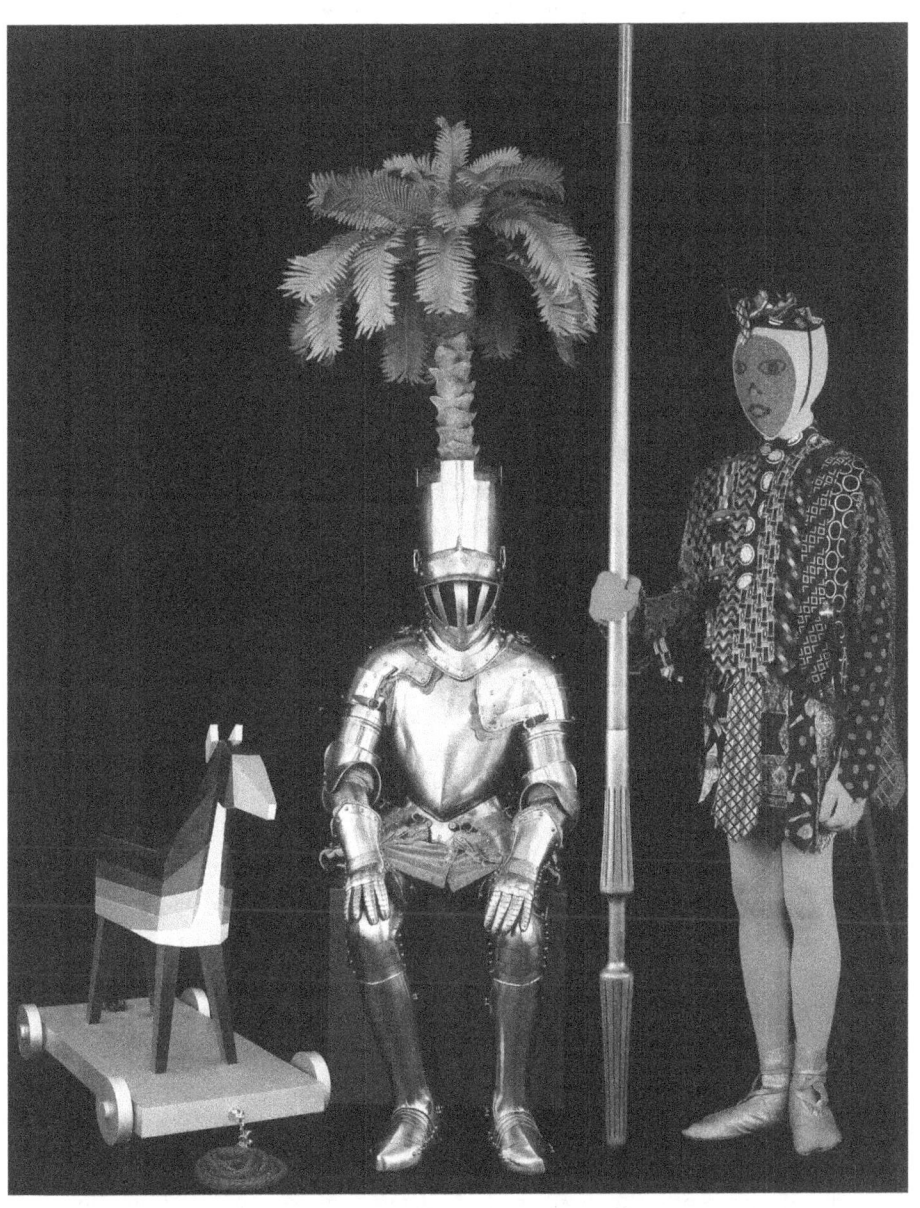

**4.09**  Lorraine O'Grady, *Family Portrait 1 (Formal, Composed)*, 2020.
Digital C-print, 50 × 40 in.

Black Lives, and the institutional structure of the art world."[111] It was here—on the occasion of a long-overdue retrospective of O'Grady's work, staged in a prominent mainstream New York museum—that O'Grady was finally welcomed as an invited guest, her presence no longer seen as trespassing.

The transformation of the institutional and art critical reception for O'Grady's work approximately forty years later speaks to the fundamental impasse presented by the anti-Blackness at the heart of the 1980s art world in which she sought inclusion. In contrast to the other three case-study artists considered in this book, for whom the notion of "failure" in their respective aims (of transforming the audience's perception of the artist or overcoming sexism in Burden's and Wilke's work, respectively) was less urgent and lacked comparable risk levels, the standards by which O'Grady's work was seen to succeed or fail within the white-run art world presented far greater stakes. Unlike Kippenberger (who deliberately sought failure as a critical element of his practice) or Burden and Wilke (whose relative failures did not mean a complete obfuscation or omission of their work), O'Grady was faced with a difficult scenario, one from which she could not be rescued, even with the help of preservers. Upon recognizing this inextricable bind, O'Grady did the only thing possible to free herself from such conventional models of achievement—she refused them altogether, enacting a kind of fugitivity from such mainstream valuations of success and failure. O'Grady's ultimate disavowal of the limited terms and conditions offered by the contemporary art world—both creatively and literally leaving it behind for some time—reflects the pursuit of an alternative possibility beyond the options presented to her, one that might be best described through Harney and Moten's formulation of fugitivity in circumventing the existing laws altogether.

The importance of futurity embedded in O'Grady's accomplices and her chosen terminology of preservers seems to intuit such belated reception for her work. To this point, O'Grady noted, "I discovered she [MBN] had an afterlife as a myth. I'm not sure I know what exactly it consists of (it's probably way too soon to figure that out), but it's there. . . . The myth will never be what I intended, but it will be something else that's real."[112] Seen slightly differently, the specifics within the mythology of MBN—the allusions to the poetry of Damas, the references to the immediate social context in which O'Grady was working, and the contemporary responses to her interventions, for instance—might have been lost in the past, but the retrospective perception of her success has only strengthened over time.

Back in 1994, O'Grady—invoking Gayatri Chakravorty Spivak—made the following statement: "It is no overstatement to say that the greatest barrier I/we face in winning back the questioning subject position is the West's continuing tradition of binary, 'either: or' logic, a philosophic system that defines the body in opposition to the mind."[113] Speaking of the ways in which postmodernism preemptively ousted the modernist authorial subject before others had a right to that access, O'Grady sought a means of repossessing agency for Black female subjectivity. As D'Souza succinctly explains, this marked an evolution of O'Grady's thinking, going "from a postmodernist emphasis on critique (manifest in the Mlle Bourgeoise Noire project, for example) toward a recognition that postmodernism's easy disposal of the 'essentialized' subject was another way of reinscribing white masculinity at the center of critical theory."[114]

Throughout her career, O'Grady engaged in a persistent interrogation of how the Western "either/or" binary—upon which the paradigm of an artist-audience duality, among other oppositional orders structured on hierarchies—was historically constructed as a means of reclaiming subjectivity on her own terms. The fragmentation that was central to postmodernism's decentered subject was still evident in the breaking open of O'Grady's authorial identity into MBN, yet the accomplice paradigm allows for the subject to coexist as central and dispersed, networked yet hierarchical. Neither artist nor audience, but something "both/and," the accomplice made this possible.

In the March 2021 issue of *Artforum*, O'Grady articulated: "The Knight is an avatar of Mlle Bourgeoise Noire forty years later, setting out to finish what she started. It will be a hard job. If you conceal everything—race, class, age, gender—what is left? What is possible?"[115] This speculative dimension to O'Grady's work might finally be answered. As a warrior trained to enter combat, the Knight revealed herself to be the one who could battle the forces perpetuating exclusion and discrimination that had long haunted O'Grady's life and work.

Yet while the character O'Grady became as the Knight might at first appear to reengage with the accomplice paradigm that guided her work as MBN in the early 1980s, there is a notable distinction. Here, this character is directed under *her* sovereign control, indicating a repositioning of power differentials with O'Grady at the helm. Her pronounced presence signaled a broader transformation that had occurred since she began her art career—changes to the historically segregated art world, the marginalization of women artists, and the access afforded to older artists. No longer a trespasser, the armor-clad O'Grady released her accomplice and went at it unaccompanied. The preservers were waiting.

# Conclusion

**In early 2003, the Friedrich Petzel Gallery** finalized a commission for an untitled work by artist Andrea Fraser. The private client—an unnamed male collector—put forth production costs as well as the purchase price for the work itself, which comprised both a performance and a copy of its recording in the form of a sixty-minute video on DVD. In January, Fraser met the collector in a hotel room at the Royalton in New York, where—in accordance with the previously agreed upon terms of the work—they proceeded to have sex. While there was no live audience, the encounter took place in front of a stationary camera that was elevated in a corner of the room; its position gave the perspective of surveillance footage, while allowing enough distance for the client to remain anonymous.

The role of the collector, neither nominal artist nor audience, in Fraser's piece is ambiguous. Given that Fraser retained authority over defining the terms of the work, she clearly held the position of artistic author. But while the nature of the collector's involvement was voluntary, it required a financial transaction and the agreement to stipulations set by Fraser. Moreover, this conscious decision to participate beyond that of a viewing audience would implicate him in an actual crime with potential legal consequences. The monetary exchange—paying for both a legal commodity (art) and an illegal one in New York State (sex work)—destabilizes the relations of power, as Fraser transformed the collector into her accomplice in the name of art.

Such a maneuvering of power differentials was deliberate; after completing the work, Fraser stated that, in contrast to claims of being exploited by the collector, "it was my idea, it was my scenario, I was producing a piece I would own. . . . I was much more concerned about using him."[1] Her construction of the work's conditions, particularly on a legal level, emphasized her interest in manipulating others as a critical part of the piece—whether the deliberate involvement of her gallery in brokering the financials for a performance that resulted in potential complicity for a criminal action shared with third parties, or requiring purchasers of the remaining copies of the DVD to sign tightly orchestrated legal documents regarding any subsequent distribution, installation, and reproduction of her work.

In contrast, Fraser did not enter into a formal agreement with the collector in the form of a written contract or release form before engaging in the sexual encounter. The transactional nature of Fraser's performance might lead us to best define the collector-participant as a client, alluding to the similarities in how art and sex are marketed, sold, and traded; the artist herself has stated that "the question I'm interested in posing is whether art is prostitution—in a metaphorical sense, of course. Is it any more prostitution because I happen to be having sex with a man than it would be if I were just selling him a piece?"[2] Yet the collector assumed responsibility that exceeds that of a straightforward art-buying client, presenting an uncertainty between subject positions that can be resolved by the model introduced in this book. The illicit nature of Fraser's 2003 performance, produced twenty years after O'Grady left the art world in 1983, puts pressure on the artist-audience binary in ways that demonstrate the ongoing relevance and continued evolution of the accomplice paradigm in art practices.

Through the introduction of a new figure occupying an intermediary subject position between the relationship of artist and audience, *Artist, Audience, Accomplice: Ethics and Authorship in Art of the 1970s and 1980s* proposes a complete revision of the relations between artistic property, agency, and authorship that have been previously described regarding body and performance art, Neo-Expressionism, and appropriation practices. In the wake of the late 1960s poststructuralist ideas concerning the decentering of the authorial subject and Conceptual art's reformulation of existing models of artistic ownership, this investigation considers how certain artists during the 1970s and 1980s were exploring different methods for mobilizing a set of previously unacknowledged individuals as critical players in their artworks. As key examples, the four artists discussed in this book illustrate a unique body of seemingly unrelated practices that collectively open onto an alternative model of the social that is at once networked yet hierarchical.

*Artist, Audience, Accomplice* analyzes how artists developed artistic strategies for putting pressure on social relationships to expose a level of exploitation and shared responsibility that only becomes visible through legal or ethical transgressions. In their respective ways, Burden, Wilke, Kippenberger, and O'Grady all created pieces that called into question the authority of art to reframe illicit actions—such as manipulation, obfuscation, disclosure, or mistreatment—as sanctioned if conducted within the framework of art. Such considerations might get us closer to understanding the scope of art's power, for better or worse.

In 1991, Vito Acconci posed a similar inquiry to readers of *Art Journal*, opening his essay with the following statement: "Three performance pieces I did in the early 1970s raised the question of how art may be illegal, *whether* it can be illegal."[3] Acconci explains how the framework of art was critical in allowing the artist to explore unlawful actions and to recognize the potential implications for such illicit engagement—but also to nullify its criminality at the same time. Expanding the legacies of the readymade through Minimalism and Conceptual art in determining a work's meaning through things extrinsic to the art object itself, Acconci explains how artists (like himself) working in the early 1970s "expand the boundaries of art by bringing into it that which, outside the realm of art, breaks the boundaries of convention and law."[4] Whether through the invocation of an artistic jury to determine the "case" of Marcel Duchamp's store-bought and apocryphally signed urinal being recognized as art in the May 1917 issue of the Dada art journal *The Blind Man* or the legal contracts conferring delegated authority to fabricators of Minimalist objects, there is a history throughout the twentieth century of artists exploring the ways in which art requires, but can also shape and alter, the legal ability to confer power. The ease with which the law can be manipulated through authorial intentionality and art institutional contexts reveals its fundamental arbitrariness and might ultimately undermine its perceived authority.

While the term *accomplice* specifically—and deliberately—implies illegality, its application throughout this book assumes more metaphorical dimensions over the course of the four chapters. By using accomplices in actions of questionable legal status and social acceptability, my case-study artists draw out the lack of clear demarcations between what is legal or not. In other words, even though what these artists were doing wasn't formally illegal, particularly in the context of art, the practices in which they engaged make us think about legality and the inconsistencies in which it is applied. For Burden to involve unwitting participants in defending his innocence against police investigation or for Kippenberger to test the outermost parameters of exploiting the intellectual property of his assistants, both use the framework of art to nullify their actions as innocuous. For Wilke and O'Grady, the direct experience of a shifting purview of the law, broadly construed, inspired artistic work meant to recalibrate such discrepancies.

In her book *The Cultural Life of Intellectual Properties: Authorship, Appropriation, and the Law*, anthropologist and legal theorist Rosemary Coombe writes: "The law creates spaces in which hegemonic struggles are enacted as well as signs and symbols whose connotations are always at risk. Legal strategies and legal institutions may lend authority to certain interpretations while denying status to others."[5] Despite ongoing efforts to combat this injustice, the law is still contingent on one's identity; whether through policies that discriminate based on racial identities, like stop-and-frisk policing that disproportionately affects people of color, or disparities in sentencings based on the racial makeup of criminals and their victims, the law continues to be unstable, often based on a person's subject position. When considered within the framework of art, as I do here, the accomplices challenge a certain set of assumptions concerning the stability of the law, the purpose of art, and the possible subject positions of those involved with the work itself.

The accomplices complicate fictions of artistic sovereignty. They move and act in ways that evade visibility, only coming into focus when legal or ethical transgressions occur, yet their presence radically reframes our understanding of established artworks by introducing an expanded field of responsibility that was heretofore overlooked. They represent the intermediary figures whose presence had been previously indiscernible, who fail to fit into the established binary of artist and audience by which art has been conventionally analyzed. They reveal the complexities behind visibility, in that the same forms of representation that bring agency to subjects are often joined by mechanisms of control and surveillance and therefore need to be taken seriously.

The acknowledgment of accomplices profoundly shifts our understanding of artworks, yet their presence cannot be accounted for through mere recognition or inclusion into existing narratives. Rather, the existence of such figures alters the stakes of certain known artworks—such as those discussed in previous chapters—as investigations of a subject's rights and concepts of responsibility. As seen with particular focus in chapter 4, inclusion within institutions that maintain structural marginalization doesn't necessarily disrupt anything; the accomplices could possibly become allies in attempts to overturn such institutions altogether. These considerations invite further reflection on what other marginalized figures might exist and present us with an opportunity to think about what their entrance into spaces previously closed off to them might do to undermine the established order.

The book maps the development of the accomplice from the practices of the early 1970s, when it was located on the periphery of performances in third-party individuals, to its increased prominence in the following decade as it became folded into the artist's authorial identity. In my estimation, the key to many of the questions in the public consciousness at the time concerning authorship, agency, and accountability was found in debates that were being explored on both aesthetic and legal levels. Just as artists began probing the ways in which they might assert their authority over other subjects as part of their work, so too did criminal, intellectual property, and privacy law cases, which evaluated and redrew some of the boundaries around questions of responsibility, artistic ownership, and personal sovereignty. By the end of the 1980s, the nature of participatory art in the United States and Western Europe shifted once again, as labor often became visibly distributed among either voluntary audiences or hired workers whose live bodies replaced the immediate presence of the artist thought to be central in such earlier works. While the scope of my research focuses on the emergence of the accomplice and its immediate transformations during a particular geographic and historical period, the accomplice paradigm introduced in this book does offer a potential framework for interrogating other forms of unrecognized labor that currently go unexamined. The way in which Fraser features her accomplice so conspicuously might represent a further evolution of this role as it appears in the twenty-first century. Moreover, the resurgence of avatars and surrogate actors in recent art practices by artists such as Cao Fei, Sondra Perry, Jacolby Satterwhite, and Martine Syms might potentially be productively analyzed using the accomplice model in considering the development of new legal questions that arise with emerging technologies or alternative forms of artistic subjecthood.

By considering the role of the accomplice in the works of Burden, Wilke, Kippenberger, and O'Grady, I present a framework for how these disparate projects are linked through distinct yet interrelated forms of *dispossession*, defined as the abrogation or deprivation of an individual's proprietary rights. In the case of Burden and Kippenberger, they dispossess others to show how such deprivation occurs in other facets of life and art: from the involuntary conscription in the Vietnam War draft to the separation from one's image within the spectacle of celebrity in the commercialized 1980s art world, for instance. In the case of Wilke and O'Grady, these artists use their own dispossession as the content of their artistic production. Both applied their experiences of unjust authorial attribution and ongoing practices of marginalization on account of gender and/or race to draw attention to the less visible forms of dispossession that continue even today. These four chapters chart an arc of increased dispossession not undertaken to merely show other people's involvement in a work of art or to add a layer of unnecessary complexity but rather to demonstrate how taking seriously the sometimes illicit—but certainly often unethical—use of accomplices in art practices allows us to explore alternative social relations in which new models of accountability and authorship may surface. This book considers the potentials and problematics of such a paradigm, particularly thinking through the hierarchies of privilege and power that are at play in using others based on gender, class, and race.

By providing the language to articulate these intermediary figures, who exceed the existing definitions of both the artist and the audience, it is my aim that the recognition of those individuals can broaden our understanding of specific artworks as well as contribute to a revised history of art. The transformative potential of such amendments centers on a means of restoring attribution to individuals—often women and people of color—whose auxiliary status often became a liability that ultimately rendered them invisible within the records of history. If the accomplice paradigm destabilizes the neatness of historical narratives centered on a strict artist-audience binary, the ambitions of this book will have been met.


There are accomplices all around us. They are evasive and elusive, yet their role remains critical in artworks that pivot on their contributions. In Fraser's 2003 performance, the collector only comes to light because of the illicit actions that transpire; his visibility in the work is intimately tied up with complicity. This exploration of shared accountability with auxiliary figures marks a continuation of the questions posed by Burden, Wilke, Kippenberger, and O'Grady—and others who may not yet be identified. Until then, the accomplices linger in the background of artworks, playing a significant but largely disregarded role that only captures a viewer's attention in the case of aberration—O'Grady breaches institutional walls, Kippenberger's assistant sues, Wilke gains legal power over her images, Burden's knife slips. In between these deviations, directives, and dispossessions, we find the accomplice.

## Introduction

1    Peter Plagens, "He Got Shot—for His Art," *New York Times*, September 2, 1973, 87.

2    B. Smith, "Art Piece Brings Arrest."

3    The reason for arrest was given in a description of *Deadman* by Burden in his self-published artist book *Chris Burden 71–73*, 54. *Avalanche* magazine editors Willoughby Sharp and Liza Béar issued an official letter defending Burden's performance. The content of this document served to situate the artist's actions for this performative intervention within the context of "an established category of contemporary sculpture" to support the artist's claim that his goal "was self-exploration rather than frivolous exhibitionism." Yet the logic behind the circumstances in which Béar and Sharp, who were based in New York and not present at the time of the performance, would have written such a letter remains unclear until the final paragraph. After general remarks by the *Avalanche* team specifying their relationship to Burden and knowledge of his career as an artist, the letter closes with the following statement: "The intervention of the police was unforeseen and inadvertent. It was an occurrence that the artist did not desire." Willoughby Sharp and Liza Béar, letter, February 1, 1973, *Avalanche* Magazine Archives, II.115. Museum of Modern Art Archives, New York.

4    Wagner, "Performance, Video," 60.

5    Wagner, "Performance, Video," 79.

6    Wagner, "Performance, Video," 60.

7    The primary framework of modern accomplice liability was established in the United States by 1948 with a provision to Title 18 of the United States Code, which deals with federal proceedings for criminal procedures.

8    18 U.S.C. § 2(a) (2012).

9    18 U.S.C. § 2. See Iannelli v. United States 420 U.S. 770 (1975); United States v. Jewell, 532 F. 2d 697 (9th Cir. 1976); United States v. Swiderski 548 F. 2d 445, 451 (end. Cir. 1977); Sanabria v. United States, 437 U.S. 54, 71 n. 26 (1978); United States v. Southard, 700 F. 2d1, 20 (1st Cir. 1983); United States v. McKnight, 799 F. 2d 443, 446 (8th Cir. 1986). Some

examples of state legislation regarding complicity and the accomplice include Hawai'i (Hawai'i Statutes, Section 702–222: "Liability for conduct of another; complicity," 1972), Washington (RCW 9A.08.020: "Liability for conduct of another—Complicity," 1975), Kentucky (502.020: "Liability for conduct of another—Complicity," created 1974, Ky. Acts Ch. 406, sec. 21, effective January 1, 1975), and New Jersey (2C:2–6: "Liability for conduct of another; complicity," 1978).

10    18 U.S.C. 2 (a) (2012), cited in Girgis, "The Mens Rea of Accomplice Liability," 462.

11    In 1979, the US Court of Appeals for the Second Circuit expanded the notion of shared responsibility in *United States v. Ruffin*, in which a defendant was held liable as a principal for inciting another to commit criminal acts, despite the fact that the defendant could not themselves perform the crime under any circumstances and instead enlisted another person—who was ultimately acquitted—to enact the crime in their place. In 1980, the US Supreme Court further affirmed in *Standefer v. United States* that the criminality of an accomplice did not depend on whether the actual perpetrator was convicted.

12    In Acconci's essay, the artist explains how potentially illicit actions are often neutralized when considered in an art context.

13    For instance, Coombe, *The Cultural Life of Intellectual Properties*; Girgis, "The Mens Rea of Accomplice Liability"; Young, *Judging the Image*; Nead and Douzinas, *Law and the Image*; and Feldman, *Art Works*.

14    A comparable transference also occurred during this period in terms of terroristic violence, in which "targets shifted from property to people—minorities, abortion providers, and federal agents." Kleinfeld, "The Rise of Political Violence in the United States," 161.

15    See Schulman, *The Seventies*.

16    See Alberro, *Conceptual Art and the Politics of Publicity*; and Buskirk, *The Contingent Object of Contemporary Art*.

17    The lawyer was Robert Projansky, who played an integral role in the development of ARRTSA.

18    Bishop, *Artificial Hells*, 19. See also Bishop, "Participation and Spectacle."

19    Bishop, *Artificial Hells*, 9.

20    Phelan, *Unmarked*, 6.

21    Phelan, *Unmarked*, 1.

22    The (largely inaccurate) term *dematerialization* in this context most notably comes from Lippard's influential text *Six Years: The Dematerialization of the Art Object from 1966 to 1972*. See also Sharp, "Body Works," 14.

23    A. Jones, *Body Art / Performing the Subject*, 1.

24    Notably Bourriaud, *Relational Aesthetics*; Lind, "The Collaborative Turn"; and Green, *The Third Hand*.

25    Bishop, *Artificial Hells*; Ward, *No Innocent Bystanders*.

26    Bishop, *Artificial Hells*, 2.

27    Bishop, "Delegated Performance," 91. See also Bishop, "The Social Turn."

28    Bishop, "Delegated Performance," 91.

29    Bishop, "Delegated Performance," 95.

30    Galenson, *Conceptual Revolutions in Twentieth-Century Art*, 201.

31    For example, Chadwick and de Courtivron, *Significant Others*.

32    For a longer discussion of this point, see C. Jones, *Machine in the Studio*.

33    For example, Rosalind Krauss describes the transformed state of art practice as the "post-medium condition." See Krauss, *A Voyage on the North Sea*.

34    The coercion of audiences harkens back to early twentieth-century Dada and Futurist performances as well as André Breton's 1929 statement in his Second Manifesto of Surrealism that "the simplest Surrealist act consists of dashing down into the street, pistol in hand, and firing blindly, as fast as you can pull the trigger, into the crowd." Breton, "Second Manifesto of Surrealism," 125.

35    Susan Sontag famously considered the foreboding aspects of Happenings in her 1962 essay "Happenings: An Art of Radical Juxtaposition."

36    Barthes's text was followed by many important writings on authorship in subsequent years. On February 22, 1969, Michel Foucault gave a lecture at the Société Française de philosophie (later published as the essay "What Is an Author?") in which he analyzed how an author's proper name became associated with a set of discourses rooted in the valorization of personal subjectivity that he termed an *author function*. That same year, Peter Wollen published *Signs and Meaning in the Cinema*, in which he explored ways of ascertaining authorship given the collaborative nature of filmmaking; shortly thereafter marked the publication of Stephen Heath's 1973 essay "Comment on 'The Idea of Authorship,'" which questioned the assumption that an author is always the originator of discourses by bringing up alternative types of creative production in which authorship is either shared or absent.

37    For instance, Norma Broude and Mary Garrard pointed out in their 1982 feminist anthology *The Expanding Discourse: Feminism and Art History* how "some art historians have observed that the death-of-the-author theories emerged, perhaps not fortuitously, just at the time when feminist scholars were attempting to gain a place for women artists within the historical canon" (4). See also Nochlin, "Why Have There Been No Great Women Artists?"; Irigaray, *This Sex Which Is Not One*; and Spivak, "Can the Subaltern Speak?"

38    Pollock, "Preface," in *Generations and Geographies in the Visual Arts*, xv.

39    Sandoval, "U.S. Third World Feminism," 1.

## Chapter 1. Abettors

1     Burden, *Chris Burden*, 24.

2     The close personal nature of the relationship between the shooter (later identified as Bruce Dunlap) and Burden is evident by the numerous appearances of this individual in earlier works by Burden, such as *Being Photographed: Looking Out, Looking In* (1971).

3     Burden quoted in notes for Crown Point Press interview, ca. 1978–79, *High Performance* Artists File: Burden, 2006.M.8, folder 8, Getty Research Institute, Los Angeles, CA.

4     Peter Plagens, "He Got Shot—for His Art," *New York Times*, September 2, 1973, 87. Other later examples of such media coverage include J. Walker, "Happenings"; Bourdon, "Body Artists without Bodies"; Calendo, "Portrait of the Artist as a Young Sculpture"; Tom Albright, "Crucifixion and Whatnot, an Artist's Schtick," *San Francisco Chronicle*, September 12, 1974, 44; and Grobel, "Chris Burden."

5     See A. Jones, "Chris Burden's Bridges, Relationality, and the Conceptual Body," 118.

6     For example, following *Shoot*, Burden claims to have received phone calls from radio stations across the country asking, "Hey man, when are you going to do your next freaky thing?" See Plagens, "He Got Shot." Additionally, according to Hunter Drohojowska-Philp, "the press hyped the apparently physical dangers, as if he were another Iggy Pop. Which was to miss the point." See Hunter Drohojowska, "Fear and Fantasy in LA: The Artwork of Chris Burden," *LA Weekly*, September 28–October 4, 1979, 4. Another example is Calendo's "Portrait of the Artist as a Young Sculpture," published in *Oui* magazine, wherein a psychedelic-inspired drawing of *Trans-Fixed* became a double-page spread that centered on Burden grimacing with his hand impaled, playing up the spectacular effects of the work. This focus is also found in Kathy O'Dell's *Contract with the Skin: Masochism, Performance Art, and the 1970s*, which emphasizes the masochistic elements of Burden's performance practice. Significantly, Burden's withdrawal from performance work by the late 1970s has been attributed to the continued media focus on the extremity of his actions. For further discussion of this point, see Måns Wrange, "A Conversation with Chris Burden."

7     Burden quoted in Liza Béar, "Chris Burden: Back to You," 12.

8     Recent examples include Justin Moyer, "Chris Burden: Why 'Extreme' Artist Was Shot, Kicked, and Crucified," *Washington Post*, May 11, 2015. Similarly, RJ Smith called Burden "modernism's Evel Knievel" in 2012. See RJ Smith, "The Sculptor of Dreams."

9     Walker, "Happenings."

10     The shooter's miscalculation sent the bullet directly into Burden's flesh. According to Burden's doctors, if the bullet had been a centimeter off, it would have shattered Burden's bone.

11    According to Phyllis Lutjeans, Chris had called her husband, Alfred, ask-
      ing him to document a performance without giving him prior knowledge
      of the circumstances. Given the legal implications of having been present
      at the site of a shooting that occurred during *Shoot*, it is significant that
      Alfred never spoke of what had happened that evening, even to his wife
      when he returned home following the performance. This reaction sug-
      gests that Alfred understood the potential consequences of having been
      the work's documenter and chose to protect his wife's innocence by not
      disclosing the event before the publication of the photographs. Personal
      interview with Phyllis Lutjeans in her home in Irvine, CA, May 16, 2016.
12    For example, Plagens, "He Got Shot."
13    Burden quoted in Plagens, "He Got Shot."
14    *West's Encyclopedia of American Law*, s.v. "abettor."
15    Model Penal Code 2.06 (2), cited in Girgis, "The Mens Rea of Accomplice
      Liability," 465.
16    Ward, "Gray Zone," 117. Ward contextualizes the shared accountabil-
      ity for a given work with an audience as emerging out of the expanded
      spatial and perceptual components of a phenomenological reading of
      Minimalism.
17    In *No Innocent Bystanders*, Ward analyzes the shifting role of the spectator
      in performance art of the 1970s, yet his scholarship maintains a focus on
      the relationship between artist and audience. My argument complicates
      Ward's maintenance of the artist-audience binary by introducing the
      subject position of the accomplice as an alternative to both conventional
      artistic roles. Rather than transforming the audience into complicit
      observers, as Ward argues, I contend that Burden's work explicitly uses
      a series of "tests" to implicate a distinct group of participants who enter
      a fluid network of shared agency with the artist yet whose visibility has
      been diminished or occluded in conventional readings of such works.
18    Ward, *No Innocent Bystanders*, 3.
19    See Buskirk, *The Contingent Object of Contemporary Art*.
20    Liza Béar, interview transcript with Chris Burden, c. 1974, *Avalanche*
      Magazine Archives, I.A.343, Museum of Modern Art Archives, New York.
      The quotation is from an archival transcript in which names are not listed
      throughout the interview. I have read the transcript and become familiar
      with Liza Béar's voice, and my expertise indicates it was likely Béar.
21    Plagens, "He Got Shot."
22    For instance, Ward primarily focuses on the events during the night of
      Burden's performance and arrest.
23    Burden's official description of *Deadman* reads: "At 8 p.m. I lay down on
      La Cienega Boulevard and was covered completely with a canvas tarpau-
      lin. Two fifteen-minute flares were placed near me to alert cars. Just before
      the flares extinguished, a police car arrived. I was arrested and booked for
      causing a false emergency to be reported. Trial took place in Beverly Hills.

After three days of deliberation, the jury failed to reach a decision, and the judge dismissed the case." Burden, *Chris Burden*, 54. This is further supported by Burden's lecture at the Rhode Island School of Design on November 12, 1974, in which he discussed his performances. For his explication of *Deadman*, Burden included the photographs taken in the courtroom and described the larger legal context and trial that occurred in the months that followed.

24 B. Smith, "Art Piece Brings Arrest." See also B. Smith, "Response to Editor's Mail Bag."

25 Smith, "Art Piece Brings Arrest."

26 Letter from "Michael" to Barbara T. Smith, Barbara T. Smith papers, 2014.M.14.Smith, box 45, folder 5, Getty Research Institute, Los Angeles, CA.

27 B. Smith, "Response to Editor's Mail Bag."

28 B. Smith, "Response to Editor's Mail Bag."

29 B. Smith, "Response to Editor's Mail Bag."

30 B. Smith, "Art Piece Brings Arrest."

31 Plagens, "He Got Shot."

32 B. Smith, "Burden Case Tried, Dismissed," *Artweek*, February 24, 1973.

33 Winer's titles were described in this way in B. Smith, "Burden Case Tried, Dismissed."

34 Winer, "Burden at Pomona," 166. Winer points out that while writing this essay, she initially mistakenly recalled Burden's location in the performance as situated against the curb. Describing such a memory error as "art blindness," she corrects herself, indicating that the artist staged his performance on the traffic side of a parked car and indeed could have been in danger himself or to others.

35 B. Smith, "Burden Case Tried, Dismissed."

36 B. Smith, "Burden Case Tried, Dismissed."

37 Valerie J. Nelson, "Obituary: James Butler, 84; Groundbreaking Lawyer, Activist, Art Collector," *Los Angeles Times*, June 4, 2005.

38 There are multiple mentions of an unnamed lawyer throughout the documentation of Burden's work from the early 1970s. Given Butler's interest in supporting and collecting art throughout his career as well as his documented involvement as Burden's legal representative for the trial of *Deadman*, it seems possible that he was the unspecified lawyer who worked for Burden during his other legal charges as well. Notably, the hammering of nails into Burden's hands for the performance of *Trans-Fixed* have been attributed to a close friend of Burden's who also worked as a lawyer. Along similar lines, while the name of Burden's lawyer who assisted him with the FBI investigation following *747* has not been credited, the fact that *Deadman*, *747*, and *Trans-Fixed* were made within a two-year window suggests that Burden's legal representation and relationship to Butler likely remained consistent throughout.

39   B. Smith, "Burden Case Tried, Dismissed."

40   B. Smith, "Burden Case Tried, Dismissed."

41   B. Smith, "Burden Case Tried, Dismissed."

42   Gamboa, "L.A. Stories," 245–46.

43   Kellie Jones makes this important point in *South of Pico*, 228.

44   B. Smith, "Burden Case Tried, Dismissed."

45   As recounted in Plagens, "He Got Shot."

46   B. Smith, "Art Piece Brings Arrest."

47   Kalman, *Right Star Rising*; and Schulman, *The Seventies*.

48   Such a point might be compared, in a greatly different context, to Martin Shaw's concept of "risk transfer" in his analysis of contemporary American warfare. See Blocker, "Aestheticizing Risk in Wartime."

49   Barbara and Chris had been romantically involved with each other since he was enrolled as an undergraduate at Pomona College.

50   Calendo, "Portrait of the Artist as a Young Sculpture," 86. Barbara's labor in this work was confirmed by Phyllis Lutjeans in an interview conducted in Irvine, CA, on May 16, 2016.

51   Burden, "Match Piece."

52   RJ Smith, "The Sculptor of Dreams," 142. Other recounted details noted that Barbara Burden had later called crying and begging Chris to either not do the performance or to modify it by moving the site of the nail to the web, rather than the palm, of his hand to avoid hitting nerves. Chris countered that positioning the nails in the center of his palms would produce the most powerful image and that he had studied medical books since he couldn't go to medical authorities for officially sanctioned assistance. See Calendo, "Portrait of the Artist as a Young Sculpture," 86.

53   Other sources have cited Alexis Smith, with whom he had become romantically involved, either during or following the end of his marriage to Barbara in 1977, as Burden's "kicker." However, given Feldman's presence at Basel that year, this seems unlikely. See RJ Smith, "The Sculptor of Dreams," 146.

54   Longtime friend Charles Hill recalled that Burden drank whiskey before the performance to loosen up his body and that Hill had received satisfaction from his task as "Chris is always pissing people off." Hill quoted in Calendo, "Portrait of the Artist as a Young Sculpture," 128.

55   Hill quoted in Drohojowska, "Fear and Fantasy in L.A."

56   Acconci himself spoke of this condition, stating: "it was the assumption of art that allowed the artist to court the 'illegal'; it can be said, further, that this assumption of art vitiated whatever rebellious value the supposedly illegal action may have had (it's not illegal, it's only art)." Acconci quoted in Ward, *No Innocent Bystanders*, 107.

57   Fuller quoted in Calendo, "Portrait of the Artist as a Young Sculpture," 132.

58   Burden quoted in Calendo, "Portrait of the Artist as a Young Sculpture," 132.

59   G. Phillips, *California Video*, 63.

60   Burden quoted in G. Phillips, *California Video*, 63.

61     Personal interview with Phyllis Lutjeans, Irvine, CA, May 16, 2016.

62     Burden quoted in Sharp and Béar, "Chris Burden," 56.

63     Personal interview with Phyllis Lutjeans, Irvine, CA, May 16, 2016.

64     Burden quoted in G. Phillips, *California Video*, 63.

65     Lutjeans described numerous dinners with the artist in her own home, his assistance in moving furniture, and even his requests to use Lutjeans's daughter Rachel in one of his performances. Personal interview with Phyllis Lutjeans, Irvine, CA, May 16, 2016.

66     Personal interview with Phyllis Lutjeans, Irvine, CA, May 16, 2016.

67     Ross, "Chris Burden's Television," 31.

68     Burden quoted in Sharp and Béar, "Chris Burden," 57.

69     This is despite the fact that in Anglo-American law, there are only limited circumstances in which a "failure to act" is grounds for criminal charges. See Freeman, "Criminal Liability and the Duty to Aid the Distressed"; and Kleinig, "Criminal Liability for Failures to Act."

70     For example, even though Burden includes seven images as documentation for *TV Hijack* in *Chris Burden 71–73*, the image of Burden holding a knife to Lutjeans's neck is often the only one reproduced (see Ward, *No Innocent Bystanders*; and Burden, Ayres, and Schimmel, *Chris Burden: A Twenty-Year Survey*). Similarly, Kristine Stiles describes the parameters of *TV Hijack* as simply "he held a knife to the throat of the woman interviewing him on television." See Stiles, "Burden of Light," 27.

71     Burden quoted in G. Phillips, *California Video*, 63.

72     Burden quoted in G. Phillips, *California Video*, 63.

73     Transcript of Burden's lecture at the Rhode Island School of Design, November 12, 1974, *High Performance* Artist Files, Burden, 2006.M.8, box 8, folder 8, Getty Research Institute, Los Angeles, CA.

74     Chris Burden, notes for Crown Point Press Interview, ca. 1978–79, *High Performance* Artist Files, Chris Burden, 2006.M.8, box 8, folder 8, Getty Research Institute, Los Angeles, CA.

75     Significantly, in his brief discussion of *TV Hijack*, Ward touches on certain points that are central to my argument. For example, he describes Burden's video crew as "accomplices," although he does not extend this notion further. Moreover, Ward's brief examination of the "association of the artist with the criminal, or outlaw" elides an analysis of how the auxiliary participants positioned around the nominal artist were transformed into culpable associates to the crime as well, and does not extend such an analysis to other artworks by Burden beyond *Deadman* and *Shoot*. Of particular note, however, is Ward's intimation that in the case of this particular performance, the station staff's "unwitting participation as a captive audience begins to suggest the range of positions upon which Burden was prepared to put pressure, in the absence of a more conventional audience, from Lutjeans to the other station workers to his own assistants, as if in the end to gesture toward possible new audience formations, while disallowing

any of them." Ward, *No Innocent Bystanders*, 105. This interest in hierarchical models of participation and the control of a subject's agency can be connected to Burden's artistic training during his undergraduate years at Pomona College under sculptor Mowry Baden, whose work often explored the manipulation of the audience. Personal telephone interview with Mowry Baden, May 21, 2016. See also Burnham, "On Being Sculpture," 45.

76 Burden quoted in Willoughby Sharp and Liza Béar, "Chris Burden: The Church of Human Energy," undated transcript of interview with handwritten edits, *Avalanche* Magazine Archives, I.A.323, Museum of Modern Art Archives, New York.

77 McDonnell, who continued a career in journalism as an editor at *Rolling Stone*, *Sports Illustrated*, *Newsweek*, and *Esquire*, had in fact been involved with Burden's work since 1971. He had written an article on Burden following *Shoot*, which he had sent to *Esquire* for publication, but the magazine ran only the photograph of the work alongside an image of Linda Lovelace "as proof that the 70s are indeed upon us."

78 Burden quoted in Sharp and Béar, "Chris Burden," 58.

79 Robbins, "A Conversation with Chris Burden," n.p.

80 *Oui* magazine was an American men's adult magazine founded in 1972; it was first published as the French equivalent to *Playboy* (under the title *Lui*) and included photographs by Helmut Newton and Jean-Paul Goude.

81 The rapid execution of Burden's works, staged in semiprivate studios, in unfrequented public spaces, or without official publicity measures to generate an outside audience, contributed to a delayed critical and legal reaction. Much public interest around Burden's work was generated by word of mouth, resulting in reporters and radio DJs contacting Burden from places as far away as Texas.

82 Robbins, "A Conversation with Chris Burden," n.p.

83 Calendo writes that "Barbara remembers him there as a stoned kid who thought that the FBI was on his tail." Calendo, "Portrait of the Artist as a Young Sculpture," 86.

84 18 U.S.C. § 912, June 25, 1948, ch. 645, 62 Stat. 742, later amended on September 13, 1994, 108 Stat. 2147.

85 According to 18 U.S.C. § 912, "whoever falsely assumes or pretends to be an officer or employee acting under the authority of the United States or any department, agency of officer thereof, and acts as such, or in such pretended character demands or obtains any money, paper document, or things of value, shall be fined under this title or imprisoned not more than three years, or both."

86 Robbins, "A Conversation with Chris Burden," n.p.

87 Roger Ebert, "Chris Burden: 'My God, Are They Going to Leave Me Here to Die?,'" *Chicago Sun-Times*, May 25, 1975.

88 Burden quoted in Seiberling, "The Art-Martyr." A similar statement by Valkanas was quoted by Ebert, who claimed that her words were "My

God, all we had to do was end it ourselves, and we thought the rules of the piece required us to do nothing."

89    Burden relayed his own personal responsibility regarding the determination of a work's temporal, logistical, and ethical scope to a hosting institution in the 1985 interactive sculpture *Samson*. First installed at the Henry Art Gallery of the University of Washington, the work was composed of two solid timber beams that were positioned horizontally in midair so that their ends, which were capped with steel, would press against the load-bearing sidewalls of the museum. Between the two beams was a one-hundred-ton jack connected to a gear box that was rigged so that each time a person entered the exhibit through an entrance turnstile, the jack would expand and increase pressure onto the supporting walls, potentially destroying the building's structural capacities. The responsibility of determining the maximum load accumulation fell thoroughly onto the host institution—calling into question the level of risk and accountability that its staff would take for the work in light of the potential for accident or danger.

90    Marioni, "Chris Burden," 153.

91    Marioni, "Chris Burden," 153.

92    Singerman, "Chris Burden's Pragmatism," 24.

93    Singerman, "Chris Burden's Pragmatism," 25.


## Chapter 2. Partners

1    Cone, "Life over Art," 26.

2    For example, in a 2015 interview, Barbara Rose describes only two of his female partners-collaborators, excluding Wilke. She writes, "The soft sculptures were sewn by Oldenburg's first wife, an impish artist and poet named Patty Mucha, whom he met at art school. They separated in the early '70s, and Oldenburg met the beautiful and brilliant Dutch art historian Coosje van Bruggen, whom he married in 1977." Rose, "Claes Oldenburg."

3    I discovered this work in her archive in Los Angeles in early 2017 with the generous assistance of the artist's sister, Marsie Scharlatt, and nephew, Andrew Scharlatt.

4    See Riane Eisler's book *The Chalice and the Blade*, which explores the distinctions between patriarchal domination and the partnership models of a relationship.

5    Wilke, "Seura Chaya," 12.

6    This letter was in a folder titled "Oldenburg Portfolio" in the Hannah Wilke Collection and Archive, Los Angeles, CA.

7    Letter in folder titled "Photos by Hannah Wilke Borrowed by the Marian Goodman Gallery and Not Returned to the Artist," Hannah Wilke Collection and Archive, Los Angeles, CA.

8   Letter in folder titled "Photos by Hannah Wilke Borrowed by the Marian Goodman Gallery and Not Returned to the Artist," Hannah Wilke Collection and Archive, Los Angeles, CA.

9   Bois, "Character Study," 128.

10  Wilke photographed Oldenburg numerous times; she was credited as a photographer on certain published photographs as well.

11  In 1974, Wilke had moved into her loft on Greene Street, where she maintained her own living and work space independent from Claes's loft on Broome Street. However, over the course of their relationship, both artists went back and forth between their respective spaces, with Hannah keeping clothing and other personal items—including her car—at Claes's through 1977.

12  Documentation of Wilke's sexual relations with other men can be found in her archive, where erotic photographs with Robert Bell and "William" are dated February 1974 and 1966–76, respectively. While this detail wouldn't necessarily be important, the facts of their relationship are key to how we view Wilke's work.

13  For example, Wilke took several intimate photographs of Vanya, a Russian man whose image was included in Wilke's *Advertisements for Living*, as well as artist Richard Hamilton, clad in only a newsboy hat, sunbathing along the shore in Cadaqués, Spain.

14  Iversen argues that text- and photo-based feminist work in the 1960s and 1970s by figures such as Mary Kelly reflect the Minimalist anti-aesthetic position by "deflating" artistic creation and reducing it "to a thing in the world, undifferentiated from other objects or insufficiently differentiated." Iversen, "The Deflationary Impulse," 83.

15  Chave, "'I Object,'" 106.

16  Hammond, "Class Notes," 35.

17  This discussion of Wilke forms part of Meyer's broader study of historically marginalized women artists in the 1970s. See Meyer, "Hard Targets."

18  Meyer, "Hard Targets," 380.

19  Meyer, "Hard Targets," 382.

20  Meyer, "Hard Targets," 368.

21  Meyer, "Hard Targets," 382.

22  The photographs are, importantly, available to researchers.

23  This point is discussed cogently by Shannon Jackson in chapter 3 of *Social Works*.

24  Wilke quoted in Berman, "A Decade of Progress," 77.

25  Oldenburg, "History of the Alphabet / Good Humor."

26  Hannah Wilke, "Art Collaborations between Claes Oldenburg and Hannah Wilke," unpublished document in the Hannah Wilke Collection and Archive, Los Angeles, CA.

27 *Lives* was staged at the Fine Arts Building, 105 Hudson Street, New York, November 29–December 20, 1975.

28 Nancy Princenthal notes that the callers included "Louise Bourgeois, Bill Jensen, Tod Williams (repeatedly, sounding very lovesick), Oldenburg, Tony Shafrazi, Francis Ford Coppola, an unidentified heavy breather, Barbara Rose, Barbara Haskell, Donald Goddard, Marsie Scharlatt, Emmy Scharlatt, and, several times, Wilke's mother, Selma Butter." Princenthal, *Hannah Wilke*, 84. This information was corroborated by Jeffrey Deitch in personal conversations with the author in 2022.

29 Deitch, *Lives*.

30 *Intercourse with . . .* text originally written by Wilke for a Guggenheim Memorial Foundation Grant, 1976. The final phrase is a refrain from the 1937 George and Ira Gershwin song "They Can't Take That Away from Me," which was prominently featured in the film *Shall We Dance* with Fred Astaire and Ginger Rogers. The content of the song concerns the memories of past lovers, which remain even after a relationship has run its course.

31 Her interest in specifically naming those who left messages for her has often been attributed only to the later 1977 video performance, but the text-based components of the earlier installation of *Intercourse with . . .* list the names and approximate dates of each caller.

32 Roberta Smith, "Art in Review: Hannah Wilke: Performalist Self-Portraits and Video/Film Performances," *New York Times*, September 27, 1996, 29.

33 Lippard, "The Pains and Pleasures of Rebirth," 75–76.

34 Chave, "'I Object,'" 104.

35 Chave, "'I Object,'" 108.

36 Adler, "Hannah Wilke," 317. While some feminists had attacked Wilke's prominent nudity in her performances as being narcissistic, more recent critiques of her work, such as those by Amelia Jones and Joanna Frueh, have argued for a positive reading of the term. For instance, Jones has argued that the act of deliberate posing that Wilke adopts throughout this series was a strategic feminist operation to undermine the modernist patriarchal system of artistic value that she terms a "radical narcissism." Enacting an exaggerated parody of female objectification—or what Craig Owens calls the "rhetoric of [the] pose"—Wilke uses her nude body to merge her exterior physicality with her interior subjectivity in a manner that circumvents and disrupts the patriarchal model of the female nude as merely performing for the male artist/viewer. See A. Jones, *Body Art / Performing the Subject*, 149; and, more generally, Wilke, *Hannah Wilke*.

37 Wilke quoted in Siegel, "Between the Censor and the Muse?," 47.

38 Wilke quoted in M. Jones, "Politicizing Art," 1.

39 Princenthal, *Hannah Wilke*, 85.

40 Van Bruggen, *Claes Oldenburg*, 8.

41 Van Bruggen, *Claes Oldenburg*, 3.

42  The details of Mucha's and Oldenburg's respective abilities are provided by Genevieve Waller's extensive research for her brilliant essay, "Unattributed Objects." It was this essay that brought the image of Oldenburg and Mucha to my attention.

43  For instance, Waller describes how Mucha's role in performing extensive sewing and fabrication for Oldenburg's 1962 Green Gallery exhibition led to his inclusion of her name, "PAT," written upside down as skywriting next to a drawing of a black biplane. Waller, "Unattributed Objects," 174n9. According to Gene Baro, "the biplane motif acknowledges the collaboration of the artist's wife in the making of the sculptures and 'getting us aloft' in their first uptown show." Oldenburg and Baro, *Claes Oldenburg*, 120. In addition, Mucha received veiled recognition in the form of bubbled lettering that Oldenburg included often in his work. In the monoprint CAP (1961), the titular letters stood for "Claes And Pat, expressing the collaboration of husband and wife." Oldenburg and Baro, *Claes Oldenburg*, 104.

44  Waller astutely points out: "in the catalogues produced for the *Mouse Museum* and *Ray Gun Wing*, Jim Dine, George Manupelli, and others were credited for the objects they added, while Muschinski and Wilke were not." Waller, "Unattributed Objects," 164.

45  For example, Claes's brother, Richard, was the director of the Museum of Modern Art from 1972 to 1995.

46  Waller presents these fascinating details in both the body of her text and a footnote in "Unattributed Objects," 164 and 174n9.

47  For example, in Oldenburg's 1979 exhibition catalog for the Museum Ludwig show, everyone from Jim Dine to Bernhard Leitner and Heidi Bechinie were named. In the *Ray Gun Wing*, certain objects were even credited as having been "made by guards at Venice Biennale" in 1964. Van Bruggen, *Claes Oldenburg*, 112.

48  Wilke died on January 28, 1993.

49  While the use of watercolor was not new to Wilke, as she had used the medium in drawings since the early 1970s, it is significant to note that her decision to use this material for her *I-Museum* drawings seems to play on its associations with Oldenburg's own project proposals. Since the late 1960s, Oldenburg had notably used watercolors in his drawings, particularly to illustrate his monumental outdoor sculptures. It seems that Wilke's own *I-Museum* knowingly deploys these references from Oldenburg as a strategic attempt to draw connections across his practice into hers.

50  Carol Vogel, "A Little 'Q' Gets Its Day on the Block," *New York Times*, September 10, 2009.

51  Such a connection was made explicit in a phrase written in her 1991 proposed exhibition drawing, in which Wilke wrote: "COUP DE COUTEAU: *the censored edition of I Object: Memoirs of a Sugar Giver where all letters previously published in Ludwig [Museum] catalogue for Marcel Duchamp were*

*censored in book "Hannah Wilke" by CO."* The phrase "coup de couteau" can be translated as a stab wound, conjuring imagery of being stabbed in the back that Wilke directed toward Oldenburg. In 1987, Wilke published a "Coup de Couteau" edition of *I Object: Memoirs of a Sugar Giver* in which she included love letters from Oldenburg (often taken from postcards he sent her on his travels) and Hamilton, her own poetry, and quotes from other writers that were used in her performances.

52    Wilke quoted in Picard, "Hannah Wilke," 18. In this interview, Wilke also mentions how one of her *Chinese Fortune Cookie* works was included in Oldenburg's *Mouse Museum* at Documenta in Kassel, Germany.

53    As noted by Roberta Smith in a review of a 1996 posthumous exhibition of Wilke's work at Ronald Feldman Fine Arts, Wilke exhibited the ray gun collection that she *herself* amassed during the late 1960s until the demise of her and Oldenburg's relationship in the late 1970s. The language used by Smith is particularly significant. She writes, "On view is the ray-gun collection that Wilke accumulated in response to the work of Claes Oldenburg, with whom she lived for several years starting in the late 1960s." Based on Smith's description, these objects appear not as a part of the original ray gun collection that Oldenburg took from Wilke and other unacknowledged laborers but rather suggest an ongoing project of recovering ownership over her labor in accumulating such objects for Oldenburg after being excluded from public acknowledgment in his *Mouse Museum / Ray Gun Wing* exhibition. R. Smith, "Art in Review."

54    Wilke quoted in Finberg, "Body Language."

55    This point was made by Marsie Scharlatt.

56    Waller, "Unattributed Objects," 168.

57    Waller is one of the only scholars, to my knowledge, who mentions their presence. Waller, "Unattributed Objects," 169.

58    Although VALIE EXPORT recounted this version of the work to *High Performance* magazine in a 1979 interview, she later denied the veracity of these events. The action was staged in an art-house movie theater, where she walked through the crowd in her crotchless pants. See EXPORT and Bourgeois, *VALIE EXPORT*.

59    Finberg, "Body Language." The earliest collaborative works were in 1974, when Wilke asked Christopher Giercke to photograph *Hannah Wilke Super-t-Art* and she hired Les Wollam to photograph the *S.O.S. Starification Object Series* photographs.

60    Goddard quoted in Takemoto, "Looking through Hannah's Eyes," 128.

61    Lippard, "The Pains and Pleasures of Rebirth," 75.

62    This solicitation of the male gaze by Wilke reverses the principles laid out in Laura Mulvey's celebrated 1975 essay, "Visual Pleasure and Narrative Cinema," in which the film theorist analyzes how the male gaze structures and limits the possibilities for women's representation as merely serving

to be the "(passive) raw material for the (active) gaze of men." Mulvey, "Visual Pleasure and Narrative Cinema," 843.

63     While the title *Advertisements for Living* is not directly named in this drawing (although it appears on one of the five supplemental sketches that Wilke made), Wilke's loose rendering of nine pictures set on a wall matches the composition of *Advertisements for Living*. As mentioned in the introduction to this chapter, in 1989 Oldenburg pursued legal action against Wilke for using his likeness in three works of art—*Advertisements for Living*, *What'll I Do*, and the *Artists Make Toys* poster—that she planned to exhibit in her first museum retrospective at the University of Missouri that same year. Although the work had already been published elsewhere, Oldenburg also refused to give permission to Wilke for reproducing textual snippets from *I Object: Memoirs of a Sugar Giver*. Thomas H. Kochheiser, director of Gallery 210, to Jane Lago, senior editor at University of Missouri Press, February 6, 1989, Hannah Wilke Collection and Archive, Los Angeles, CA. Kochheiser writes: "Because of certain legal problems that have recently arisen concerning the inclusion of Claes Oldenburg images in the Hannah Wilke catalogue, I am instructing you to pull all such images out of the work. I would also like you to pull Hannah's written piece, 'I Object' from the catalogue. Even though it has been previously published, because it contains personal correspondence from Oldenburg, I feel it would be prudent to take it out to head off any additional problems." Only Oldenburg's postcard texts were removed from *I Object*, however.

64     The other two artworks under legal debate in 1989 were *What'll I Do* and *Artists Make Toys*, both of which included photographs of Oldenburg and Wilke together in a romantic context taken from the period when they shared a personal relationship. The photograph of Oldenburg's likeness in *Artists Make Toys* was included as part of a poster for a 1974 group exhibition at the Clocktower in New York and therefore had already been circulated widely in public with his approval. Wilke selected the photograph. Waller points out: "By choosing a photograph of herself with Oldenburg, rather than one of him alone, Wilke promoted herself as an artist equal to Oldenburg, made their romantic relationship conspicuously public, but at the same time generated an inference that she was merely some pretty toy, debunking the 'seriousness' generally attributed to established male artists and the relative lack of respect commanded by female artists." Waller, "Unattributed Objects," 164. See also Cottingham, "Some Naked Truths and Her Legacy in the 1990s," 59.

65     As in many of his other projects, Oldenburg had enlisted outside labor to realize *Bedroom Ensemble*. In this case, it was artist Richard Artschwager, who had come to fine art from a design and woodworking background and helped Oldenburg by fabricating many of the objects in this installation. See Koplos and Metcalf, *Makers*, 291. In 1965, Oldenburg and Artschwager were interviewed together for an article in *Craft Horizons*

in which Oldenburg discussed the delegation of labor within his practice with various individuals, including his then wife Mucha. He asserted that the use of others in making his work was a deliberate choice: "Up to 1963, I had been doing things where I was the only one involved, and then I wanted to get other people into it, using them almost as part of the material. She [Mucha] happened to be a good seamstress, so I took advantage of her right away." This sentiment continued when Oldenburg discussed the role of the Dutch carpenter employed in addition to Artschwager for *Bedroom Ensemble*, claiming, "I didn't burden him with the idea. I just said that I want this thing to be this way, and he didn't ask why, which is a great help. . . . We had a couple of toasts on the last night and he said he almost felt like an artist." Oldenburg quoted in McDevitt, "The Object," 56.

66    While Princenthal suggests Oldenburg's treatment of Wilke was a form of exploitation, describing the logic behind Wilke's art as a "willingness to speak out, in her work, against a man who spurned her," I contend that Wilke's artistic strategy was more tactical, using Oldenburg's manipulation as material for her own artistic response following his pursuit of legal action. Princenthal, *Hannah Wilke*, 86.

67    Hamilton appeared in her 1980 work *Venus Envy*, a photograph taken from Wilke's perspective in which he is positioned between her bare legs, looking up at her. Reversing the traditional paradigm of the male artist's gaze focused onto a female subject, often depicted nude, here Wilke uses her camera to capture her male lover between her legs, exposing his vulnerability and identity as she maintains dominion over her oblique representation.

68    Richard Hamilton to Sue Denny at University of Missouri Press, February 22, 1989, Hannah Wilke Collection and Archive, Los Angeles, CA.

69    Hamilton to Sue Denny, February 22, 1989.

70    It seems that Wilke was referring to Oldenburg's *Sculpture in the Form of a Bicycle Saddle* (1976). In an untitled archival document stipulating the scope of her labor in works attributed only to Oldenburg, Wilke asserts: "The idea to make this work in marble originated with me. In 1976 I arranged for Rene Lavaggi, my assistant at the School of Visual Arts, to carve the work in marble according to Claes' maquette. I helped pick out the marble and followed the progress of the work while teaching at the school. Made crucial decision about reshaping part of the work when it was almost completed. Documented Claes and Rene on film several times while the work was being done. Throughout the time of our relationship, I gave general assistance on numerous projects, helping to make decisions on color scale, types of paper for prints, etc.; sewing, painting and other forms of fabrication; discussing ideas and concepts for specific works and general directions. Acted as technical and aesthetic advisor on visits to various places where fabrications of some of Claes's work was done. Searched out fabrics, vinyl, leather and other materials. Accompanied him to Akron and gave advice on projects in which he was going to use rubber,

particularly since I worked with rubber in my own art. Helped with fiber-glass works on visits to factory. Early visits to Lipincott Foundry in New Haven for fabrication in metal. Gave Claes all my tools for working in clay so that he could make models for Q sculpture. Clay models also the basis for the Alphabet Good Humor Bar." Written statement by Hannah Wilke, undated, Hannah Wilke Collection and Archive, Los Angeles, CA.

71    In her archive, Wilke titled an undated document "Other Important Issues Concerning Oldenburg," which outlined various ways in which he restricted her work, including asking Alanna Heiss, director of the Institute of Art and Urban Resources, for all the *Artists Make Toys* posters, which she refused because she thought he intended to destroy them.

72    This reading of *Even-tu-ally* is supported by the artist's sister, Marsie Scharlatt, who wrote to art historian Richard Meyer: "In response to this action [the removal of the three illustrations from the catalog], Wilke persevered, creating work in defiance that included *Even-tu-ally* (1969–91), a photograph of Wilke lying in an Oldenburg installation superimposed with a letter from Richard Hamilton giving her permission to use his image in her work." Marsie Scharlatt, email to Richard Meyer, August 12, 2006, quoted in Meyer, "Hard Targets," 381n52.


## Chapter 3. Assistants

1    In many ways, Carpenter was typical of Kippenberger's assistants in that he was hired because of specific characteristics that his employer actively sought out, such as formal training, the ambition to pursue one's artistic career, and an individualized style that could be incorporated into Kippenberger's own production.

2    Carpenter, "I Was an Assistant," 120.

3    Carpenter, "I Was an Assistant," 120.

4    In 1991, Kippenberger gave an interview with artist and critic Jutta Koether in which he discussed the *Heavy Burschi* series and Carpenter's role in that project. In response to a question regarding his use of materials, Kippenberger quickly shifted the discussion to explicitly acknowledge the role of his assistant, a gesture that suggests Carpenter was seen as a vital aspect of Kippenberger's work. "These sorts of paintings or commentaries are simply too good, done far too well, which turns them into kitsch. So I decided to turn them further into a kind of double kitsch." Kippenberger quoted in Koether, "Martin Kippenberger," 95.

5    Bolter and Grusin, *Remediation*, 45.

6    Bolter and Grusin, *Remediation*, 33–34.

7    Act on Copyright and Related Rights (Urheberrechtsgesetz, UrhG), trans. Ute Reusch, Copyright Act of 9 September 1965 (Federal Law Gazette I, p. 1273), as last amended by Article 25 of the Act of 23 June 2021 (Federal

Law Gazette I, p. 1858), Federal Ministry of Justice, https://www.gesetze -im-internet.de/englisch_urhg/englisch_urhg.pdf.

8       See Fielkow, "Clashing Rights under United States Copyright Law."

9       Even the name "Büro" refers to Warhol's reformulation of the isolated art studio and his assumption of a managerial position in delegating labor among his collaborators at the Factory. Caroline A. Jones's description of Warhol's authorial persona can be productively compared to Kippenberger's, as she writes, "Warhol enforces the necessity of viewing the artist as a nonunitary author, a shifting absence (or Derridean 'trace') that can only ever be temporarily constituted in the viewer's/reader's mind." See C. Jones, *Machine in the Studio*, 198.

10      Beginning in 1979, Kippenberger focused attention on his musical endeavors. He released eight albums throughout his lifetime, many of which demonstrated a method of distributing labor among auxiliary agents and appropriating that of others. For further details on Kippenberger's musical works, see Licht, "Martin Kippenberger's *MUSIK 1979–1995*."

11      Jones has noted that Warhol's "superstars" were "unpaid, untrained, undirected." See C. Jones, *Machine in the Studio*, 236.

12      Although established in 1957, Andy Warhol Enterprises Inc. became central to Warhol's various creative operations in the 1970s, when he began diversifying his artistic output to include commercial endeavors and assuming a pseudo-corporate persona (for instance, he had previously solicited product endorsements in the *Village Voice* in 1966 and claimed to want to sell shares in his "company" on Wall Street in 1969).

13      Fremont quoted in Unruh, "Interview with Vincent Fremont," 150.

14      As Alison Gingeras has pointed out, Warhol's wholehearted embrace of the commodification of art often came as a shock to those who saw his canonical Pop art from the 1960s as a deadpan yet subversive critique of such commercialization: "To them, his indulgent participation in the spheres of entertainment and commerce in the '70s and '80s confirmed his capitulation to the system he once 'critiqued' (however deadpan or ambiguously)." Gingeras, "Performing the Self," 253.

15      Notably, two important exhibitions dealing with related themes were also staged in 1986; see Wallis, *Damaged Goods: Desire and the Economy of the Object* (at the New Museum); and Bois, *Endgame: Reference and Simulation in Recent Painting and Sculpture* (at the Institute of Contemporary Art, Boston).

16      Gianni Jetzer points out that this work revealed how these artists "operated simultaneously in two different contexts: in the art world, with intellectual, political, and moral standards and positions, and in the realm of pure entertainment." Jetzer, "Brand New," 34.

17      Two major examples of such branded commercialization include Keith Haring's Pop Shop, a storefront that the artist opened in SoHo in 1986 that was intended to make his work accessible—through the purchase of

cheaper, novelty items that featured the artist's signature—to a wide-ranging audience, and the art collective General Idea's Boutique, which was a dollar-sign-shaped booth selling commodity objects that either documented or actually were editioned artworks as part of the larger project *1984 Miss General Idea Pavilion*.

18   Gingeras points out that in German, since the title was "slightly silly sounding to a native German speaker, the artist exchanged the more conventional formulation *'male mich'* (paint me) with *'male mir'* (paint for me). This nuance in the title's wording revealed that the canvases on display were not painted by the artist's own hand." Gingeras, *Martin Kippenberger*, 9.

19   While some scholars have debated the identity of Siebert, Raimar Stange has supported this identification. See Stange, "One of You among You with You," 68.

20   This tactic of hiring a commercial sign painter reappeared in Kippenberger's *Paris Bar* (1991/93).

21   Such a model recalls John Baldessari's *Commissioned Paintings* (1969), in which he paid sign painters to create photorealistic renderings of a hand pointing to an object based on slides given to them by the artist.

22   Yet there are distinctions between copyright, which protects economic interests, and authors' rights, which govern creative authorship. In modern copyright law, which covers a wide domain of creative endeavors, sole authorial attribution and artistic ownership are awarded to the primary controlling actor who produces original content—which could be an employer. If others contribute new material, however, these creators have authorial rights—but only if such input was generated outside the scope of employment. See Woodmansee, *The Author, Art, and the Market*, 42–51.

23   Sáiz and Castro, "Trademarks in Branding," 1106.

24   See Schéré, "Where Is the Morality?"; and Sarraute, "Current Theory on the Moral Right of Authors and Artists under French Law." Notably, Buskirk points out that the "early articulation of *droit moral* was part of an attempt to wrest control over artistic production from the hands of the sovereign at the time of the French Revolution." Buskirk, *The Contingent Object*, 49.

25   Buskirk, *The Contingent Object*, 49.

26   German Copyright Act (Urheberrechtsgesetz, UrhG), art. 13–15.

27   Diederichsen, "The Poor Man's Sports Car Descending a Staircase," 148.

28   Diederichsen, "The Poor Man's Sports Car," 148.

29   Carpenter, "Back Seat Driver," 27.

30   Decter, "Martin Kippenberger," 94.

31   Alberro, *Conceptual Art and the Politics of Publicity*, 13.

32   While initially exhibited together as a cohesive installation, the individual works have since been divided into the various sculptural modules.

33    Sanchez, "Cerberus," 39. The concept of input-output processes was the subject of numerous Kippenberger works, as noted by Sanchez. These include his self-portrait in which he conceived of himself as a motor in a car (*The Capitalist Futuristic Painter in His Car*, 1985) and the series of profit-analysis charts (*Profit Peaks*, 1985), as well as the publication of his book *Input-Output: Umzüge 1957–1988* (Input-Output: Moves 1957–1988). More generally, Sanchez's discussion in "Cerberus" of Kippenberger's use of assistants through his late 1980s art practice was particularly useful for the purposes of this chapter. Notably, Kippenberger's phrase is used as the title for Schmidt-Wulffen's "Living Vehicle."

34    Diederichsen, "The Poor Man's Sports Car Descending a Staircase," 148.

35    Williams, *Permission to Laugh*, 70.

36    Carpenter, "Back Seat Driver," 27.

37    Williams, *Permission to Laugh*, 96.

38    Bell, "Martin Kippenberger's Self-Portraits," 24.

39    Bell, "Martin Kippenberger's Self-Portraits," 21.

40    Galenson, *Conceptual Revolutions*, 26–29.

41    He returned to the Picasso mythology in his later series *Jacqueline: The Paintings Pablo Couldn't Paint Anymore* (1996), eight portrait paintings of Picasso's widow and muse based on photographs of her taken in the studio after Picasso's death.

42    Jetzer, "Brand New," 20.

43    Basquiat's position in the art world was particularly complicated; as John A. Walker points out in his book *Art and Celebrity*, Basquiat was one of the only Black or minority artists who achieved such commercial success and notoriety in the mainstream, white-run art world of the early 1980s, yet his celebrity was often used as a token example of multiculturalism by the gallery system. See J. A. Walker, *Art and Celebrity*, 233.

44    J. A. Walker, *Art and Celebrity*, 265.

45    D. Phillips, "Bright Lights, Big City," 82.

46    In fact, Sherman has explicitly noted that her *Disaster* works were specifically created to be less palatable "when I was responding to my ambivalence about the 'collector frenzy.'" Sherman quoted in Morris, *The Essential Cindy Sherman*, 82.

47    Buskirk, *The Contingent Object of Contemporary Art*; and Alberro, *Conceptual Art and the Politics of Publicity*.

48    Buchloh, "Conceptual Art 1962–1969."

49    Williams, *Permission to Laugh*, 97.

50    Goldstein, "The Problem Perspective," 39.

51    Rugoff, *Just Pathetic*, 2.

52    Kelley quoted in Goldstein, "The Problem Perspective," 39.

53    Owens, "The Allegorical Impulse," 69.

54   Owens, "The Allegorical Impulse," 69.

55   Williams addresses Kippenberger's relationship to Owens's formulation of postmodern allegory: "Kippenberger throws into question the way in which meaning is produced and received by deliberately constructing a visual environment that lures one into its superficial system only to deny a singularly humorous reading." Williams, *Permission to Laugh*, 77.

56   Hermes, "On an Untitled White Installation," 32.

57   Hermes, "On an Untitled White Installation," 35.

58   According to Sanchez: "As a painter in the 1980s, he had been a linear input-output system, consuming fuel and outputting waste in the form of exhaust. By reinputting these outputs into assistants like Carpenter, and then re-uptaking these outputs again, Kippenberger turned the 'piss bridge' into a piss loop. . . . Through this perverse form of 'systemic lavage,' as Kippenberger put it, the two-headed dog processed waste into meta-waste, like a recycling system running in reverse." Sanchez, "Cerberus," 41.

59   Carpenter, "I Was an Assistant," 121.

60   Agamben, "The Assistants," 35.

61   Agamben, "The Assistants," 29.

62   Agamben, "The Assistants," 30–31.

63   In 1993, Francis Alÿs introduced a similar concept, hiring sign painters in Mexico City to make enlarged copies of his own small-scale oil paintings. After generating multiple copies, Alÿs would then introduce a new "model" painting based on a combination of the variations made by the sign painters. This cycle of reuse would perpetuate across multiple generations of copies.

64   Bell, "Martin Kippenberger's Self-Portraits," 25.

65   Hermes, "Latex and Rubber Paintings 1990/91," 147–49.

66   Bell, "Martin Kippenberger's Self-Portraits," 25.

67   Sanchez, "Cerberus," 43.

68   Notable examples of this promulgation of his persona through social networks include his acceptance of a teaching position at the Städelschule in Frankfurt (1990–92), where he delegated his first lecture as a visiting professor entirely to Krebber, who read an interview between Kippenberger and Diederichsen rather than offering a more conventional talk.

69   In 1991, a series of drawings was published in a catalog titled *Heavy Mädel* that corresponded with dual exhibitions staged at both Galerie Gisela Capitain and the Pace/MacGill Gallery in New York that year. In an exhibition review published in *Mousse* magazine on February 24, 2023, the *Heavy Mädel* drawings were described as being made by Carpenter, just as was the case with the *Heavy Burschi* works.

70   Cherix, "Martin Kippenberger," 30.

71    While there is photographic documentation of Kippenberger wielding a handsaw on one of the silkscreens, it is unclear whether he completed the destructive procedures of *Content on Tour* alone or with the help of his assistant.

## Chapter 4. Preservers

1     O'Grady, "Performance Statement #3," 47.
2     Crenshaw, "Demarginalizing the Intersection of Race and Sex."
3     O'Grady, "Performance Statement #3," 47.
4     O'Grady, "Performance Statement #3," 47.
5     O'Grady, "*Mlle Bourgeoise Noire 1955*," 9.
6     O'Grady ended up graduating a year later but remained associated with her entering class.
7     As one of the cofounders of the Négritude movement, Damas—along with Aimé Césaire and Léopold Sédar Senghor—had repudiated European colonization and sought to establish a new Black consciousness rooted in the collective pride for shared Pan-African values and culture.
8     Both performance scripts for MBN's interventions at JAM and the New Museum were printed in a document beginning "diptych . . ." in her archive, among other places. Lorraine O'Grady, untitled statement, performances binder, 1980–1983, box 9, folder 1, Papers of Lorraine O'Grady, MSS.3, Wellesley College Archives, Wellesley, MA.
9     O'Grady has expressed that "aging didn't interest me as a subject." O'Grady, "Interview with Laura Cottingham," 227.
10    O'Grady, *Writing in Space, 1973–2019*; Morris and D'Souza, *Lorraine O'Grady*; Sparling Williams, *Speaking Out of Turn*.
11    These questions were stated in front of an audience at the 2018 opening of the exhibition *Soul of a Nation: Art in the Age of Black Power* at the Crystal Bridges Museum of American Art. See O'Grady, "The *Mlle Bourgeoise Noire* Project, 1980–1983."
12    While both terms speak to unlawful entry by an outsider, *invasion* connotes a visible and aggressive takeover in the hopes of gaining territorial or proprietary control, whereas *trespassing* describes a surreptitious interference of another's property or rights performed without permission.
13    McMillan, *Embodied Avatars*, 12. McMillan notably opens his book's introduction with a brief discussion of O'Grady's MBN character in this context; his analysis aligns in many ways with my thinking of O'Grady's practice.
14    O'Grady, "Interview with Linda Montano," 80. As Catherine Damman has pointed out, this critique of the carefulness with which art was treated could be directed to various institutional workers as well: "such gloves are worn not just by the debutante but by the art handler and conservator, too—which is to say that the performance eviscerates not only artists who

play it safe, but also the entire system of extracted value and its preservation that parades under the banner of 'art'." Damman, "Risk Everything," 121.

15  Sparling Williams, *Speaking Out of Turn*, 69.

16  Beginning in the mid-1960s, the Black Arts Movement (cofounded by Amiri Baraka) advocated for developing a visual language rooted in a distinctly Black identity that could be readily accessible by Black audiences of all backgrounds—in contrast to what was considered the elitism of white-dominated abstraction. As Kellie Jones has noted, the interest in ancestral Africa by Black artists in the late 1960s and 1970s can be attributed to multiple factors: the increased prominence of independent African nations and the related growth of "black cultural nationalism" as well as the turn away from radical forms of artistic activism in the United States in favor of seeking an "African spiritual home" in the wake of the substantial violence that occurred as a reaction to the Black Power movement after 1969. K. Jones, *South of Pico*, 186.

17  Kingsley, "Black Artists."

18  O'Grady, "A Day at the Races," 173.

19  O'Grady has articulated this point throughout her career, noting that even though the avant-garde is a product of the middle class—made by and for those who have the time and resources to train this intellectualization of art—many Black avant-garde artists disavowed their class status. In a 1990 letter to Lucy Lippard, O'Grady looked back to the moment of the early 1980s, stating: "Eight or nine years ago, I sensed the white artworld being enthralled by several black artists who I felt were playing a deceptive game. Though they were producing good work, I didn't see how people like Ntozake Shange and Candace Hill and Joe Lewis could avoid paying a heavy price for in a sense denying what they were (in the case of Candace and Zake, doctors' daughters, than whom there are no more privileged people in the black community). Neither they nor their white patrons seemed to see the anomaly in their projecting their work as 'representative,' while invisibly dressing themselves in the glamour of the Street." Lorraine O'Grady to Lucy Lippard, February 25, 1990, box 31, folder 5, Papers of Lorraine O'Grady, MSS.3, Wellesley College Archives, Wellesley, MA.

20  O'Grady, "Email Q&A with Courtney Baker," unpublished email exchange, 1998, http://lorraineogrady.com/wp-content/uploads/2015/11/Courtney -Baker-Lorraine-OGrady_Email-Interview_Unpublished.pdf.

21  Kingsley, "Black Artists," 113.

22  Kingsley, "Black Artists," 114.

23  Goode Bryant quoted in Greenberger, "How New York's Legendary Just Above."

24  O'Grady, "*Rivers* and Just Above Midtown," 215.

25  O'Grady, "Interview with Linda Montano," 80.

26  O'Grady, "Interview with Linda Montano," 80.

27  O'Grady, "Interview with Linda Montano," 81.

28 *Outlaw Aesthetics* pamphlet, 2, box 10, folder 1, Papers of Lorraine O'Grady, MSS.3, Wellesley College Archives, Wellesley, MA.

29 O'Grady, "Interview with Laura Cottingham," 225.

30 Goode Bryant quoted in Steinhauer, "Just Watch Me."

31 O'Grady, "Email Q&A with Courtney Baker," n.p.

32 Harney and Moten, *The Undercommons*.

33 See Collins, *Transforming America*; Kalman, *Right Star Rising*; and Wilentz, *The Age of Reagan*.

34 Bowser, "Race Relations in the 1980s," 307.

35 Harney and Moten, *The Undercommons*, 28.

36 D'Souza, "Introduction," xxvi.

37 O'Grady, "My 1980s," 206.

38 O'Grady, "Email Q&A with Courtney Baker," n.p.

39 Cindy Sherman expressed her decision to begin using photography in the 1970s due to its perceived lesser importance within the hierarchies of media, which allowed women to make their mark without predetermined valuations set in place. This was affirmed by curator and museum director Lisa Phillips: "to Sherman, the secondary status of photography in the art-world forms a perfect corollary to the status of women in patriarchal society, and she uses each situation to question our assumptions of the other." L. Phillips, "Cindy Sherman's Cindy Shermans," 13.

40 This point is emphasized by McMillan; see *Embodied Avatars*, 6.

41 Sims, "Aspects of Performance in the Work of Black American Women Artists," 208. She also points out that "the fact that it is mostly women who have been involved in performance art might have something to do with the suspect status that it has within black American art circles." Sims, "Aspects of Performance in the Work of Black American Women Artists," 208.

42 Sims, "Aspects of Performance in the Work of Black American Women Artists," 208.

43 O'Grady, "*Mlle Bourgeoise Noire* and Feminism," 111.

44 Mlle Bourgeoise Noire to "Advanced Black Artists," 1982, box 10, folder 4, Papers of Lorraine O'Grady, MSS.3, Wellesley College Archives, Wellesley, MA.

45 Janet Henry to Mlle Bourgeoise Noire, box 10, folder 4, Papers of Lorraine O'Grady, MSS.3, Wellesley College Archives, Wellesley, MA.

46 It is worth noting that the equitable status of such tests is widely debated.

47 O'Grady, "The *Mlle Bourgeoise Noire* Project, 1980–1983," 252.

48 Thelma Golden quoted in D'Souza, "Introduction to 'My 1980s,'" 203.

49 This exclusion was not limited to this one publication; in November 1981, *ARTnews* published "New Faces in Alternative Spaces," which focused on the activities of PS1, Franklin Furnace, Artists Space, and others—but gave only comparatively limited attention to JAM. Notably, this article contained a substantial discussion of Fashion Moda, an alternative art

space in the South Bronx, which had Joe Lewis, a young Black director, at its helm. See D. Phillips, "New Faces in Alternative Spaces."

50   O'Grady has expressed: "I often say that I was 'post-black' before I was 'black.'" O'Grady, "My 1980s," 207.

51   The extent to which Antin documented her activities draws comparison with the work of other white women artists working in the mid to late 1970s and early 1980s, such as Lynn Hershman Leeson and Sophie Calle.

52   O'Grady, "Interview with Laura Cottingham," 223.

53   Gumpert and Rifkin, *Persona*, 3.

54   O'Grady, "The *Mlle Bourgeoise Noire* Project," 254.

55   O'Grady, "The *Mlle Bourgeoise Noire* Project," 254.

56   Lorraine O'Grady, untitled statement, performances binder, 1980–1983, box 9, folder 1, Papers of Lorraine O'Grady, MSS.3, Wellesley College Archives, Wellesley, MA.

57   O'Grady, "The *Mlle Bourgeoise Noire* Project," 255.

58   As this photographic documentation indicates, the work continued outside the walls of the New Museum; yet these other actions were integral components of her performance. According to a short list of documentary photographs of *Mlle Bourgeoise Noire Goes to the New Museum* located in the artist's archives, the work began while O'Grady was getting made up into character, and it ends with a final spread featuring a photo taken by Simpson described in shorthand as "L [Lorraine] laughing, arms raised, on street, R [Richard DeGussi] clapping hands, GM [George Mingo] pointing." The presence of these other performers as integral to the work expands conventional readings of the *Mlle Bourgeoise Noire* project in important ways. The piece does not begin or end with the provocative act of MBN whipping herself or reciting her poem; it extends temporally and socially to include other actions and individuals. While these photographs deserve further study, it exceeds the scope of the present study. See box 10, folder 8, Papers of Lorraine O'Grady, MSS.3, Wellesley College Archives, Wellesley, MA.

59   Sparling Williams, *Speaking Out of Turn*, 87.

60   Lorraine O'Grady to John Perrault, November 2, 1981, box 10, folder 8, Papers of Lorraine O'Grady, MSS.3, Wellesley College Archives, Wellesley, MA.

61   This point is also made by Sparling Williams, *Speaking Out of Turn*, 87–88.

62   The discarded weaponry is an interesting feature also found in Wilke's *So Help Me Hannah* photographs and the related text-and-image collages. The need for armament was notably not shared by the white male artists discussed in this book.

63   Lippard, "Open Season," 92.

64   It seems this letter was unprinted by the *Village Voice*; it was, however, mailed to O'Grady. See Ed Jones to *Village Voice* editor, October 12, 1981,

box 10, folder 8, Papers of Lorraine O'Grady, MSS.3, Wellesley College Archives, Wellesley, MA.

65    Lorraine O'Grady to John Perrault, November 2, 1981, box 10, folder 8, Papers of Lorraine O'Grady, MSS.3, Wellesley College Archives, Wellesley, MA.

66    Ed Jones to *Village Voice* editor, October 12, 1981, box 10, folder 8, Papers of Lorraine O'Grady, MSS.3, Wellesley College Archives, Wellesley, MA.

67    Lorraine O'Grady to John Perrault, November 2, 1981, box 10, folder 8, Papers of Lorraine O'Grady, MSS.3, Wellesley College Archives, Wellesley, MA.

68    For instance, Cherise Smith's book *Enacting Others* explores how women artists adopt markers of different racial, gender, and ethnic traits to explore the nature of identity.

69    Under artist Martha Wilson's direction since its formation in 1976, Franklin Furnace staged ephemeral works around the time of O'Grady's attendance by artists such as Ana Mendieta, William Pope.L, Shirin Neshat, and Tehching Hsieh. Wilson's own pioneering performance-based practice was likely influential for O'Grady as well. Through video and photographic works, Wilson assumed various personas and undertook role-playing as a means of exploring female subjectivity. Beginning her career at a moment when Conceptual art was dominated by white male artists, Wilson started to create what she termed "invasions" into other identities in the early 1970s. Manipulating her appearance with makeup, costume, and pose, Wilson investigated female gender stereotypes in projects such as her celebrated photo series *A Portfolio of Models* (1974) and later satirical emulations of political female figures, including Nancy Reagan, Barbara Bush, and Tipper Gore. She also enacted male personas while in drag, as in her 1972/96 *Posturing: Drag* photographic work, in which she played a man posing for the camera in female drag, thereby creating a double reversal of gender: a woman emulating a man—who is himself emulating a woman.

70    The gendered divisions of performance's practitioners further contributed to works by Black women—such as Senga Nengudi and Maren Hassinger—being sidelined in the 1980s art world; their work defied the figurative or representational trend of artwork produced under the influence of BAM in what Kellie Jones calls an "indeterminacy of practice." K. Jones, *South of Pico*, 189.

71    While the creation of invented personas by Black women artists was largely limited to O'Grady, Pindell, and Piper, many Black women artists adopted the medium of performance more broadly in the 1970s and 1980s—including Faith Ringgold, Candace Hill-Montgomery, Kaylynn Sullivan, Joyce Scott, and others. See Sims, "Aspects of Performance in the Work of Black American Women Artists."

72    In her 1973 video *The Mythic Being*, Piper spoke of the conceptual underpinnings of this work, asking rhetorically: "What would happen if there

was a being who had exactly my history, only a completely different visual appearance to the rest of society? And that's why I dress as a man."

73    O'Grady, "Interview with Linda Montano," 81.

74    O'Grady, "Interview with Linda Montano," 81.

75    O'Grady, "Interview with Laura Cottingham," 235.

76    O'Grady, "Interview with Linda Montano," 79.

77    O'Grady, "*Mlle Bourgeoise Noire* and Feminism," 111.

78    O'Grady, "Interview with Jarrett Earnest," 244.

79    Pindell, "On Making a Video—Free, White and 21" (1992), in *The Heart of the Question*, 65.

80    O'Grady, "Interview with Laura Cottingham," 236.

81    O'Grady, "Interview with Linda Montano," 82.

82    Lorraine O'Grady to Joe Overstreet, May 7, 1983, box 10, folder 4, Papers of Lorraine O'Grady, MSS.3, Wellesley College Archives, Wellesley, MA.

83    O'Grady, "A Day at the Races," 174.

84    O'Grady, "The Black and White Show, 1982," 185.

85    Fekner's *Toxic Junkie* mural, which was commissioned by O'Grady to be painted across the street from the gallery entrance, became emblematic of the East Village art scene. However, despite its appearance in photographs published in prominent publications such as *Art in America*, the work was not discussed in the context of *The Black and White Show*. For instance, see Robinson and McCormick, "Slouching toward Avenue D."

86    Mlle Bourgeoise Noire a.k.a. Lorraine O'Grady to Elizabeth C. Baker, October 22, 1984, box 10, folder 4, Papers of Lorraine O'Grady, MSS.3, Wellesley College Archives, Wellesley, MA.

87    Mlle Bourgeoise Noire a.k.a. Lorraine O'Grady to Elizabeth C. Baker, October 22, 1984, box 10, folder 4, Papers of Lorraine O'Grady, MSS.3, Wellesley College Archives, Wellesley, MA.

88    O'Grady, "The Black and White Show, 1982."

89    O'Grady, "Email Q&A with Courtney Baker," n.p.

90    O'Grady contributed an important essay titled "Black Dreams" to issue 15 of *Heresies*. Therein she describes her feelings of in-betweenness and not belonging as a light-skinned biracial woman. The text recounts her experiences trying to find a therapist to help analyze her dreams, which predominantly focused on racial issues. She describes how she would present a happy appearance to white therapists, hiding her concerns about racial inequality and her experience as a Black middle-class woman whose peers often were "still trying to be white." O'Grady, "Black Dreams," 70.

91    O'Grady, "Statement for Moira Roth," 25.

92    O'Grady, "Statement for Moira Roth," 25.

93    O'Grady, "Interview with Amanda Hunt on *Art Is . . .* ," 62.

94    O'Grady, "Statement for Moira Roth," 25.

95    O'Grady quoted in Whitley, "Mlle Bourgeoise Noire Throws Down the Whip," 54.

96    O'Grady, "This Will Have Been," 14.

97    O'Grady, "Interview with Amanda Hunt on *Art Is . . .*," 62.

98    O'Grady, "Interview with Amanda Hunt on *Art Is . . .*," 62.

99    Lorraine O'Grady, *Art Is . . .* project description on personal website, March 15, 2022, https://lorraineogrady.com/art/art-is/.

100   O'Grady, "Statement for Moira Roth," 26.

101   In early 1981, the *New York Times* reported the previous year as the worst-ever twelve-month period for crime in New York City since the beginning of the city's recording of crime statistics. See Leonard Buder, "1980 Called Worst Year of Crime in City History," *New York Times*, February 25, 1981. In March 1982, *The Atlantic* published an article by James Q. Wilson and George L. Kelling, who called for a strict enforcement of "quality-of-life" misdemeanors as a preventative tool for more serious criminal actions. Drawing connections between low-level and serious crimes, this so-called broken windows policing policy—which disproportionally affects communities of color—was not put into effect by the NYPD until the 1990s. However, the history of ongoing prejudicial policing tactics was undoubtedly felt by the Harlem audience at the 1983 African American Parade. Wilson and Kelling, "Broken Windows."

102   Damman, "Risk Everything," 122.

103   As noted by D'Souza and her cocurator Morris in their introduction to the exhibition catalog for O'Grady's 2021 *Both/And* exhibition, O'Grady has expressed that several interpretations of *Art Is . . .* willingly overlook the important racial critique that is central to the work, instead preferring to emphasize it as a humanistic community-building endeavor of generating subjects of art from people of all races. See Morris and D'Souza, "Introduction," 17.

104   O'Grady, "Interview with Amanda Hunt on *Art Is . . .*," 61.

105   Lorraine O'Grady, *Art Is . . .* project description on personal website, March 15, 2022, https://lorraineogrady.com/art/art-is/.

106   Lorraine O'Grady, email to Aruna D'Souza, March 18, 2019, published in O'Grady, *Writing in Space, 1973–2019*, 294n5.

107   O'Grady, "Email Q&A with Courtney Baker," n.p. Piper and Hammons were some of the first to receive recognition from white institutions. Piper had her first retrospective in 1987 at the Alternative Museum; she later became the recipient of a Guggenheim Fellowship in 1989 and had exhibitions at the Whitney Museum of American Art and the Hirshhorn Museum in 1990 and 1991, respectively. In 1988, Lowery Stokes Sims and Leslie King-Hammond curated *Art as a Verb*, an important show of avant-garde Black artists at the Maryland Institute College of Art that later traveled to the Studio Museum in Harlem. The following year, Hammons had a show in 1989 at the white-run alternative art space Exit Art, followed by a 1990 solo exhibition at PS1. He was awarded a Guggenheim Fellowship

(1984), Prix de Rome (1990), and a MacArthur Fellowship (1991). *The Decade Show*, also from 1990, was coproduced by three major institutions: the Studio Museum, the New Museum, and the Museum of Contemporary Hispanic Art. Following a premise reminiscent of MBN's *The Black and White Show*, *The Decade Show* presented work by ninety-four artists of diverse backgrounds, including Native American, Black, Hispanic, and Asian artists alongside those of European descent. In 1993, the Whitney Biennial reflected the changing social landscape; that year's biennial, curated by Thelma Golden and Elisabeth Sussman, featured a considerable amount of work in the show made by artists of color.

108 O'Grady quoted in Velasco, "1000 Words," 133. In an email to me on July 8, 2022, O'Grady clarified the nature of the *Greetings and Theses* performance video. Because of the COVID-19 pandemic, O'Grady was unable to stage her *Greetings and Theses* performance with a live audience as planned and subsequently filmed a performance for the camera that constitutes an independent artwork of the same name that was presented at the Brooklyn Museum on July 28, 2022. While the live performance and the one captured on video share many similarities, O'Grady expressed that her initial plans for *Greetings and Theses* were not executed in full.

109 Each of the Knight's appearances in the six *Announcement of a New Persona* photographs depict her with slight variations in dress: wearing a padded black protective gambeson, a helmeted headdress that appears to grow different varieties of palm trees, or a lance or sword. These key details of the Knight's costume refer to the European medieval tradition, which long fascinated the artist, as well as to Caribbean folklore and history, part of O'Grady's Jamaican heritage and meant to act as symbols of the Global South.

110 These were also textually represented in the *Greetings and Theses* performance video.

111 D'Souza, "Announcement of a New Persona (Performances to Come!)," 182.

112 O'Grady, "Email Q&A with Courtney Baker," n.p.

113 O'Grady, "Olympia's Maid," 102.

114 D'Souza, introduction to O'Grady, "Olympia's Maid," 94.

115 O'Grady quoted in Velasco, "1000 Words," 133.

## Conclusion

1 Fraser quoted in Praxis, "In Conversation," n.p.

2 Fraser quoted in Praxis, "In Conversation," n.p.

3 Acconci, "Some Notes on Illegality in Art," 69.

4 Acconci, "Some Notes on Illegality in Art," 71.

5 Coombe, *The Cultural Life of Intellectual Properties*, 11.

Acconci, Vito. "Some Notes on Illegality in Art." *Art Journal* 50, no. 3 (1991): 69–74.

Adler, Esther. "Hannah Wilke." In *WACK! Art and the Feminist Revolution*, edited by Cornelia Butler and Lisa Gabrielle Mark, 317–18. Los Angeles: Museum of Contemporary Art, 2007.

Agamben, Giorgio. "The Assistants." In *Profanations*, translated by Jeff Fort, 29–35. New York: Zone Books, 2007.

Alberro, Alexander. *Conceptual Art and the Politics of Publicity*. Cambridge, MA: MIT Press, 2003.

Barthes, Roland. "The Death of the Author." In *Image-Music-Text*, translated by Stephen Heath, 142–48. New York: Hill and Wang, 1977.

Béar, Liza. "Chris Burden: Back to You." *Avalanche*, no. 9 (May 1974): 12–13.

Bell, Kirsty. "Martin Kippenberger's Self-Portraits: The Importance of Ernest's Jacket." In *Martin Kippenberger: Catalogue Raisonné of the Paintings*, vol. 3, *1987–1992*, edited by Gisela Capitain, Regina Fiorito, and Lisa Franzen, 10–26. Cologne: Walther König, 2017.

Berman, Avis. "A Decade of Progress, but Could a Female Chardin Make a Living?" *ARTnews* 79, no. 8 (October 1980): 73–79.

Bishop, Claire. *Artificial Hells: Participatory Art and the Politics of Spectatorship*. London: Verso, 2012.

Bishop, Claire. "Delegated Performance, Outsourcing Authenticity." *October* 140 (Spring 2012): 91–112.

Bishop, Claire. "Participation and Spectacle: Where Are We Now?" In *Living as Form: Socially Engaged Art from 1991–2011*, edited by Nato Thompson, 34–45. New York: Creative Time Books, 2012.

Bishop, Claire. "The Social Turn: Collaboration and Its Discontents." *Artforum* 44, no. 6 (February 2006): 178–83.

Blocker, Jane. "Aestheticizing Risk in Wartime: The SLA to Iraq." In *The Aesthetics of Risk*, edited by John C. Welchman, 191–223. Zurich: JRP/ Ringier, 2008.

Bois, Yve-Alain. "Character Study: Sophie Calle." *Artforum* 38, no. 8 (April 2000): 126–31.

Bois, Yve-Alain. *Endgame: Reference and Simulation in Recent Painting and Sculpture.* Boston: Institute of Contemporary Art; Cambridge, MA: MIT Press, 1986. Exhibition catalog.

Bolter, Jay David, and Richard Grusin. *Remediation: Understanding New Media.* Cambridge, MA: MIT Press, 2000.

Bourdon, David. "Body Artists without Bodies." *Village Voice*, February 24, 1975, 85–86.

Bourriaud, Nicolas. *Relational Aesthetics.* Dijon: Les Presses du Réel, 2002.

Bowser, Benjamin P. "Race Relations in the 1980s: The Case of the United States." *Journal of Black Studies* 15, no. 3 (March 1985): 307–24.

Breton, André. "Second Manifesto of Surrealism." In *Manifestos of Surrealism*, by André Breton, 117–94. Translated by Richard Seaver and Helen R. Lane. Ann Arbor: University of Michigan Press, 1972.

Broude, Norma, and Mary Garrard, eds. *The Expanding Discourse: Feminism and Art History.* New York: Icon Editions, 1992.

Buchloh, Benjamin H. D. "Conceptual Art 1962–1969: From the Aesthetic of Administration to the Critique of Institutions." *October* 55 (Winter 1990): 105–43.

Burden, Chris. *Chris Burden 71–73.* Los Angeles: Chris Burden, 1974.

Burden, Chris. "Match Piece." In *Chris Burden: 71–73*, by Chris Burden, 46. Los Angeles: Chris Burden, 1974.

Burden, Chris, Anne Ayres, and Paul Schimmel. *Chris Burden: A Twenty-Year Survey.* Newport Beach, CA: Newport Harbor Art Museum, 1988. Exhibition catalog.

Burnham, Jack. "On Being Sculpture." *Artforum* 7, no. 9 (May 1969): 44–45.

Buskirk, Martha. *The Contingent Object of Contemporary Art.* Cambridge, MA: MIT Press, 2003.

Calendo, John. "Portrait of the Artist as a Young Sculpture." *Oui* 4, no. 4 (April 1975): 84–86, 126–28, 130, 132.

Carpenter, Merlin. "Back Seat Driver." In *Gitarren, die nicht Gudrun heißen: Hommage à Martin Kippenberger*, edited by Thomas Groetz, 26–32. Berlin: Galerie Max Hetzler, 2002.

Carpenter, Merlin. "I Was an Assistant (to Kippenberger, Büttner, and Oehlen)." *Texte zur Kunst* 1 (1990): 119–21.

Chadwick, Whitney, and Isabelle de Courtivron, eds. *Significant Others: Creativity and Intimate Partnership.* London: Thames and Hudson, 1993.

Chave, Anna. "'I Object': Hannah Wilke's Feminism." *Art in America* 97, no. 3 (March 2009): 104–9, 159.

Cherix, Christophe. "Martin Kippenberger." In *Print/out: 20 Years in Print*, edited by Christophe Cherix, Kim Conaty, and Sarah J. S. Suzuki, 29–48. New York: Museum of Modern Art, 2012.

Collins, Robert M. *Transforming America: Politics and Culture during the Reagan Years.* New York: Columbia University Press, 2007.

Cone, Tim. "Life over Art: Oldenburg's Privacy, Wilke's Publicity." *Arts Magazine* 64, no. 1 (September 1989): 25–26.

Coombe, Rosemary. *The Cultural Life of Intellectual Properties: Authorship, Appropriation, and the Law.* Durham, NC: Duke University Press, 1998.

Cottingham, Laura. "Some Naked Truths and Her Legacy in the 1990s." In *Hannah Wilke: A Retrospective*, edited by Elisabeth Delin Hansen, Kirsten Dybbøl, and Donald Goddard, 56–62. Copenhagen: Nikolaj Copenhagen Contemporary Art Center, 1998.

Crenshaw, Kimberlé. "Demarginalizing the Intersection of Race and Sex: A Black Feminist Critique of Antidiscrimination Doctrine, Feminist Theory and Antiracist Politics." *University of Chicago Legal Forum* 1, no. 8 (1989): 139–67.

Damman, Catherine. "Risk Everything." *Artforum* 59, no. 5 (March 2021): 118–25.

Decter, Joshua. "Martin Kippenberger: Metro Pictures." *Artforum* 32, no. 8 (April 1994): 94–95.

Deitch, Jeffrey, ed. *Lives: Artists Who Deal with Peoples' Lives (Including Their Own) as the Subject and/or The Medium of Their Work.* New York: Fine Arts Building, 1975. Exhibition catalog.

Diederichsen, Diedrich. "The Poor Man's Sports Car Descending a Staircase: Kippenberger as Sculptor." In *Martin Kippenberger: The Problem Perspective*, edited by Ann Goldstein, 119–56. Cambridge, MA: MIT Press, 2008. Exhibition catalog.

Drohojowska, Hunter. "Fear and Fantasy in LA: The Artwork of Chris Burden," *LA Weekly*, September 28–October 4, 1979, 4–5, 8.

D'Souza, Aruna. "Announcement of a New Persona (Performances to Come!) (2020)." In *Lorraine O'Grady: Both/And*, edited by Catherine Morris and Aruna D'Souza, 182–83. New York: Dancing Foxes Press, 2021. Exhibition catalog.

D'Souza, Aruna. "Introduction." In *Writing in Space, 1973–2019*, by Lorraine O'Grady, x–xxxv. Edited by Aruna D'Souza. Durham, NC: Duke University Press, 2020.

D'Souza, Aruna. "Introduction to 'My 1980s.'" In *Writing in Space, 1973–2019*, by Lorraine O'Grady, 203–4. Edited by Aruna D'Souza. Durham, NC: Duke University Press, 2020.

Eisler, Riane. *The Chalice and the Blade: Our History, Our Future.* San Francisco: Harper and Row, 1987.

EXPORT, VALIE, and Caroline Bourgeois. *VALIE EXPORT.* Montreuil: Ed. De l'Oeil, 2003.

Feldman, Franklin, and Stephen E. Weil. *Art Works: Law, Policy, Practice.* New York: Practicing Law Institute, 1974.

Fielkow, Colleen Creamer. "Clashing Rights under United States Copyright Law: Harmonizing an Employer's Economic Right with the Artist-Employee's Moral Rights in a Work Made for Hire." *DePaul*

*Journal of Art, Technology and Intellectual Property Law* 7, no. 2 (Spring 1997): 218–63.

Finberg, Bonnie. "Body Language: Hannah Wilke Interview." *Cover*, September 1989, 16.

Foucault, Michel. "What Is an Author?" In *Modernity and Its Discontents*, edited by Steven B. Smith, 299–314. New Haven, CT: Yale University Press, 2018.

Freeman, Samuel. "Criminal Liability and the Duty to Aid the Distressed." *University of Pennsylvania Law Review* 142 (1994): 1455–92.

Galenson, David. *Conceptual Revolutions in Twentieth-Century Art*. Cambridge: Cambridge University Press, 2012.

Gamboa, Harry, Jr. "L.A. Stories: A Roundtable." *Artforum* 50, no. 2 (October 2011): 240–49, 339–40.

Gingeras, Alison. *Martin Kippenberger: Lieber Maler, male mir*. New York: Gagosian Gallery, 2005. Exhibition catalog.

Gingeras, Alison. "Performing the Self: Martin Kippenberger." *Artforum* 43, no. 2 (October 2004): 253–55, 304–5.

Girgis, Sherif. "The Mens Rea of Accomplice Liability: Supporting Intentions." *Yale Law Journal* 123 (2013): 460–94.

Goldstein, Ann. "The Problem Perspective." In *Martin Kippenberger: The Problem Perspective*, edited by Ann Goldstein, 38–103. Cambridge, MA: MIT Press, 2008. Exhibition catalog.

Green, Charles. *The Third Hand: Collaboration in Art from Conceptualism to Postmodernism*. Minneapolis: University of Minnesota Press, 2001.

Greenberger, Alex. "How New York's Legendary Just Above Midtown Gallery Spurred Generations of Black Artists to Success." *ARTnews*, April 6, 2021.

Grobel, Larry. "Chris Burden: Picasso Used Canvas. Michelangelo Used Marble. Chris Burden Uses His Body." *Playgirl*, April 1978, 48–51, 64, 66, 76.

Gumpert, Lynn, and Ned Rifkin. *Persona*. New York: New Museum, 1981. Exhibition catalog.

Hammond, Harmony. "Class Notes." *Heresies* 1, no. 3 (1977): 34–36.

Harney, Stefano, and Fred Moten. *The Undercommons: Fugitive Planning and Black Study*. Wivenhoe: Minor Compositions, 2013.

Heath, Stephen. "Comment on 'The Idea of Authorship.'" *Screen* 14, no. 3 (Autumn 1973): 86–91.

Hermes, Manfred. "Latex and Rubber Paintings 1990/91." In *Nach Kippenberger = After Kippenberger*, edited by Eva Meyer-Hermann and Susanne Neuburger, 147–49. Vienna: Schlebrügge, 2003.

Hermes, Manfred. "On an Untitled White Installation." In *Martin Kippenberger: Sehr gute Bilder*, edited by Udo Kittelmann, 21–40. Berlin: Nationalgalerie, Staatliche Museen zu Berlin, 2013. Exhibition catalog.

Irigaray, Luce. *This Sex Which Is Not One*. Translated by Catherine Porter with Carolyn Burke. Ithaca, NY: Cornell University Press, 1985.

Iversen, Margaret. "The Deflationary Impulse: Postmodernism, Feminism and the Anti-Aesthetic." In *Thinking Art: Beyond Traditional Aesthetics*, edited by Andrew Benjamin and Peter Osborne, 81–93. London: Institute of Contemporary Arts, 1991.

Jackson, Shannon. *Social Works: Performing Art, Supporting Publics*. New York: Routledge, 2011.

Jetzer, Gianni. "Brand New: Art and Commodity in the 1980s." In *Brand New: Art and Commodity in the 1980s*, edited by Gianni Jetzer, 20–35. New York: Rizzoli Electa; Washington, DC: Hirshhorn Museum and Sculpture Garden, 2018. Exhibition catalog.

Jones, Amelia. *Body Art / Performing the Subject*. Minneapolis: University of Minnesota Press, 1998.

Jones, Amelia. "Chris Burden's Bridges, Relationality, and the Conceptual Body." In *Chris Burden: Extreme Measures*, edited by Lisa Phillips, 110–31. New York: Skira Rizzoli and New Museum, 2013. Exhibition catalog.

Jones, Caroline A. *Machine in the Studio: Constructing the Postwar American Artist*. Chicago: University of Chicago Press, 1996.

Jones, Kellie. *South of Pico: African American Artists in Los Angeles in the 1960s and 1970s*. Durham, NC: Duke University Press, 2017.

Jones, Marvin. "Politicizing Art: Hannah Wilke's Art, Politics, Religion and Feminism." *New Common Good*, May 1985, 1, 9–11.

Kalman, Laura. *Right Star Rising: A New Politics, 1974–1980*. New York: W. W. Norton, 2010.

Kingsley, April. "Black Artists: Up against the Wall." *Village Voice*, September 11, 1978, 113.

Kippenberger, Martin. *Input-Output: Umzüge 1957–1988*. Cologne: Galerie Gisela Capitain, 1989.

Kleinfeld, Rachel. "The Rise of Political Violence in the United States." *Journal of Democracy* 32, no. 4 (October 2021): 160–76.

Kleinig, John. "Criminal Liability for Failures to Act." *Law and Contemporary Problems* 49, no. 3 (Summer 1986): 161–80.

Koether, Jutta. "Martin Kippenberger: An Artist Doesn't Have to Be New, an Artist Has to Be Good." *Flash Art*, March/April 2006, 92–96.

Koplos, Janet, and Bruce Metcalf. *Makers: A History of American Studio Craft*. Chapel Hill: University of North Carolina Press, 2010.

Krauss, Rosalind. "Video: The Aesthetics of Narcissism." *October* 1 (Spring 1976): 50–64.

Krauss, Rosalind. *A Voyage on the North Sea: Art in the Age of the Post-medium Condition*. London: Thames and Hudson, 2000.

Le Feuvre, Lisa. "Introduction: Strive to Fail." In *Failure*, edited by Lisa Le Feuvre, 12–21. London: Whitechapel Gallery; Cambridge, MA: MIT Press, 2010.

Licht, Alan. "Martin Kippenberger's *MUSIK 1979–1995.*" *Artforum* 49, no. 5 (January 2011): 51.

Lind, Maria. "The Collaborative Turn." In *Taking the Matter into Common Hands: On Contemporary Art and Collaborative Practices*, edited by Johanna Billing, Maria Lind, and Lars Nilsson, 15–31. London: Black Dog, 2007.

Lippard, Lucy. "Open Season." *Village Voice*, October 7–13, 1981, 91–92.

Lippard, Lucy. "The Pains and Pleasures of Rebirth: Women's Body Art." *Art in America* 64, no. 3 (May/June 1976): 73–81.

Lippard, Lucy. *Six Years: The Dematerialization of the Art Object from 1966 to 1972.* New York: Praeger, 1973.

Marioni, Tom. "Chris Burden: Body Culture." In *Chris Burden: Extreme Measures*, edited by Lisa Phillips, 150–61. New York: Skira Rizzoli and New Museum, 2013. Exhibition catalog.

McDevitt, Jan. "The Object: Still Life. Interviews with the New Object Makers, Richard Artschwager and Claes Oldenburg on Craftsmanship, Art, and Function." *Craft Horizons* 25, no. 5 (September/October 1965): 28–56.

McMillan, Uri. *Embodied Avatars: Genealogies of Black Feminist Art and Performance.* New York: New York University Press, 2015.

Meyer, Richard. "Hard Targets: Male Bodies, Feminist Art, and the Force of Censorship in the 1970s." In *WACK! Art and the Feminist Revolution*, edited by Cornelia H. Butler and Lisa Gabrielle Mark, 362–83. Los Angeles: Museum of Contemporary Art, 2007. Exhibition catalog.

Morris, Catherine. *The Essential Cindy Sherman.* New York: Abrams / Wonderland Press, 2002.

Morris, Catherine, and Aruna D'Souza. "Introduction." In *Lorraine O'Grady: Both/And*, edited by Catherine Morris and Aruna D'Souza, 10–20. Brooklyn: Dancing Foxes Press, 2021. Exhibition catalog.

Morris, Catherine, and Aruna D'Souza, eds. *Lorraine O'Grady: Both/And.* Brooklyn: Dancing Foxes Press, 2021. Exhibition catalog.

Mulvey, Laura. "Visual Pleasure and Narrative Cinema." In *Film Theory and Criticism: Introductory Readings*, edited by Leo Braudy and Marshall Cohen, 833–44. New York: Oxford University Press, 1999.

Nead, Lynda, and Costas Douzinas, eds. *Law and the Image: The Authority of Art and the Aesthetics of Law.* Chicago: University of Chicago Press, 1999.

Nochlin, Linda. "Why Have There Been No Great Women Artists?" *ARTnews* 69, no. 9 (January 1971): 22–39, 67–71.

O'Dell, Kathy. *Contract with the Skin: Masochism, Performance Art, and the 1970s.* Minneapolis: University of Minnesota Press, 1998.

O'Grady, Lorraine. "*The Black and White Show*, 1982." In *Writing in Space, 1973–2019*, by Lorraine O'Grady, 184–97. Edited by Aruna D'Souza. Durham, NC: Duke University Press, 2020.

O'Grady, Lorraine. "Black Dreams." In *Writing in Space, 1973–2019*, by Lorraine O'Grady, 69–76. Edited by Aruna D'Souza. Durham, NC: Duke University Press, 2020.

O'Grady, Lorraine. "A Day at the Races: Lorraine O'Grady on Jean-Michel Basquiat and the Black Art World." In *Writing in Space, 1973–2019*, by Lorraine O'Grady, 169–75. Edited by Aruna D'Souza. Durham, NC: Duke University Press, 2020.

O'Grady, Lorraine. "Interview with Amanda Hunt on *Art Is . . .* , 1983." In *Writing in Space, 1973–2019*, by Lorraine O'Grady, 60–63. Edited by Aruna D'Souza. Durham, NC: Duke University Press, 2020.

O'Grady, Lorraine. "Interview with Jarrett Earnest." In *Writing in Space, 1973–2019*, by Lorraine O'Grady, 239–49. Edited by Aruna D'Souza. Durham, NC: Duke University Press, 2020.

O'Grady, Lorraine. "Interview with Laura Cottingham." In *Writing in Space, 1973–2019*, by Lorraine O'Grady, 221–38. Edited by Aruna D'Souza. Durham, NC: Duke University Press, 2020.

O'Grady, Lorraine. "Interview with Linda Montano." In *Writing in Space, 1973–2019*, by Lorraine O'Grady, 77–83. Edited by Aruna D'Souza. Durham, NC: Duke University Press, 2020.

O'Grady, Lorraine. "*Mlle Bourgeoise Noire 1955*." In *Writing in Space, 1973–2019*, by Lorraine O'Grady, 8–10. Edited by Aruna D'Souza. Durham, NC: Duke University Press, 2020.

O'Grady, Lorraine. "*Mlle Bourgeoise Noire* and Feminism." In *Writing in Space, 1973–2019*, by Lorraine O'Grady, 110–11. Edited by Aruna D'Souza. Durham, NC: Duke University Press, 2020.

O'Grady, Lorraine. "The *Mlle Bourgeoise Noire* Project, 1980–1983." In *Writing in Space, 1973–2019*, by Lorraine O'Grady, 250–59. Edited by Aruna D'Souza. Durham, NC: Duke University Press, 2020.

O'Grady, Lorraine. "My 1980s." In *Writing in Space, 1973–2019*, by Lorraine O'Grady, 203–12. Edited by Aruna D'Souza. Durham, NC: Duke University Press, 2020.

O'Grady, Lorraine. "Olympia's Maid: Reclaiming Black Female Subjectivity." In *Writing in Space, 1973–2019*, by Lorraine O'Grady, 94–109. Edited by Aruna D'Souza. Durham, NC: Duke University Press, 2020.

O'Grady, Lorraine. "Performance Statement #3: Thinking Out Loud: About Performance Art and My Place in It (1983)." In *Writing in Space, 1973–2019*, by Lorraine O'Grady, 43–49. Edited by Aruna D'Souza. Durham, NC: Duke University Press, 2020.

O'Grady, Lorraine. "*Rivers* and Just Above Midtown." In *Writing in Space, 1973–2019*, by Lorraine O'Grady, 213–16. Edited by Aruna D'Souza. Durham, NC: Duke University Press, 2020.

O'Grady, Lorraine. "Statement for Moira Roth re: *Art Is*. . . ." In *Writing in Space, 1973–2019*, by Lorraine O'Grady, 23–26. Edited by Aruna D'Souza. Durham, NC: Duke University Press, 2020.

O'Grady, Lorraine. "This Will Have Been: My 1980s." *Art Journal* 71, no. 2 (Summer 2012): 6–17.

O'Grady, Lorraine. *Writing in Space, 1973–2019*. Edited by Aruna D'Souza. Durham, NC: Duke University Press, 2020.

Oldenburg, Claes. "History of the Alphabet / Good Humor." In *Claes Oldenburg: The Alphabet in L.A.*, n.p. Los Angeles: Margo Leavin Gallery, 1975.

Oldenburg, Claes. *Notes in Hand*. New York: E. P. Dutton, 1971.

Oldenburg, Claes, and Gene Baro. *Claes Oldenburg: Drawings and Prints*. New York: Chelsea House Publishers, 1969.

Owens, Craig. "The Allegorical Impulse: Toward a Theory of Postmodernism." *October* 12 (Spring 1980): 67–86.

Phelan, Peggy. *Unmarked: The Politics of Performance*. London: Routledge, 1993.

Phillips, Deborah C. "Bright Lights, Big City." *ARTnews*, September 1985, 82–91.

Phillips, Deborah C. "New Faces in Alternative Spaces." *ARTnews*, November 1981, 90–100.

Phillips, Glenn, ed. *California Video: Artists and Histories*. Los Angeles: Getty Research Institute / J. Paul Getty Museum, 2008.

Phillips, Lisa. "Cindy Sherman's Cindy Shermans." In *Cindy Sherman*, by Cindy Sherman, Lisa Phillips, Peter Schjeldahl, and Whitney Museum of American Art, 13–16. New York: Whitney Museum of American Art, 1987. Exhibition catalog.

Picard, Lil. "Hannah Wilke: Sexy Objects." *Interview*, January 1973, 18, 44.

Pindell, Howardena. *The Heart of the Question: The Writings and Paintings of Howardena Pindell*. New York: Midmarch Arts, 1997.

Pollock, Griselda, ed. *Generations and Geographies in the Visual Arts: Feminist Readings*. New York: Routledge, 1996.

Praxis. "In Conversation: Andrea Fraser." *Brooklyn Rail*, October 2004.

Princenthal, Nancy. *Hannah Wilke*. Munich: Prestel, 2010.

Robbins, David. "A Conversation with Chris Burden." Unpublished interview for *Interview* magazine, March 1980. http://theenemyreader.org /a-conversation-with-chris-burden/.

Robinson, Walter, and Carlo McCormick. "Slouching toward Avenue D." *Art in America* 72, no. 6 (Summer 1984): 134–62.

Rose, Barbara. "Claes Oldenburg." *Interview*, December 2015.

Ross, David A. "Chris Burden's Television." In *Chris Burden: A Twenty-Year Survey*, by Chris Burden, Anne Ayres, and Paul Schimmel, 30–34. Newport Beach: Newport Harbor Art Museum, 1988. Exhibition catalog.

Rugoff, Ralph. *Just Pathetic.* Los Angeles: Rosamund Felsen Gallery, 1990. Exhibition catalog.

Sáiz, Patricio, and Rafael Castro. "Trademarks in Branding: Legal Issues and Commercial Practices." *Business History* 50, no. 8 (2018): 1105–26.

Sanchez, Michael. "Cerberus." In *Martin Kippenberger: Catalogue Raisonné of the Paintings,* vol. 3, *1987–1992,* edited by Gisela Capitain, Regina Fiorito, and Lisa Franzen, 37–45. Cologne: Walther König, 2017.

Sandoval, Chela. "U.S. Third World Feminism: The Theory and Method of Oppositional Consciousness in the Postmodern World." *Genders* 10 (Spring 1991): 1–24.

Sarraute, Raymond. "Current Theory on the Moral Right of Authors and Artists under French Law." *American Journal of Comparative Law* 16, no. 4 (Autumn 1968): 465–86.

Schéré, Elizabeth. "Where Is the Morality? Moral Rights in International Intellectual Property and Trade Law." *Fordham International Law Journal* 41, no. 3 (2018): 773–84.

Schmidt-Wulffen, Stephan. "Living Vehicle." In *Gitarren, die nicht Gudrun heißen: Hommage à Martin Kippenberger,* edited by Thomas Groetz, 15–20. Berlin: Galerie Max Hetzler, 2003.

Schulman, Bruce. *The Seventies: The Great Shift in American Culture, Society, and Politics.* New York: The Free Press, 2001.

Seiberling, Dorothy. "The Art-Martyr." *New York Magazine,* May 24, 1976, 64.

Sharp, Willoughby. "Body Works." *Avalanche* 1 (Fall 1970): 14–17.

Sharp, Willoughby, and Liza Béar. "Chris Burden: The Church of Human Energy." *Avalanche,* no. 8 (Summer/Fall 1973): 54–61.

Siegel, Judy. "Between the Censor and the Muse? Hannah Wilke: Censoring the Muse?" *Women Artists News,* Winter 1986, 4, 46–48.

Sims, Lowery Stokes. "Aspects of Performance in the Work of Black American Women Artists." In *Feminist Art Criticism: An Anthology,* edited by Arlene Raven, Cassandra L. Langer, and Joanna Frueh, 207–25. Ann Arbor, MI: UMI Research Press, 1988.

Singerman, Howard. "Chris Burden's Pragmatism." In *Chris Burden: A Twenty-Year Survey,* by Chris Burden, Anne Ayres, and Paul Schimmel, 19–29. Newport, CA: Newport Harbor Art Museum, 1988. Exhibition catalog.

Smith, Barbara T. "Art Piece Brings Arrest." *Artweek* 4, no. 1 (January 6, 1973): 3.

Smith, Barbara T. "Burden Case Tried, Dismissed." *Artweek* 4, no. 8 (February 24, 1973): 2.

Smith, Barbara T. "Response to Editor's Mail Bag." *Artweek* 4, no. 6 (February 10, 1973): 2.

Smith, Cherise. *Enacting Others: Politics of Identity in Eleanor Antin, Nikki S. Lee, Adrian Piper, and Anna Deavere Smith.* Durham, NC: Duke University Press, 2011.

Smith, RJ. "The Sculptor of Dreams." *Los Angeles Magazine,* November 2012.

Sontag, Susan. "Happenings: An Art of Radical Juxtaposition." In *Against Interpretation and Other Essays,* 263–73. New York: Picador, 2001.

Sparling Williams, Stephanie. *Speaking Out of Turn: Lorraine O'Grady and the Art of Language.* Berkeley: University of California Press, 2021.

Spivak, Gayatri Chakravorty. "'Can the Subaltern Speak?" In *Can the Subaltern Speak? Reflections on the History of an Idea,* edited by Rosalind C. Morris, 21–78. New York: Columbia University Press, 2010.

Stange, Raimar. "One of You among You with You." *Modern Painters,* Winter 2002, 66–69.

Steinhauer, Jillian. "Just Watch Me." *New York Magazine,* March 2, 2021.

Stiles, Kristine. "Burden of Light." In *Chris Burden,* edited by Fred Hoffman, 22–37. Newcastle, England: Locus Plus, 2007.

Takemoto, Tina. "Looking through Hannah's Eyes: Interview with Donald Goddard." *Art Journal* 67, no. 2 (Summer 2008): 126–39.

Unruh, Allison. "Interview with Vincent Fremont." In *Andy Warhol Enterprises,* edited by Sarah Urist Green and Allison Unruh, 147–57. Hatje Cantz Verlag: Ostfildern, 2010.

Van Bruggen, Coosje. *Claes Oldenburg: Mouse Museum / Ray Gun Wing.* Cologne: Museum Ludwig, 1979. Exhibition catalog.

Velasco, David. "1000 Words: Lorraine O'Grady." *Artforum* 59, no. 5 (March 2021): 130–33.

Wagner, Anne M. "Performance, Video, and the Rhetoric of Presence." *October* 91 (Winter 2000): 59–80.

Wagner, Anne M. *Three Artists (Three Women): Modernism and the Art of Hesse, Krasner, and O'Keeffe.* Berkeley: University of California Press, 1996.

Walker, Jeffrey. "Happenings: Is Violence Art?" *Penthouse,* February 1975, 36.

Walker, John A. *Art and Celebrity.* London: Pluto Press, 2003.

Waller, Genevieve. "Unattributed Objects: The *Mouse Museum,* the *Ray Gun Wing,* and Four Artists." In *Sculpture and the Vitrine,* edited by John C. Welchman, 159–78. Farnham: Ashgate, 2012.

Wallis, Brian. *Damaged Goods: Desire and the Economy of the Object.* New York: New Museum of Contemporary Art, 1986. Exhibition catalog.

Ward, Frazer. "Gray Zone: Watching *Shoot.*" *October* 95 (Winter 2001): 115–30.

Ward, Frazer. *No Innocent Bystanders: Performance Art and Audience.* Hanover, NH: Dartmouth College Press, 2012.

*West's Encyclopedia of American Law.* 2nd ed. Minneapolis: West Publishing Company, 2005. Online.

Whitley, Zoé. "Mlle Bourgeoise Noire Throws Down the Whip: Alter Ego as Fierce Critic of Institutions." In *Lorraine O'Grady: Both/And*, edited by Catherine Morris and Aruna D'Souza, 46–79. Brooklyn: Dancing Foxes Press, 2021. Exhibition catalog.

Wilentz, Sean. *The Age of Reagan: A History, 1974–2008.* New York: HarperCollins, 2008.

Wilke, Hannah. *Hannah Wilke: A Retrospective.* Edited by Thomas H. Kochheiser and Joanna Frueh. Columbia: University of Missouri Press, 1989. Exhibition catalog.

Wilke, Hannah. "Seura Chaya." *New Observations* 58 (June 1988): 12–13.

Williams, Gregory. *Permission to Laugh: Humor and Politics in Contemporary German Art.* Chicago: University of Chicago Press, 2012.

Wilson, James Q., and George L. Kelling. "Broken Windows." *The Atlantic*, March 1982, 29–38.

Winer, Helene. "Burden at Pomona." In *Chris Burden: Extreme Measures*, edited by Lisa Phillips, 163–66. New York: Skira Rizzoli and New Museum, 2013. Exhibition catalog.

Wollen, Peter. *Signs and Meaning in the Cinema.* London: British Film Institute; Secker and Warburg, 1969.

Woodmansee, Martha. *The Author, Art, and the Market: Rereading the History of Aesthetics.* New York: Columbia University Press, 1994.

Wrange, Måns. "A Conversation with Chris Burden." In *Chris Burden*, n.p. Stockholm: Magasin 3 Stockholm Konsthall, 1999.

Young, Alison. *Judging the Image: Art, Value, Law.* London: Routledge, 2005.

*Page numbers in italics refer to illustrations.*

www.ingramcontent.com/pod-product-compliance
Lightning Source LLC
Chambersburg PA
CBHW051210170526
45166CB00005B/1830